2017
Insurance
Fact
Book

TO THE READER

Disruption is everywhere, and insurance is poised to lead through it.

The past few years have been busy ones for the insurance industry. Under pressure from low interest rates and excess capital, mergers and acquisition activity has been on the rise. Cybercrime is growing; global geopolitical unrest is burgeoning; social forces like the sharing economy are disrupting how we live and how we work. The daily commute may change soon, as the auto industry creeps closer to producing self-driving vehicles — for personal as well as commercial use. Threats such as terror persist. Even catastrophes are changing in scope. And the cultivation of insuretech and big data will undoubtedly forge new risks, while also presenting new opportunities.

Fortunately, insurance continues to provide stability against risks—both new and old—and is a valuable partner in building resilience.

This year, the Insurance Information Institute (I.I.I.) has added even more data to the Insurance Fact Book. You will see an expanded section on cybercrime. We also included new I.I.I. data on consumer sentiment, all in support of the I.I.I.'s mission: improving public understanding of what insurance does, and how it works. Since its inception more than 50 years ago, the Insurance Fact Book has provided information to help consumers, journalists, businesses, policymakers and researchers understand the trends and statistics shaping the insurance industry.

Interest in cyber insurance and risk continues to expand beyond expectations, and as such we are excited to add a bonus feature in this year's edition, an excerpt from our white paper, "Cyberrisk: Threat and Opportunity." Main topics covered include the growth in cyber liability interest, the rising frequency and severity of cyberattacks and the insurance industry and cyberrisk.

The Insurance Fact Book is meant to be used along with the institute's website, www.iii.org, which features information for consumers, researchers, public policymakers and businesses alike. The I.I.I. remains a vital source for the media, which rely on I.I.I. spokespersons, the Insurance Fact Book and Insurance Handbook, videos and other materials for credible, timely information. Social networks are another way to stay in touch with the I.I.I. We welcome you to like our Facebook page and follow us on Twitter at @iiiorg and @III_Research.

As always, we would like to thank the many associations, consultants and others who collect industry statistics and who have generously given permission to use their data. Thank you especially to all of our members for their longstanding support, and we would also like to extend a warm welcome to all our new members.

Sean Kevelighan
Chief Executive Officer
Insurance Information Institute

The I.I.I. Insurance Fact Book is published by the Insurance Information Institute, a primary source for information, analysis and referral on insurance subjects. The Fact Book contains material from numerous sources. Because these sources define and collect data in various ways, and moreover, are constantly refining the data, differences among similar data may occur.
©2017 Insurance Information Institute. ISBN 978-0-932387-77-6

Insurance Industry At A Glance V

Chapter 1: World Insurance Markets 1

Premiums...1
Reinsurance 3
Leading Companies 4
International Sales 6
Captives And Other Risk-Financing Options 7
Microinsurance And Emerging Markets 9

Chapter 2: U.S. Insurance Industry, All Sectors 13

Premiums...13
Leading Companies 15
Health...16
Employment And Other Economic Contributions 17
Mergers And Acquisitions..20
Companies By State...23
Premium Taxes By State 24

Chapter 3: Distribution 25

Property/Casualty...25
Life 27
Annuities 28

Chapter 4: Retirement 29

Overview..29
IRAs..32
401(k)s 33
Mutual Funds 33
Annuities 34

Chapter 5: Life/Health Financial Data 37

Financial Results...37
Investments...39
Payouts..40
Premiums By Line...41
Leading Companies 47

Chapter 6: Property/Casualty Financial Data...49

Financial Results...49
Investments...56
Surplus Lines 58
Concentration...59
Reinsurance 60
Premiums By State...61
Incurred Losses By State...62
Guaranty Funds 63

Chapter 7: Property/Casualty Insurance By Line **65**
   Premiums 65
   Auto: Premiums 73
   Auto: Costs/Expenditures 76
   Auto: Claims 81
   Auto: High-Risk Markets 82
   Auto: Uninsured Motorists 84
   Auto: Laws 86
   Homeowners: Premiums 100
   Homeowners: High-Risk Markets 101
   Homeowners: Costs/Expenditures 106
   Homeowners: Claims 108
   Flood Insurance 112
   Earthquake Insurance 116
   Commercial Lines 117
Chapter 8: Losses **133**
   Major Catastrophes: World 133
   Major Catastrophes: United States 136
   Major Catastrophes U.S.: Hurricanes, Winter Storms, Floods, Tornadoes,
    Earthquakes, Terrorism, Nuclear Incidents, Hail, Wildfires 140
   Fire 159
   Crime: Arson, Property 163
   Crime: Cyber And Identity Theft 166
   Motor Vehicles: Crashes 171
   Motor Vehicles: Theft 182
   Recreation 184
   Aviation 188
   Workplace 190
   Home 194
   Causes Of Death 195
Chapter 9: Factors Affecting Costs **197**
   Cost Of Goods And Services 197
   Fraud 200
   Litigiousness 203
Appendices **211**
   Special Report: Cyberrisk: Threat And Opportunity 211
   I.I.I. Resources 229
   2016: A Look Back 231
   State Insurance Departments 233
   Insurance And Related Service Organizations 235
Insurance Information Institute Members **244**
Insurance Information Institute Staff **246**
Index **247**

Insurance Industry At A Glance

- The U.S. insurance industry's net premiums written totaled $1.2 trillion in 2015, with premiums recorded by life/health (L/H) insurers accounting for 55 percent and premiums by property/casualty (P/C) insurers accounting for 45 percent, according to S&P Global Market Intelligence.

- P/C insurance consists primarily of auto, home and commercial insurance. Net premiums written for the sector totaled $519.8 billion in 2015.

- The L/H insurance sector consists primarily of annuities and life insurance. Net premiums written for the sector totaled $635.6 billion in 2015.

- Health insurance is generally considered separate. The sector includes private health insurance companies as well as government programs. P/C and L/H insurers also write some health insurance.

- There were 5,926 insurance companies in 2015 in the United States (including territories), including P/C (2,544), life/annuities (872), health (859), fraternal (85), title (56), risk retention groups (239) and other companies (1,261), according to the National Association of Insurance Commissioners.

- Insurance carriers and related activities contributed $450.3 billion, or 2.6 percent, of U.S. gross domestic product in 2014, according to the U.S. Bureau of Economic Analysis.

- The U.S. insurance industry employed 2.5 million people in 2015, according to the U.S. Department of Labor. Of those, 1.5 million worked for insurance companies, including L/H insurers (851,100 workers), P/C insurers (599,700 workers) and reinsurers (25,100 workers). The remaining 1.1 million people worked for insurance agencies, brokers and other insurance-related enterprises.

- Total P/C cash and invested assets were $1.5 trillion in 2015, according to S&P Global Market Intelligence. L/H cash and invested assets totaled $3.7 trillion in 2015. The total of cash and invested assets for both sectors was $5.2 trillion. The majority of these assets were in bonds (62 percent of P/C assets and 74 percent of L/H assets).

- P/C and L/H insurance companies paid $19.2 billion in premium taxes in 2015, or $60 for every person living in the United States, according to the U.S. Department of Commerce.

- P/C insurers paid out $15.2 billion in property losses related to catastrophes in 2015, compared with $15.5 billion in 2014 according to the Property Claims Services division of Verisk Analytics®. There were 39 catastrophes in 2015, compared with 31 in 2014.

U.S. P/C And L/H Insurance Premiums, 2015 ($ billions)

L/H	55%	$635.6
P/C	45	519.8

Source: NAIC data, sourced from S&P Global Market Intelligence, Insurance Information Institute.

Chapter 1

World Insurance Markets

PREMIUMS

World Life And Nonlife Insurance In 2015

Outside the United States, the insurance industry is divided into life and nonlife, or general insurance, rather than life/health and property/casualty. Swiss Re's 2015 world insurance study is based on direct premium data from 147 countries, with detailed information on the largest 88 markets. World insurance premiums rose 3.8 percent in 2015, adjusted for inflation, compared with 3.5 percent in 2014. Nonlife premiums rose 3.6 percent in 2015, adjusted for inflation, following 2.4 percent growth in 2014. Life insurance premiums grew by 4.0 percent after inflation in 2015, slower than the 4.3 percent growth achieved in 2014.

Top 10 Countries By Life And Nonlife Direct Premiums Written, 2015[1] (US$ millions)

Rank	Country	Life premiums	Nonlife premiums[2]	Total premiums Amount	Total premiums Percent change from prior year	Total premiums Percent of total world premiums
1	United States[3,4]	$552,506	$763,766	$1,316,721	3.6%	28.90%
2	Japan[5,6]	343,816	105,891	449,707	-5.6	9.88
3	P.R. China[7]	210,763	175,737	386,500	17.7	8.49
4	United Kingdom[5]	214,492	105,685	320,176	-5.2	7.03
5	France[7]	150,143	80,402	230,545	-14.5	5.06
6	Germany[8]	96,725	116,538	213,263	-16.4	4.68
7	Italy[5]	124,848	40,189	165,037	-15.3	3.62
8	South Korea[6]	98,218	55,402	153,620	-3.3	3.37
9	Canada[5,9]	49,331	65,637	114,968	-9.5	2.52
10	Taiwan	79,627	16,352	95,979	0.4	2.11

[1]Before reinsurance transactions. [2]Includes accident and health insurance. [3]Nonlife premiums include state funds; life premiums include an estimate of group pension business. [4]Life premiums are provisional. [5]Estimated. [6]April 1, 2015, to March 31, 2016. [7]Provisional. [8]Nonlife premiums are provisional. [9]Life premiums are net premiums.

Source: Swiss Re, *sigma*, No. 3/2016.

World Life And Nonlife Insurance Direct Premiums Written, 2015 ($ billions)

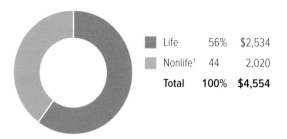

Life	56%	$2,534
Nonlife[1]	44	2,020
Total	**100%**	**$4,554**

[1]Includes accident and health insurance.
Source: Swiss Re, *sigma*, No. 3/2016.

World Life And Nonlife Insurance Direct Premiums Written, 2013-2015[1] (US$ millions)

Year	Life	Nonlife[2]	Total
2013	$2,547,486	$2,040,966	$4,588,451
2014	2,655,593	2,099,118	4,754,710
2015	2,533,818	2,019,967	4,553,785

[1]Before reinsurance transactions. [2]Includes accident and health insurance.
Source: Swiss Re, *sigma* database, *sigma* 3/2016.

Top 10 Countries By Total Insurance Premiums Per Capita And Percent Of Gross Domestic Product (GDP), 2015[1]

Rank	Country	Total premiums per capita	Rank	Country	Total premiums as a percent of GDP
1	Cayman Islands	$12,619.3	1	Cayman Islands	20.24%
2	Switzerland	7,370.3	2	Taiwan	18.97
3	Hong Kong	6,271.2	3	Hong Kong	14.76
4	Luxembourg	5,401.3	4	South Africa	14.69
5	Finland	4,963.2	5	Finland	11.86
6	Denmark	4,914.2	6	South Korea[2]	11.42
7	Netherlands	4,763.1	7	Japan[2]	10.82
8	United Kingdom	4,358.5	8	Netherlands	10.72
9	United States	4,095.8	9	United Kingdom	9.97
10	Taiwan	4,094.1	10	Denmark	9.43
	World	**$621.2**		**World**	**6.23%**

[1]Includes nonlife and life insurance and cross-border business. [2]April 1, 2015, to March 31, 2016.
Source: Swiss Re, *sigma*, No. 3/2016.

REINSURANCE

Each year the Reinsurance Association of America (RAA) provides an overview of the countries from which U.S. insurance companies obtain reinsurance, i.e., the countries to which they have ceded, or transferred, some of their risk. The analysis includes premiums that a U.S. insurance company cedes to offshore, i.e., foreign, reinsurance companies that are not part of the insurer's own corporate group (*unaffiliated offshore reinsurers* in the chart below), as well as business ceded to overseas reinsurers that are part of the insurer's corporate family (*affiliated offshore reinsurers* in the chart below).

The RAA report compares U.S. insurance premiums ceded to U.S. professional reinsurance companies to the U.S. premiums ceded to offshore, i.e., foreign, companies. U.S. professional rein- surance companies accounted for 36.6 percent of the U.S. premium written that was ceded in 2014, while offshore companies accounted for 63.4 percent. However, a number of U.S.-based reinsurers are owned by foreign companies. Taking this into consideration, foreign reinsurers accounted for 91.5 percent of premiums ceded, while U.S. professional reinsurers accounted for 8.5 percent.

U.S. Reinsurance Premiums Ceded To Unaffiliated And Affiliated Offshore Reinsurers By Country, 2012-2014[1] (US$ millions)

Rank	Country	Unaffiliated offshore reinsurers			Affiliated offshore reinsurers			2014 total
		2012	2013	2014	2012	2013	2014	
1	Bermuda	$9,387	$10,019	$9,962	$23,918	$25,471	$25,465	$35,427
2	Switzerland	1,151	1,426	2,192	9,013	10,803	11,815	14,007
3	United Kingdom	4,719	5,137	4,980	544	477	512	5,492
4	Germany	2,883	3,712	3,740	1,318	1,579	1,541	5,281
5	Cayman Islands	2,963	3,301	2,981	591	982	1,096	4,077
6	Turks and Caicos	873	1,084	1,445	234	237	291	1,736
7	Channel Islands	2,883	1,252	1,323	NA	NA	NA	1,323
8	Barbados	652	658	761	NA	NA	NA	761
9	Ireland	454	565	441	194	180	168	609
10	British Virgin Islands	434	462	499	NA	NA	NA	499
11	Japan	NA	NA	NA	294	-1,857	464	464
12	France	NA	NA	NA	256	336	337	337
13	Spain	NA	NA	NA	278	266	259	259
	Total, countries shown	$26,398	$27,615	$28,372	$36,640	$38,474[2]	$41,949	$70,321
	Total, all countries	$26,790	$29,176	$30,211	$36,929	$38,741[2]	$42,295	$72,506

[1]Ranked by 2014 total reinsurance premiums. [2]Includes -$1.86 billion in affiliated premiums ceded to Japan. NA=Data not available.
Source: Reinsurance Association of America.

LEADING COMPANIES

Top 10 Global Insurance Companies By Revenues, 2015[1] (US$ millions)

Rank	Company	Revenues	Country	Industry
1	Berkshire Hathaway	$210,821	U.S.	Property/casualty
2	AXA	129,250	France	Life/health
3	Allianz	122,948	Germany	Property/casualty
4	Japan Post Holdings	118,762	Japan	Life/health
5	Ping An Insurance	110,308	China	Life/health
6	Assicurazioni Generali	102,567	Italy	Life/health
7	China Life Insurance	101,274	China	Life/health
8	State Farm Insurance Cos.	75,697	U.S.	Property/casualty
9	MetLife	69,951	U.S.	Life/health
10	Munich Re	69,433	Germany	Property/casualty

[1]Based on an analysis of companies in the Global Fortune 500. Includes stock and mutual companies.
Source: Fortune.

Top 10 Global Property/Casualty Reinsurers By Net Reinsurance Premiums Written, 2013 (US$ millions)

Rank	Company	Net reinsurance premiums written	Country
1	Munich Reinsurance Co.	$22,545.9	Germany
2	Swiss Re Ltd.	14,542.0	Switzerland
3	Hannover Re S.E.	12,905.8	Germany
4	Berkshire Hathaway Reinsurance Group	11,440.0	U.S.
5	Lloyd's of London	11,363.7	U.K.
6	Scor S.E.	5,931.9	France
7	Everest Re Group Ltd.	5,004.8	Bermuda
8	PartnerRe Ltd.	4,479.1	Bermuda
9	Korean Reinsurance Co.	3,499.0[1]	South Korea
10	Transatlantic Holdings Inc.	3,248.0	U.S.

[1]Fiscal year ending March 31, 2013.
Source: Business Insurance, September 1, 2014.

Top 10 Global Insurance Brokers By Revenues, 2015[1] (US$ millions)

Rank	Company	Brokerage revenues	Country
1	Marsh & McLennan Cos. Inc.	$12,912	U.S.
2	Aon P.L.C.	11,661	U.K.
3	Willis Towers Watson P.L.C.[2]	8,124	U.K.
4	Arthur J. Gallagher & Co.	3,990	U.S.
5	Jardine Lloyd Thompson Group P.L.C.	1,698	U.K.
6	BB&T Insurance Holdings Inc.	1,676	U.S.
7	Brown & Brown Inc.	1,657	U.S.
8	Hub International Ltd.	1,470	U.S.
9	Lockton Cos. L.L.C.[3]	1,329	U.S.
10	Wells Fargo Insurance Services USA Inc.	1,316	U.S.

Revenue generated by the world's 10 largest brokers increased to $45.8 billion in 2015 from $25.9 billion in 2006.

[1]Revenue generated by insurance brokerage and related services. [2]Reflects the 2016 merger of Willis Group Holdings P.L.C., Towers Watson & Co. and Gras Savoye & Cie. [3]Fiscal year ending April 30, 2015.
Source: Business Insurance, July 18, 2016.

Top 10 Global Reinsurance Brokers By Gross Reinsurance Revenues, 2013[1] (US$ 000)

Rank	Company	Gross reinsurance revenues	Country
1	Aon Benfield	$1,505,000	U.K.
2	Guy Carpenter & Co. L.L.C.[2]	1,131,267	U.S.
3	Willis Re	860,000	U.K.
4	JLT Reinsurance Brokers Ltd.	375,869	U.K.
5	Cooper Gay Swett & Crawford Ltd.	158,466	U.K.
6	Miller Insurance Services L.L.P.[3]	93,528	U.K.
7	UIB Holdings Ltd.[2]	67,463	U.K.
8	THB Group Ltd.	58,094	U.K.
9	BMS Group Ltd.	54,300	U.K.
10	Lockton Re[3]	46,029	U.K.

[1]Includes all reinsurance revenue reported through holding and/or subsidiary companies. [2]Includes aviation reinsurance business placed by Marsh L.L.C. [3]Fiscal year ending April 30, 2013.
Source: Business Insurance, October 27, 2014.

INTERNATIONAL SALES

The U.S. Department of Commerce provides estimates on two methods of international delivery of insurance services: cross-border trade, in which a domestic company transacts directly with a foreign company (for example, a European firm purchasing insurance from a U.S. firm through a broker); and sales by subsidiaries of multinational corporations (for example, sales to the European market through a European-based subsidiary of a U.S. insurer). The combination of these methods of delivery creates a broad measure of insurance services provided and received from abroad.

U.S. Insurance Sales Abroad, 2008-2014 (US$ millions)

Year	Sold directly[1]	Sold through majority-owned foreign affiliates of U.S. multinational corporations[2]
2008	$13,403	$61,794
2009	14,586	61,609
2010	14,397	58,379
2011	15,114	59,942
2012	16,790	64,346
2013	17,058	64,805
2014	17,417	NA

[1]Largely based on premiums. Includes adjustments for "normal" i.e., expected losses and premium supplements (income due to policy holders). Bureau of Economic Analysis (BEA) refers to this category as "cross border sales." Includes property/casualty, life insurance and reinsurance. [2]Based on sales by primary industry of the affiliate; there could be other services, such as financial services, included in the data. NA=Data not available.
Source: U.S. Department of Commerce, BEA, International Division.

Insurance Business In The U.S. Written By Subsidiaries Of Foreign Controlled Companies, 2010-2014 (US$ millions)

	Gross premiums written				2014	
	2010	2011	2012	2013	Amount	Percentage of total
Life	$132,870	$139,311	$141,524	$143,429	$150,000	66.3%
Nonlife	78,504	82,199	69,668	74,219	76,306	33.7
Total[1]	$211,374	$221,511	$211,192	$217,648	$226,306	100.0%

[1]Calculated from unrounded data.
Source: Organization for Economic Cooperation and Development.

CAPTIVES AND OTHER RISK-FINANCING OPTIONS

A number of alternatives to traditional commercial insurance have emerged to respond to fluctuations in the marketplace. Captives—a special type of insurance company set up by a parent company, trade association or group of companies to insure the risks of its owner or owners—emerged during the 1980s when businesses had trouble obtaining some types of commercial insurance coverage. Today alternative risk transfer (ART) arrangements include self insurance, risk retention groups and risk purchasing groups and more recent innovations such as catastrophe bonds and microinsurance.

Leading Captive Domiciles, 2014-2015

Rank[1]	Domicile	Number of captives		Rank[1]	Domicile	Number of captives	
		2014	2015			2014	2015
1	Bermuda	800	797	12	Hawaii	194	197
2	Cayman Islands	759	708	13	Montana	177	196
3	Vermont	587	596	14	District of Columbia	191	193
4	Utah	422	450	15	Puerto Rico	152[2]	182[3]
5	Delaware	333	323	16	South Carolina	158	167
6	Anguilla	379	319	17	British Virgin Islands	146	142
6	Guernsey	321	319	18	Tennessee	70[2]	127
8	Nevis	281	268	19	Isle of Man	122	115
9	Barbados	231[2]	236	20	Arizona	114	110
10	Luxembourg	224	217		**Total, top 20**	**5,821**	**5,864**
11	Nevada	160	202		**Total, all captives**	**6,839**	**6,939**

[1]Domiciles with the same number of captives receive the same rank. [2]Restated. [3]Estimate.

Source: Business Insurance, February 29, 2016.

The Securitization Of Insurance Risk: Catastrophe Bonds

Catastrophe (cat) bonds are one of a number of innovative risk transfer products that have emerged as an alternative to traditional insurance and reinsurance products. Insurers and reinsurers typically issue cat bonds through a special purpose vehicle, a company set up specifically for this purpose. Cat bonds pay high interest rates and diversify an investor's portfolio because natural disasters occur randomly and are not associated with economic factors. Depending on how the cat bond is structured, if losses reach the threshold specified in the bond offering, the investor may lose all or part of the principal or interest.

Catastrophe bond issuance in 2015, at $5.92 billion, was less than the record high of $7.9 billion in 2014, according to the GC Securities division of MMC Securities Corp. Catastrophe bond issuance was markedly low in the fourth quarter of 2015, in contrast with a record first quarter. Catastrophe bond risk capital outstanding fell slightly to $22.44 billion in 2015, from $22.77 billion in 2014. GC Securities expects in the absence of a major market disruption, issuance in 2016 will be similar to the last several years as new sponsors incorporate alternative capital into their strategies.

Top 10 Catastrophe Bond Transactions, 2015 (US$ millions)

Rank	Special purpose vehicle	Sponsor name	Risk amount	Peril	Risk location
1	Alamo Re Ltd. Series 2015-1	TWIA	$700	Hurricane	Texas
2	Kilimanjaro Re Ltd. Series 2015-1	Everest Re	625	Hurricane and earthquake	U.S.
3	Cranberry Re Ltd. Series 2015-1	MPIUA	300	Hurricane	Massachusetts
4	Acorn Re Ltd. Series 2015-1	Kaiser Permanente	300	Earthquake	U.S. and Mexico
5	Galileo Re Ltd. 2015-1	Catlin	300	Hurricane and earthquake	U.S., Canada, Europe
6	Merna Re Ltd.	State Farm	300	Earthquake	New Madrid
7	Everglades Re II Ltd.	Florida Citizens	300	Hurricane	Florida
8	Long Point Re III Ltd.	Travelers	300	Hurricane and earthquake	U.S.
9	Nakama Re Ltd. 2015-1	Zenkyoren	300	Earthquake	Japan
10	Kizuna Re II Ltd. Series 2015-1	Tokio Marine & Fire	290	Earthquake	Japan

Source: GC Securities, a division of MMC Securities Corp., a U.S. registered broker-dealer, member FINRA/SIPC and Guy Carpenter.

**Catastrophe Bonds, Risk Capital Outstanding And Annual Issued,
2006-2015** (US$ billions)

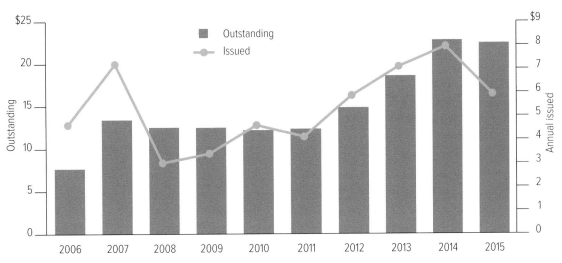

Source: GC Securities, a division of MMC Securities Corp., a registered broker-dealer, member FINRA/SIPC and Guy Carpenter.

MICROINSURANCE AND EMERGING MARKETS

A growing number of insurers are tapping into markets in developing countries through microinsurance projects, which provide low-cost insurance to individuals generally not covered by traditional insurance or government programs. Microinsurance products tend to be much less costly than traditional products and thus extend protection to a much wider market. Microinsurance products vary in type and structure but are generally distinguished by high volumes, low cost and efficient administration. Microinsurance policies may be offered along with a small loan, with premiums that are a small percentage of the loan amount. The approach is an outgrowth of the microfinancing projects developed by Bangladeshi Nobel Prize-winning banker and economist Muhammad Yunus, which helped millions of low-income individuals in Asia and Africa to set up businesses and buy houses. Today a number of innovative microinsurance products have been developed to protect the working poor against the financial impact of losses. A 2014 A.M. Best report states that about 500 million people globally have microinsurance and that there is increasing evidence from numerous academic studies that its impact has been beneficial for the poor in many ways. A 2015 Microinsurance Network report found that in the three major microinsurance regions of Africa, Asia and Oceania, and Latin America and the Caribbean, between 2012 and 2014, 263.4 million lives and properties were insured, generating $2.1 billion in microinsurance premiums. In terms of microinsurance premiums, both Latin America and Asia accounted for 39 percent of premiums while Africa accounted for 22 percent.

Insurance In Emerging Markets

With limited growth prospects in the insurance markets of developed countries, insurers see emerging economies as presenting significant potential for growth and profitability. Premium growth in developing countries has been outpacing growth in industrialized countries. Swiss Re's 2016 *sigma* report on world insurance markets found that premiums in emerging countries rose 9.8 percent in 2015, after adjusting for inflation, following a 7.6 percent rise in 2014. Growth in developing markets outpaced growth in advanced markets, which increased by 2.5 percent in 2015 after rising 2.6 percent in 2014. Emerging markets accounted for 18.7 percent of total global premium volume in 2015, up from 17.4 percent in 2014.

Swiss Re identifies emerging markets as countries in South and East Asia, Latin America and the Caribbean, Central and Eastern Europe, Africa, the Middle East (excluding Israel), Central Asia and Turkey. Emerging market premiums rose to $849.7 billion in 2015 from $828.3 billion in 2014, driven by increases in both the nonlife and life sectors. Nonlife sector premiums had 7.8 percent growth in 2015, adjusted for inflation, compared with 8.6 percent in 2014. Life sector premiums grew faster in 2015, up 11.7 percent after inflation, compared with 6.8 percent in 2014.

Insurance In Emerging Markets, 2015

	Direct premiums written, 2015[1]	Percent change from 2014[2]	Share of world market	Premiums as a percent of GDP[3]	Premiums per capita
Total industry					
Advanced markets	$3,704,063	2.5%	81.34%	8.12%	$3,440
Emerging markets	849,723	9.8	18.66	2.92	135
Total	**$4,553,785**	**3.8%**	**100.00%**	**6.23%**	**$621**
Life					
Advanced markets	2,089,765	2.5	82.47	4.61	1,954
Emerging markets	444,052	11.7	17.53	1.52	71
Total	**$2,533,818**	**4.0%**	**100.00%**	**3.47%**	**$346**
Nonlife					
Advanced markets	1,614,298	2.6	79.92	3.51	1,486
Emerging markets	405,670	7.8	20.08	1.39	64
Total	**$2,019,967**	**3.6%**	**100.00%**	**2.77%**	**$276**

[1]Expressed in millions of U.S. dollars. [2]Inflation-adjusted. [3]Gross domestic product.
Source: Swiss Re, *sigma*, No. 3/2016.

According to Swiss Re, China is the largest emerging market country based on insurance premiums written (including life and nonlife business) with $386.5 billion in premiums written in 2015, followed by India with $71.8 billion and Brazil with $69.1 billion. However when measured by insurance density, Macao ranked first, with $2,104 in premiums per capita (including life and nonlife business).

Top 10 Emerging Markets By Insurance Density, 2015[1]

Rank	Country	Total premiums[2] Per capita (US $)	As a percent of GDP[3]
1	Macao	$2,104	1.86%
2	Qatar	1,268	1.54
3	United Arab Emirates	1,102	2.35
4	Slovenia	1,058	5.01
5	Trinidad and Tobago	843	4.44
6	South Africa	843	14.69
7	Chile	630	4.74
8	Czech Republic	592	3.27
9	Mauritius	589	6.43
10	Bahrain	585	2.45

[1]Based on total insurance premiums per capita. Excludes cross-border business. [2]Life and nonlife premiums. Data are estimated for Qatar, United Arab Emirates, Trinidad and Tobago, South Africa and Bahrain and provisional for the Czech Republic. [3]Gross domestic product.
Source: Swiss Re, *sigma*, No. 3/2016.

Total Insurance Premiums, Emerging Markets, 2015[1] (US$ billions, end of year)

Emerging Asia	61.69%	$524,211
Latin America and Caribbean	18.61	158,146
Africa	7.55	64,123
Central and Eastern Europe	6.32	53,693
Middle East and Central Asia	5.83	49,549
Total	**100.00%**	**$849,722**

[1]Includes life and nonlife insurance premiums.
Source: Insurance Information Institute using data from Swiss Re, *sigma*, No. 3/2016.

2015 Emerging Markets Premiums

Emerging Asia: This sector is the largest emerging market, accounting for $524 billion or 61.7 percent of total emerging markets premium. China has by far the largest emerging market share in Asia, with total premiums of $387 billion, or 74 percent of the sector. In emerging Asia, life premiums grew 16 percent in 2015, due in part to economic recovery in India and the Philippines, and the continuing expansion in Indonesia and Vietnam. Nonlife premiums grew 15 percent, driven by growth in China's motor, guarantee and credit and agricultural insurance.

Latin America and the Caribbean: The second-largest emerging market, which made up $158.1 billion or 18.6 percent of the total emerging sector, had a 7.5 percent increase in life premiums in 2015, mostly due to strong growth in Brazil and Chile. Nonlife premiums rose in Argentina, Mexico and Peru, but were down in Venezuela and Brazil.

Africa: In 2015 total insurance premiums in Africa were $64.1 billion or 7.5 percent of all emerging markets. Life premium growth at 2.8 percent was lower than 5.1 percent in 2014. In South Africa, which held 86 percent of premiums in the region, nonlife premium growth slowed to 2.3 percent in 2015 from 4.6 percent during the previous year, as consumer incomes suffered from a weaker economy. Nonlife premium growth was lower in 2015, at 1.3 percent, about the same as in 2014. South Africa registered 2.5 percent growth.

Central and Eastern Europe: The area made up $53.7 billion or 6.3 percent of emerging markets premium in 2015. Life insurance premiums slipped 3.5 percent in 2015, the third year of lower premiums, following a 2.0 percent drop in 2014. The decrease was mainly caused by declines in Poland (4.9 percent) and the Czech Republic (down 13 percent), the two largest markets in the region. Nonlife premiums fell 4.9 percent in 2015, almost entirely due to a 12 percent decline in Russia, as the economy faltered, and a 24 percent drop in Ukraine.

The Middle East, Central Asia and Turkey: The smallest region of the emerging markets sector accounted for $49.5 billion or 5.8 percent of total premiums in 2015. Life insurance in the region grew 7.6 percent, up from 3.2 percent growth in 2014. The region's largest market, the United Arab Emirates, saw 9.3 percent growth. Nonlife premiums were up by 9.7 percent in 2015 in the sector as premiums rose 20 percent in Saudi Arabia, reflecting rising rates in motor and medical insurance, and up 12 percent in Turkey due to increases in motor, aviation and other lines of insurance.

Chapter 2

U.S. Insurance Industry, All Sectors

PREMIUMS

Net Premiums Written, Property/Casualty And Life/Health

There are three main insurance sectors. Property/casualty (P/C) consists mainly of auto, home and commercial insurance. Life/health (L/H) consists mainly of life insurance and annuity products. Most private health insurance is written by insurers whose main business is health insurance. However, L/H and P/C insurers also write this coverage. P/C net premiums written rose by 3.4 percent while L/H net premiums written fell by 1.4 percent in 2015.

Property/Casualty And Life/Health Insurance Net Premiums Written, 2006-2015 ($000)

Year	Property/casualty[1]	Life/health[2]	Total
2006	$447,803,479	$564,983,111	$1,012,786,590
2007	446,179,922	596,111,873	1,042,291,795
2008	440,318,983	607,250,216	1,047,569,199
2009	423,528,077	491,600,805	915,128,882
2010	425,878,773	560,494,920	986,373,693
2011	441,562,154	602,268,835	1,043,830,989
2012	460,486,285	623,258,729	1,083,745,014
2013	481,517,971	560,091,205	1,041,609,176
2014	502,635,327	644,509,707	1,147,145,034
2015	519,848,590	635,567,361	1,155,415,951
Percent change, 2006-2015	**16.1%**	**12.5%**	**14.1%**

[1]Net premiums written after reinsurance transactions, excludes state funds. [2]Premiums, annuity considerations (fees for annuity contracts) and deposit-type funds for life/health insurance companies.

Source: NAIC data, sourced from S&P Global Market Intelligence, Insurance Information Institute.

Property/Casualty And Life/Health Insurance Premiums, 2015[1] (US$ billions)

■	Life/health	55%	$635.6
■	Property/casualty	45	519.8
	Total	**100%**	**$1,155.4**

[1]Property/casualty: net premiums written after reinsurance transactions, excludes state funds; life/health: premiums, annuity considerations (fees for annuity contracts) and deposit-type funds.
Source: NAIC data, sourced from S&P Global Market Intelligence, Insurance Information Institute.

Growth In U.S. Premiums, Property/Casualty And Life/Health Insurance, 2006-2015 (Percent change from prior year)

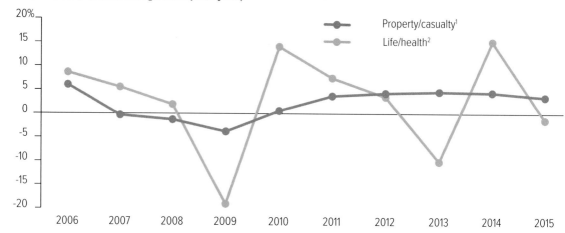

[1]Net premiums written after reinsurance transactions, excludes state funds. [2]Premiums and annuity considerations (fees for annuity contracts) for life/health insurance companies.

Source: NAIC data, sourced from S&P Global Market Intelligence, Insurance Information Institute.

Direct Premiums Written, Property/Casualty And Life/Health

Property/Casualty And Life/Health Insurance Direct Premiums Written, 2006-2015 ($000)

Year	Property/casualty[1]	Life/health[2]	Total
2006	$508,324,604	$600,580,462	$1,108,905,066
2007	510,979,916	645,611,925	1,156,591,841
2008	498,690,753	661,930,391	1,160,621,144
2009	483,081,379	608,246,237	1,091,327,616
2010	484,404,467	612,939,920	1,097,344,387
2011	502,005,179	656,938,393	1,158,943,571
2012	523,881,547	684,868,448	1,208,749,995
2013	546,250,329	646,652,656	1,192,902,985
2014	570,782,893	662,304,443	1,233,087,337
2015	591,758,049	681,097,036	1,272,855,085
Percent change, 2006-2015	**16.4%**	**13.4%**	**14.8%**

[1]Direct premiums written before reinsurance transactions, excludes state funds. [2]Premiums, annuity considerations (fees for annuity contracts) and deposit-type funds for life/health insurance companies.

Source: NAIC data, sourced from S&P Global Market Intelligence, Insurance Information Institute.



LEADING COMPANIES

Top 10 Writers Of Property/Casualty Insurance By Direct Premiums Written, 2015 ($000)

Rank	Group/company	Direct premiums written[1]	Market share[2]
1	State Farm Mutual Automobile Insurance	$59,361,685	10.0%
2	Allstate Corp.	30,180,756	5.1
3	Berkshire Hathaway Inc.	29,967,354	5.1
4	Liberty Mutual	29,848,412	5.1
5	Travelers Companies Inc.	23,200,304	3.9
6	Progressive Corp.	21,346,246	3.6
7	Chubb Ltd.[3]	20,671,147	3.5
8	Nationwide Mutual Group	19,577,849	3.3
9	American International Group (AIG)	19,066,161	3.2
10	Farmers Insurance Group of Companies[4]	19,050,733	3.2

[1]Before reinsurance transactions, includes state funds. [2]Based on U.S. total, includes territories. [3]Chubb Ltd. data reflect the 2015 merger with Ace Ltd. [4]Data for Farmers Insurance Group of Companies and Zurich Financial Group (which owns Farmers' management company) are reported separately by S&P Global Market Intelligence.

Source: NAIC data, sourced from S&P Global Market Intelligence, Insurance Information Institute.

Top 10 Writers Of Life Insurance/Annuities By Direct Premiums Written, 2015 ($000)

Rank	Group/company	Direct premiums written[1]	Market share[2]
1	MetLife Inc.	$102,487,074	16.4%
2	Prudential Financial Inc.	43,134,670	6.9
3	New York Life Insurance Group	29,647,519	4.8
4	Jackson National Life Group	27,457,195	4.4
5	AEGON	24,983,201	4.0
6	American International Group (AIG)	24,976,781	4.0
7	Principal Financial Group Inc.	23,416,059	3.8
8	Massachusetts Mutual Life Insurance Co.	23,117,904	3.7
9	Lincoln National Corp.	22,676,916	3.6
10	AXA	19,478,236	3.1

[1]Includes life insurance, annuity considerations, deposit-type contract funds and other considerations; excludes accident and health insurance. Before reinsurance transactions. [2]Based on U.S. total, includes territories.

Source: NAIC data, sourced from S&P Global Market Intelligence, Insurance Information Institute.

HEALTH

Healthcare Expenditures

Nearly half of the nation's healthcare costs are covered under Medicaid, Medicare and other public programs.

The Nation's Healthcare Dollar: Where It Came From, 2014[1]

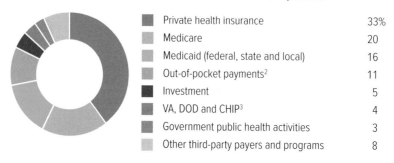

■	Private health insurance	33%
■	Medicare	20
■	Medicaid (federal, state and local)	16
■	Out-of-pocket payments[2]	11
■	Investment	5
■	VA, DOD and CHIP[3]	4
■	Government public health activities	3
■	Other third-party payers and programs	8

[1]Sum of components may not add to 100 percent due to rounding. [2]Includes co-payments, deductibles, and any amounts not covered by health insurance. [3]Department of Veterans Affairs, Department of Defense and Children's Health Insurance Program.
Source: Centers for Medicare and Medicaid Services, Office of the Actuary, National Health Statistics Group.

National healthcare expenditures rose 5.3 percent to $3.0 trillion in 2014, according to the U.S. Department of Health and Human Services' Centers for Medicare and Medicaid Services (CMS). The 2014 increase was larger than 2013's 2.9 percent rise, primarily due to the major coverage expansions under the Affordable Care Act, particularly for Medicaid and private health insurance. Between 1970 and 1993, the beginning of the shift to managed care, healthcare expenditures rose 11.5 percent on an average annual basis. In 2014 the health spending share of the U.S. gross domestic product rose to 17.5 percent from 17.3 percent in 2013 and was the highest level on record. Healthcare spending rose to $9,523 per capita in 2014 from $9,115 in 2013, a 4.5 percent increase. CMS projected that annual health expenditures grew 5.5 percent in 2015 and will average 5.8 percent a year through 2025, due to changes in economic growth, faster growth in medical prices and population aging.

National Health Expenditures, Average Annual Percent Growth From Prior Year, 1993-2019

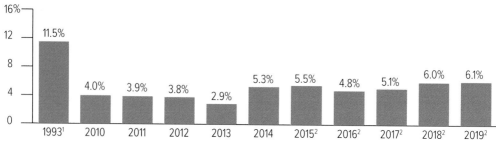

[1]Average annual growth from 1970 through 1993; marks the beginning of the shift to managed care. [2]Projected.
Source: Centers for Medicare and Medicaid Services, Office of the Actuary.

EMPLOYMENT AND OTHER ECONOMIC CONTRIBUTIONS

Property/casualty (P/C) and life/health insurance companies contribute to our economy far beyond their core function of helping to manage risk. Insurers contributed $450.3 billion, or 2.6 percent, to the nation's gross domestic product in 2014. The taxes they pay include special levies on insurance premiums, which amounted to $19.2 billion in 2015, or 2.1 percent of all taxes collected by the states. Insurance companies invested $748.9 billion in state and local municipal bonds and loans in 2015, helping to fund the building of roads, schools and other public projects. They provide businesses with capital for research, expansions and other ventures through their holdings in stocks and bonds, a figure which totaled $4.1 trillion in 2015. The industry is also a major contributor to charitable causes. The Insurance Industry Charitable Foundation, established by the P/C insurance industry in 1994, and McKinsey and Co. said that the insurance industry increased charitable giving by an average of 15 percent per year since 2011 for a total of $575 million in 2014. By mid-2015 the industry had contributed more than $23.5 million in local community grants and nearly 200,000 volunteer hours to hundreds of community nonprofit organizations. The sector is also a large employer, providing some 2.5 million jobs, or 2.1 percent of U.S. employment in 2015.

Employment In Insurance, 2006-2015 (Annual averages, 000)

| | Insurance carriers | | | | Insurance agencies, brokerages and related services | | | |
| | Direct insurers[1] | | | | | | | |
Year	Life and health[2]	Property/ casualty	Reinsurers	Total	Insurance agencies and brokers	Other insurance-related activities[3]	Total	Total industry
2006	790.6	649.1	28.0	1,467.7	662.4	249.0	911.4	2,379.1
2007	787.1	647.0	27.0	1,461.1	677.8	252.7	930.5	2,391.6
2008	800.8	646.7	27.9	1,475.4	671.6	258.1	929.6	2,405.1
2009	802.8	632.9	27.5	1,463.2	653.3	254.2	907.4	2,370.6
2010	804.1	614.3	26.8	1,445.2	642.3	253.1	895.5	2,340.6
2011	788.9	611.6	25.6	1,426.1	649.2	261.1	910.3	2,336.4
2012	811.3	599.5	25.7	1,436.4	659.6	272.3	931.8	2,368.3
2013	813.2	593.7	26.2	1,433.1	672.3	283.5	955.8	2,388.9
2014	829.0	594.7	25.1	1,448.7	720.0	297.1	1,017.1	2,465.8
2015	851.1	599.7	25.1	1,475.9	762.4	306.2	1,068.6	2,544.5

[1]Establishments primarily engaged in initially underwriting insurance policies. [2]Includes establishments engaged in underwriting annuities, life insurance and health and medical insurance policies. [3]Includes claims adjusters, third-party administrators of insurance funds and other service personnel such as advisory and insurance ratemaking services.

Source: U.S. Department of Labor, Bureau of Labor Statistics.

Insurance Carriers And Related Activities Employment By State, 2015[1]

State	Number of employees	State	Number of employees
Alabama	37,524	Montana	8,712
Alaska	2,633	Nebraska	33,842
Arizona	65,141	Nevada	19,067
Arkansas	21,734	New Hampshire	17,877
California	307,212	New Jersey	101,744
Colorado	54,861	New Mexico	12,288
Connecticut	68,387	New York	197,029
Delaware	8,300	North Carolina	80,192
D.C.	4,566	North Dakota	10,777
Florida	212,509	Ohio	137,212
Georgia	103,297	Oklahoma	31,497
Hawaii	10,485	Oregon	33,958
Idaho	13,203	Pennsylvania	156,862
Illinois	152,766	Rhode Island	12,022
Indiana	62,742	South Carolina	41,933
Iowa	55,942	South Dakota	12,174
Kansas	39,792	Tennessee	62,775
Kentucky	43,623	Texas	270,730
Louisiana	35,878	Utah	26,593
Maine	13,750	Vermont	5,038
Maryland	48,407	Virginia	67,591
Massachusetts	81,755	Washington	55,526
Michigan	80,165	West Virginia	11,148
Minnesota	81,552	Wisconsin	79,910
Mississippi	18,809	Wyoming	3,437
Missouri	66,833	**United States**	**3,181,800**

[1]Total full-time and part-time employment. Note: Does not match data shown elsewhere due to the use of different surveys. Data as of September 2016.

Source: U.S. Department of Commerce, Bureau of Economic Analysis, Regional Economic Information System.

Gross Domestic Product

Insurance Sector's Share Of Gross Domestic Product (GDP), 2010-2014 ($ billions)

Year	Total GDP	Insurance carriers and related activities	
		GDP	Percent of total GDP
2010	$14,964.4	$365.2	2.4%
2011	15,517.9	379.5	2.4
2012	16,155.3	402.6	2.5
2013	16,663.2	410.3	2.5
2014	17,348.1	450.3	2.6

Source: U.S. Department of Commerce, Bureau of Economic Analysis.

Gross domestic product (GDP) is the total value of all final goods and services produced in the economy. The GDP growth rate is the primary indicator of the state of the economy.

The insurance industry contributed $450.3 billion to the $17.3 trillion GDP in 2014.

Ownership Of Municipal Bonds

Insurance companies help fund the construction of schools, roads and healthcare facilities as well as a variety of other public sector projects through their investments in municipal bonds. The property/casualty insurance industry invested $330 billion in such bonds in 2015, and the life insurance industry invested $159 billion, according to the Federal Reserve.

Insurance Company Holdings Of U.S. Municipal Securities And Loans, 2011-2015
($ billions, end of year)

	2011	2012	2013	2014	2015
Property/casualty insurance companies	$331.0	$328.1	$326.4	$322.1	$330.4
Life insurance companies	121.8	131.5	141.6	147.8	158.5
Total	**$452.8**	**$459.6**	**$468.0**	**$469.9**	**$488.9**

Source: Board of Governors of the Federal Reserve System, June 9, 2016.

MERGERS AND ACQUISITIONS

The number of global insurance-related mergers and acquisitions (M&A) rose to 796 transactions in 2015 from 732 in 2014, reflecting continued low interest rates, high levels of industry capital and low-growth economies in developed countries, according to an analysis by Conning Research. The value of M&A transactions rose to $238.2 billion in 2015, almost four times higher than the $67.0 billion total in 2014. There were 24 underwriter transactions valued at $1 billion or more in 2015, compared with only nine in 2014.

In 2015 the number of insurance-related deals in which a U.S. firm was either a buyer or a target rose 11.5 percent, to 564 in 2015 from 506 transactions in 2015. The value of properties acquired in 2015 deals quadrupled to a record $193.8 billion from $37.5 billion in 2014, according to Conning data. The number of non-U.S. insurance M&A transactions (i.e., where a non-U.S. company was both buyer and seller) increased 6.4 percent to 232 in 2015 from 218 in 2014. The overall reported value of non-U.S. deals rose by 50.5 percent to $44.4 billion in 2015 from $29.5 billion in 2014.

Reported Global Insurance-Related Mergers And Acquistions By Sector, U.S. And Non-U.S. Acquirers, 2015

Sector	Number of transactions			Transaction values ($ millions)		
	U.S.[1]	Non-U.S.[2]	Total	U.S.[1]	Non-U.S.[2]	Total
Underwriting						
Property/casualty	36	59	95	$39,607	$23,364	$62,971
Life/annuity	17	40	57	11,798	18,857	30,655
Health/managed care	22	3	25	100,832	16	100,848
Total	**75**	**102**	**177**	**$152,237**	**$42,237**	**$194,474**
Distribution and services						
Distribution	401	107	508	18,695	1,020	19,715
Services	88	17	105	22,905	735	23,640
Total	**489**	**124**	**613**	**41,600**	**1,755**	**43,355**
Total, all sectors	**564**	**232[3]**	**796**	**$193,837**	**$44,400[3]**	**$238,237**

[1]Includes transactions where a U.S. company was the acquirer and/or the target. [2]Includes transactions where a non-U.S. company was the acquirer and the target. [3]Includes six transactions for multiline companies not noted in the chart.

Source: Conning Research & Consulting, Inc. analysis.

In 2015, four consolidation transactions among U.S. health/managed care insurers accounted for about $100 billion or about half of the total U.S. reported M&A transaction value of $195 billion, according to Conning research. (These deals are under review by state attorneys general and the Justice Department has sued to block the mergers.) Major transactions in the property/casualty sector include ACE's acquisition of Chubb and Tokio Marine Holdings acquisition of HCC Insurance Holdings.

Top 10 Global Insurance-Related Mergers And Acquisitions Announced, 2015 ($ millions)

Rank	Buyer (country)	Target (country)	Sector	Transaction value
1	Anthem, Inc. (U.S.)[1]	Cigna Corp. (U.S.)	Health	$54,200
2	Aetna, Inc. (U.S.)[1]	Humana Inc. (U.S.)	Health	37,000
3	Ace Ltd. (U.S.)	Chubb Corp. (U.S.)	Property/casualty	28,300
4	Willis Group (U.K.)	Towers Watson (U.S.)	Distribution	18,000
5	OptumRx (U.S.)	Catamaran Corp. (U.S.)	Insurance services	12,800
6	Tokio Marine Holdings, Inc. (Japan)	HCC Insurance Holdings, Inc. (U.S.)	Property/casualty	7,500
7	EXOR S.p.A. (Italy)	PartnerRe Ltd. (Bermuda)	Property/casualty	6,900
8	Centene Corp. (U.S.)	Health Net, Inc. (U.S.)	Health	6,800
9	Vista Equity Partners (U.S.)	Solera Holdings (U.S.)	Insurance services	6,500
10	Mitsui Sumitomo Insurance Co. Ltd. (Japan)	Amlin plc (U.K.)	Property/casualty	5,330

[1]These deals are currently under review by the U.S. Department of Justice.
Source: Conning Research & Consulting Inc. analysis.

In the first 10 months of 2016, there were 55 insurance deals affecting whole insurance companies in the United States, compared with 78 in all of 2015. There were 31 property/casualty company deals so far in 2016, only five deals fewer than in all of 2015. 2016 included a $3.4 billion deal for Arch Capital Group to acquire United Guaranty Corp. Meanwhile, there were eight managed care deals, about half of the 2015 total of 17 deals. In 2015 Anthem's announced purchase of Cigna, and Aetna's planned purchase of Humana together totaled $83 billion, according to S&P. The continued scrutiny of these two deals may have dampened merger activity in this sector in 2016.

U.S. Insurance-Related Mergers And Acquisitions, 2006-2015[1] ($ millions)

Year	Underwriting mergers and acquisitions					
	Property/casualty		Life/annuity		Health/managed care	
	Number of transactions	Transaction values	Number of transactions	Transaction values	Number of transactions	Transaction values
2006	48	$35,221	23	$5,055	20	$646
2007	65	14,000	19	8,000	52	10,000
2008	59	16,294	14	382	19	1,691
2009	63	3,507	22	840	18	640
2010	60	6,419	20	23,848	15	692
2011	77	12,458	34	3,063	25	4,703
2012	46	4,651	21	6,083	26	18,520
2013	39	4,397	18	3,299	15	33
2014	53	6,723	10	7,978	15	864
2015	36	39,607	17	11,798	22	100,832

Year	Distribution and insurance services mergers and acquisitions				Total U.S. mergers and acquisitions	
	Distribution		Insurance services			
	Number of transactions	Transaction values	Number of transactions	Transaction values	Number of transactions	Transaction values
2006	246	$944	69	$1,156	406	$43,022
2007	311	15,000	72	6,000	519	52,000
2008	284	5,812	94	7,256	470	31,435
2009	176	615	41	8,771	320	14,373
2010	243	1,727	98	13,823	436	46,509
2011	351	2,608	105	31,892	592	54,724
2012	323	4,225	62	9,673	478	43,152
2013	317	8,246	57	3,349	446	19,324
2014	349	2,581	79	19,390	506	37,536
2015	401	18,695	88	22,905	564	193,837

[1]Includes transactions where a U.S. company was the acquirer and/or the target.

Source: Conning Research & Consulting Inc., proprietary database.

COMPANIES BY STATE

An insurance company is said to be *domiciled* in the state that issued its primary license; it is *domestic* in that state. Once it receives its primary license, it may seek licenses in other states as an out-of-state insurer. These out-of-state insurers are called *foreign* insurers. An insurer incorporated in a foreign country is called an *alien* insurer in states where it is licensed.

Domestic Insurance Companies By State, Property/Casualty And Life/Annuities, 2015

State	Property/ casualty	Life/ annuities	State	Property/ casualty	Life/ annuities
Alabama	19	6	Montana	14	1
Alaska	7	0	Nebraska	34	28
Arizona	40	29	Nevada	11	3
Arkansas	11	29	New Hampshire	51	1
California	100	14	New Jersey	68	3
Colorado	11	10	New Mexico	13	1
Connecticut	69	27	New York	179	80
Delaware	100	29	North Carolina	60	9
D.C.	6	0	North Dakota	13	3
Florida	122	10	Ohio	136	38
Georgia	33	12	Oklahoma	36	24
Hawaii	17	3	Oregon	17	3
Idaho	8	1	Pennsylvania	181	26
Illinois	193	55	Rhode Island	21	2
Indiana	66	27	South Carolina	22	9
Iowa	71	38	South Dakota	18	3
Kansas	28	12	Tennessee	15	13
Kentucky	7	7	Texas	199	120
Louisiana	30	35	Utah	10	16
Maine	11	3	Vermont	13	1
Maryland	31	4	Virginia	18	4
Massachusetts	50	17	Washington	8	7
Michigan	71	23	West Virginia	19	0
Minnesota	38	11	Wisconsin	170	20
Mississippi	14	15	Wyoming	2	1
Missouri	45	25	**United States[1]**	**2,526**	**858**

[1]Excludes territories. Excludes health insurers, risk retention groups, fraternals, title and other insurers.

Source: U.S. Department of Commerce, Bureau of the Census.

According to the National Association of Insurance Commissioners, in the U.S. (including territories) there were 5,926 insurance companies in 2015, including property/casualty (P/C) (2,554), life/annuities (872), health (859), fraternal (85), title (56), risk retention groups (239) and other companies (1,261).

Many insurance companies are part of larger organizations. According to A.M. Best, in 2015 the P/C insurance industry contained about 1,205 organizations or groups (as opposed to 2,655 companies), including 734 stock (or public) organizations, 386 mutual organizations (firms owned by their policyholders) and 66 reciprocals (a type of self-insurance). The remainder consisted of Lloyd's organizations and state funds.

PREMIUM TAXES BY STATE

All insurance companies pay a state tax based on their premiums. Other payments are made to states for licenses and fees, income and property taxes, sales and use taxes, unemployment compensation taxes and franchise taxes.

Insurance companies, including life/health and property/casualty companies, paid $19.2 billion in premium taxes to the 50 states and the District of Columbia in 2015. On a per capita basis, this works out to $60 for every person living in the United States.

Premium taxes accounted for 2.1 percent of all taxes collected by the states and the District of Columbia in 2015.

Premium Taxes By State, Property/Casualty And Life/Health Insurance, 2015 ($000)

State	Amount	State	Amount
Alabama	$312,030	Montana	$97,404
Alaska	66,456	Nebraska	31,036
Arizona	466,788	Nevada	293,922
Arkansas	190,884	New Hampshire	107,740
California	2,444,573	New Jersey	648,090
Colorado	257,795	New Mexico	122,280
Connecticut	189,362	New York	1,431,361
Delaware	93,763	North Carolina	529,936
DC	106,407	North Dakota	58,008
Florida	690,160	Ohio	544,523
Georgia	419,653	Oklahoma	325,954
Hawaii	150,872	Oregon	62,340
Idaho	84,498	Pennsylvania	792,921
Ilinois	379,773	Rhode Island	95,174
Indiana	221,100	South Carolina	248,418
Iowa	109,593	South Dakota	83,022
Kansas	211,766	Tennessee	809,567
Kentucky	146,481	Texas	1,986,919
Louisiana	438,179	Utah	119,280
Maine	98,353	Vermont	57,950
Maryland	444,691	Virginia	451,037
Massachusetts	367,832	Washington	555,976
Michigan	322,999	West Virginia	155,687
Minnesota	437,806	Wisconsin	184,166
Mississippi	299,127	Wyoming	29,648
Missouri	376,811	**United States**	**$19,150,111**

Source: U.S. Department of Commerce, Bureau of the Census.

Chapter 3

Distribution

PROPERTY/CASUALTY

Overview

Many insurance companies use a number of different channels to distribute their products. In the early days of the U.S. insurance industry, insurers hired agents, often on a part-time basis, to sign up applicants for insurance. Some agents, known nowadays as *captive* or *exclusive* agents, represented a single company. Others, the equivalent of today's independent agent, worked for a number of companies. At the same time that the two agency systems were expanding, commercial insurance brokers, who were often underwriters, began to set up shop in cities. While agents usually represented insurers, brokers represented clients who were buying insurance. These three distribution channels (captive agents, independent agents and brokers) exist in much the same form today. But with the development of information technology, which provides faster access to company representatives and makes the exchange of information for underwriting purposes much easier, alternative distribution channels sprang up, including direct sales by telephone, mail and the internet. In addition, insurers are using other types of outlets, such as banks, workplaces, associations and car dealers, to access potential policyholders.

Online Property/Casualty Insurance Sales

Online insurance distribution systems have evolved to encompass all the devices consumers use to conduct business—mobile, tablet and desktop/laptops. As with all online retail businesses, insurers have responded to consumer preferences and developed websites to enable shoppers and customers to view the same website content using different devices. According to J.D. Power and Associates' *2015 Insurance Website Evaluation Study*, although 10 of the 20 largest insurers included in the study use specialized web design, it is not enough to meet shopper and customer demand. The study also found differences among existing customers and shoppers. Service satisfaction for existing customers was down slightly in 2015 from a year ago, and was down for three-quarters of the respondents. Four out of 10 customers use their insurer's website to pay bills, and satisfaction with this task declined the most in 2015, albeit only slightly. Customers said the most difficult tasks were obtaining or printing ID cards and viewing policy information. In contrast, policy shoppers' satisfaction was up significantly and rose for 19 of the 20 insurers. By task, satisfaction with obtaining a quote and comparing prices rose the most. Shoppers said the most difficult task was researching policy information.

The Insurance Information Institute's *Pulse* poll found that among policyholders who compared prices for auto and homeowners insurance at renewal, talking to an agent in person was the preferred method of comparing prices. In November 2015, 69 percent of respondents who were auto insurance customers compared prices, and 50 percent said they talked to an agent in person. More than one-third (39 percent) went online to compare prices and about the same number (37 percent) called a company by phone. (Respondents could report more than one method.) Of the 44 percent of homeowner policyholders who checked prices in May 2016, about a third of those (29 percent) talked to an agent in person, while 24 percent compared prices over the phone. Seventeen percent went online.

There were an estimated 38,000 independent agencies in the United States in 2016, down from 38,500 in 2014, according to the Independent Insurance Agents and Brokers of America's (IIABA) 2016 Agency Universe survey.

The IIABA says the 2016 decrease reflects the increase in mergers and acquisitions along with stable rates of exclusive agency conversions from captive to independent and new agency formation.

Between 2014 and 2016 the estimated percentage of small agencies (less than $150,000 in revenue) rose to 21 percent from 15 percent, while jumbo agencies (revenue of $10 million or more) now account for 1.6 percent of agencies, compared with 0.8 percent in 2014.

Property/Casualty Insurance Distribution

Agency writers, whose products are sold by independent agents or brokers representing several companies—and direct writers, which sell their own products through captive agents by mail, telephone, or via the internet and other means—each account for about half of the property/casualty (P/C) market. There is a degree of overlap as many insurers use multiple channels.

A.M. Best organizes insurance into two main distribution channels: agency writers and direct writers. Its *agency writers* category includes insurers that distribute through independent agencies, brokers, general agents and managing general agents. Its *direct writers* category includes insurers that distribute through the internet, exclusive/captive agents, direct response and affinity groups.

- In 2015 direct writers accounted for 51.4 percent of P/C insurance net premiums written and agency writers accounted for 46.1 percent, according to A.M. Best.*
- In the personal lines market, direct writers accounted for 71.2 percent of net premiums written in 2015 and agency writers accounted for 27.0 percent. Direct writers accounted for 68.4 percent of the homeowners market and agency writers accounted for 27.9 percent. Direct writers accounted for 72.4 percent of the personal auto market and agency writers accounted for 26.6 percent.*
- Agency writers accounted for 67.1 percent of commercial P/C net premiums written, and direct writers accounted for 29.5 percent.*

*Unspecified distribution channels accounted for the remainder.

LIFE

Life Insurance Distribution

Life Individual Market Share By Distribution Channel, 2006-2015
(Based on first year collected premiums)

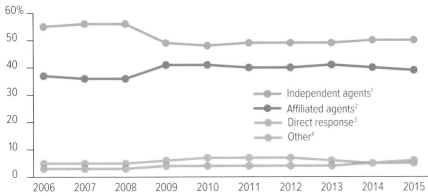

Legend:
- Independent agents[1]
- Affiliated agents[2]
- Direct response[3]
- Other[4]

In 2015 independent agents held 50 percent of the new individual life insurance sales market, followed by affiliated (i.e., captive) agents with 39 percent, direct marketers with 6 percent and others accounting for the remaining 5 percent, according to LIMRA, a life insurance trade association.

[1]Includes brokers, stockbrokers and personal producing general agents. [2]Includes career, multiline exclusive and home service agents. [3]No producers are involved. Excludes direct marketing efforts involving agents. [4]Includes financial institutions, worksite and other channels.
Source: LIMRA's *U.S. Individual Life Insurance Sales Survey* and LIMRA estimates.

Online Life Insurance Sales

Although half of consumers prefer to purchase life insurance in person with a financial adviser, the second most popular method was online, with 21 percent of respondents preferring this method, according to the *2016 Insurance Barometer Study* survey by Life Happens and LIMRA. These proportions did not change from the 2015 survey. Less than 10 percent of respondents chose purchasing life insurance at their workplace, email, mail or over the phone. When asked why they prefer to purchase life insurance online, three-quarters of those consumers said the major reason was the convenience and the ability to purchase at their own time and pace, according to LIMRA. Three out of five respondents cited the ability to research and the ease and speed of purchasing life insurance online as major reasons. Other reasons were the ability to comparison shop (58 percent) and lack of pressure to buy (55 percent) and comfort and confidence (45 percent). Nearly 30 percent of respondents have purchased or attempted to purchase life insurance through the internet, half within the past year. However, few actually completed their application online, and most were directed to meet with a financial advisor or agent. Half of online shoppers used a quoting engine website in 2016, compared with about 40 percent a year ago. This proportion rose to almost three-quarters for millennials (ages 18 to 35). Eighty-eight percent of consumers say they would use the internet to research life insurance before purchasing coverage, about the same number as a year earlier. Ninety-five percent of millennials would use the internet to research life insurance. That amount falls for older age groups, down to 70 percent for consumers age 65 and older.

ANNUITIES

Annuities Distribution

Insurance agents, including career agents, who sell the products of a single life insurance company, and independent agents, who represent several insurers, accounted for 37 percent of annuity sales in 2015. State and federal regulators require sellers of variable annuities to register with the Financial Industry Regulatory Authority (FINRA) and the Securities and Exchange Commission (SEC).

Sales Of Individual Annuities By Distribution Channels, 2011 and 2015

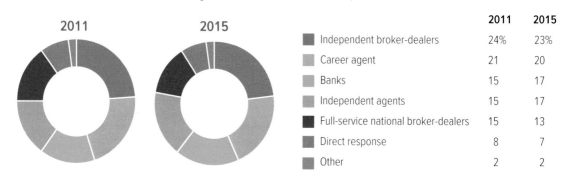

	2011	2015
Independent broker-dealers	24%	23%
Career agent	21	20
Banks	15	17
Independent agents	15	17
Full-service national broker-dealers	15	13
Direct response	8	7
Other	2	2

Source: *U.S. Individual Annuity Yearbook - 2015*, LIMRA Secure Retirement Institute.

Chapter 4

Retirement

OVERVIEW

In addition to Social Security and private savings, a large number of Americans rely on investments in formal plans to prepare for retirement. Employer-sponsored retirement plans, individual retirement accounts (IRAs) and annuities play an important role in the U.S. retirement system. Such retirement assets totaled $24 trillion at the end of 2015, slightly less than the same period in 2014, according to the Investment Company Institute (ICI). The largest components of retirement assets were IRAs and employer-sponsored defined contribution plans, holding $7.3 trillion and $6.7 trillion, respectively, at the close of 2015. An ICI report found that 60 percent of U.S. households (75 million households) reported that they had employer-sponsored retirement plans, IRAs or both in mid-2015.

U.S. Retirement Assets, 2011 And 2015 ($ trillions, year-end)

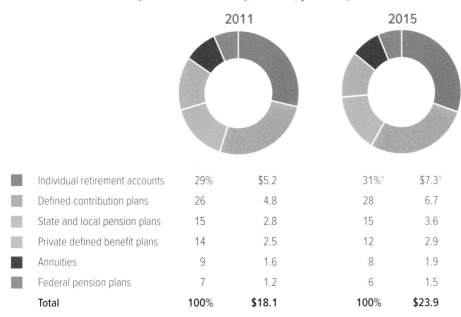

	2011		2015	
Individual retirement accounts	29%	$5.2	31%[1]	$7.3[1]
Defined contribution plans	26	4.8	28	6.7
State and local pension plans	15	2.8	15	3.6
Private defined benefit plans	14	2.5	12	2.9
Annuities	9	1.6	8	1.9
Federal pension plans	7	1.2	6	1.5
Total	**100%**	**$18.1**	**100%**	**$23.9**

[1]Estimated.

Source: Investment Company Institute, "*The U.S. Retirement Market, First Quarter 2016.*"

Workplace plans play a major part in retirement savings. In 2015, 61.3 percent of Americans' retirement assets were held in private or public employer-sponsored plans, according to the Investment Company Institute. These workplace plans include private pension plans, defined contribution plans such as 401(k) plans and state and local and federal pension plans. Almost one-third (30.6 percent) of all retirement assets were in individual retirement accounts (IRAs) and 8.1 percent were in annuities. In 2006, 65.9 percent of the nation's retirement assets were held in private or public employer-sponsored plans, 25.5 percent were held in IRAs and 8.6 percent were held in annuities. In 2015, 55 percent of households had employer-sponsored benefit plans. Thirty-two percent had assets in IRAs, and 27 percent had both IRAs and employer-sponsored retirement plans.

U.S. Retirement Assets, By Type, 2006-2015 ($ trillions, end of year)

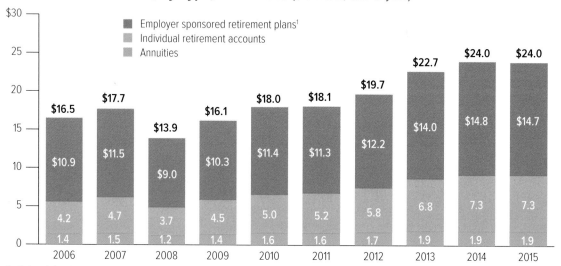

[1]Includes defined contribution plans, private defined benefits plans, state and local and federal pension plans.

Source: 2016 Investment Company Fact Book: A Review of Trends and Activities in the U.S. Investment Company Industry, Investment Company Institute.

Defined Benefit And Defined Contribution Retirement Plans

There are two basic types of workplace retirement plans: defined benefit and defined contribution plans. In a defined benefit plan, the income the employee receives in retirement is guaranteed, based on predetermined benefit formulas. In a defined contribution plan, a type of savings plan in which taxes on earnings are deferred until funds are withdrawn, the amount of retirement income depends on the contributions made and the earnings generated by the securities purchased. The employer generally matches the employee contribution up to a certain level, and the employee selects investments from among the options the employer's plan offers. 401(k) plans fall into this category, as do 403(b) plans for nonprofit organizations and 457 plans for government workers.

Retirement Funds Asset Mix, 2015

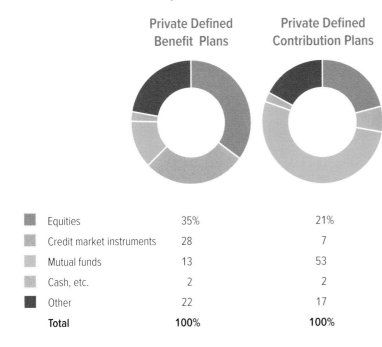

	Private Defined Benefit Plans	Private Defined Contribution Plans
Equities	35%	21%
Credit market instruments	28	7
Mutual funds	13	53
Cash, etc.	2	2
Other	22	17
Total	**100%**	**100%**

In defined benefit plans, equities held the largest share by type of investment in 2015, with 35 percent, followed by credit market instruments, with 28 percent and mutual funds, with 13 percent.

In defined contribution plans, mutual funds held the largest share, with 53 percent. Equities ranked second, with 21 percent, followed by other assets (such as guaranteed investment contracts) with 17 percent.

Source: Board of Governors of the Federal Reserve System, June 9, 2016.

IRAs

Traditional IRAs are defined as those first allowed under the Employee Retirement Income Security Act of 1974.

An individual retirement account (IRA) is a personal savings plan that allows individuals to set aside money for retirement, while offering tax advantages. Amounts in a traditional IRA, including earnings, generally are not taxed until distributed to the holder. Unlike traditional IRAs, Roth IRAs do not allow holders to deduct contributions, but qualified distributions are tax-free. Other variations include Simplified Employee Pensions (SEP), which enable businesses to contribute to traditional IRAs set up for their workers, Savings Incentive Match Plans for Employees (SIMPLE) plans and a similar arrangement for small businesses and Keogh plans for the self-employed. According to the Investment Company Institute, 40 million households, or more than three out of 10, had at least one type of IRA as of mid-2015, Of these, 30 million households had traditional IRAs, 20 million had Roth IRAs and nearly 7 million had a SEP, SIMPLE or other employer-sponsored IRA.

IRA Market Shares By Holder, 2011 And 2015 (Market value, end of year)

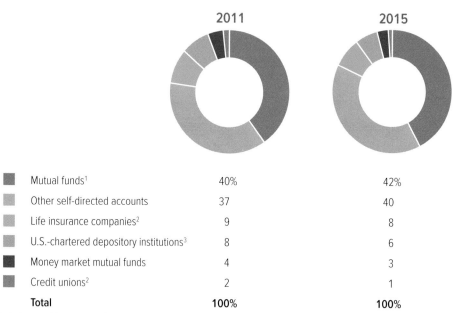

		2011	2015
■	Mutual funds[1]	40%	42%
■	Other self-directed accounts	37	40
■	Life insurance companies[2]	9	8
■	U.S.-chartered depository institutions[3]	8	6
■	Money market mutual funds	4	3
■	Credit unions[2]	2	1
	Total	**100%**	**100%**

[1]Excludes variable annuities. [2]Includes Keogh accounts. [3]Includes savings banks, commercial banks and Keogh accounts.
Source: Board of Governors of the Federal Reserve System, June 9, 2016.

401(k)s

A 401(k) plan is a retirement plan offered by an employer to its workers, allowing employees to set aside tax-deferred income for retirement purposes. It is a type of defined contribution plan. (See page 30.) With $4.7 trillion in assets at year-end 2015, 401(k) plans held the largest share of employer-sponsored defined contribution plan assets, according to the Investment Company Institute (ICI). At the end of 2015 employer-sponsored defined contribution plans, including 401(k) plans and other defined contribution plans, held an estimated $6.7 trillion in assets, according to the ICI.

Average Asset Allocation For All 401(k) Plan Balances, 2014[1]

Equity funds	43%
Balanced funds	25
Bond funds	8
Company stock	7
Guaranteed investment contracts and other stable value funds	6
Money funds	4
Other and unknown	7
Total	**100%**

[1]Percentages are dollar-weighted averages.

Source: Investment Company Institute, *ICI Research Perspective*, vol. 22 no. 3.

MUTUAL FUNDS

Mutual funds held in defined contribution plans and IRAs accounted for $7.1 trillion, or 30 percent, of the $24.0 trillion U.S. retirement market at the end of 2015, according to the Investment Company Institute.

Mutual Fund Retirement Assets By Type Of Plan, 2015[1] ($ billions, end of year)

IRAs	49.1%	$3,499
401(k) plans	39.3	2,805
403(b) plans	6.0	429
Other defined contribution plans	5.6	396
Total	**100%**	**$7,130**

At the end of 2015, 44 percent of mutual fund assets was invested in domestic equity funds, 14 percent in foreign equity funds, 23 percent in hybrid funds, 14 percent in bond funds and 5 percent in money market funds.

[1]Preliminary data. Excludes defined benefit plans.

Source: Investment Company Institute, *2016 Investment Company Fact Book*.

ANNUITIES

Sales Of Fixed And Variable Annuities

Annuities play an important role in retirement planning by helping individuals guard against outliving their assets. In its most general sense, an annuity is an agreement for an entity (generally a life insurance company) to pay another a stream or series of payments. While there are many types of annuities, key features can include tax savings, protection from creditors, investment options, lifetime income and benefits to heirs.

There are many types of annuities. Among the most common are fixed and variable. Fixed annuities guarantee the principal and a minimum rate of interest. Generally, interest credited and payments made from a fixed annuity are based on rates declared by the company, which can change only yearly. In contrast, variable annuity account values and payments are based on the performance of a separate investment portfolio, thus their value may fluctuate daily.

There is a variety of fixed annuities and variable annuities. One type of fixed annuity, the equity indexed annuity, contains features of fixed and variable annuities. It provides a base return, just as other fixed annuities do, but its value is also based on the performance of a specified stock index. The return can go higher if the index rises. The 2010 Dodd-Frank Act included language keeping equity indexed annuities under state insurance regulation. Variable annuities are subject to both state insurance regulation and federal securities regulation. Fixed annuities are not considered securities and are only subject to state insurance regulation.

Annuities can be deferred or immediate. Deferred annuities generally accumulate assets over a long period of time, with withdrawals taken as a single sum or as an income payment beginning at retirement. Immediate annuities allow purchasers to convert a lump sum payment into a stream of income that begins right away. Annuities can be written on an individual or group basis. (See the Life/Health Premiums By Line table, page 41.)

Annuities can be used to fund structured settlements, arrangements in which an injury victim in a lawsuit receives compensation in a number of tax-free payments over time, rather than as a lump sum.

Individual variable annuity sales in the U.S. fell 5.1 percent in 2015, following a 3.6 percent drop the previous year. Fixed annuity sales grew 7.0 percent in 2015, after a 14.8 percent increase in 2014.

Individual Annuity Considerations, 2011-2015[1] ($ billions)

Year	Variable	Fixed	Total Amount	Percent change from prior year
2011	$157.9	$80.5	$238.4	7.2%
2012	147.4	72.3	219.7	-7.8
2013	145.4	84.4	229.8	4.6
2014	140.1	96.9	237.0	3.1
2015	133.0	103.7	236.7	-0.1

[1]Based on LIMRA's estimates of the total annuity sales market. Includes some considerations (i.e., premiums) that though bought in group settings involve individual buying decisions.
Source: LIMRA.

Deferred Annuity Assets, 2006-2015 ($ billions, end of year)

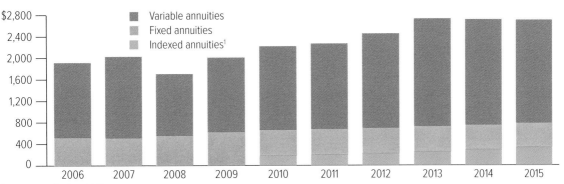

Legend:
- Variable annuities
- Fixed annuities
- Indexed annuities[1]

[1]Not reported before 2010.

Source: LIMRA Secure Retirement Institute.

Individual Immediate Annuity Sales, 2011-2015[1] ($ billions)

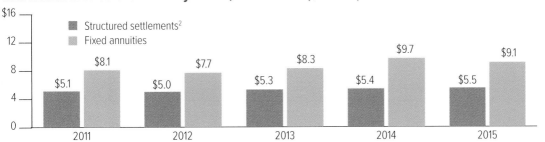

Legend:
- Structured settlements[2]
- Fixed annuities

	Structured settlements	Fixed annuities
2011	$5.1	$8.1
2012	$5.0	$7.7
2013	$5.3	$8.3
2014	$5.4	$9.7
2015	$5.5	$9.1

[1]Includes variable individual annuities sales which were less than $0.1 billion. [2]Single premium contracts bought by property/casualty insurers to distribute awards in personal injury or wrongful death lawsuits over a period of time, rather than as lump sums.

Source: LIMRA Secure Retirement Institute.

Top 10 Writers Of Annuities By Direct Premiums Written, 2015[1] ($000)

Rank	Group/company	Direct premiums written	Market share[2]
1	Jackson National Life Group	$24,613,402	9.5%
2	American International Group (AIG)	21,103,210	8.2
3	Lincoln National Corp.	15,945,646	6.2
4	Prudential Financial Inc.	14,247,941	5.5
5	Voya Financial Inc.	13,557,649	5.3
6	TIAA	11,913,597	4.6
7	New York Life Insurance Group	11,312,531	4.4
8	MetLife Inc.	11,056,363	4.3
9	Allianz Group	10,778,426	4.2
10	AXA	10,101,559	3.9

[1]Includes individual and group annuities. [2]Based on U.S. total, includes territories.

Source: NAIC data, sourced from S&P Global Market Intelligence, Insurance Information Institute.

Top 10 Writers Of Individual Annuities By Direct Premiums Written, 2015 ($000)

Rank	Group/company	Direct premiums written	Market share[1]
1	Jackson National Life Group	$21,845,270	11.1%
2	American International Group (AIG)	14,653,077	7.4
3	Lincoln National Corp.	12,866,640	6.5
4	New York Life Insurance Group	10,786,682	5.5
5	Allianz Group	10,778,426	5.5
6	Prudential Financial Inc.	9,093,778	4.6
7	MetLife Inc.	8,665,101	4.4
8	AEGON	7,871,417	4.0
9	AXA	7,579,613	3.9
10	American Equity Investment	7,061,478	3.6

[1]Based on U.S. total, includes territories.

Source: NAIC data, sourced from S&P Global Market Intelligence, Insurance Information Institute.

Top 10 Writers Of Group Annuities By Direct Premiums Written, 2015 ($000)

Rank	Group/company	Direct premiums written	Market share[1]
1	Voya Financial Inc.	$11,308,978	18.5%
2	American International Group (AIG)	6,450,133	10.6
3	TIAA	5,834,204	9.6
4	Prudential Financial Inc.	5,154,163	8.4
5	Great-West Insurance Group	4,755,022	7.8
6	Massachusetts Mutual Life Insurance Co.	3,312,402	5.4
7	Lincoln National Corp.	3,079,006	5.0
8	OneAmerica Financial Partners	3,027,904	5.0
9	Jackson National Life Group	2,768,132	4.5
10	AXA	2,521,946	4.1

[1]Based on U.S. total, includes territories.

Source: NAIC data, sourced from S&P Global Market Intelligence, Insurance Information Institute.

Chapter 5

Life/Health Financial Data

FINANCIAL RESULTS

Life/Health Sector

Whether measured by premium income or by assets, traditional life insurance is no longer the primary business of many companies in the life/health insurance industry. The emphasis has shifted to the underwriting of annuities. Annuities are contracts that accumulate funds and/or pay out a fixed or variable income stream. An income stream can be for a set period of time or over the lifetimes of the contract holder or his or her beneficiaries.

Nevertheless, traditional life insurance products such as universal life and term life for individuals as well as group life remain an important part of the business, as do disability income and health insurance.

Life insurers invest primarily in corporate bonds but also significantly in corporate equities. Besides annuities and life insurance products, life insurers may offer other types of financial services such as asset management.

2015 Financial Results

According to S&P Global Market Intelligence, in 2015 the life insurance industry posted a 7.3 percent increase in net income after taxes despite continued low interest rates and soft equity markets that resulted in a $2.2 billion decrease in capital gains. Premiums were down 1.4 percent in 2015, compared with 2014, when premiums were at their highest level since the Great Recession. Expenses fell 4.5 percent in 2015 and net gains from operations before federal income tax rose 11.0 percent, after having fallen 22.1 percent in 2014. Capital and surplus rose to $367.4 billion in 2015, from $354.0 billion in 2014, according to S&P Global Market Intelligence.

Investments

The life/health insurance industry's cash and invested assets totaled $3.7 trillion in 2015, according to S&P Global Market Intelligence. Almost three-quarters of these assets were invested in bonds (see page 39). About 11 percent of life insurers' assets were held in real estate loans.

Life/Health Insurance Industry Income Statement, 2011-2015 ($ billions, end of year)

	2011	2012	2013	2014	2015	Percent change, 2014-2015[1]
Revenue						
Life insurance premiums	$122.8	$130.5	$126.0	$133.8	$151.4	13.2%
Annuity premiums and deposits	327.0	339.9	279.4	352.8	324.0	-8.2
Accident and health premiums	151.1	151.4	153.3	156.6	158.8	1.4
Credit life, credit accident and health premiums	1.6	1.6	1.4	1.4	1.4	-0.4
Other premiums and considerations	2.1	2.2	2.3	2.6	2.5	-2.2
Total premiums, consideration and deposits	**$604.5**	**$625.7**	**$562.6**	**$647.3**	**$638.2**	**-1.4%**
Net investment income	167.3	166.5	167.1	171.7	170.8	-0.6
Reinsurance allowance	-16.3	-30.8	-21.2	-15.0	-86.4	NA
Separate accounts revenue	26.1	29.5	31.4	34.3	35.2	2.7
Other income	53.3	41.5	42.8	39.5	90.5	128.9
Total revenue	**$835.0**	**$832.5**	**$782.7**	**$877.8**	**$848.2**	**-3.4%**
Expense						
Benefits	238.9	241.8	250.7	251.8	263.9	4.8
Surrenders	237.3	245.7	248.7	281.5	273.0	-3.0
Increase in reserves	141.2	83.8	86.2	108.7	80.5	-25.9
Transfers to separate accounts	32.4	61.6	-0.8	-16.5	36.9	NA
Commissions	51.4	52.6	53.0	52.1	55.5	6.6
General and administrative expenses	56.4	57.2	58.5	59.0	60.1	1.9
Insurance taxes, licenses and fees	7.8	8.0	8.2	10.0	10.5	5.0
Other expenses	8.1	6.7	-0.4	65.8	-4.9	NA
Total expenses	**$773.5**	**$757.4**	**$704.1**	**$812.4**	**$775.5**	**-4.5%**
Net income						
Policyholder dividends	15.1	15.2	15.7	16.4	18.3	11.2
Net gain from operations before federal income tax	28.0	59.6	62.9	49.0	54.4	11.0
Federal income tax	4.7	9.9	8.6	10.1	10.6	4.6
Net income before capital gains	**$22.9**	**$49.7**	**$54.3**	**$38.9**	**$43.8**	**12.7%**
Net realized capital gains (losses)	-8.5	-9.4	-12.0	-1.3	-3.5	NA
Net income	**$14.4**	**$40.3**	**$42.3**	**$37.6**	**$40.3**	**7.3%**
Pre-tax operating income	28.0	59.6	62.9	49.0	54.4	11.0

[1]Calculated from unrounded data. NA=Not applicable.

Source: NAIC data, sourced from S&P Global Market Intelligence, Insurance Information Institute.

INVESTMENTS

Investments, Life/Health Insurers, 2013-2015[1] ($ billions, end of year)

Investment type	Amount			Percent of total investments		
	2013	2014	2015	2013	2014	2015
Bonds	$2,601.2	$2,684.9	$2,734.1	74.70%	73.93%	73.82%
Stocks	**80.4**	**86.2**	**84.9**	**2.31**	**2.37**	**2.29**
Preferred stock	8.3	9.1	9.6	0.24	0.25	0.26
Common stock	72.1	77.0	75.2	2.07	2.12	2.03
Mortgage loans on real estate	**353.1**	**373.0**	**404.2**	**10.14**	**10.27**	**10.91**
First lien real estate mortgage loans	350.1	368.4	397.4	10.05	10.14	10.73
Real estate loans less first liens	3.1	4.6	6.8	0.09	0.13	0.18
Real estate	**22.4**	**21.9**	**23.7**	**0.64**	**0.60**	**0.64**
Occupied properties	5.4	5.5	5.5	0.16	0.15	0.15
Income generating properties	16.0	16.0	17.8	0.46	0.44	0.48
Properties for sale	0.9	0.4	0.4	0.03	0.01	0.01
Cash, cash equivalent and short term investments	94.8	100.0	103.3	2.72	2.75	2.79
Contract loans including premium notes	128.4	130.1	126.8	3.69	3.58	3.42
Derivatives	37.8	56.5	53.8	1.09	1.56	1.45
Other invested assets	145.5	161.8	154.9	4.18	4.46	4.18
Receivables for securities	3.2	2.2	2.3	0.09	0.06	0.06
Securities lending reinvested collateral assets	13.8	11.2	11.7	0.40	0.31	0.32
Write-ins for invested assets	1.6	4.0	4.1	0.05	0.11	0.11
Total cash and invested assets	**$3,482.2**	**$3,631.7**	**$3,703.9**	**100.00%**	**100.00%**	**100.00%**

[1]Data are net admitted assets of life/health insurers.
Source: NAIC data, sourced from S&P Global Market Intelligence, Insurance Information Institute.

Investments, Life/Health Insurers, Bond Portfolio, 2015[1]

Industrial and miscellaneous	75.8%
All government and revenue bonds	23.0
Parents, subsidiaries and affiliates	1.2

[1]Long-term bonds with maturity dates over one year, as of December 31, 2015.
Source: NAIC data, sourced from S&P Global Market Intelligence, Insurance Information Institute.

PAYOUTS

Life insurance benefits and claims totaled $617 billion in 2015. This includes life insurance death benefits, annuity benefits, disability benefits and other payouts, compared with $642 billion in 2014. The largest payout, $273 billion, was for surrender benefits and withdrawals from life insurance contracts made to policyholders who terminated their policies early or withdrew cash from their policies.

Life Insurance Industry Benefits And Claims, 2011-2015 ($000)

	2011	2012	2013	2014	2015
Death benefits	$60,609,925	$61,699,965	$62,537,003	$65,961,376	$72,321,581
Matured endowments, excluding annual pure endowments	767,092	415,088	368,210	350,488	397,554
Annuity benefits	70,873,226	70,296,382	74,882,585	69,583,732	73,535,200
Disability, accident and health benefits[1]	104,964,677	107,507,088	110,806,435	113,589,753	115,472,213
Coupons, pure endowment and similar benefits	16,075	17,179	17,222	18,992	18,237
Surrender benefits, withdrawals for life contracts	237,281,666	245,728,327	248,702,088	281,532,892	272,998,652
Group conversions	27,884	27,891	52,893	28,088	48,382
Interest and adjustments on deposit type contracts	9,829,729	7,321,437	8,195,240	7,749,827	8,009,313
Payments on supplementary contracts with life contingencies	1,690,841	1,809,677	1,985,919	2,237,030	2,120,777
Increase in aggregate reserve	131,334,694	76,439,405	78,027,832	100,983,247	72,537,076
Total benefits and claims	**$617,395,809**	**$571,262,436**	**$585,575,427**	**$642,035,425**	**$617,455,351**

[1]Excludes benefits paid by health insurance companies and property/casualty insurance companies.

Source: NAIC data, sourced from S&P Global Market Intelligence, Insurance Information Institute.

PREMIUMS BY LINE

Annuities are the largest life/health product line, as measured by premiums written, followed by life, and accident and health insurance. Life insurance policies can be sold on an individual, or ordinary, basis or to groups such as employees and associations. Accident and health insurance includes medical expenses, disability income and long-term care. Other lines include credit life, which pays the balance of a loan if the borrower dies or becomes disabled, and industrial life, small policies whose premiums are generally collected by an agent on a weekly basis.

Direct Premiums Written By Line, Life/Health Insurance Industry, 2013-2015 ($000)

	2013		2014		2015	
Lines of insurance	Direct premiums written[1]	Percent of total	Direct premiums written[1]	Percent of total	Direct premiums written[1]	Percent of total
Annuities						
Ordinary individual annuities	$198,862,072	30.8%	$205,448,744	31.0%	$206,964,955	30.4%
Group annuities	120,091,136	18.6	119,716,314	18.1	127,014,242	18.6
Total	**$318,953,208**	**49.3%**	**$325,165,057**	**49.1%**	**$333,979,197**	**49.0%**
Life						
Ordinary life	129,961,179	20.1	132,935,453	20.1	136,272,726	20.0
Group life	33,531,921	5.2	34,378,152	5.2	37,823,537	5.6
Credit life (group and individual)	990,170	0.2	960,229	0.1	920,257	0.1
Industrial life	146,248	[2]	142,962	[2]	131,020	[2]
Total	**$164,629,519**	**25.5%**	**$168,416,797**	**25.4%**	**$175,147,541**	**25.7%**
Accident and health[3]						
Group	94,510,273	14.6	98,108,859	14.8	108,825,848	16.0
Other	67,592,828	10.5	69,655,745	10.5	62,232,501	9.1
Credit	966,052	0.1	954,502	0.1	908,567	0.1
Total	**$163,069,153**	**25.2%**	**$168,719,106**	**25.5%**	**$171,966,915**	**25.2%**
All other lines	777	[2]	3,482	[2]	3,383	[2]
Total, all lines[4]	**$646,652,656**	**100.0%**	**$662,304,443**	**100.0%**	**$681,097,036**	**100.0%**

[1]Before reinsurance transactions. [2]Less than 0.1 percent. [3]Excludes accident and health premiums reported on the property/casualty and health annual statements. [4]Excludes deposit-type funds.

Source: NAIC data, sourced from S&P Global Market Intelligence, Insurance Information Institute.

Private Health Insurance

Most private health insurance is written by companies that specialize in that line of business. However, life/health and property/casualty insurers also write this coverage, referred to as accident and health insurance on their annual statements. Total private health insurance direct written premiums were $770.8 billion in 2015, including: $593.2 billion from the health insurance segment; $172.0 billion from the life/health segment; and $5.6 billion from property/casualty annual statements, according to S&P Global Market Intelligence.

In 2015, 29 million Americans did not have health insurance, according to a U.S. Census Bureau report, compared with 33 million in 2014. The percentage of uninsured Americans in 2015 was 9.1 percent, down from 10.4 percent in 2014. There is other evidence not directly comparable to the Census Bureau data of falling uninsured rates: according to the Gallup-Healthways Well-Being Index, the percentage of Americans without health insurance fell to 10.8 percent in the first seven months of 2016, compared with 11.7 percent in 2015.

In 2015, 90.9 percent of Americans had private or government health insurance coverage compared with 89.6 percent in 2014.

Healthcare Coverage, 2015

	Number	Percent of total
Insured[1]	**289,903**	**90.9%**
Private health insurance	214,238	67.2
Government health insurance	118,395	37.1
Uninsured	**28,966**	**9.1**
Total[2]	**318,869**	**100.0%**

[1]Includes individuals with some form of insurance i.e., government, private and a combination of both and is not a total of people who have either private or government health insurance. [2]Differs from Census Bureau estimates of the total population because of different survey methods.

Source: U.S. Department of Commerce, Census Bureau.

Other findings from the Census Bureau

- The percentage of Americans insured by private coverage increased from 66.0 percent in 2014 to 67.2 percent in 2015, up 1.2 percentage points.
- The rate insured by government plans grew from 36.5 percent in 2014 to 37.1 percent in 2015, up, by 0.6 percentage points, or by half of the gain in private plans.
- For the second consecutive year, the percentage of Americans without health insurance fell for every year of age under age 65.
- The percentage of uninsured children under the age of 19 fell from 6.2 percent in 2014 to 5.3 percent in 2015.
- In 2015 the uninsured rate decreased for 47 states and the District of Columbia, when compared with 2014. Three states did not record a statistically significant change in the uninsured rate: North Dakota, South Dakota and Wyoming.

Top 10 Health Insurance Groups By Direct Premiums Written, 2015 ($000)

Rank	Group/company	Direct premiums written[1]	Market share
1	UnitedHealth Group Inc.	$67,486,464	11.4%
2	Anthem Inc.	54,715,501	9.2
3	Humana Inc.	51,405,175	8.7
4	HealthCare Service Corp.	32,644,621	5.5
5	Aetna Inc.	24,417,307	4.1
6	Centene Corp.	20,261,187	3.4
7	Independence Health Group Inc.	14,291,608	2.4
8	WellCare Health Plans Inc.	12,229,584	2.1
9	Kaiser Foundation Health Plan Inc.	11,934,022	2.0
10	Molina Healthcare Inc.	11,918,163	2.0

[1]Based on health insurer annual statement data. Excludes health insurance data from the property/casualty and life/health annual statements. Excludes territories.

Source: NAIC data, sourced from S&P Global Market Intelligence, Insurance Information Institute.

Disability Insurance

Disability insurance pays an insured person an income when he or she is unable to work because of an accident or illness.

Individual Disability Insurance, New Issues Sale, 2015[1]

	Annualized premiums	Percent change, 2014-2015	Number of policies	Percent change, 2014-2015
Guaranteed renewable	$227,683,997	1%	378,196	-3%
Noncancellable	335,343,117	6	167,579	8
Total	**$563,027,114**	**4%**	**545,775**	[2]

Annualized premiums for new disability income policies rose by 4 percent in 2015, following a 1 percent increase the previous year.

[1]Short-term and long-term individual disability income insurance. Based on a LIMRA survey of 19 personal disability insurance companies. Excludes commercial disability income. [2]Less than one-half of 1 percent.

Source: LIMRA.

Individual Disability Insurance In Force, 2015[1]

	Number of policies	Percent change, 2014-2015	Annualized premiums	Percent change, 2014-2015
Noncancellable	2,394,345	[2]	$4,261,491,419	[3]
Guaranteed renewable	1,692,589	[2]	1,191,483,346	[3]
Total	**4,086,934**	[2]	**$5,452,974,765**	[3]

[1]Short-term and long-term individual disability income insurance. Based on a LIMRA survey of 21 personal disability insurance companies. Excludes commercial disability income. [2]Less than -0.5 percent. (3) Less than 0.5 percent.
Source: LIMRA.

Long-Term Care Insurance

Long-term care (LTC) insurance pays for services to help individuals who are unable to perform certain activities of daily living without assistance or who require supervision due to a cognitive impairment such as Alzheimer's disease. According to the U.S. Department of Health and Human Services, about 70 percent of individuals over age 65 will require at least some type of LTC services. There were 47.8 million people age 65 and older in 2015, accounting for 14.9 percent of the U.S. population, or about one in every seven Americans, according to the U.S. Census Bureau. By 2030 the Census Bureau projects there will be about 74.1 million older people and about 88.0 million in 2050.

Individual Long-Term Care (LTC) Insurance, 2015[1]

	Lives	Percent change, 2014-2015	Preumiums ($ millions)	Percent change, 2014-2015
New business	104,332	-20%	$261	-17%
In-force[2]	<4,765,000	-1	≈10,100	1

[1]Based on LIMRA International's Individual LTC Sales survey. [2]Includes estimates for non-participants.
< =Less than. ≈ =Approximately.
Source: LIMRA's Individual Long-Term Care Insurance Sales and In Force Survey, 2015.

Life/Health Insurers Direct Premiums Written And Annuity Considerations By State, 2015[1] ($ millions)

State	Life Insurance	Annuities	Accident and health insurance[2]	Deposit-type contract funds	Other considerations	Total
Alabama	$2,077	$2,969	$1,487	$292	$477	$7,301
Alaska	532	380	333	24	175	1,443
Arizona	2,287	4,726	3,826	314	1,330	12,483
Arkansas	1,103	1,502	1,002	88	230	3,924
California	15,840	24,497	14,286	2,510	8,374	65,508
Colorado	2,627	4,692	3,420	1,031	980	12,750
Connecticut	3,228	4,195	2,865	7,581	2,256	20,126
Delaware	1,176	2,483	550	57,516	506	62,231
D.C.	397	619	781	200	1,279	3,276
Florida	8,839	18,664	12,584	1,542	3,699	45,328
Georgia	4,636	5,462	5,151	631	2,741	18,621
Hawaii	718	1,273	998	82	419	3,490
Idaho	576	977	560	88	239	2,440
Illinois	6,693	9,799	6,086	1,327	2,881	26,786
Indiana	2,616	5,264	3,986	1,309	838	14,013
Iowa	1,677	3,022	1,327	7,122	2,502	15,649
Kansas	1,418	2,588	3,269	1,819	380	9,474
Kentucky	1,494	2,444	1,594	246	718	6,497
Louisiana	2,225	3,575	1,964	218	629	8,612
Maine	522	1,170	823	93	175	2,783
Maryland	2,911	5,118	3,253	698	1,156	13,135
Massachusetts	4,768	7,072	3,110	1,000	3,509	19,458
Michigan	4,379	9,317	3,392	910	1,832	19,829
Minnesota	4,198	4,650	1,511	1,014	1,939	13,311
Mississippi	1,169	1,527	1,442	112	171	4,420
Missouri	2,751	6,651	3,714	926	1,028	15,069
Montana	360	529	362	29	111	1,391
Nebraska	1,008	1,584	1,271	459	385	4,707
Nevada	952	2,117	1,120	292	407	4,889

(table continues)

Life/Health Insurers Direct Premiums Written And Annuity Considerations By State, 2015[1] ($ millions) (Cont'd)

State	Life Insurance	Annuities	Accident and health insurance[2]	Deposit-type contract funds	Other considerations	Total
New Hampshire	$600	$1,748	$655	$189	$558	$3,750
New Jersey	6,301	11,514	5,420	1,493	2,910	27,637
New Mexico	626	997	757	79	354	2,813
New York	11,738	17,808	9,209	26,564	8,967	74,286
North Carolina	4,490	7,232	4,610	1,492	2,930	20,754
North Dakota	449	629	305	62	217	1,661
Ohio	4,937	11,600	6,796	3,806	2,236	29,376
Oklahoma	1,411	2,074	1,599	199	546	5,829
Oregon	1,175	2,415	1,782	241	1,160	6,773
Pennsylvania	6,373	13,469	6,331	5,670	3,322	35,166
Rhode Island	510	1,277	476	64	281	2,608
South Carolina	2,041	3,824	1,973	196	476	8,509
South Dakota	818	640	374	72	91	1,996
Tennessee	2,876	4,765	2,839	1,568	1,065	13,112
Texas	11,038	16,911	16,182	1,399	3,114	48,644
Utah	1,314	2,253	998	348	585	5,499
Vermont	252	542	347	44	191	1,377
Virginia	4,158	6,262	4,108	746	1,806	17,081
Washington	2,341	4,687	2,902	466	1,373	11,769
West Virginia	631	1,221	656	96	182	2,787
Wisconsin	2,500	5,489	3,569	622	1,108	13,289
Wyoming	284	427	324	22	43	1,100
United States[3]	$150,041	$256,650	$158,281	$134,910	$74,879	$774,761

[1]Direct premiums written before reinsurance transactions, excludes state funds. [2]Excludes accident and health premiums reported on property/casualty and health annual statements. [3]Excludes territories, dividends and other nonstate specific data.

Source: NAIC data, sourced from S&P Global Market Intelligence, Insurance Information Institute.

LEADING COMPANIES

Top 20 Writers Of Life Insurance By Direct Premiums Written, 2015 ($000)

Rank	Group/company	Direct premiums written[1]	Market share
1	MetLife Inc.	$13,356,783	8.6%
2	Northwestern Mutual Life Insurance Co.	10,123,987	6.5
3	New York Life Insurance Group	8,822,267	5.7
4	Prudential Financial Inc.	8,626,713	5.5
5	Lincoln National Corp.	6,731,270	4.3
6	Massachusetts Mutual Life Insurance Co.	6,176,245	4.0
7	Manulife Financial Corp.	4,755,479	3.1
8	AEGON	4,483,372	2.9
9	State Farm Mutual Automobile Insurance	4,232,704	2.7
10	Securian Financial Group	3,815,847	2.5
11	Guardian Life Insurance Co. of America	3,648,750	2.3
12	Aflac Inc.	3,497,524	2.2
13	American International Group (AIG)	3,442,794	2.2
14	Nationwide Mutual Group	3,256,741	2.1
15	AXA	3,062,949	2.0
16	Pacific MHC	3,011,195	1.9
17	Voya Financial Inc.	2,701,363	1.7
18	Hartford Financial Services	2,475,131	1.6
19	Dai-ichi Life Insurance Co. Ltd.	2,391,647	1.5
20	Sammons Enterprises Inc.	2,271,588	1.5

[1]Before reinsurance transactions. Based on U.S. total, includes territories. Excludes annuities, accident and health, deposit-type contract funds and other considerations.

Source: NAIC data, sourced from S&P Global Market Intelligence, Insurance Information Institute.

Top 10 Writers Of Individual Life Insurance By Direct Premiums Written, 2015 ($000)

Rank	Group/company	Direct premiums written[1]	Market share
1	Northwestern Mutual Life Insurance Co.	$10,123,987	8.3%
2	New York Life Insurance Group	7,015,574	5.8
3	MetLife Inc.	6,735,071	5.5
4	Lincoln National Corp.	5,949,566	4.9
5	Prudential Financial Inc.	5,081,952	4.2
6	Massachusetts Mutual Life Insurance Co.	4,765,228	3.9
7	Manulife Financial Corp.	4,749,494	3.9
8	State Farm Mutual Automobile Insurance	4,189,927	3.5
9	AEGON	4,145,928	3.4
10	Aflac Inc.	3,481,111	2.9

[1]Before reinsurance transactions. Based on U.S. total, includes territories. Excludes annuities, accident and health, deposit-type contract funds and other considerations.

Source: NAIC data, sourced from S&P Global Market Intelligence, Insurance Information Institute.

Top 10 Writers Of Group Life Insurance By Direct Premiums Written, 2015 ($000)

Rank	Group/company	Direct premiums written[1]	Market share
1	MetLife Inc.	$6,590,929	19.7%
2	Prudential Financial Inc.	3,544,761	10.6
3	Securian Financial Group	2,315,845	6.9
4	Cigna Corp.	1,807,734	5.4
5	New York Life Insurance Group	1,806,693	5.4
6	Nationwide Mutual Group	1,444,782	4.3
7	Massachusetts Mutual Life Insurance Co.	1,411,017	4.2
8	Unum Group	1,384,939	4.2
9	Hartford Financial Services	1,292,513	3.9
10	Aetna Inc.	1,064,110	3.2

[1]Before reinsurance transactions. Based on U.S. total, includes territories. Excludes annuities, accident and health, deposit-type contract funds and other considerations.

Source: NAIC data, sourced from S&P Global Market Intelligence, Insurance Information Institute.

Chapter 6

Property/Casualty Financial Data

FINANCIAL RESULTS

2015 Financial Results

In 2015 the property/casualty insurance industry had moderate profits, with a return on average surplus of 8.4 percent, virtually the same as in 2014. Challenged by continuing low interest rates and a slumping stock market, the industry posted modest premium growth and a combined ratio below 100 for the third straight year, according to data compiled by ISO®, a Verisk Analytics® business, and the Property Casualty Insurers Association of America (PCI). Policyholder surplus slipped slightly to $673.7 billion as of end-2015, but was still extraordinarily strong. The combined ratio rose slightly to 97.8 from 97.0 in 2014, resulting in underwriting profit of $8.7 billion, compared with $12.2 billion in 2014. Net income after taxes (profits) totaled $56.6 billion, slightly higher than $55.9 billion a year earlier. Net written premiums crossed the half-trillion-dollar mark (to $514.0 billion). The industry's net investment income was $47.2 billion, compared to $46.4 billion in 2014 (up 1.9 percent).

Property/Casualty Insurance Industry Income Analysis, 2011-2015[1] ($ billions)

	2011	2012	2013	2014	2015
Net premiums written	$438.0	$456.7	$477.0	$497.0	$514.0
Percent change	3.4%	4.3%	4.4%	4.2%	3.4%
Premiums earned	$434.4	$448.9	$467.4	$487.9	$505.8
Losses incurred	290.8	277.7	259.4	277.7	290.6
Loss adjustment expenses incurred	53.8	55.5	55.6	57.3	59.6
Other underwriting expenses	124.2	128.9	134.6	138.3	144.3
Policyholder dividends	1.9	2.1	2.5	2.4	2.5
Net underwriting gain/loss	-36.2	-15.4	15.2	12.2	8.7
Net investment income	49.2	48.0	47.3	46.4	47.2
Miscellaneous income/loss	2.5	2.4	1.5	-2.7	1.4
Operating income	15.4	35.0	64.1	55.9	57.3
Realized capital gain	7.0	6.2	11.4	10.3	9.4
Federal and foreign income tax	3.0	6.1	12.0	10.3	10.1
Net income after taxes	19.5	35.1	63.4	55.9	56.6

The property/casualty insurance industry had an underwriting gain of $8.7 billion in 2015, down 28.7 percent from $12.2 billion in 2014, although catastrophe losses fell slightly to $15.2 billion in 2015 from $15.5 billion in 2014.

[1]Data in this chart exclude state funds and other residual market insurers and may not agree with similar data shown elsewhere from different sources.

Source: ISO®, a Verisk Analytics® business.

Premiums, Expenses And Combined Ratio

Insurers use various measures to gauge financial performance. The combined ratio after dividends is a measure of underwriting profitability. It reflects the percentage of each premium dollar an insurer spends on claims and expenses. The combined ratio does not take investment income into account. A combined ratio above 100 indicates an underwriting loss.

Net Premiums Written And Combined Ratio, Property/Casualty Insurance, 2006-2015 ($ billions)

Year	Net premiums written[1]	Annual percent change	Combined ratio after dividends[2]	Annual point change[3]	Year	Net premiums written[1]	Annual percent change	Combined ratio after dividends[2]	Annual point change[3]
2006	$447.8	6.0%	92.4	-8.2 pts.	2011	$441.6	3.7%	108.3	5.8 pts.
2007	446.2	-0.4	95.6	3.2	2012	460.5	4.3	103.1	-5.2
2008	440.3	-1.3	105.2	9.5	2013	481.5	4.6	96.4	-6.8
2009	423.5	-3.8	100.4	-4.8	2014	502.6	4.4	97.2	0.8
2010	425.9	0.6	102.5	2.1	2015	519.8	3.4	97.9	0.8

[1]After reinsurance transactions, excludes state funds. [2]After dividends to policyholders. A drop in the combined ratio represents an improvement; an increase represents a deterioration. [3]Calculated from unrounded numbers.

Source: NAIC data, sourced from S&P Global Market Intelligence, Insurance Information Institute.

Property/Casualty Insurance Industry Underwriting Expenses, 2015[1]

Expense	Percent of premiums
Losses and related expenses[2]	
Loss and loss adjustment expense (LAE) ratio	**69.3%**
Incurred losses	57.4
Defense and cost containment expenses incurred	4.5
Adjusting and other expenses incurred	7.4
Underwriting expenses[3]	
Expense ratio	**27.9%**
Net commissions and brokerage expenses incurred	10.9
Taxes, licenses and fees	2.5
Other acquisition and field supervision expenses incurred	7.6
General expenses incurred	6.9
Dividends to policyholders[2]	**0.6%**
Combined ratio after dividends[4]	**97.7%**

[1]After reinsurance transactions. [2]As a percent of net premiums earned ($511.5 billion in 2015). [3]As a percent of net premiums written ($519.8 billion in 2015). [4]Sum of loss and LAE, expense and dividends ratios.

Source: NAIC data, sourced from S&P Global Market Intelligence, Insurance Information Institute.

Profitability: Insurance And Other Selected Industries

Profitability of property/casualty (P/C) insurance companies using generally accepted accounting principles (GAAP) lags other industries. The median return on shareholders' equity for the Fortune 500 Combined Industrial and Service Businesses for the years 2006 to 2015 exceeded that of the P/C industry in every year. Insurers are required to use statutory accounting principles (SAP), which are more conservative than GAAP, when filing annual financial reports with state regulators and the Internal Revenue Service. Insurers outside the United States use standards that differ from SAP and GAAP. Some insurers support a move toward uniform global standards. The P/C industry's GAAP rate of return in 2015 was 7.4 percent, about the same as 7.5 percent in 2014.

Annual Rate Of Return: Net Income After Taxes As A Percent Of Equity, 2006-2015

Year	Property/casualty[1]		Life/health		Selected other industries[2]			Fortune 500 combined industrials and service[8]
	Statutory accounting[3]	GAAP accounting[4]	Life/health insurance[5]	Healthcare insurance[6]	Diversified financial[7]	Commercial banks	Electric and gas utilities	
2006	14.4%	12.7%	12.0%	19.0%	15.0%	15.0%	11.0%	15.4%
2007	12.4	10.9	11.0	19.0	-1.0	11.0	11.0	15.2
2008	0.6	0.1	1.0	11.0	8.0	3.0	13.0	13.1
2009	5.9	5.0	4.0	14.0	9.0	4.0	9.0	10.5
2010	6.6	5.6	7.0	12.0	10.0	8.0	10.0	12.7
2011	3.5	3.0	8.0	15.0	12.0	8.0	10.0	14.5
2012	6.1	5.3	7.0	12.0	18.0	9.0	8.0	15.0
2013	10.2	8.9	7.0	13.0	18.0	9.0	9.0	13.7
2014	8.4	7.5	9.0	12.0	22.0	9.0	10.0	14.2
2015	8.4	7.4	8.0	12.0	22.0	8.0	9.0	13.3

[1]Excludes state funds for workers compensation and other residual market carriers. [2]Return on equity on a GAAP accounting basis, Fortune. [3]Statutory net income after taxes, divided by the average of current and prior year-end policyholders' surplus. Calculated by ISO. Statutory accounting is used by insurers when preparing the Annual Statements they submit to regulators. [4]Estimated from statutory data. Equals GAAP net income divided by the average of current and prior-year-end GAAP net worth. Calculated by ISO. [5]Return on equity on a GAAP accounting basis, Fortune. Combined stock and mutual companies, calculated by the Insurance Information Institute. [6]Healthcare insurance and managed care. [7]Companies whose major source of revenue comes from providing diversified financial services. These companies are not specifically chartered as insurance companies, banks or savings institutions, or brokerage or securities companies, but they may earn revenue from these sources. [8]Fortune 500 Combined Industrial and Service Businesses median return on shareholders' equity.

Source: ISO®, a Verisk business®; Fortune.

Property/Casualty Insurance Cycle

Most industries are cyclical to some extent. The property/casualty (P/C) insurance industry cycle is characterized by periods of soft market conditions, in which premium rates are stable or falling and insurance is readily available, and by periods of hard market conditions, where rates rise, coverage may be more difficult to find and insurers' profits increase.

A dominant factor in the P/C insurance cycle is intense competition within the industry. Premium rates drop as insurance companies compete vigorously to increase market share. As the market softens to the point that profits diminish or vanish completely, the capital needed to underwrite new business is depleted. In the up phase of the cycle, competition is less intense, underwriting standards become more stringent, the supply of insurance is limited due to the depletion of capital, and, as a result, premiums rise. The prospect of higher profits draws more capital into the marketplace, leading to more competition and the inevitable down phase of the cycle.

The chart below shows both nominal and inflation-adjusted growth of P/C net premiums written over four decades and three hard markets. Premiums can be accounted for in several ways. This chart uses net premiums written, which reflect premium amounts after deductions for reinsurance transactions.

During the last three hard markets, inflation-adjusted net premiums written grew 7.7 percent annually (1975 to 1978), 10.0 percent (1984 to 1987) and 6.3 percent (2001 to 2004).

Percent Change From Prior Year, Net Premiums Written, P/C Insurance, 1975-2015[1]

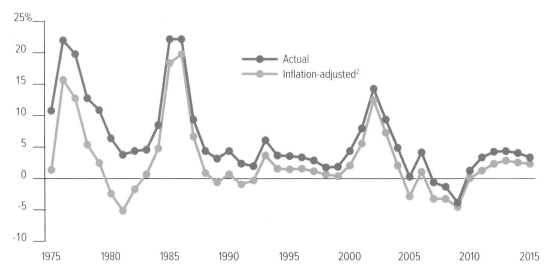

[1]Excludes state funds and other residual market insurers. [2]Adjusted for inflation by ISO using the GDP implicit price deflator.
Source: ISO®, a Verisk Analytics® business.

Operating Results

In many years the insurance industry does not generate profits from its underwriting operations. Investment income from a number of sources—including capital and surplus accounts, money set aside as loss reserves and unearned premium reserves—generally offsets these losses. Underwriting results were favorable in 2006, 2007 and 2009, according to S&P Global Market Intelligence. The industry posted underwriting losses in 2010 through 2012, including 2011's $35.3 billion loss, the largest since 2001's $50.3 billion loss. Results for 2015 showed an underwriting gain of $11.2 billion, about $3.1 billion less than a year earlier.

Operating Results, Property/Casualty Insurance, 2006-2015[1] ($ millions)

Year	Net underwriting gain/loss	Net investment income earned	Net realized capital gains/ losses	Policyholder dividends	Taxes[2]	Net income after taxes[3]
2006	$34,753	$55,719	$3,670	$3,611	$22,651	$67,479
2007	21,637	56,320	8,817	2,814	19,857	63,138
2008	-19,810	53,430	-19,609	2,211	7,730	4,446
2009	1,579	48,640	-7,895	2,141	8,481	32,492
2010	-8,422	48,833	8,003	2,709	8,951	37,716
2011	-35,305	51,000	6,891	2,315	3,026	19,532
2012	-13,827	49,605	8,525	2,656	6,267	37,565
2013	17,500	48,830	17,212	3,018	11,948	70,061
2014	14,259	54,914	11,748	2,932	10,396	64,704
2015	11,188	48,879	9,579	3,017	10,199	57,990

[1]Excludes state funds. [2]Includes federal and foreign taxes. [3]Does not equal the sum of the columns shown due to the omission of miscellaneous income.

Source: NAIC data, sourced from S&P Global Market Intelligence, Insurance Information Institute.

Operating Results, Property/Casualty Insurance, 2006-2015[1] ($ billions)

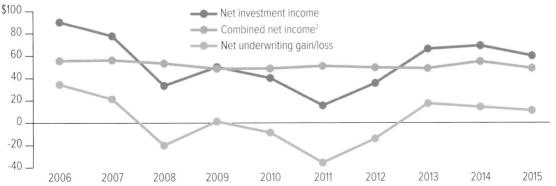

[1]Excludes state funds. [2]Net underwriting gain/loss plus net investment income.

Source: NAIC data, sourced from S&P Global Market Intelligence, Insurance Information Institute.

Policyholders' Surplus

A property/casualty insurer must maintain a certain level of surplus to underwrite risks. This financial cushion is known as capacity. When the industry is hit by high losses, such as a major hurricane, capacity is diminished. It can be restored by increases in net income, favorable investment returns, reinsuring more risk and/or raising additional capital.

Consolidated Assets And Policyholders' Surplus, P/C Insurance, 2006-2015 ($ millions)

Year	Net admitted assets	Annual percent change	Statutory liabilities	Annual percent change	Policy-holders' surplus	Annual percent change	Total net premiums written[1]	Annual percent change[1]
2006	$1,549,509	11.7%	$1,045,931	9.9%	$503,578	15.7%	$448,967	5.2%
2007	1,468,776	-5.2	940,758	-10.1	528,016	4.9	446,378	-0.6
2008	1,405,742	-4.3	943,732	0.3	462,006	-12.5	440,681	-1.3
2009	1,456,852	3.6	936,261	-0.8	520,591	12.7	423,545	-3.9
2010	1,514,190	3.9	947,390	1.2	566,800	8.9	426,380	0.7
2011	1,537,222	1.5	974,699	2.9	562,522	-0.8	441,925	3.6
2012	1,594,419	3.7	996,473	2.2	597,946	6.3	460,930	4.3
2013	1,684,070	5.6	1,016,275	2.0	667,795	11.7	481,757	4.5
2014	1,736,476	3.1	1,046,318	3.0	690,158	3.3	502,883	4.4
2015	1,747,725	0.6	1,056,502	1.0	691,223	0.2	520,332	3.5

[1]After reinsurance transactions, excludes state funds. May not match total premiums written shown elsewhere in this book because of the use of different exhibits from S&P Global Market Intelligence.

Source: NAIC data, sourced from S&P Global Market Intelligence, Insurance information Institute.

Policyholders' surplus dropped substantially in 2008, reflecting the deterioration in global financial markets.

Policyholders' surplus reached a record $691.2 billion in 2015, rising 0.2 percent from 2014.

Percent Change From Prior Year, Net Premiums Written And Policyholders' Surplus, P/C Insurance, 2006-2015[1]

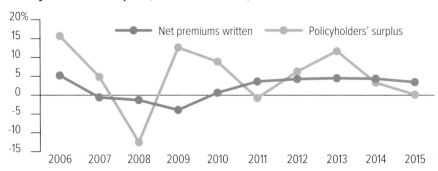

[1]After reinsurance transactions, excludes state funds.

Source: NAIC data, sourced from S&P Global Market Intelligence, Insurance Information Institute.

The Combined Ratio

The combined ratio represents the percentage of each premium dollar an insurer spends on claims and expenses. The following chart shows the components of the combined ratio, a measure of the industry's underwriting performance.

The combined ratio is the sum of the loss ratio and the expense ratio. The loss ratio expresses the relationship between losses and premiums in percentage terms. The expense ratio expresses the relationship between underwriting expenses and premiums.

Components Of The Combined Ratio, Property/Casualty Insurance, 2006-2015[1]

Year	Loss ratio[2]	Expense ratio[3]	Combined ratio	Dividends to policyholders[4]	Combined ratio after dividends
2006	65.2	26.4	91.6	0.8	92.4
2007	67.7	27.3	94.9	0.6	95.5
2008	77.1	27.5	104.6	0.4	105.0
2009	72.5	28.0	100.5	0.5	101.0
2010	73.6	28.3	101.8	0.5	102.4
2011	79.3	28.4	107.7	0.4	108.1
2012	74.2	28.2	102.5	0.5	102.9
2013	67.4	28.2	95.6	0.5	96.2
2014	68.7	27.8	96.5	0.5	97.0
2015	69.2	28.1	97.3	0.5	97.8

[1]Excluding state funds and other residual market insurers. [2]Incurred loss and loss adjustment expenses as a percent of earned premiums.
[3]Other underwriting expenses as a percent of written premiums. [4]Dividends to policyholders as a percent of earned premiums.
Source: ISO®, a Verisk Analytics® business.

Property/Casualty Insurance Combined Ratio, 1975-2015[1]

[1]Excludes state funds and other residual insurers.
Source: ISO®, a Verisk Analytics® business.

INVESTMENTS

Cash and invested assets of property/casualty insurance companies totaled $1.53 trillion in 2015. This represents 87 percent of total assets, which were $1.75 trillion. Most of these assets were invested in highly liquid securities (high-quality stocks and bonds, for example, rather than real estate), which can be sold quickly to pay claims in the event of a major catastrophe.

Investments, Property/Casualty Insurers, 2013-2015[1] ($ millions, end of year)

Investment type	Amount			Percent of total investments		
	2013	2014	2015	2013	2014	2015
Bonds	$927,346	$941,943	$949,702	62.47%	61.45%	62.01%
Stocks	329,642	345,762	340,252	22.21	22.56	22.22
Preferred	11,550	14,630	14,025	0.78	0.95	0.92
Common	318,092	331,133	326,227	21.43	21.60	21.30
Mortgage loans on real estate	7,972	10,008	12,441	0.54	0.65	0.81
First liens	7,765	9,820	12,209	0.52	0.64	0.80
Other than first liens	207	188	232	0.01	0.01	0.02
Real estate	9,975	10,165	11,685	0.67	0.66	0.76
Properties occupied by company	8,484	8,598	8,716	0.57	0.56	0.57
Properties held for income production	1,249	1,286	2,693	0.08	0.08	0.18
Properties held for sale	243	282	276	0.02	0.02	0.02
Cash, cash equivalent and short-term investments	83,645	90,754	87,516	5.63	5.92	5.71
Derivatives	578	637	652	0.04	0.04	0.04
Other invested assets	118,344	126,582	121,291	7.97	8.26	7.92
Receivable for securities	1,494	1,104	2,530	0.10	0.07	0.17
Securities lending reinvested collateral assets	2,746	2,681	2,618	0.18	0.17	0.17
Aggregate write-in for invested assets	2,776	3,282	2,860	0.19	0.21	0.19
Total cash and invested assets	**$1,484,518**	**$1,532,917**	**$1,531,547**	**100.00%**	**100.00%**	**100.00%**

[1]Includes cash and net admitted assets of property/casualty insurers.
Source: NAIC data, sourced from S&P Global Market Intelligence, Insurance Information Institute.

Bonds

Property/casualty insurers invest primarily in safe, liquid securities, mainly bonds. These provide stability against underwriting results, which can vary considerably from year to year. The vast majority of bonds are government issued or are high-grade corporates. Bonds in or near default accounted for less than 1 percent (0.16 percent) of all short- and long-term bonds owned by insurers at the end of 2015, according to S&P Global Market Intelligence.

Investments, Property/Casualty Insurers, 2015

Investments by type[1]

Bonds	62.01%
Common stock	21.30
Cash and short-term investments	5.71
Real estate[2]	1.58
Preferred stock	0.92
Other	8.48

Bond portfolio
(Represents 62.0% of total investments)

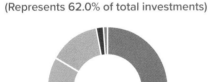

Industrial and miscellaneous	42.4%
Special revenue	26.6
Governments	15.5
States, territories and others	13.9
Parent, subsidiaries and affiliates	1.3
Hybrid securities	0.3

Common stock portfolio
(Represents 21.3% of total investments)

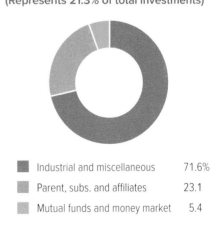

Industrial and miscellaneous	71.6%
Parent, subs. and affiliates	23.1
Mutual funds and money market	5.4

[1]Cash and invested net admitted assets, as of December 31, 2015. [2]Includes mortgage loans on real estate.

Source: NAIC data, sourced from S&P Global Market Intelligence, Insurance Information Institute.

SURPLUS LINES

The surplus lines market exists to assume risks that licensed companies decline to insure or will only insure at a very high price, with many exclusions or with a very high deductible. To be eligible to seek coverage in the surplus lines market, a diligent effort must have been made to place insurance with an admitted company, usually defined by a certain number of declinations, or rejections, by licensed insurers, typically three to five. Many states provide an export list of risks that can be insured in the surplus lines market. This obviates the diligent search requirement.

The terms applied to the surplus lines market—nonadmitted, unlicensed and unauthorized— do not mean that surplus lines companies are barred from selling insurance in a state or are unregulated. They are just less regulated. Each state has surplus lines regulations, and each surplus lines company is overseen for solvency by its home state. More than half of the states maintain a list of eligible surplus lines companies and some a list of those that are not eligible to do business in that state.

Nonadmitted direct premiums written for the top 10 U.S. surplus lines writers rose 9.6 percent to $13.10 billion in 2015 from $11.95 billion in 2014.

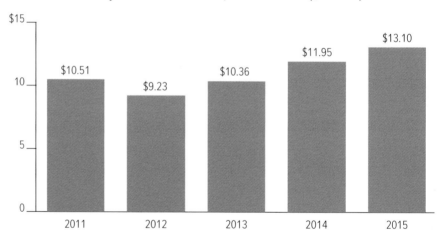

Nonadmitted Direct Premiums Written For The Top 10 U.S.- Based Surplus Lines Writers, 2011-2015 ($ billions)

2011	$10.51
2012	$9.23
2013	$10.36
2014	$11.95
2015	$13.10

Source: *Business Insurance*, October, 2016.

Top 10 U.S-Based Surplus Lines Insurance Companies By Nonadmitted Direct Premiums Written, 2015

Rank	Company	Parent	Nonadmitted direct premiums written
1	Lexington Insurance Co.	American International Group Inc.	$3,783,299,430
2	Nationwide Mutual Insurance Co.[1]	Nationwide Mutual Insurance Co.	1,733,825,799
3	Associated Electric & Gas Ins. Services Inc.	AEGIS	1,250,510,000
4	Markel Corp.	Markel Corp.	1,173,396,130
5	Steadfast Insurance Co	Zurich Insurance Group Ltd.	1,108,275,644
6	Ironshore Specialty Insurance Co.	Ironshore Inc.	1,009,566,789[2]
7	AIG Specialty Insurance Co.	American International Group Inc.	931,710,609
8	Indian Harbor Insurance Co.	XL Group P.L.C.	796,445,484
9	National Fire & Marine Insurance Co.	Berkshire Hathaway Reinsurance Group.	722,736,828
10	Axis Surplus Insurance Co.	Axis Capital Holdings Ltd.	603,264,518

[1]Formerly Scottsdale Insurance Company and Western Heritage Insurance Company. [2]Business Insurance estimate.

Source: Business Insurance, October, 2016.

CONCENTRATION

According to ISO®, a Verisk Analytics® business, concentration in the property/casualty insurance sector as measured by the Herfindahl-Hirschman Index (HHI) increased from 229 in 1980 to 357 in 2008, and then fell, albeit irregularly, to 344 in 2014. The U.S. Department of Justice classifies any market with an HHI under 1,500 as unconcentrated and any market with an HHI over 2,500 as highly concentrated.

Market Share Trends By Size Of Insurer, 1994-2014[1]

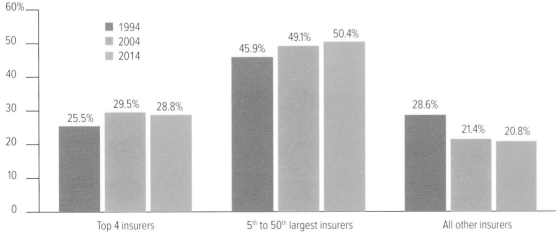

[1]Based on net premiums written. Excludes state funds and other residual market carriers.

Source: ISO®, a Verisk Analytics® business.

REINSURANCE

Reinsurance is essentially insurance for insurance companies. It is a way for primary insurers to protect against unforeseen or extraordinary losses. Reinsurance also serves to limit liability on specific risks, to increase individual insurers' capacity to write business and to help insurers stabilize their business in the face of the wide swings in profit and loss margins which are inherent in the insurance business.

Net Premiums Written, U.S. Property/Casualty Reinsurers, 2006-2015 ($000)

Year	Net premiums written	Annual percent change	Combined ratio[1]	Annual point change
2006	$26,625,918	0.4%	94.2	-31.8 pts.
2007	24,548,841	-7.8	93.5	-0.7
2008	26,440,426	7.7	100.4	6.9
2009	25,548,851	-3.4	92.3	-8.1
2010	25,722,426	0.7	94.5	2.2
2011	27,897,553	8.5	107.1	12.6
2012	31,649,616	13.4	96.2	-10.9
2013	29,144,853	-7.9	86.8	-9.4
2014	50,012,241[2]	71.6	91.0	4.2
2015	41,466,073	-17.1	92.3	1.3

[1]After dividends to policyholders. [2]Includes National Indemnity Co.'s loss portfolio and quota share agreements with affiliated GEICO companies.
Source: Reinsurance Association of America.

Top 10 U.S. Property/Casualty Reinsurers Of U.S. Business By Gross Premiums Written, 2015 ($000)

Rank	Company[1]	Country of parent company	Gross premiums written
1	National Indemnity Company (Berkshire Hathaway)[2]	U.S.	$18,349,736
2	Munich Re America	Germany	6,669,622
3	QBE North America (Combined)	Australia	5,084,876
4	Everest Reinsurance Company	Bermuda	5,009,780
5	Swiss Reinsurance America Corporation	Switzerland	4,330,306
6	XL Reinsurance America	Ireland	3,802,990
7	Transatlantic Reinsurance	U.S.	3,219,832
8	Odyssey Reinsurance Group	Canada	2,267,041
9	Partner Reinsurance Company of the U.S.	Bermuda	1,778,845
10	AXIS Reinsurance Company	Bermuda	1,237,862

[1]See Reinsurance Underwriting Review 2015 notes posted at http://www.reinsurance.org for list of affiliated companies included. [2]Underwriting results exclude assumptions from affiliated General Re Group.
Source: Reinsurance Association of America.

PREMIUMS BY STATE

Direct premiums written represent premium amounts before reinsurance transactions. This contrasts with charts based on net premiums written, i.e., premium amounts after reinsurance transactions.

Direct Premiums Written, P/C Insurance By State, 2015[1] ($000)

State	Total, all lines	State	Total, all lines
Alabama	$7,788,908	Montana	$2,240,077
Alaska	1,667,043	Nebraska	4,485,562
Arizona	9,605,269	Nevada	4,486,525
Arkansas	4,738,870	New Hampshire	2,284,780
California	69,464,495	New Jersey	20,102,839
Colorado	10,727,291	New Mexico	3,087,127
Connecticut	8,225,865	New York	43,283,391
Delaware	2,342,982	North Carolina	14,223,016
D.C.	1,729,032	North Dakota	2,488,807
Florida	44,925,094	Ohio	15,483,542
Georgia	17,119,570	Oklahoma	7,814,964
Hawaii	2,339,270	Oregon	6,206,281
Idaho	2,460,311	Pennsylvania	22,992,115
Illinois	24,234,963	Rhode Island	2,233,945
Indiana	10,596,498	South Carolina	8,329,788
Iowa	6,183,482	South Dakota	2,355,727
Kansas	6,195,200	Tennessee	10,531,541
Kentucky	6,926,410	Texas	49,124,353
Louisiana	10,881,835	Utah	4,150,335
Maine	2,136,170	Vermont	1,394,114
Maryland	10,654,571	Virginia	12,601,788
Massachusetts	13,696,275	Washington	10,609,797
Michigan	18,144,575	West Virginia	2,911,489
Minnesota	11,010,676	Wisconsin	9,940,655
Mississippi	4,899,035	Wyoming	1,115,145
Missouri	10,624,938	**United States**	**$583,796,332**

In 2015 California accounted for the largest amount of direct premiums written, followed by Texas, Florida, New York and Illinois, according to S&P Global Market Intelligence.

Among the states with the most premiums, California experienced the highest increase in 2015 from 2014 (5.7 percent), followed by Illinois, with a 5.2 percent increase. Premiums rose 4.6 percent in Florida and 3.5 percent in both New York and Texas.

Nationally, direct premiums written rose 3.7 percent in 2015.

[1]Before reinsurance transactions, includes state funds, excludes territories.

Source: NAIC data, sourced from S&P Global Market Intelligence, Insurance Information Institute.

INCURRED LOSSES BY STATE

Property/casualty (P/C) insurers pay out billions of dollars each year to settle claims. Many of the payments go to businesses, such as auto repair companies, that help claimants get their lives back together after an accident, fire, windstorm or other incident that caused the injury or property damage. Insurance claim payments support local businesses, enabling them to provide jobs and pay taxes that support the local economy. When P/C insurance claims are paid, funds flow to the industries that supply claimants with the goods and services necessary for their recovery. The chart below shows incurred losses, i.e., losses occurring during a fixed period, whether or not adjusted or paid during the same period.

Incurred Losses By State, Property/Casualty Insurance, 2015[1] ($000)

State	Incurred losses	State	Incurred losses	State	Incurred losses
Alabama	$4,093,192	Louisiana	$5,609,416	Oklahoma	$4,491,760
Alaska	719,288	Maine	1,044,592	Oregon	3,346,175
Arizona	5,446,616	Maryland	6,409,320	Pennsylvania	13,301,894
Arkansas	2,910,023	Massachusetts	8,836,136	Rhode Island	1,565,774
California	39,547,703	Michigan	11,187,648	South Carolina	5,073,633
Colorado	6,396,637	Minnesota	5,731,502	South Dakota	1,194,828
Connecticut	4,533,879	Mississippi	2,520,682	Tennessee	5,766,943
Delaware	1,383,315	Missouri	6,369,204	Texas	29,009,021
D.C.	878,280	Montana	1,309,551	Utah	2,171,672
Florida	22,014,264	Nebraska	2,322,393	Vermont	628,825
Georgia	10,489,728	Nevada	2,819,262	Virginia	6,617,186
Hawaii	1,014,650	New Hampshire	1,156,725	Washington	6,373,962
Idaho	1,414,387	New Jersey	11,946,823	West Virginia	1,422,841
Illinois	13,392,906	New Mexico	1,897,250	Wisconsin	4,948,732
Indiana	5,771,409	New York	24,944,776	Wyoming	510,973
Iowa	3,153,050	North Carolina	7,503,427		
Kansas	2,997,963	North Dakota	1,119,926		
Kentucky	4,331,174	Ohio	7,974,601	**United States**	**$327,615,917**

[1] Losses occurring within a fixed period whether or not adjusted or paid during the same period, on a direct basis before reinsurance.

Source: NAIC data, sourced from S&P Global Market Intelligence, Insurance Information Institute.

GUARANTY FUNDS

All 50 states, Washington, D.C., Puerto Rico and the Virgin Islands have procedures under which solvent property/casualty (P/C) insurance companies cover claims against insolvent insurers. New York has a pre-assessment system, under which estimates are made annually of how much will be needed in the coming year to fulfill the system's obligations to pay the claims of insolvent insurers. Some states—including New Jersey, New York and Pennsylvania—have separate pre-assessment funds for workers compensation. Florida has a post-assessment fund, which covers the claims of insolvent workers compensation insurers and self-insurers.

The P/C lines of insurance covered by guaranty funds and the maximum amount paid on any claim vary from state to state. Assessments are used to pay claims against companies that became insolvent in the past as well as for current insolvencies. A similar system for life and health insurers is coordinated by the National Organization of Life and Health Insurance Guaranty Associations.

Property/Casualty Guaranty Fund Net Assessments, 2006-2015

Year	Net assessments[1]	Year	Net assessments[1]
2006	$1,344,487,899	2012	$450,415,322
2007	943,164,094	2013	456,953,717
2008	368,451,899	2014	481,082,306
2009	522,881,688	2015	458,510,638
2010	171,159,059	**Total, inception-2015[2]**	**$16,702,976,899**
2011	138,652,497		

At $458 million, guaranty fund net assessments in 2015 were down 4.7 percent from $481 million in 2014.

Net assessments in 2014 were at their highest level since 2009, when they totaled $523 million.

[1]Assessments less refunds and abatements (cancellations of uncalled portions of assessments when funds on hand are sufficient to pay claims). [2]Includes pre-1978 net assessments.

Source: National Conference of Insurance Guaranty Funds.

Property/Casualty Guaranty Fund Net Assessments By State, 2015

State	Net assessments[1]	State	Net assessments[1]
Alabama	$7,117,657	Montana	0
Alaska	5,050,002	Nebraska	$3,200,000
Arizona	0	Nevada	7,485,495
Arkansas	0	New Hampshire	0
California	228,506,804	New Jersey	128,576,628
Colorado	0	New Mexico	0
Connecticut	973,820	New York	0
Delaware	0	North Carolina	5,625,000
D.C.	3,915,999	North Dakota	0
Florida	0	Ohio	0
Georgia	0	Oklahoma	-7,800,000
Hawaii	38,847,339	Oregon	0
Idaho	0	Pennsylvania	19,265,000
Illinois	5,147,731	Rhode Island	-1,815,432
Indiana	0	South Carolina	14,249,530
Iowa	0	South Dakota	831,387
Kansas	0	Tennessee	0
Kentucky	0	Texas	0
Louisiana	0	Utah	0
Maine	-1,125,799	Vermont	0
Maryland	0	Virginia	0
Massachusetts	0	Washington	459,477
Michigan	0	West Virginia	0
Minnesota	0	Wisconsin	0
Mississippi	0	Wyoming	0
Missouri	0	**United States**	**$458,510,638**

[1]Assessments less refunds and abatements (cancellations of uncalled portions of assessments when funds on hand are sufficient to pay claims). Negative numbers represent net refunds.

Source: National Conference of Insurance Guaranty Funds.

Chapter 7

Property/Casualty Insurance By Line

PREMIUMS BY LINE

Premiums can be accounted for in two major ways: net premiums written, which reflect premium amounts after deductions for reinsurance and direct premiums written, which are calculated before reinsurance transactions.

Premiums Written By Line, Property/Casualty Insurance, 2015 ($ billions)

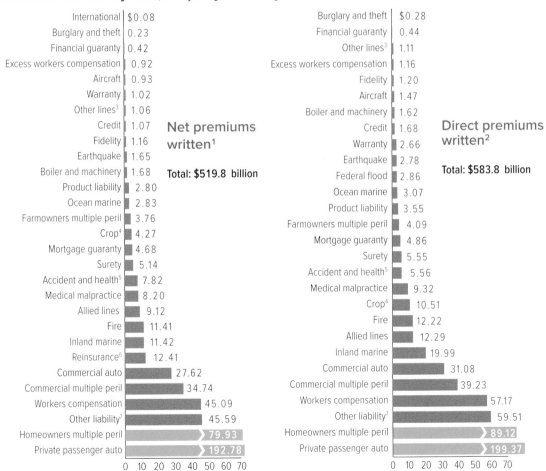

Net premiums written[1]

Total: $519.8 billion

Line	$ billions
International	$0.08
Burglary and theft	0.23
Financial guaranty	0.42
Excess workers compensation	0.92
Aircraft	0.93
Warranty	1.02
Other lines[3]	1.06
Credit	1.07
Fidelity	1.16
Earthquake	1.65
Boiler and machinery	1.68
Product liability	2.80
Ocean marine	2.83
Farmowners multiple peril	3.76
Crop[4]	4.27
Mortgage guaranty	4.68
Surety	5.14
Accident and health[5]	7.82
Medical malpractice	8.20
Allied lines	9.12
Fire	11.41
Inland marine	11.42
Reinsurance[6]	12.41
Commercial auto	27.62
Commercial multiple peril	34.74
Workers compensation	45.09
Other liability[7]	45.59
Homeowners multiple peril	79.93
Private passenger auto	192.78

Direct premiums written[2]

Total: $583.8 billion

Line	$ billions
Burglary and theft	$0.28
Financial guaranty	0.44
Other lines[3]	1.11
Excess workers compensation	1.16
Fidelity	1.20
Aircraft	1.47
Boiler and machinery	1.62
Credit	1.68
Warranty	2.66
Earthquake	2.78
Federal flood	2.86
Ocean marine	3.07
Product liability	3.55
Farmowners multiple peril	4.09
Mortgage guaranty	4.86
Surety	5.55
Accident and health[5]	5.56
Medical malpractice	9.32
Crop[4]	10.51
Fire	12.22
Allied lines	12.29
Inland marine	19.99
Commercial auto	31.08
Commercial multiple peril	39.23
Workers compensation	57.17
Other liability[7]	59.51
Homeowners multiple peril	89.12
Private passenger auto	199.37

[1]After reinsurance transactions, excludes state funds. [2]Before reinsurance transactions, includes some state funds. [3]Includes miscellaneous coverages. [4]Includes federally sponsored multiple peril crop and private market crop-hail. [5]Premiums from certain insurers that write health insurance but file financial statements with state regulators on a property/casualty rather than life/health basis. [6]Only includes nonproportional reinsurance, an arrangement in which a reinsurer makes payments to an insurer whose losses exceed a predetermined amount. [7]Coverages protecting against legal liability resulting from negligence, carelessness or failure to act.

Source: NAIC data, sourced from S&P Global Market Intelligence, Insurance Information Institute.

Personal vs. Commercial

The property/casualty (P/C) insurance industry is divided into two main segments: personal lines and commercial lines. Personal lines include coverage for individuals, mainly auto and homeowners. Commercial lines include the many kinds of insurance products designed for businesses. In 2015 private passenger auto insurance was the largest line of insurance, based on net premiums written, making up 37 percent of all P/C insurance (commercial and personal combined) and 71 percent of personal insurance. Homeowners multiple peril insurance is the second largest line. Other liability is the largest commercial line and third-largest P/C line. It accounted for 9 percent of all P/C net premiums and 18 percent of all commercial premiums.

Net Premiums Written, Personal And Commercial Lines, 2015 ($ billions)

Personal lines	52.0%	$272.7
Commerical lines	48.0	247.1
Total	**100.0%**	**$519.8**

Source: NAIC data, sourced from S&P Global Market Intelligence, Insurance Information Institute.

Net Premiums Written By Line, Property/Casualty Insurance 2013-2015[1] ($ millions)

Lines of insurance	2013	2014	2015	Percent change from prior year			Percent of total, 2015
				2013	2014	2015	
Private passenger auto	$174,899.0	$183,451.5	$192,782.5	4.1%	4.9%	5.1%	37.1%
Liability	107,446.4	112,354.9	116,298.9	3.9	4.6	3.5	22.4
Collision and comprehensive	67,452.7	71,096.6	76,483.6	4.4	5.4	7.6	14.7
Commercial auto	23,891.4	25,694.2	27,622.0	8.2	7.5	7.5	5.3
Liability	18,355.1	19,570.6	20,897.1	8.1	6.6	6.8	4.0
Collision and comprehensive	5,536.3	6,123.6	6,724.9	8.6	10.6	9.8	1.3
Fire	11,229.4	11,501.5	11,414.8	4.0	2.4	-0.8	2.2
Allied lines	9,251.9	9,209.8	9,119.6	13.4	-0.5	-1.0	1.8
Crop[2]	4,942.5	4,772.6	4,265.4	-7.1	-3.4	-10.6	0.8
Federal flood[3]	5.1	8.5	3.0	1,110.4	67.3	-64.8	[4]
Farmowners multiple peril	3,511.7	3,628.1	3,762.6	7.1	3.3	3.7	0.7
Homeowners multiple peril	72,773.2	77,914.4	79,931.1	7.3	7.1	2.6	15.4

(table continues)

Net Premiums Written By Line, Property/Casualty Insurance 2013-2015[1] ($ millions) (Cont'd)

Lines of insurance	2013	2014	2015	Percent change from prior year			Percent of total, 2015
				2013	2014	2015	
Commercial multiple peril	$33,245.1	$34,375.1	$34,741.5	5.5%	3.4%	1.1%	6.7%
Mortgage guaranty	4,329.9	4,180.0	4,681.9	9.2	-3.5	12.0	0.9
Ocean marine	2,863.5	2,910.4	2,831.6	5.9	1.6	-2.7	0.5
Inland marine	10,147.9	10,990.0	11,417.3	5.7	8.3	3.9	2.2
Financial guaranty	710.5	488.5	418.8	2.6	-31.2	-14.3	0.1
Medical malpractice	8,531.2	8,475.5	8,201.4	-2.1	-0.7	-3.2	1.6
Earthquake	1,587.0	1,641.8	1,650.2	-0.4	3.5	0.5	0.3
Accident and health[5]	7,538.6	7,731.8	7,819.2	-5.1	2.6	1.1	1.5
Workers compensation	41,147.2	43,546.7	45,090.5	6.2	5.8	3.5	8.7
Excess workers compensation	844.1	920.2	924.3	3.5	9.0	0.4	0.2
Product liability	2,718.9	2,674.2	2,796.8	5.6	-1.6	4.6	0.5
Other liability[6]	42,075.3	44,181.3	45,585.3	9.8	5.0	3.2	8.8
Aircraft	1,067.7	1,005.7	929.0	-8.0	-5.8	-7.6	0.2
Fidelity	1,124.2	1,165.3	1,161.4	2.5	3.7	-0.3	0.2
Surety	4,868.8	5,000.4	5,139.9	3.7	2.7	2.8	1.0
Burglary and theft	207.2	226.2	230.4	-6.2	9.2	1.8	4
Boiler and machinery	1,979.5	1,999.0	1,682.1	4.9	1.0	-15.9	0.3
Credit	1,167.3	1,191.0	1,070.0	-19.9	2.0	-10.2	0.2
Warranty	1,155.3	1,020.2	1,017.8	-16.7	-11.7	-0.2	0.2
International	113.2	125.1	82.0	6.9	10.6	-34.4	4
Reinsurance[7]	12,458.6	11,532.9	12,411.4	-15.1	-7.4	7.6	2.4
Other lines[8]	1,132.4	1,073.0	1,064.7	2.9	-5.2	-0.8	0.2
Total, all lines [9]	$481,518.0	$502,635.3	$519,848.6	4.6%	4.4%	3.4%	100.0%

[1]After reinsurance transactions, excludes state funds. [2]Includes federally sponsored multiple peril crop and crop-hail provided by the private market. [3]Excludes flood insurance provided by the National Flood Insurance Program through participating private insurers. [4]Less than 0.1 percent. [5]Premiums from certain insurers that write health insurance but file financial statements with state regulators on a property/casualty basis. [6]Coverages protecting against legal liability resulting from negligence, carelessness or failure to act. [7]Only includes nonproportional reinsurance, an arrangement in which a reinsurer makes payments to an insurer whose losses exceed a predetermined amount. [8]Includes miscellaneous coverages. [9]May not match total premiums shown elsewhere in this book because of the use of different exhibits from S&P Global Market Intelligence.

Source: NAIC data, sourced from S&P Global Market Intelligence, Insurance Information Institute.

Direct Premiums Written, Property/Casualty Insurance, By State By Line, 2015[1] ($000)

State	Private passenger auto		Commercial auto		Homeowners multiple peril
	Liability	Coll./comp.	Liability	Coll./comp.	
Alabama	$1,508,342	$1,282,032	$332,404	$112,408	$1,657,676
Alaska	275,311	176,403	53,597	17,242	164,273
Arizona	2,384,847	1,623,295	361,338	94,409	1,519,049
Arkansas	903,538	776,709	231,834	98,807	863,215
California	13,076,221	10,171,421	2,532,792	737,019	7,462,747
Colorado	2,172,631	1,462,220	351,663	131,784	2,024,785
Connecticut	1,652,325	1,018,396	307,229	75,802	1,408,185
Delaware	531,599	234,045	89,433	18,828	244,064
D.C.	161,084	144,789	34,675	8,303	151,109
Florida	11,507,025	4,266,241	1,741,263	332,358	8,772,206
Georgia	4,209,292	2,648,118	731,313	194,876	2,844,022
Hawaii	411,791	279,008	84,856	21,748	368,755
Idaho	458,875	327,863	104,101	49,276	315,632
Illinois	3,689,342	2,961,992	1,015,310	314,375	3,423,857
Indiana	1,870,338	1,412,730	442,786	181,571	1,851,696
Iowa	768,221	794,093	222,219	146,781	731,293
Kansas	838,873	817,742	182,763	118,571	1,104,651
Kentucky	1,731,028	907,113	289,741	99,006	1,115,395
Louisiana	2,373,772	1,433,621	545,084	107,638	1,851,819
Maine	356,032	297,110	93,909	39,450	387,943
Maryland	2,563,615	1,734,216	413,885	114,678	1,628,226
Massachusetts	2,647,008	2,009,122	584,015	194,661	2,155,538
Michigan	5,153,560	2,922,954	618,902	282,383	2,658,451
Minnesota	1,851,128	1,390,794	357,317	182,120	2,013,736
Mississippi	912,578	751,930	244,087	93,934	957,972
Missouri	1,841,243	1,510,163	393,455	163,444	1,912,187
Montana	339,566	291,454	96,894	57,029	300,539
Nebraska	582,233	516,969	140,435	103,582	649,522
Nevada	1,342,378	611,390	197,144	33,972	535,066
New Hampshire	395,181	374,013	89,479	33,361	383,096
New Jersey	4,851,134	2,237,735	1,053,833	194,960	2,556,089
New Mexico	768,815	450,507	139,010	46,631	489,700
New York	7,724,377	4,220,344	1,912,401	321,298	5,220,744
North Carolina	2,777,884	2,379,626	561,356	176,543	2,376,336
North Dakota	205,695	246,377	91,591	73,512	196,937
Ohio	3,351,659	2,642,568	654,731	241,300	2,785,059
Oklahoma	1,325,907	1,086,545	311,135	134,858	1,595,082
Oregon	1,664,350	747,023	248,739	73,318	749,220
Pennsylvania	4,442,481	3,398,391	985,726	364,695	3,248,515
Rhode Island	532,672	272,326	80,395	20,320	370,153
South Carolina	2,004,321	1,270,757	289,557	88,193	1,601,721
South Dakota	229,958	252,966	66,454	52,439	221,501
Tennessee	1,974,694	1,582,309	392,528	185,811	1,909,045
Texas	9,683,925	7,828,538	2,275,072	707,959	7,994,072
Utah	988,494	594,727	181,504	68,619	489,732
Vermont	173,906	172,454	42,935	22,176	190,047
Virginia	2,753,821	2,112,626	480,476	143,741	2,126,210
Washington	2,947,369	1,480,636	420,902	126,933	1,585,812
West Virginia	671,203	515,921	123,786	42,953	427,551
Wisconsin	1,556,803	1,226,494	382,244	167,266	1,344,070
Wyoming	173,265	195,442	59,221	32,618	188,617
United States	**$119,311,710**	**$80,062,258**	**$23,637,523**	**$7,445,556**	**$89,122,918**

[1] Includes some state funds. Source: NAIC data, sourced from S&P Global Market Intelligence, Insurance Information Institute.

Direct Premiums Written, Property/Casualty Insurance, By State By Line, 2015[1] ($000)

Farmowners multiple peril	Commercial multiple peril	Workers compensation	Excess workers compensation	Medical malpractice	Product liability
$74,050	$568,579	$349,379	$22,482	$122,485	$33,851
633	107,869	281,738	4,829	23,547	4,370
15,988	610,403	841,693	13,249	220,314	36,666
28,608	323,955	259,624	7,888	64,074	17,710
209,485	4,552,394	12,334,022	239,208	752,021	463,741
78,943	761,544	1,057,358	13,034	160,999	64,623
5,894	638,210	892,281	23,420	157,007	57,727
5,756	303,839	197,234	1,659	33,662	7,579
0	163,331	198,170	2,635	26,459	5,254
23,481	2,221,245	2,650,681	60,679	572,191	209,081
118,657	981,971	1,446,665	39,563	241,936	89,599
460	174,298	261,805	5,311	27,272	9,310
57,224	195,885	368,128	1,897	30,210	12,906
170,482	1,721,225	2,826,687	60,481	499,549	160,032
201,698	803,114	889,525	13,038	116,197	82,981
194,132	373,834	770,150	10,427	66,109	40,974
233,692	380,403	473,902	11,026	61,133	39,258
158,011	506,951	512,806	19,112	106,286	29,057
13,541	530,484	834,136	50,313	102,058	44,140
4,607	226,195	220,659	3,113	46,581	8,271
26,987	636,161	962,920	12,084	276,782	47,936
3,257	1,124,973	1,150,611	24,079	300,740	101,034
142,183	1,066,692	1,197,085	35,167	190,342	89,938
145,046	707,248	998,846	1,208	78,305	87,711
22,557	328,052	361,104	11,493	48,354	19,101
169,216	764,843	923,617	39,372	141,780	56,364
65,832	174,613	287,327	6,290	41,208	11,084
216,270	262,711	388,612	5,547	33,171	23,443
7,843	310,843	364,126	17,891	71,348	59,778
3,150	231,881	265,035	4,058	37,784	13,200
2,622	1,424,250	2,434,552	37,039	423,483	205,513
25,354	225,469	296,101	6,521	51,208	10,255
41,296	3,706,915	5,523,560	59,256	1,651,460	302,454
58,237	935,094	1,487,632	28,957	180,665	86,663
115,129	143,982	7,042	0	9,754	14,861
163,692	1,265,653	20,656	74,265	265,801	114,097
161,694	527,709	810,551	24,391	99,583	42,861
64,656	459,370	678,682	11,690	93,174	36,359
103,859	1,704,178	2,724,970	43,210	655,048	143,084
276	150,488	213,035	1,864	31,129	11,223
13,152	471,680	729,091	10,982	65,229	42,802
116,988	128,504	180,816	1,297	17,003	11,132
143,342	696,206	858,644	20,336	229,468	56,039
285,031	2,674,326	2,741,890	31,155	295,300	297,827
13,563	259,607	422,609	4,083	63,050	30,635
14,677	135,019	196,611	1,406	16,305	6,592
75,397	779,795	981,402	25,197	193,276	54,397
71,375	791,229	24,346	24,203	160,753	54,248
14,364	204,764	323,086	4,990	63,887	11,987
175,143	686,942	1,941,027	9,159	78,561	81,717
28,801	101,855	6,291	276	23,777	5,993
$4,086,331	**$39,226,781**	**$57,168,518**	**$1,180,828**	**$9,317,817**	**$3,547,454**

[1]Includes some state funds. Source: NAIC data, sourced from S&P Global Market Intelligence, Insurance Information Institute.

Direct Premiums Written, Property/Casualty Insurance, By State By Line, 2015[1] ($000)

State	Other liability	Fire	Allied lines	Inland marine	Ocean marine	Surety
Alabama	$594,528	$204,159	$196,178	$276,700	$37,875	$65,448
Alaska	154,052	51,660	29,906	146,994	37,391	27,527
Arizona	794,500	130,857	119,302	326,234	19,143	92,080
Arkansas	317,625	148,588	118,168	202,279	16,690	38,058
California	7,237,187	1,185,644	788,076	2,613,836	280,178	700,960
Colorado	1,103,463	142,584	156,788	352,254	12,813	118,973
Connecticut	1,007,433	130,236	111,834	293,180	87,409	65,330
Delaware	330,898	29,215	25,762	77,982	7,658	21,302
D.C.	364,576	30,606	28,050	111,023	3,642	127,412
Florida	4,493,713	1,292,683	2,633,607	1,210,054	313,912	355,920
Georgia	1,428,160	327,497	266,334	569,795	55,871	142,469
Hawaii	264,065	68,302	92,178	97,662	15,693	39,707
Idaho	192,078	30,361	27,323	101,675	5,071	20,355
Illinois	3,805,176	367,963	322,788	747,640	92,191	208,310
Indiana	852,538	320,670	185,235	312,147	29,554	74,002
Iowa	540,735	107,291	119,701	194,324	7,598	46,593
Kansas	422,832	99,850	146,407	188,697	8,857	62,238
Kentucky	454,986	124,202	100,240	259,232	26,726	78,982
Louisiana	869,399	337,373	466,070	418,461	185,278	106,015
Maine	156,732	41,940	41,209	94,505	26,244	16,679
Maryland	999,564	147,039	120,137	323,970	96,325	153,869
Massachusetts	1,740,127	297,693	208,668	455,437	86,661	139,365
Michigan	1,227,428	313,377	172,071	519,758	65,390	88,290
Minnesota	1,059,133	192,982	290,126	362,785	24,997	86,685
Mississippi	306,401	136,349	126,563	182,656	17,810	42,560
Missouri	943,874	210,796	182,225	331,130	37,043	74,987
Montana	158,709	30,730	30,578	96,631	3,435	29,629
Nebraska	320,853	58,524	79,597	166,990	5,422	38,339
Nevada	345,528	81,307	70,405	172,582	6,696	73,946
New Hampshire	188,396	36,823	29,167	83,979	11,249	15,683
New Jersey	2,331,570	372,581	334,645	550,979	135,249	161,294
New Mexico	220,414	38,929	42,186	102,292	2,764	42,947
New York	7,131,634	820,460	653,181	1,510,929	406,485	366,065
North Carolina	1,146,112	278,303	277,822	511,480	44,524	132,591
North Dakota	178,072	34,746	49,373	88,736	1,570	28,262
Ohio	1,553,922	382,665	240,699	539,840	52,694	138,829
Oklahoma	599,589	164,860	189,727	247,880	20,981	64,115
Oregon	512,151	96,489	72,262	242,845	32,858	57,396
Pennsylvania	2,494,374	441,435	297,035	652,790	60,086	227,544
Rhode Island	224,372	45,407	39,834	86,344	45,318	13,319
South Carolina	486,009	213,072	182,313	291,455	28,162	74,922
South Dakota	120,143	28,442	33,594	70,927	1,063	26,285
Tennessee	914,507	244,852	181,959	393,089	55,573	85,805
Texas	4,835,733	1,590,866	1,829,521	1,961,471	311,755	533,181
Utah	386,273	102,523	50,515	149,880	10,467	41,991
Vermont	105,338	22,338	13,607	48,653	5,163	8,263
Virginia	1,249,637	222,575	182,854	413,208	64,187	140,060
Washington	1,075,503	205,542	142,402	457,716	130,224	138,073
West Virginia	200,993	62,128	36,752	76,566	3,704	36,305
Wisconsin	964,089	158,564	137,281	254,510	35,530	55,469
Wyoming	103,853	19,266	17,988	47,996	1,053	29,727
United States	**$59,508,974**	**$12,223,345**	**$12,290,243**	**$19,990,177**	**$3,074,234**	**$5,554,157**

[1]Includes some state funds. Source: NAIC data, sourced from S&P Global Market Intelligence, Insurance Information Institute.

Direct Premiums Written, Property/Casualty Insurance, By State By Line, 2015[1] ($000)

Fidelity	Burglary and theft	Boiler and machinery	Financial guaranty	Aircraft	Earthquake	Federal flood
$13,501	$2,933	$26,949	$2,005	$16,211	$8,029	$26,362
2,215	663	9,777	79	31,312	25,182	1,759
12,516	3,432	25,326	2,075	56,999	8,840	17,487
10,040	2,014	15,920	1,716	21,218	31,615	10,736
121,784	32,558	158,166	51,102	139,449	1,615,393	163,226
22,948	4,531	21,672	3,613	32,300	10,800	14,331
26,639	4,562	21,316	4,040	33,283	8,277	43,032
3,465	1,720	4,070	22,247	13,943	1,173	14,944
13,524	2,743	6,525	151	2,123	2,610	1,250
63,636	17,041	67,360	7,099	98,909	23,490	812,917
31,760	8,319	40,670	875	62,561	14,871	51,622
5,116	620	5,425	4,108	11,053	11,557	32,891
2,824	602	7,031	130	12,689	3,597	3,361
63,495	15,025	67,352	11,329	60,200	67,210	28,816
18,801	4,031	63,322	1,059	21,460	36,466	17,316
14,280	2,205	23,553	3,186	11,351	5,844	10,124
11,951	2,181	19,307	2,034	17,732	7,119	6,513
10,663	1,986	25,151	3,212	7,251	41,992	15,373
13,635	4,135	29,527	7,006	44,951	6,262	255,937
4,026	667	9,137	356	3,312	2,035	7,514
27,222	4,633	24,053	4,946	16,944	12,270	32,062
41,042	7,064	38,419	4,337	13,568	20,926	63,632
32,852	8,398	55,183	2,064	26,382	8,340	16,165
29,089	5,297	33,922	4,795	28,714	6,850	6,650
8,212	1,839	14,423	2,064	11,779	17,364	32,290
24,065	4,916	27,942	5,746	24,566	91,411	16,251
2,747	457	5,659	41	9,581	4,692	2,834
7,922	1,441	13,615	598	11,804	2,701	7,354
6,829	2,076	10,993	1,203	19,707	19,481	6,731
3,561	949	6,499	365	5,791	2,579	7,326
45,759	9,657	47,948	23,016	22,479	19,597	197,323
3,902	627	8,967	1,008	7,990	2,525	8,593
149,415	30,746	117,613	226,759	62,777	53,503	170,628
34,941	5,434	41,313	2,140	27,512	13,809	87,145
3,174	415	12,391	760	7,340	989	6,245
41,484	10,475	59,869	3,708	55,226	29,806	26,795
11,741	2,260	19,335	224	17,088	18,858	8,697
10,433	2,780	18,214	1,085	24,010	79,096	19,241
51,450	11,066	71,085	9,584	31,414	16,953	54,655
4,253	873	5,530	1,261	12,051	2,421	18,122
10,164	2,281	22,195	1,030	11,055	40,740	111,255
3,535	436	6,741	0	6,552	1,007	3,304
18,367	6,598	30,688	189	23,843	78,908	18,844
77,540	24,802	135,384	14,286	157,714	35,706	284,365
6,779	1,795	10,604	652	26,459	44,999	1,982
4,064	419	4,684	1,140	2,211	28,341	4,591
31,122	7,497	31,846	682	40,971	18,759	60,388
17,699	4,945	35,805	1,156	35,357	169,354	28,038
4,010	720	8,282	253	2,960	1,281	13,093
23,644	4,714	40,524	250	18,172	5,864	9,753
1,558	298	7,979	0	5,528	2,952	1,279
$1,205,395	$277,874	$1,615,261	$442,766	$1,465,850	$2,784,445	$2,861,144

[1]Includes some state funds. Source: NAIC data, sourced from S&P Global Market Intelligence, Insurance Information Institute.

Direct Premiums Written, Property/Casualty Insurance, By State By Line, 2015[1] ($000)

State	Credit	Warranty	Accident and health	Multiple peril crop	Private crop	Mortgage guaranty	Misc.
Alabama	$27,134	$9,157	$62,312	$61,103	$642	$68,348	$25,647
Alaska	6,163	2,209	12,116	83	0	16,912	1,229
Arizona	17,320	15,948	86,661	18,919	2,310	109,755	24,313
Arkansas	13,320	4,546	50,357	110,612	9,785	31,627	7,993
California	159,694	177,398	461,636	488,837	15,077	458,719	84,501
Colorado	16,170	20,856	80,851	168,919	16,397	131,372	16,073
Connecticut	27,769	11,447	41,866	5,139	0	61,253	5,346
Delaware	13,053	7,425	68,871	10,042	64	20,827	624
D.C.	6,963	105	98,278	0	0	32,943	696
Florida	85,946	444,037	202,527	82,588	425	253,800	108,979
Georgia	45,000	38,540	150,730	131,588	1,449	175,638	29,811
Hawaii	5,695	2,592	13,675	1,378	0	20,725	2,214
Idaho	2,965	3,806	18,022	58,257	15,360	30,420	2,389
Illinois	63,109	183,354	254,847	689,548	83,739	223,611	35,926
Indiana	26,552	35,895	242,662	347,136	26,566	102,094	13,319
Iowa	9,244	4,166	70,376	714,656	125,599	48,589	5,832
Kansas	11,839	145,332	61,752	616,745	50,477	45,762	5,563
Kentucky	35,416	14,903	50,641	144,031	11,401	41,149	4,369
Louisiana	23,811	8,350	55,456	77,895	1,890	60,806	22,972
Maine	6,266	3,988	10,350	9,288	0	16,948	1,105
Maryland	18,362	19,188	67,719	31,010	87	128,027	9,655
Massachusetts	33,189	15,160	84,963	3,710	0	131,418	15,856
Michigan	89,595	544,363	197,210	194,520	7,721	181,245	36,566
Minnesota	18,301	32,223	111,295	635,566	109,826	142,170	15,811
Mississippi	19,109	4,934	55,368	120,168	2,928	26,753	18,303
Missouri	31,541	34,039	168,151	379,106	21,464	88,452	11,551
Montana	697	993	25,161	143,431	4,897	15,041	2,298
Nebraska	4,505	4,539	64,391	555,728	183,986	28,363	6,395
Nevada	22,267	6,013	28,097	13,026	54	42,712	5,095
New Hampshire	5,523	6,127	17,557	465	0	28,936	3,570
New Jersey	69,511	28,787	147,809	2,627	27	153,542	27,230
New Mexico	4,610	3,926	23,143	25,729	1,908	27,309	7,785
New York	159,612	66,954	406,851	39,664	28	169,550	56,431
North Carolina	45,478	46,890	130,692	161,872	7,578	156,490	21,894
North Dakota	1,022	1,199	8,508	863,655	85,246	11,157	1,064
Ohio	55,579	50,616	188,784	250,088	14,217	162,779	45,987
Oklahoma	20,167	14,035	60,774	172,484	7,863	41,936	12,033
Oregon	26,401	5,120	59,390	28,452	3,226	73,876	14,376
Pennsylvania	63,702	76,073	352,105	56,735	148	181,376	28,348
Rhode Island	4,160	803	24,672	123	0	17,304	3,898
South Carolina	19,964	7,225	86,719	62,619	233	79,868	11,022
South Dakota	1,917	1,339	20,017	691,370	46,663	11,575	1,759
Tennessee	36,331	39,707	153,407	92,082	3,549	90,865	13,957
Texas	233,165	372,370	504,478	836,373	56,310	379,260	134,976
Utah	13,518	29,034	61,894	5,230	164	84,819	4,136
Vermont	6,014	6,531	4,980	5,043	0	10,058	140,549
Virginia	23,907	23,034	120,135	62,950	2,672	160,555	18,413
Washington	26,837	50,679	82,840	117,650	15,081	155,252	31,838
West Virginia	6,136	3,892	32,256	2,016	3	12,741	2,907
Wisconsin	18,435	30,129	156,804	252,426	13,619	101,506	9,946
Wyoming	839	552	23,646	17,993	2,685	13,142	656
United States	**$1,683,822**	**$2,660,530**	**$5,563,802**	**$9,560,677**	**$953,362**	**$4,859,375**	**$1,113,204**

[1]Includes some state funds. Source: NAIC data, sourced from S&P Global Market Intelligence, Insurance Information Institute.

AUTO: PREMIUMS

Total Auto Net Premiums Written By Sector, 2015 ($ billions)

Private passenger auto	87.5%	$192.8
Commercial auto	12.5	27.6

Liability	62.2%	$137.2
Collision/ comprehensive	37.8	83.2

Source: NAIC data, sourced from S&P Global Market Intelligence, Insurance Information Institute.

Auto Share Of P/C Industry Net Premiums Written, 2015 ($ billions)

Private passenger auto	37.1%	$192.8
Commercial auto	5.3	27.6
All other P/C	57.6	299.4

Source: NAIC data, sourced from S&P Global Market Intelligence, Insurance Information Institute.

Private Passenger Automobile Insurance, 2006-2015 ($000)

	Liability				Collision/comprehensive			
Year	Net premiums written[1]	Annual percent change	Combined ratio[2]	Annual point change[3]	Net premiums written[1]	Annual percent change	Combined ratio[2]	Annual point change[3]
2006	$95,325,685	1.0%	98.6	0.2 pts.	$65,125,977	0.4%	91.4	0.7 pts.
2007	94,974,640	-0.4	101.8	3.1	64,700,792	-0.7	93.4	2.0
2008	94,545,647	-0.5	103.5	1.7	64,054,581	-1.0	95.8	2.4
2009	94,990,682	0.5	106.2	2.7	62,630,693	-2.2	93.0	-2.8
2010	97,672,826	2.8	105.9	-0.3	62,595,851	-0.1	93.4	0.4
2011	100,369,441	2.8	103.8	-2.1	62,948,280	0.6	99.6	6.3
2012	103,429,677	3.0	103.2	-0.6	64,619,667	2.7	100.2	0.6
2013	107,446,382	3.9	103.6	0.4	67,452,663	4.4	98.7	-1.5
2014	112,354,903	4.6	103.8	0.3	71,096,640	5.4	100.2	1.5
2015	116,298,871	3.5	107.9	4.1	76,483,627	7.6	99.4	-0.8

[1]After reinsurance transactions, excludes state funds. [2]After dividends to policyholders. A drop in the combined ratio represents an improvement; an increase represents a deterioration. [3]Calculated from unrounded numbers.

Source: NAIC data, sourced from S&P Global Market Intelligence, Insurance Information Institute.

Percent Change From Prior Year, Net Premiums Written, Private Passenger Auto Insurance, 2006-2015

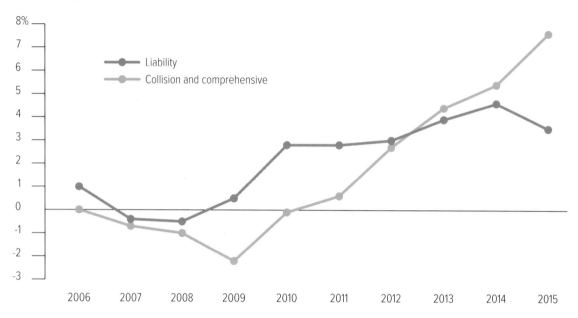

Source: NAIC data, sourced from S&P Global Market Intelligence, Insurance Information Institute.

Top 10 Writers Of Private Passenger Auto Insurance By Direct Premiums Written, 2015
($000)

Rank	Group/company	Direct premiums written[1]	Market share[2]
1	State Farm Mutual Automobile Insurance	$36,545,896	18.3%
2	Berkshire Hathaway Inc.	22,808,382	11.4
3	Allstate Corp.	20,036,973	10.0
4	Progressive Corp.	17,518,721	8.8
5	USAA Insurance Group	10,562,100	5.3
6	Farmers Insurance Group of Companies[3]	9,985,969	5.0
7	Liberty Mutual	9,942,667	5.0
8	Nationwide Mutual Group	7,468,708	3.7
9	American Family Mutual	3,694,271	1.9
10	Travelers Companies Inc.	3,377,404	1.7

[1]Before reinsurance transactions, includes state funds. [2]Based on U.S. total, includes territories. [3]Data for Farmers Insurance Group of Companies and Zurich Financial Group (which owns Farmers' management company) are reported separately by S&P Global Market Intelligence.

Source: NAIC data, sourced from S&P Global Market Intelligence, Insurance Information Institute.

Commercial Automobile Insurance, 2006-2015 ($000)

Year	Liability				Collision/comprehensive			
	Net premiums written[1]	Annual percent change	Combined ratio[2]	Annual point change[3]	Net premiums written[1]	Annual percent change	Combined ratio[2]	Annual point change[3]
2006	$19,704,282	-31.5%	95.7	3.7 pts.	$6,949,388	28.9%	88.4	0.3 pts.
2007	18,803,425	-4.6	95.4	-0.3	6,630,652	-4.6	91.0	2.5
2008	17,833,085	-5.2	97.4	2.0	5,989,108	-9.7	94.7	3.7
2009	16,581,981	-7.0	100.6	3.1	5,347,981	-10.7	96.9	2.3
2010	16,249,433	-2.0	97.1	-3.5	4,870,380	-8.9	101.6	4.7
2011	16,382,082	0.8	101.1	4.0	4,647,376	-4.6	112.0	10.4
2012	16,984,612	3.7	106.6	5.5	5,099,427	9.7	109.2	-2.9
2013	18,355,088	8.1	107.2	0.7	5,536,307	8.6	105.2	-3.9
2014	19,570,622	6.6	103.7	-3.5	6,123,604	10.6	103.2	-2.0
2015	20,897,124	6.8	111.4	7.7	6,724,902	9.8	100.9	-2.3

[1]After reinsurance transactions, excludes state funds. [2]After dividends to policyholders. A drop in the combined ratio represents an improvement; an increase represents a deterioration. [3]Calculated from unrounded numbers.

Source: NAIC data, sourced from S&P Global Market Intelligence, Insurance Information Institute.

Top 10 Writers Of Commercial Auto Insurance By Direct Premiums Written, 2015 ($000)

Rank	Group/company	Direct premiums written[1]	Market share[2]
1	Progressive Corp.	$2,187,740	7.0%
2	Travelers Companies Inc.	2,026,479	6.5
3	Nationwide Mutual Group	1,721,820	5.5
4	Liberty Mutual	1,512,741	4.8
5	Zurich Insurance Group[3]	1,487,295	4.8
6	American International Group (AIG)	1,128,691	3.6
7	Berkshire Hathaway Inc.	1,072,074	3.4
8	Old Republic International Corp.	1,071,187	3.4
9	Auto-Owners Insurance Co.	677,075	2.2
10	AmTrust Financial Services	646,737	2.1

[1]Before reinsurance transactions, includes state funds. [2]Based on U.S. total, includes territories. [3]Data for Farmers Insurance Group of Companies and Zurich Financial Group (which owns Farmers' management company) are reported separately by S&P Global Market Intelligence.

Source: NAIC data, sourced from S&P Global Market Intelligence, Insurance Information Institute.

AUTO: COSTS/EXPENDITURES

AAA's 2016 *Your Driving Costs* study found that the average cost to own and operate an average sedan was $8,558 in 2015, down 1.6 percent from $8,698 in 2014. The decline reflects reduced gasoline costs offsetting increases in maintenance, insurance, finance charges and other costs. Average insurance costs for sedans rose 9.6 percent, or $107, to $1,222 in 2015 from $1,115 in 2014. AAA insurance cost estimates are based on a full coverage policy for a 47-year old male with a clean driving record for a policy with $100,000/$300,000 bodily injury liability coverage with a $500 deductible for collision and a $100 deductible for comprehensive coverage. Figures are not comparable with the National Association of Insurance Commissioners' Auto Expenditures data below.

Average expenditures for auto insurance are projected to have risen 3.4 percent in 2014 to $870 and 3.3 percent in 2015 to $899, according to the Insurance Information Institute (I.I.I.).

78 percent of insured drivers purchase comprehensive coverage in addition to liability insurance, and 72 percent buy collision coverage, based on an analysis by I.I.I. of NAIC data.

Average Expenditures For Auto Insurance, 2004-2013

Year	Average expenditure	Percent change
2004	$842.65	1.5%
2005	831.58	-1.3
2006	817.99	-1.6
2007	798.54	-2.4
2008	790.66	-1.0
2009	786.65	-0.5
2010	791.85	0.7
2011	797.73	0.7
2012	814.63	2.1
2013	841.23	3.3

Source: © 2016 National Association of Insurance Commissioners (NAIC).

Auto Insurance Expenditures, By State

The tables on the following pages show estimated average expenditures for private passenger automobile insurance by state from 2009 to 2013, providing approximate measures of the relative cost of automobile insurance to consumers in each state. To calculate average expenditures the National Association of Insurance Commissioners (NAIC) assumes that all insured vehicles carry liability coverage but not necessarily collision or comprehensive coverage. The average expenditure measures what consumers actually spend for insurance on each vehicle. It does not equal the sum of liability, collision and comprehensive expenditures because not all policyholders purchase all three coverages.

Expenditures are affected by the coverages purchased as well as other factors. In states with a healthy economy, people are more likely to purchase new cars. Since new car owners are more likely to purchase physical damage coverages, these states will have a higher average expenditure. The NAIC notes that urban population, traffic density and per capita income have a significant impact on premiums. The latest report shows that high premium states tend also to be highly urban, with higher wage and price levels and greater traffic density. Tort liability and other auto laws, auto repair costs, liability coverage requirements, theft rates and other factors can also affect auto insurance prices.

Top 10 Most Expensive And Least Expensive States For Auto Insurance, 2013[1]

Rank	Most expensive states	Average expenditure		Rank	Least expensive states	Average expenditure
1	New Jersey	$1,254.10		1	Idaho	$553.38
2	D.C.	1,187.49		2	Iowa	572.14
3	New York	1,181.86		3	South Dakota	580.99
4	Louisiana	1,146.29		4	Maine	592.82
5	Florida	1,143.83		5	North Dakota	604.58
6	Michigan	1,131.40		6	Wisconsin	621.05
7	Delaware	1,101.12		7	Indiana	621.71
8	Rhode Island	1,066.25		8	North Carolina	624.76
9	Connecticut	1,011.27		9	Nebraska	638.74
10	Massachusetts	1,007.98		10	Wyoming	639.71

[1]Based on average automobile insurance expenditures.

Source: ©2016 National Association of Insurance Commissioners (NAIC).

Top 10 Most Expensive And Least Expensive Cities For Auto Insurance, 2014[1]

Rank	Most expensive cities	Average car insurance price		Rank	Least expensive cities	Average car insurance price
1	Detroit, MI	$10,723		1	Winston-Salem, NC	$969
2	New Orleans, LA	4,310		2	Greensboro, NC	1,090
3	Grand Rapids, MI	4,042		3	Raleigh, NC	1,098
4	Newark, NJ	3,525		4	Durham, NC	1,101
5	Baton Rouge, LA	3,364		5	Charlotte, NC	1,123
6	Hialeah, FL	3,272		6	Boise, ID	1,222
7	Jersey City, NJ	3,267		7	Rochester, NY	1,249
8	Louisville, KY	3,256		8	Fayetteville, NC	1,295
9	Miami, FL	3,169		9	Spokane, WA	1,308
10	Philadelphia, PA	2,931		10	Montgomery, AL	1,376

[1]Based on a 26-year-old male without any history of accidents, insuring a 2012 Toyota Camry. Assumes $100,000/$300,000/$50,000 liability limits with a $500 deductible. To calculate city averages, NerdWallet used only ZIP codes within city limits and not in the city's metro area.

Source: NerdWallet.

Average Expenditures For Auto Insurance By State, 2009-2013

State	2013				
	Liability	Collision	Comprehensive	Avg. expenditure	Rank[1]
Alabama	$372.44	$292.40	$146.91	$673.51	38
Alaska	555.04	361.42	141.68	889.28	14
Arizona	490.78	254.85	180.88	811.45	18
Arkansas	380.78	301.90	185.45	703.04	36
California	464.53	361.24	97.67	782.63	22
Colorado	473.55	255.36	158.40	777.74	23
Connecticut	635.62	347.07	126.34	1,011.27	9
Delaware	783.30	291.67	112.21	1,101.12	7
D.C.	634.70	451.59	230.19	1,187.49	2
Florida	860.43	242.48	106.83	1,143.83	5
Georgia	485.40	313.28	150.65	800.58	19
Hawaii	457.09	291.89	95.18	739.26	29
Idaho	339.50	203.02	108.06	553.38	51
Illinois	424.92	278.01	116.34	744.75	27
Indiana	362.97	229.17	112.35	621.71	45
Iowa	291.24	205.15	171.71	572.14	50
Kansas	342.20	247.31	238.75	668.93	39
Kentucky	522.34	254.45	128.20	772.80	24
Louisiana	723.93	380.26	203.52	1,146.29	4
Maine	333.69	245.85	95.40	592.82	48
Maryland	596.17	327.89	147.29	979.28	11
Massachusetts	589.38	361.12	129.97	1,007.98	10
Michigan	742.31	377.45	144.45	1,131.40	6
Minnesota	441.79	210.01	171.80	744.51	28
Mississippi	434.88	299.27	190.98	768.20	26
Missouri	399.08	257.09	163.62	704.22	34
Montana	389.29	256.63	198.81	678.58	37
Nebraska	347.57	220.73	205.38	638.74	43
Nevada	648.19	284.79	114.77	935.90	12
New Hampshire	391.92	279.36	102.02	733.02	31
New Jersey	882.10	363.80	122.37	1,254.10	1
New Mexico	464.51	261.94	162.39	722.66	32
New York	791.14	354.69	155.65	1,181.86	3
North Carolina	355.19	263.06	120.72	624.76	44
North Dakota	284.03	228.38	226.05	604.58	47
Ohio	374.53	251.13	113.02	659.37	40
Oklahoma	443.88	290.08	197.45	768.25	25
Oregon	562.95	206.78	86.53	783.46	21
Pennsylvania	497.28	301.49	131.71	841.42	16
Rhode Island	719.53	372.15	118.86	1,066.25	8
South Carolina	495.96	242.85	165.41	794.40	20
South Dakota	290.24	200.83	227.50	580.99	49
Tennessee	400.64	292.01	136.73	704.20	35
Texas	502.67	357.37	198.56	895.44	13
Utah	465.64	248.39	106.91	733.55	30
Vermont	343.85	272.27	118.70	655.66	41
Virginia	415.86	263.54	130.00	718.72	33
Washington	569.42	243.50	101.12	838.30	17
West Virginia	506.60	319.49	195.28	858.85	15
Wisconsin	354.56	207.71	127.49	621.05	46
Wyoming	323.34	260.15	220.96	639.71	42
United States	**$518.49**	**$296.99**	**$138.82**	**$841.23**	

[1]Ranked highest to lowest by average expenditure. Note: Average expenditure=Total written premium/liability car years. A car year is equal to 365 days of insured coverage for a single vehicle.

Average Expenditures For Auto Insurance By State, 2009-2013

2012 Avg. expenditure	Rank	Average expenditure percent change, 2012-2013	Avg. expenditure 2011	2010	2009
$659.06	37	2.2%	$653.37	$651.22	$652.07
873.15	13	1.8	873.11	890.35	896.74
781.71	18	3.8	776.56	804.97	842.21
679.46	35	3.5	665.49	662.44	657.13
747.82	23	4.7	740.50	746.15	756.16
737.95	26	5.4	723.61	730.42	741.28
986.73	9	2.5	969.41	965.22	952.36
1,065.37	6	3.4	1,048.03	1,030.98	1,021.42
1,154.91	2	2.8	1,139.43	1,133.87	1,127.72
1,128.31	4	1.4	1,090.58	1,037.36	1,006.20
768.34	20	4.2	754.06	748.89	754.61
735.18	27	0.6	748.45	765.83	786.33
534.56	51	3.5	535.11	548.03	554.80
731.57	28	1.8	727.33	733.45	727.82
637.37	40	-2.5	621.38	624.27	620.31
561.26	49	1.9	551.72	546.59	530.96
632.07	42	5.8	625.92	625.17	622.16
759.70	21	1.7	744.53	722.70	698.85
1,112.53	5	3.0	1,110.63	1,121.44	1,100.09
582.71	47	1.7	577.38	582.29	597.87
966.29	11	1.3	956.14	947.74	928.92
976.65	10	3.2	942.12	890.83	860.49
1,048.87	7	7.9	983.62	954.75	913.28
718.61	29	3.6	696.00	693.08	692.08
748.44	22	2.6	740.14	745.17	737.77
683.82	34	3.0	674.60	678.03	668.29
658.42	38	3.1	654.56	657.42	655.61
616.78	44	3.6	602.39	592.56	575.26
905.82	12	3.3	904.91	930.43	944.16
717.15	30	2.2	705.88	706.24	717.56
1,219.97	1	2.8	1,186.24	1,157.30	1,100.66
695.09	32	4.0	691.74	703.64	717.96
1,153.46	3	2.5	1,111.27	1,078.88	1,057.82
611.18	45	2.2	600.04	599.90	609.80
576.08	48	4.9	549.73	528.81	509.72
634.91	41	3.9	619.73	619.45	616.33
740.11	25	3.8	716.21	703.03	677.71
741.51	24	5.7	723.72	724.47	722.85
827.75	16	1.7	812.79	812.15	811.15
1,034.51	8	3.1	1,004.12	984.95	969.02
772.14	19	2.9	748.26	737.77	737.74
556.51	50	4.4	538.49	525.16	512.47
673.90	36	4.5	649.98	641.17	634.24
858.54	14	4.3	842.58	848.11	860.42
713.20	31	2.9	712.74	716.97	717.28
643.47	39	1.9	633.51	630.11	645.79
691.80	33	3.9	679.60	673.72	667.51
809.56	17	3.6	806.02	815.29	826.59
846.74	15	1.4	834.04	830.10	815.00
598.84	46	3.7	600.23	613.41	590.54
623.70	43	2.6	619.88	621.15	624.10
$814.63		**3.3%**	**$797.73**	**$791.85**	**$786.65**

The NAIC does not rank state average expenditures and does not endorse any conclusion drawn from these data.
Source: © 2016 National Association of Insurance Commissioners (NAIC).

Auto Insurance Claims And Expenses

The combined ratio after dividends is a measure of underwriting profitability. It reflects the percentage of each premium dollar an insurer spends on claims (the claims ratio) and percentage of each premium dollar that goes toward expenses (the expense ratio). The combined ratio does not take investment income into account. The private passenger auto combined ratio after dividends was 104.6 in 2015, reflecting a claims ratio of 79.8 percent and an expense ratio 24.3 percent. A combined ratio above 100 indicates an underwriting loss.

Private Passenger Auto Insurance Industry Underwriting Expenses, 2015[1]

Expense	Percent of premiums
Losses and related expenses[2]	
Loss and loss adjustment expense (LAE) ratio	79.8%
Incurred losses	67.5
Defense and cost containment expenses incurred	2.7
Adjusting and other expenses incurred	9.6
Operating expenses[3]	
Expense ratio	24.3%
Net commissions and brokerage expenses incurred	8.9
Taxes, licenses and fees	2.1
Other acquisition and field supervision expenses incurred	7.9
General expenses incurred	5.3
Dividends to policyholders[2]	0.5%
Combined ratio after dividends[4]	104.6%

[1]After reinsurance transactions. [2]As a percent of net premiums earned ($189.2 billion in 2015). [3]As a percent of net premiums written ($192.8 billion in 2015). [4]Sum of loss and LAE, expense and dividends ratios.

Source: NAIC data, sourced from S&P Global Market Intelligence, Insurance Information Institute.

AUTO: CLAIMS

Liability insurance pays for the policyholder's legal responsibility to others for bodily injury or property damage. Collision and comprehensive insurance cover property damage and theft to the policyholder's car.

Private Passenger Auto Insurance Losses, 2006-2015[1]

Year	Liability							
	Bodily injury[2]		Property damage[3]	
	Claim frequency[4]	Claim severity[5,6]	Claim frequency[4]	Claim severity[5,6]
2006	0.98	$12,907	3.40	$2,796
2007	0.90	13,361	3.46	2,847
2008	0.91	14,067	3.42	2,903
2009	0.89	13,891	3.49	2,869
2010	0.91	14,406	3.53	2,881
2011	0.92	14,848	3.56	2,958
2012	0.95	14,690	3.50	3,073
2013	0.95	15,441	3.55	3,231
2014	0.87	16,640	3.66	3,290
2015	0.91	17,024	3.73	3,493

Year	Physical damage[7]			
	Collision		Comprehensive[8]	
	Claim frequency[4]	Claim severity[5]	Claim frequency[4]	Claim severity[5]
2006	4.87	$3,194	2.40	$1,528
2007	5.20	3,109	2.48	1,524
2008	5.35	3,005	2.57	1,551
2009	5.48	2,869	2.75	1,389
2010	5.69	2,778	2.62	1,476
2011	5.75	2,861	2.79	1,490
2012	5.57	2,950	2.62	1,585
2013	5.71	3,144	2.57	1,621
2014	5.95	3,161	2.80	1,567
2015	6.05	3,350	2.73	1,671

In 2015 less than 1 percent of people with liability insurance had a bodily injury liability claim, while 3.7 percent of those with liability insurance had a property damage liability claim, according to ISO.

In 2015, 6.0 percent of collision insurance policyholders had a claim, while 2.7 percent of people with comprehensive coverage had a claim.

In 2015 the average auto liability claim for property damage was $3,493; the average auto liability claim for bodily injury was $17,024.

In 2015 the average collision claim was $3,350; the average comprehensive claim was $1,671.

[1]For all limits combined. Data are for paid claims. [2]Excludes Massachusetts and most states with no-fault automobile insurance laws. [3]Excludes Massachusetts, Michigan and New Jersey. [4]Claim frequency is claims per 100 car years. A car year is equal to 365 days of insured coverage for one vehicle. [5]Claim severity is the size of the loss. [6]Includes loss adjustment expenses. [7]Excludes Massachusetts, Michigan and Puerto Rico. Based on coverage with a $500 deductible. [8]Excludes wind and water losses.

Source: ISO®, a Verisk Analytics® business.

Incurred Losses For Auto Insurance, 2011-2015[1] ($000)

	2011	2012	2013	2014	2015
Private passenger auto					
Liability	$64,110,267	$64,310,776	$65,135,976	$67,879,783	$72,027,357
Physical damage	36,454,102	40,589,159	41,275,620	41,754,861	45,313,540
Commercial auto					
Liability	8,798,119	9,363,647	10,515,806	11,305,679	11,933,884
Physical damage	2,911,013	3,164,880	3,250,740	3,255,581	3,627,601
Total	**$112,273,501**	**$117,428,462**	**$120,178,142**	**$124,195,904**	**$132,902,382**

[1]Losses occurring within a fixed period, whether or not adjusted or paid during the same period, after reinsurance transactions.
Source: NAIC data, sourced from S&P Global Market Intelligence, Insurance Information Institute.

AUTO: HIGH-RISK MARKETS

The Shared/Residual Market

All states and the District of Columbia use special systems to guarantee that auto insurance
is available to those who cannot obtain it in the private market. These systems are commonly
known as assigned risk plans, although that term technically applies to only one type of plan. The
assigned risk and other plans are known in the insurance industry as the shared, or residual, market.
Policyholders in assigned risk plans are assigned to various insurance companies doing business in
the state. In the voluntary, or regular, market, auto insurers are free to select policyholders.

The percentage of vehicles insured in the shared market is dropping, in part because of the
evolution of the nonstandard sector of the voluntary market. The nonstandard market is a niche
market for drivers who have a worse than average driving record or drive specialized cars such
as high-powered sports cars or custom-built cars. It is made up of both small specialty companies,
whose only business is the nonstandard market, and well-known auto insurance companies with
nonstandard divisions.

Insured Vehicles

In 2014, 198 million private passenger vehicles were insured in the United States excluding Texas,
up from 195 million in 2013, according to AIPSO. The figures include cars insured by private auto
insurers in the voluntary market as well as those insured in the so-called shared or residual markets
set up by states to cover hard-to-insure risks. In 2014 California had the most insured private passenger cars (26.2 million), followed by Florida (12.2 million) and New York (9.4 million), including vehicles
in the voluntary and residual markets.

Private Passenger Cars Insured In The Shared And Voluntary Markets, 2014

State	Voluntary market	Shared market	Total	Shared market as a percent of total
Alabama	3,761,830	1	3,761,831	1
Alaska	498,512	23	498,535	0.461%
Arizona	4,465,315	0	4,465,315	1
Arkansas	2,135,039	4	2,135,043	1
California	26,193,318	331	26,193,649	0.001
Colorado	4,007,532	0	4,007,532	1
Connecticut	2,513,014	105	2,513,119	0.004
Delaware	648,565	1	648,566	1
D.C.	245,775	110	245,885	0.045
Florida	12,175,011	178	12,175,189	0.001
Georgia	7,372,180	0	7,372,180	1
Hawaii	868,883	3,126	872,009	0.358
Idaho	1,126,812	2	1,126,814	1
Illinois	8,153,935	311	8,154,246	0.004
Indiana	4,797,686	2	4,797,688	1
Iowa	2,492,910	8	2,492,918	1
Kansas	2,286,148	1,709	2,287,857	0.075
Kentucky	3,196,910	278	3,197,188	0.009
Louisiana	3,012,620	1	3,012,621	1
Maine	1,038,587	4	1,038,591	1
Maryland	4,022,954	42,872	4,065,826	1.054
Massachusetts	4,320,839	62,401	4,383,240	1.424
Michigan	6,215,682	4,959	6,220,641	0.080
Minnesota	3,934,513	4	3,934,517	1
Mississippi	1,958,600	5	1,958,605	1
Missouri	4,337,047	0	4,337,047	1
Montana	792,550	9	792,559	0.001
Nebraska	1,557,743	-2	1,557,741	1
Nevada	1,868,413	0	1,868,413	1
New Hampshire	939,602	172	939,774	0.018

From 2010 to 2014, 1.05 percent of vehicles were insured in the shared market annually, compared with 3.6 percent in 1995 and 1.4 percent in 2000 (excluding Texas).

In 2014 the number of vehicles in the shared market nationwide rose by about 676,000 vehicles, or 34.4 percent compared with 2013, due to a significant rise in the number of cars in the shared market in North Carolina.

In 2014 North Carolina had the highest percentage of cars in the shared market, 30.1 percent, up from 23.5 percent in 2013.

(table continues)

Rhode Island ranked second by percentage of cars in the shared market with 1.9 percent, followed by Massachusetts with 1.4 percent.

In 2014 the number of cars in shared market plans rose 41.1 percent in North Carolina, 5.9 percent in Maryland and 4.5 percent in Rhode Island. The number fell 26.7 percent in Massachusetts, following a 17.5 percent drop in 2013.

Private Passenger Cars Insured In The Shared And Voluntary Markets, 2014 (Cont'd)

State	Voluntary market	Shared market	Total	Shared market as a percent of total
New Jersey	5,461,412	23,201	5,484,613	0.423%
New Mexico	1,534,787	0	1,534,787	[1]
New York	9,445,133	41,894	9,487,027	0.442
North Carolina	5,666,816	2,437,076	8,103,892	30.073
North Dakota	673,309	3	673,312	[1]
Ohio	8,350,922	0	8,350,922	[1]
Oklahoma	2,791,740	9	2,791,749	[1]
Oregon	2,750,778	1	2,750,779	[1]
Pennsylvania	8,774,172	6,897	8,781,069	0.079
Rhode Island	672,178	13,235	685,413	1.931
South Carolina	3,637,020	0	3,637,020	[1]
South Dakota	743,255	1	743,256	[1]
Tennessee	4,514,935	4	4,514,939	[1]
Texas[2]	NA	NA	NA	NA
Utah	1,943,746	6	1,943,752	[1]
Vermont	500,041	38	500,079	0.008
Virginia	6,312,905	413	6,313,318	0.007
Washington	4,835,225	1	4,835,226	[1]
West Virginia	1,338,054	10	1,338,064	0.001
Wisconsin	4,098,048	1	4,098,049	[1]
Wyoming	539,771	0	539,771	[1]
United States	**195,522,772**	**2,639,404**	**198,162,176**	**1.332%**

[1] Less than 0.001 percent. [2] Texas information is no longer available.
NA=Data not available.
Source: AIPSO.

AUTO: UNINSURED MOTORISTS

Uninsured and underinsured motorist coverage reimburses policyholders in an accident involving an uninsured, underinsured or hit-and-run driver. Twenty states and the District of Columbia have mandatory requirements for uninsured or underinsured motorist coverage. More than half of the states have passed laws and begun to develop and implement online auto insurance verification systems to identify uninsured motorists.

In 2012, 12.6 percent of motorists, or about one in eight drivers, was uninsured, according to a 2014 study by the Insurance Research Council (IRC). The percentage has been declining in recent years. Oklahoma had the highest percentage of uninsured motorists, 26 percent, and Massachusetts had the lowest, 4 percent. IRC measures the number of uninsured motorists based on insurance claims, using a ratio of insurance claims made by people who were injured by uninsured drivers relative to the claims made by people who were injured by insured drivers.

Estimated Percentage Of Uninsured Motorists, 1992-2012[1]

Year	Percent	Year	Percent	Year	Percent
1992	15.6%	1999	12.8%	2006	14.3%
1993	16.0	2000	13.4	2007	13.8
1994	15.1	2001	14.2	2008	14.3
1995	14.2	2002	14.5	2009	13.8
1996	13.8	2003	14.9	2010	12.3
1997	13.2	2004	14.6	2011	12.2
1998	13.0	2005	14.6	2012	12.6

[1]Percentage of uninsured drivers, as measured by the ratio of uninsured motorists (UM) claims to bodily injury (BI) claim frequencies.
Source: Insurance Research Council.

Top 10 Highest And Lowest States By Estimated Percentage Of Uninsured Motorists, 2012[1]

Highest			Lowest		
Rank	State	Percent uninsured	Rank	State	Percent uninsured
1	Oklahoma	25.9%	1	Massachusetts	3.9%
2	Florida	23.8	2	Maine	4.7
3	Mississippi	22.9	3	New York	5.3
4	New Mexico	21.6	4	Utah	5.8
5	Michigan	21.0	5	North Dakota	5.9
6	Tennessee	20.1	6	Pennsylvania	6.5
7	Alabama	19.6	7	Nebraska	6.7
8	Rhode Island	17.0	8	Idaho	6.7
9	Colorado	16.2	9	South Carolina	7.7
10	Washington	16.1	10	South Dakota	7.8

[1]Percentage of uninsured drivers, as measured by the ratio of uninsured motorists (UM) claims to bodily injury (BI) claim frequencies.
Source: Insurance Research Council.

Estimated Percentage Of Uninsured Motorists By State, 2012[1]

State	Uninsured	Rank[2]	State	Uninsured	Rank[2]	State	Uninsured	Rank[2]
Alabama	19.6%	7	Kentucky	15.8%	12	North Dakota	5.9%	47
Alaska	13.2	21	Louisiana	13.9	16	Ohio	13.5	17
Arizona	10.6	29	Maine	4.7	50	Oklahoma	25.9	1
Arkansas	15.9	11	Maryland	12.2	22	Oregon	9.0	36
California	14.7	13	Massachusetts	3.9	51	Pennsylvania	6.5	46
Colorado	16.2	9	Michigan	21.0	5	Rhode Island	17.0	8
Connecticut	8.0	41	Minnesota	10.8	28	South Carolina	7.7	43
Delaware	11.5	27	Mississippi	22.9	3	South Dakota	7.8	42
D.C.	11.9	24	Missouri	13.5	18	Tennessee	20.1	6
Florida[3]	23.8	2	Montana	14.1%	15	Texas	13.3	19
Georgia	11.7	26	Nebraska	6.7	44	Utah	5.8	48
Hawaii	8.9	37	Nevada	12.2	23	Vermont	8.5	39
Idaho	6.7	45	New Hampshire	9.3	34	Virginia	10.1	31
Illinois	13.3	20	New Jersey	10.3	30	Washington	16.1	10
Indiana	14.2	14	New Mexico	21.6	4	West Virginia	8.4	40
Iowa	9.7	32	New York	5.3	49	Wisconsin	11.7	25
Kansas	9.4	33	North Carolina	9.1	35	Wyoming	8.7	38

[1]Percentage of uninsured drivers, as measured by the ratio of uninsured motorists (UM) claims to bodily injury (BI) claim frequencies. [2]Rank calculated from unrounded data. [3]In Florida, compulsory auto laws apply to personal injury protection (PIP) and physical damage, but not to third-party bodily injury coverage. Source: Insurance Research Council.

AUTO: LAWS

Automobile Financial Responsibility Laws

Most states require motor vehicle owners to buy a minimum amount of bodily injury and property damage liability insurance before they can legally drive their vehicles. All states have financial responsibility laws, which means that people involved in an accident will be required to furnish proof of financial responsibility up to a certain amount. To comply with these laws, most drivers purchase liability insurance. Despite these laws a significant percentage of drivers are uninsured.

Motorcycle insurance is compulsory in every state except Hawaii, Montana, New Hampshire and Washington. Minimum liability limits and the insurance required by state law are the same for motorcycles as for autos and other motor vehicles.

The chart that follows shows mandatory requirements for bodily injury (BI), property damage (PD) liability, no-fault personal injury protection (PIP), and uninsured (UM) and underinsured (UIM) motorists coverage. It also indicates which states have only financial responsibility (FR) laws.

Automobile Financial Responsibility Limits By State

State	Insurance required	Minimum liability limits[1]
Alabama	BI & PD liability	25/50/25
Alaska	BI & PD liability	50/100/25
Arizona	BI & PD liability	15/30/10
Arkansas	BI & PD liability, PIP	25/50/25
California	BI & PD liability	15/30/5[2]
Colorado	BI & PD liability	25/50/15
Connecticut	BI & PD liability, UM, UIM	20/40/10
Delaware	BI & PD liability, PIP	15/30/10
D.C.	BI & PD liability, PIP, UM	25/50/10
Florida	PD liability, PIP	10/20/10[3]
Georgia	BI & PD liability	25/50/25
Hawaii	BI & PD liability, PIP	20/40/10
Idaho	BI & PD liability	25/50/15
Illinois	BI & PD liability, UM, UIM	25/50/20
Indiana	BI & PD liability	25/50/10
Iowa	BI & PD liability	20/40/15
Kansas	BI & PD liability, PIP	25/50/25
Kentucky	BI & PD liability, PIP	25/50/10[3]
Louisiana	BI & PD liability	15/30/25
Maine	BI & PD liability, UM	50/100/25[4]
Maryland	BI & PD Liability, PIP, UM, UIM	30/60/15
Massachusetts	BI & PD liability, PIP, UM	20/40/5
Michigan	BI & PD liability, PIP	20/40/10
Minnesota	BI & PD liability, PIP, UM, UIM	30/60/10
Mississippi	BI & PD liability	25/50/25
Missouri	BI & PD liability, UM	25/50/10
Montana	BI & PD liability	25/50/20
Nebraska	BI & PD liability, UM, UIM	25/50/25
Nevada	BI & PD liability	15/30/10
New Hampshire	FR only, UM	25/50/25[4]
New Jersey	BI & PD liability, PIP, UM, UIM	15/30/5[5]

(table continues)

Automobile Financial Responsibility Limits By State (Cont'd)

State	Insurance required	Minimum liability limits[1]
New Mexico	BI & PD liability	25/50/10
New York	BI & PD liability, PIP, UM	25/50/10[6]
North Carolina	BI & PD liability, UM, UIM[7]	30/60/25
North Dakota	BI & PD liability, PIP, UM, UIM	25/50/25
Ohio	BI & PD liability	25/50/25
Oklahoma	BI & PD liability	25/50/25
Oregon	BI & PD liability, PIP, UM, UIM[7]	25/50/20
Pennsylvania	BI & PD liability, PIP	15/30/5
Rhode Island	BI & PD liability	25/50/25[3]
South Carolina	BI & PD liability, UM	25/50/25
South Dakota	BI & PD liability, UM, UIM	25/50/25
Tennessee	BI & PD liability	25/50/15[3]
Texas	BI & PD liability	30/60/25
Utah	BI & PD liability, PIP	25/65/15[3]
Vermont	BI & PD liability, UM, UIM	25/50/10
Virginia	BI & PD liability (8), UM, UIM	25/50/20
Washington	BI & PD liability	25/50/10
West Virginia	BI & PD liability, UM	20/40/10
Wisconsin	BI & PD liability, UM	25/50/10
Wyoming	BI & PD liability	25/50/20

[1]The first two numbers refer to bodily injury (BI) liability limits and the third number to property damage (PD) liability. For example, 20/40/10 means coverage up to $40,000 for all persons injured in an accident, subject to a limit of $20,000 for one individual, and $10,000 coverage for property damage. [2]Low-cost policy limits for low-income drivers in the California Automobile Assigned Risk Plan are 10/20/3. [3]Instead of policy limits, policyholders can satisfy the requirement with a combined single limit policy. Amounts vary by state. [4]In addition, policyholders must carry coverage for medical payments. Amounts vary by state. [5]Basic policy (optional) limits are 10/10/5. Uninsured and underinsured motorist coverage not available under the basic policy but uninsured and underinsured motorist coverage is required under the standard policy. Special Automobile Insurance Policy available for certain drivers which only covers emergency treatment and a $10,000 death benefit. [6]In addition, policyholders must have 50/100 for wrongful death coverage. [7]UIM mandatory in policies with UM limits exceeding certain limits. Amount vary by state. [8]Compulsory to buy insurance or pay an uninsured motorists vehicle (UMV) fee to the state Department of Motor Vehicles.

Source: Property Casualty Insurers Association of America; state departments of insurance.

State Auto Insurance Laws Governing Liability Coverage

State auto insurance laws governing liability coverage fall into four broad categories: no-fault, choice no-fault, tort liability and add-on. The major differences are whether there are restrictions on the right to sue and whether the policyholder's own insurer pays first-party (i.e., the insured's) benefits, up to the state maximum amount, regardless of who is at fault in the accident.

No-fault: The no-fault system is intended to lower the cost of auto insurance by taking small claims out of the courts. Each insurance company compensates its own policyholders for the cost of minor injuries regardless of who was at fault in the accident. These first-party benefits, known as personal injury protection (PIP), are a mandatory coverage in no-fault states but benefits vary by state. In states with the most extensive benefits, a policyholder receives compensation for medical fees, lost wages, funeral costs and other out-of-pocket expenses.

The term no-fault can be confusing because it is often used to denote any auto insurance system in which each driver's own insurance company pays for certain losses, regardless of fault. In its strict form, the term no-fault applies only to states where insurance companies pay first-party benefits and where there are restrictions on the right to sue.

Victims in no-fault states may sue for severe injuries if the case meets certain conditions. These conditions are known as the tort liability threshold, and may be expressed in verbal terms such as death or significant disfigurement (verbal threshold) or in dollar amounts of medical bills (monetary threshold).

Choice no-fault: In choice no-fault states, drivers may select one of two options: a no-fault auto insurance policy, usually with a verbal threshold, or a traditional tort liability policy.

Tort liability: In traditional tort liability states, there are no restrictions on lawsuits. A policyholder at fault in a car crash can be sued by the other driver and by the other driver's passengers for the pain and suffering the accident caused as well as for out-of-pocket expenses such as medical costs.

Add-on: In add-on states, drivers can purchase medical coverage and other first-party benefits from their own insurance company as they do in no-fault states but there are no restrictions on lawsuits. The term add-on is used because in these states first-party benefits have been added on to the traditional tort liability system. In add-on states, first-party coverage may not be mandatory and the benefits may be lower than in true no-fault states.

In the following 28 states auto liability is based on the traditional tort liability system. In these states, there are no restrictions on lawsuits:

Alabama
Alaska
Arizona
California
Colorado
Connecticut
Georgia
Idaho
Illinois
Indiana
Iowa
Louisiana
Maine
Mississippi
Missouri
Montana
Nebraska
Nevada
New Mexico
North Carolina
Ohio
Oklahoma
Rhode Island
South Carolina
Tennessee
Vermont
West Virginia
Wyoming

State Auto Insurance Laws Governing Liability Coverage

True no-fault	First-party benefits (PIP)[1]		Restrictions on lawsuits		Thresholds for lawsuits	
	Compulsory	Optional	Yes	No	Monetary	Verbal
Florida	X		X			X
Hawaii	X		X		X	
Kansas	X		X		X	
Kentucky	X		X	X[2]	X[2]	
Massachusetts	X		X		X	
Michigan	X		X			X
Minnesota	X		X		X	
New Jersey	X		X	X[2]		X[2,3]
New York	X		X			X
North Dakota	X		X		X	
Pennsylvania	X		X	X[2]		X[2]
Puerto Rico	X		X		X	
Utah	X		X		X	
Add-On						
Arkansas	X			X		
Delaware	X			X		
D.C.		X	X[4]	X[4]		
Maryland	X			X		
New Hampshire		X		X		
Oregon	X			X		
South Dakota		X		X		
Texas		X		X		
Virginia		X		X		
Washington		X		X		
Wisconsin		X		X		

[1]Personal injury protection. [2]Choice no-fault state. Policyholder can choose a policy based on the no-fault system or traditional tort liability. [3]Verbal threshold for the Basic Liability Policy, the Special Policy and the Standard Policy where the policyholder chooses no-fault. The Basic and Special Policies contain lower amounts of coverage. [4]The District of Columbia is neither a true no-fault nor add-on state. Drivers are offered the option of no-fault or fault-based coverage, but in the event of an accident a driver who originally chose no-fault benefits has 60 days to decide whether to receive those benefits or file a claim against the other party.

Source: Property Casualty Insurers Association of America.

Seatbelt Laws

Thirty-four states and the District of Columbia have a primary seatbelt enforcement law, which allows law enforcement officers to stop a car for noncompliance with seatbelt laws. The other states have secondary laws; officials can only issue seatbelt violations if they stop motorists for other infractions. New Hampshire, the only state that does not have a seatbelt law that applies to adults, has a child restraint law. Seatbelts were in use 88.5 percent of the time nationwide in 2015; states with primary seatbelt laws had an average 91.2 percent usage rate, 12.6 points higher than the 78.6 percent in states with secondary laws.

State Seatbelt Use Laws

State	2015 usage rate	Primary/ secondary enforcement[1]	Age requirements	Maximum fine, first offense	Damages reduced[2]
Alabama	93.3%	P	15+ yrs. in front seat	$25	
Alaska	89.3	P	16+ yrs. in all seats	15	X
Arizona	86.6	S	8+ yrs. in front seat; 8-15 in all seats	10	X
Arkansas	77.7	P	15+ yrs. in front seat	25	
California	97.3	P	16+ yrs. in all seats	20	X
Colorado	85.2	S	16+ yrs. in front seat	71	X
Connecticut	85.4	P	7+ yrs. in front seat	15	
Delaware	90.4	P	16+ yrs. in all seats	25	
D.C.	95.5	P	16+ yrs. in all seats	50	
Florida	89.4	P	6+ yrs. in front seat; 6-17 yrs. in all seats	30	X
Georgia	97.3	P	8-17 yrs. in all seats; 18+ yrs. in front seat	15-25	
Hawaii	92.8	P	8+ yrs. in all seats	45	
Idaho	81.1	S	7+ yrs. in all seats	10	
Illinois	95.2	P	16+ yrs. in all seats	25	
Indiana	91.9	P	16+ yrs. in all seats	25	
Iowa	93.0	P	18+ yrs. in front seat	25	X
Kansas	82.1	P[4]	14+ yrs. in all seats	10-60	
Kentucky	86.7	P	7 and younger and more than 57 inches tall in all seats; 8+ yrs. in all seats	25	
Louisiana	85.9	P	13+ yrs. in all seats	50	
Maine	85.5	P	18+ yrs. in all seats	50	
Maryland	92.9	P[4]	16+ yrs. in all seats	50	
Massachusetts	74.1	S	13+ yrs. in all seats	25[5]	
Michigan	92.8	P	16+ yrs. in front seat	25	X
Minnesota	94.0	P	7 and younger and more than 57 inches tall in all seats; 8+ in all seats	25	

(table continues)

State Seatbelt Use Laws (Cont'd)

State	2015 usage rate	Primary/ secondary enforcement[1]	Age requirements	Maximum fine, first offense	Damages reduced [2]
Mississippi	79.6	P	7+ yrs. in front seat	$25	
Missouri	79.9	[3]	16+ yrs. in front seat	10	X
Montana	77.0	S	6+ yrs. in all seats	20	
Nebraska	79.6	S	18+ yrs. in front seat	25	X
Nevada	92.1	S	6+ yrs. in all seats	25	
New Hampshire	69.5	No law for adults			
New Jersey	91.4	P[4]	7 yrs. and younger and more than 57 inches; 8+ yrs. in all seats	20	X
New Mexico	93.3	P	18+ yrs. in all seats	25	
New York	92.2	P	16+ yrs. in front seat	50	X
North Carolina	89.9	P[4]	16+ yrs. in all seats	25	
North Dakota	80.4	S	18+ yrs. in front seat	20	X
Ohio	83.9	S	8-14 yrs. in all seats; 15+ yrs. in front seat	30 driver/ 20 passenger	X
Oklahoma	84.5	P	9+ yrs. in front seat	20	
Oregon	95.5	P	16+ yrs. in all seats	110	X
Pennsylvania	82.7	[3]	18+ yrs. in front seat	10	
Rhode Island	86.7	P	18+ yrs. in all seats	40	
South Carolina	91.6	P	6+ yrs. in all seats	25	
South Dakota	73.6	S	18+ yrs. in front seat	20	
Tennessee	86.2	P	16+ yrs. in front seat	25	
Texas	90.5	P	7 yrs. and younger who are 57 inches or taller; 8+ yrs. in all seats	200	
Utah	87.2	P	16+ yrs. in all seats	45	
Vermont	85.0	S	18+ yrs. in all seats	25	
Virginia	80.9	S	18+ yrs. in front seat	25	
Washington	94.6	P	16+ yrs. in all seats	124	
West Virginia	89.0	P	8+ yrs. in front seat; 8-17 yrs. in all seats	25	X
Wisconsin	85.8	P	8+ yrs. in all seats	10	X
Wyoming	79.8	S	9+ yrs. in all seats	25 driver/ 10 passenger	
United States	**88.5%**				

[1]Primary enforcement means police may stop a vehicle and issue a fine for noncompliance with seatbelt laws. Secondary enforcement means that police may issue a fine for not wearing a seatbelt only if the vehicle has been stopped for other traffic violations. [2]Court awards for compensation for injury may be reduced if seatbelt laws were violated. [3]Primary enforcement for children; ages vary. [4]Secondary for rear seat occupants, ages vary. [5]Drivers fined additional $25 for every unrestrained passenger 12-16 years old.

Source: U.S. Department of Transportation, National Highway Traffic Safety Administration (NHTSA); Insurance Institute for Highway Safety.

Drunk Driving Laws

In 2015, 10,265 people died in the United States in alcohol-impaired crashes, up 3.2 percent from 9,943 in 2014, according to the National Highway Traffic Safety Administration. In 2015 alcohol-impaired crash fatalities accounted for 29 percent of all crash fatalities, slightly lower than 30 percent of all crash fatalities in 2014. A major factor in the long-term downward trend in alcohol-impaired deaths is the enactment, beginning in the 1980s, of state laws designed to deter drunk driving. By 2004 every state and the District of Columbia had lowered the limit defining drunk driving from a 0.10 percent blood alcohol concentration to 0.08 percent. All states have enacted more stringent restrictions for drivers under the legal drinking age (21 years old in all states).

State Laws Curbing Drunk Driving

| | License revocation | | | | Mandatory ignition interlocks[1] | | | |
| | | | | | | First offenders | | |
State	Admin. license rev./ susp.[2]	Mandatory 90-day license rev./ susp.[3]	Open container law[4]	All offenders	All	High-BAC offenders only[5]	Repeat offenders
Alabama	X	X	X	X	X		X
Alaska	X	X		X	X		X
Arizona	X	X	X	X	X		X
Arkansas	X	X		X	X		X
California	X	X	X		In 4 counties		X
Colorado	X	X	X	X	X		X
Connecticut	X			X	X		X
Delaware	X	X		X	X		X
D.C.	X		X				
Florida	X	X	X			X	X
Georgia	X	X	X				X
Hawaii	X	X	X	X	X		X
Idaho	X	X	X				X
Illinois	X	X	X	X	X		X
Indiana	X	X	X				
Iowa	X	X	X			X	X
Kansas	X		X	X	X		X
Kentucky			X			X	X
Louisiana	X	X		X	X		X
Maine	X	X	X	X	X		X
Maryland	X	X*	X	X*		X	X
Massachusetts	X		X				X

(table continues)

State Laws Curbing Drunk Driving (Cont'd)

State	License revocation		Open container law[4]	Mandatory ignition interlocks[1]			
	Admin. license rev./ susp.[2]	Mandatory 90-day license rev./ susp.[3]		All offenders	First offenders		Repeat offenders
					All	High-BAC offenders only[5]	
Michigan			X			X	X
Minnesota	X	X	X			X	X
Mississippi	X	X		X	X		X
Missouri	X			X	X		X
Montana			X				
Nebraska	X	X	X	X	X		X
Nevada	X	X	X			X	X
New Hampshire	X	X	X		X	X	X
New Jersey			X			X	X
New Mexico	X	X	X	X	X		X
New York	[6]		X	X	X		X
North Carolina	X		X			X	X
North Dakota	X	X	X				
Ohio	X	X	X				X
Oklahoma	X	X	X			X	X
Oregon	X	X	X	X	X		X
Pennsylvania			X			X**	X
Rhode Island		X	X	X	X		X
South Carolina			X			X	X
South Dakota			X				
Tennessee				X	X		X
Texas	X	X	X	X	X		X
Utah	X	X	X	X	X		X
Vermont	X	X	X	X	X		X
Virginia	X		X	X	X		X
Washington	X	X	X	X	X		X
West Virginia	X	X	X	X	X		X
Wisconsin	X	X	X			X	X
Wyoming	X	X				X	X

[1]Ignition interlock devices analyze a driver's breath for alcohol and disable the ignition if a driver has been drinking. States identified mandate the devices on offenders' vehicles. [2]On-the-spot drivers license suspension or revocation if blood alcohol concentration (BAC) is over the legal limit or the driver refuses to take a BAC test. [3]Mandatory penalty for violation of the implied consent law, which means that drivers who refuse to take a breath alcohol test when stopped or arrested for drunk driving will have their license revoked or suspended. [4]Prohibits unsealed alcohol containers and alcohol consumption in motor vehicle passenger compartments for all occupants. Counts only laws meeting federal requirements. [5]Usually 0.15 percent BAC or higher. [6]Administrative license suspension lasts until prosecution is complete.

Source: Insurance Institute for Highway Safety; Governors Highway Safety Administration.

Alcohol Server Liability Laws

Most states have enacted liquor liability laws which hold businesses and/or people who serve liquor liable for the damage a drunk driver causes.

Statutes Or Court Cases Holding Alcoholic Beverage Servers Liable

State	Commercial servers Statute[1]	Court[2]	Social hosts Statute[3]	Court	State	Commercial servers Statute[1]	Court[2]	Social hosts Statute[3]	Court
Alabama	X		X	X	Montana	X	X	X	
Alaska	X		X		Nebraska			X	
Arizona	X	X	X	X	Nevada			X[4]	
Arkansas	X	X			New Hampshire	X		X	X
California	X		X		New Jersey	X		X	X
Colorado	X	X	X		New Mexico	X		X	X
Connecticut	X	X		X[4,5]	New York	X		X	
Delaware					North Carolina	X	X	X	X[4]
D.C.		X[4]			North Dakota	X		X	
Florida	X		X	X	Ohio	X	X	X	X[4]
Georgia	X		X		Oklahoma	X	X		
Hawaii		X	X		Oregon	X		X	
Idaho	X	X	X		Pennsylvania	X	X		X[4]
Illinois	X		X	X	Rhode Island	X			
Indiana	X	X	X	X	South Carolina	X	X	X	X[4]
Iowa	X	X	X	X[4]	South Dakota				
Kansas					Tennessee	X			
Kentucky	X	X		X[4]	Texas	X	X	X	X
Louisiana	X	X	X	X	Utah	X		X	X
Maine	X		X		Vermont	X		X	X
Maryland					Virginia				
Massachusetts	X	X	X	X	Washington	X	X	X	X[4]
Michigan	X		X	X[4]	West Virginia	X	X[4]		
Minnesota	X		X	X	Wisconsin	X	X	X	X
Mississippi	X	X	X	X	Wyoming	X		X	X[4]
Missouri	X								

[1]Indicates some form of liability is permitted by statute. [2]States where common-law liability has not been specifically overruled by statute or where common-law actions are specifically recognized in addition to statutory liability. [3]Indicates that language is capable of being read broadly enough to include noncommercial servers. [4]For guests under the age of 21. [5]Only if host either purveyed or supplied alcohol.

Source: Property Casualty Insurers Association of America.

Older Drivers

In 2014, about 14.5 percent of the total U.S. resident population (46.2 million people) were 65 years old and older. In 2014, 5,709 people age 65 and older were killed in traffic crashes, accounting for 17 percent of all traffic fatalities that year. Recognizing the need for older drivers to retain their mobility and independence, some states issue restricted licenses. Depending on ability, older drivers may be limited to driving during daylight hours or on non-freeway types of roads. In most states restrictions such as these can be placed on anyone's drivers license regardless of age, if his or her medical condition warrants it.

State Drivers License Renewal Laws Including Requirements For Older Drivers

State	Length of regular renewal cycle (years)	Renewal for older drivers		Require older drivers to pass tests		Age limits on mail or online renewal
		Length (years)	Age	Age	Type of test	
Alabama	4					
Alaska	5			69	Vision	69
Arizona	12	5	65			
Arkansas	8					
California[1]	5			70	Vision	70
Colorado	5					66
Connecticut	6	2 or 6	65			
Delaware	8					
D.C.	8			70	Medical	70
Florida	8	6	80	80	Vision	
Georgia	8	8*	59			64
Hawaii	8	2	72			
Idaho	4 or 8	4	63			70
Illinois	4	2	81[2]	75	Road, vision	75
Indiana	6	3	75[2]			75
Iowa	8	2	72	70	Vision	70
Kansas	6	4	65			
Kentucky	4					
Louisiana	6			70	Vision	70
Maine	6	4	65	40 and 62	Vision	62
Maryland	8			40	Vision	
Massachusetts	5			75	Vision	75
Michigan	4					

(table continues)

State Drivers License Renewal Laws Including Requirements For Older Drivers (Cont'd)

State	Length of regular renewal cycle (years)	Renewal for older drivers		Require older drivers to pass tests		Age limits on mail or online renewal
		Length (years)	Age	Age	Type of test	
Minnesota	4					
Mississippi	4 or 8					
Missouri	6	3	70			
Montana	8	4	75			
Nebraska	5			72	Vision	72
Nevada	4 or 8	4	65	71	Vision	
New Hampshire	5			75	Road	
New Jersey	4	2-4	70			
New Mexico	4 or 8	4	67[2]	75	Vision	75
New York	8					
North Carolina	8	5	66			
North Dakota	6	4	78			
Ohio	4					
Oklahoma	4					
Oregon	8			50	Vision	
Pennsylvania	4	2-4	65			
Rhode Island	5	2	75			
South Carolina	10	5	65	65	Vision	
South Dakota	5			65	Vision	
Tennessee	8					
Texas	6	2	85	79	Vision	79
Utah	5			65	Vision	
Vermont	2-4					
Virginia	8	5	75	75	Vision	75
Washington	6					70
West Virginia	8					
Wisconsin	8					
Wyoming	4					

[1]Specifically requires doctors to report a diagnosis of dementia. [2]These states have special renewal requirements for other age groups: Illinois (1 year for drivers 87 and older); Indiana (2 years for drivers 85 and older); and New Mexico (1 year for drivers 75 and older).

Note: Specific requirements vary by state; contact state department of motor vehicles for more information.

Source: Insurance Institute for Highway Safety; Governors Highway Safety Administration.

State Young Driver Laws[1]

State	Learners permit required for a minimum period	Graduated licensing		Driver may not operate a cellphone in learner and/or intermediate stages[4]
		Intermediate phase		
		Restrictions on night driving[2]	Passenger restrictions[3]	
Alabama	6 months	X	X	Talk
Alaska	6 months	X	X	
Arizona	6 months	X	X	
Arkansas	6 months	X	X	Talk
California	6 months	X	X	Talk
Colorado	12 months	X	X	Talk
Connecticut	6 months	X	X	Talk
Delaware	6 months	X	X	Talk
D.C.	6 months	X	X	Talk
Florida	12 months	X		
Georgia	12 months	X	X	Talk
Hawaii	6 months	X	X	Talk
Idaho	6 months	X	X	
Illinois	9 months	X	X	Talk
Indiana	6 months	X	X	Talk
Iowa	12 months	X		Talk
Kansas	12 months	X	X	Talk
Kentucky	6 months	X	X	Talk
Louisiana	6 months	X	X	Talk
Maine	6 months	X	X	Talk
Maryland	9 months	X	X	Talk
Massachusetts	6 months	X	X	Talk
Michigan	6 months	X	X	Talk
Minnesota	6 months	X	X	Talk
Mississippi	12 months	X		
Missouri	6 months	X	X	Text
Montana	6 months	X	X	
Nebraska	6 months	X	X	Talk
Nevada	6 months	X	X	
New Hampshire	none[5]	X	X	Talk

(table continues)

State Young Driver Laws[1] (Cont'd)

State	Learners permit required for a minimum period	Graduated licensing Intermediate phase Restrictions on night driving[2]	Passenger restrictions[3]	Driver may not operate a cellphone in learner and/or intermediate stages[4]
New Jersey	6 months	X	X	Talk
New Mexico	6 months	X	X	Talk
New York	6 months	X	X	
North Carolina	12 months	X	X	Talk
North Dakota	6-12 months[6]	X		Talk
Ohio	6 months	X	X	Talk
Oklahoma	6 months	X	X	Talk[7]
Oregon	6 months	X	X	Talk
Pennsylvania	6 months	X	X	
Rhode Island	6 months	X	X	Talk
South Carolina	6 months	X	X	
South Dakota	6 months	X		Talk
Tennessee	6 months	X	X	Talk
Texas	6 months	X	X	Talk, text
Utah	6 months	X	X	Talk
Vermont	12 months		X	Talk
Virginia	9 months	X	X	Talk
Washington	6 months	X	X	Talk
West Virginia	6 months	X	X	Talk
Wisconsin	6 months	X	X	Talk
Wyoming	10 days	X	X	

[1]Designed to aid young novice drivers between the ages of 15 and 18 gain driving experience. To date they apply only to drivers under the age of 18. All states have lower blood alcohol content laws for under-21 drivers which range from none to 0.02 percent, in contrast with 0.08 percent for drivers over the age of 21 in all states. Includes graduated licensing as defined by the National Highway Traffic Safety Administration. Every state has a graduated licensing law. [2]Intermediate stage; varies by state with regard to age of driver, night hours that driving is restricted, who must accompany driver during night hours and how long and what stage the restrictions are lifted. Exceptions may be made for work, school or religious activities and emergencies. [3]Intermediate stage; limits the number of teenage passengers a young driver may have in the vehicle. [4]Only includes states with restrictions on the use of cellphones for talking or texting by young drivers. Does not reference cellphone laws such as bans on handheld cellphones that apply to all drivers in some states. [5]New Hampshire does not issue learners permits. [6]Under age 16: 12 months; 16-18: 6 months. [7]Banned for non-life threatening purposes.

Source: Insurance Institute for Highway Safety.

HOMEOWNERS: PREMIUMS

Homeowners Insurance

Homeowners insurance accounted for 15.4 percent of all property/casualty (P/C) insurance premiums and 29.3 percent of personal property/casualty lines insurance in 2015.

According to the Insurance Information Institute, the vast majority (93 percent) of homeowners have basic homeowners insurance, as it is generally a requirement of mortgage lenders. Homeowners insurance is a package policy, providing both property and personal liability insurance. The typical policy covers the house, garage and other structures on the property—as well as personal property inside the house—against a wide variety of perils, such as fire, windstorm, vandalism and accidental water damage. The typical homeowners policy includes theft coverage on personal property anywhere in the world and liability coverage for accidental harm caused to others. It also reimburses the policyholder for the additional cost of living elsewhere while his or her house is being repaired or rebuilt after a fire or other disaster.

Earthquake damage and flood damage caused by external flooding are not covered by standard homeowners policies but special policies can be purchased separately. Flood coverage is provided by the federal government's National Flood Insurance Program and some private insurers.

Homeowners Multiple Peril Insurance, 2006-2015 ($000)

Year	Net premiums written[1]	Annual percent change	Combined ratio[2]	Annual point change[3]
2006	$55,822,275	5.3%	89.5	-15.6 pts.
2007	57,053,137	2.2	93.9	4.4
2008	57,375,139	0.6	115.4	21.5
2009	58,478,195	1.9	105.7	-9.7
2010	61,659,466	5.4	106.0	0.3
2011	64,131,058	4.0	121.0	15.0
2012	67,847,033	5.8	103.0	-18.1
2013	72,773,216	7.3	89.6	-13.4
2014	77,914,406	7.1	91.6	2.0
2015	79,931,147	2.6	91.3	-0.3

[1]After reinsurance transactions, excludes state funds. [2]After dividends to policyholders. A drop in the combined ratio represents an improvement; an increase represents a deterioration. [3]Calculated from unrounded numbers.

Source: NAIC data, sourced from S&P Global Market Intelligence, Insurance Information Institute.

Top 10 Writers Of Homeowners Insurance By Direct Premiums Written, 2015 ($000)

Rank	Group/company	Direct premiums written[1]	Market share[2]
1	State Farm Mutual Automobile Insurance	$17,516,715	19.6%
2	Allstate Corp.	7,926,984	8.9
3	Liberty Mutual	5,993,803	6.7
4	Farmers Insurance Group of Companies[3]	5,284,511	5.9
5	USAA Insurance Group	5,000,407	5.6
6	Travelers Companies Inc.	3,305,427	3.7
7	Nationwide Mutual Group	3,249,456	3.6
8	American Family Insurance Group	2,609,366	2.9
9	Chubb Ltd.[4]	2,485,193	2.8
10	Erie Insurance Group	1,471,544	1.7

[1]Before reinsurance transactions, includes state funds. [2]Based on U.S. total, includes territories. [3]Data for Farmers Insurance Group of Companies and Zurich Financial Group (which owns Farmers' management company) are reported separately by S&P Global Market Intelligence. [4]Chubb Ltd. data reflect the 2015 merger with Ace Ltd.

Source: NAIC data, sourced from S&P Global Market Intelligence, Insurance Information Institute.

HOMEOWNERS: HIGH-RISK MARKETS

The Census Bureau reported that in Florida, 75.7 percent of the state's population resided in coastal counties, compared with 32.3 percent in Louisiana and 9.9 percent in North Carolina. Nationally, 52 percent of the population resided in coastal counties outside of Alaska, according to the U.S. Census Bureau. The population of most counties along the Pacific, Atlantic and Gulf coasts grew between 2000 and 2010, creating an almost unbroken chain of coastal counties with population densities of 319 people per square mile or more running from New Hampshire through northern Virginia, according to the U.S. Census Bureau.

Between 1960-2010, California had the largest growth in population in the United States, some 13 million people. By percent change, Florida had the most growth, 270 percent.

Top 10 States, By Population Change In Coastal Counties, 1960-2010

	By number change				By percent change	
Rank	State	Number change		Rank	State	Percent change
1	California	13,130,000		1	Florida	270.1%
2	Florida	10,360,000		2	Alaska	239.8
3	Texas	3,732,000		3	New Hampshire	198.0
4	Washington	2,578,000		4	Texas	161.9
5	Virginia	1,903,000		5	Virginia	150.8
6	New York	1,400,000		6	Washington	144.4
7	New Jersey	1,275,000		7	South Carolina	125.1
8	Maryland	938,000		8	Hawaii	115.2
9	Massachusetts	826,000		9	North Carolina	114.4
10	Hawaii	728,000		10	California	107.2

Source: U.S. Department of Commerce, Census Bureau

Coastal Area Growth

A report by AIR Worldwide on the insured value of properties in coastal areas of the U.S. (the cost of rebuilding) shows that over the five years from 2007 to 2012 the compound annual growth rate slowed to 4 percent from 7 percent, due to the sharp decrease in the number of housing starts. This, in turn, kept the cost of labor and building materials in check. But as the economy recovers, particularly the demand for new housing, AIR expects the growth rate to accelerate. Among the 18 coastal states studied, New York has the highest coastal property values, but Florida has the largest proportion of total value in coastal counties, at 79 percent, compared with 62 percent for New York. The total insured value of residential and commercial properties in U.S. coastal counties exceeds $10 trillion, with New York and Florida accounting for nearly $3 trillion each. Of the $10.6 trillion in insured coastal properties, $4.7 trillion, or 44 percent, were residential and $6.0 trillion, or 56 percent, were commercial.

Estimated Value Of Insured Coastal Properties Vulnerable To Hurricanes By State, 2012[1] ($ billions)

Rank	State	Commercial	Residential	Total coastal	Total exposure[2]	Coastal as a percent of total
1	New York	$2,105.6	$817.5	$2,923.1	$4,724.2	62%
2	Florida	1,359.9	1,502.4	2,862.3	3,640.1	79
3	Texas	653.8	521.5	1,175.3	4,580.7	26
4	Massachusetts	456	393.6	849.6	1,561.4	54
5	New Jersey	374.6	339.3	713.9	2,129.9	34
6	Connecticut	271.7	296.1	567.8	879.1	65
7	Louisiana	153.5	140.0	293.5	823.0	36
8	South Carolina	129.9	109.4	239.3	843.6	28
9	Virginia	95.2	87.1	182.3	1,761.7	10
10	Maine	73.3	91.3	164.6	285.5	58
11	North Carolina	65.8	97.7	163.5	1,795.1	9
12	Alabama	61.6	56.6	118.2	917.8	13
13	Georgia	57.4	49.3	106.7	1,932.2	6
14	Delaware	31.8	50.1	81.9	208.9	39
15	New Hampshire	28.5	35.5	64.0	278.7	23
16	Mississippi	29.6	31.0	60.6	468.5	13
17	Rhode Island	22.6	35.7	58.3	207.5	28
18	Maryland	8.7	8.6	17.3	1,293.4	1
	Total, states shown	$5,979.5	$4,662.7	$10,642.2	$28,331.4	38%
	Total, United States	5,979.5	4,662.7	$10,642.2	$64,624.3	16%

[1]Includes residential and commercial Gulf and East Coast properties, as of December 31, 2012. Ranked by value of total insured coastal property. [2]Total exposure is an estimate of the actual total value of all property in the state that is insured or can be insured, including the full replacement value of structures and their contents, additional living expenses and the time value of business interruption coverage.

Source: AIR Worldwide.

Residual Market Property Plans

A myriad of different programs in place across the United States provide insurance to high-risk policy-holders who may have difficulty obtaining coverage from the standard market. Residual, shared or involuntary market programs make basic insurance coverage more readily available. Today, property insurance for the residual market is provided by Fair Access to Insurance Requirements (FAIR) Plans, Beach and Windstorm Plans, and two state-run insurance companies in Florida and Louisiana: Florida's Citizens Property Insurance Corp. and Louisiana's Citizens Property Insurance Corp. Established in the late 1960s to ensure the continued provision of insurance in urban areas, FAIR Plans often provide property insurance in both urban and coastal areas. Beach and Windstorm Plans cover predominantly wind-only risks in designated coastal areas. Over the past four decades FAIR and Beach and Windstorm plans experienced explosive growth both in the number of policies and in exposure value. However, latest dat show that between 2011 and 2015, total policies fell by 34.3 percent and exposure dropped by 47.7 percent.

Insurance Provided By FAIR Plans, Fiscal Years 2006-2015 [1]

Year	Number of policies			Exposure[2] ($000)	Direct premiums written ($000)
	Habitational	Commercial	Total		
2006	2,389,299	172,070	2,561,369	$601,859,916	$4,063,324
2007	2,412,252	114,053	2,526,305	684,829,667	4,431,381
2008	2,190,189	90,876	2,281,065	612,749,753	3,727,311
2009	2,043,969	86,575	2,130,544	614,905,551	3,038,712
2010	2,378,736	83,243	2,461,979	662,633,180	3,448,576
2011	2,658,662	51,657	2,710,319	715,289,876	3,942,021
2012	2,518,808	71,776	2,590,584	635,705,150	4,059,446
2013	2,484,816	64,359	2,549,175	445,635,335	3,685,283
2014	2,015,536	61,285	2,076,821	424,732,706	3,029,772
2015	1,728,423	51,443	1,779,866	373,829,442	2,198,182

[1]Includes the Texas FAIR Plan; Florida's Citizens Property Insurance Corp., which includes FAIR and Beach Plans; the Louisiana Citizens Property Insurance Corp., which includes FAIR and Beach Plans and premiums written after 2007; and North Carolina after 2010. [2]Exposure is the estimate of the aggregate value of all insurance in force in all FAIR Plans in all lines (except liability, where applicable, and crime) for 12 months ending September through December.

Source: Property Insurance Plans Service Office (PIPSO).

Insurance Provided By FAIR Plans By State, Fiscal Year 2015[1]

State	Number of policies			Exposure[2] ($000)	Direct premiums written ($000)
	Habitational	Commercial	Total		
California	123,162	4,701	127,863	$45,551,156	$76,448
Connecticut	2,538	80	2,618	487,144	3,632
Delaware	1,732	76	1,808	281,471	617
D.C.	276	42	318	89,000	287
Florida[3]	671,641	29,456	701,097	150,495,190	1,267,754
Georgia	24,865	1,872	26,737	3,741,795	25,554
Illinois	6,067	81	6,148	678,952	6,921
Indiana	2,029	50	2,079	230,413	2,123
Iowa	1,437	50	1,487	96,174	999

(table continues)

Insurance Provided By FAIR Plans By State, Fiscal Year 2015[1] (Cont'd)

State	Number of policies			Exposure[2] ($000)	Direct premiums written ($000)
	Habitational	Commercial	Total		
Kansas	17,482	197	17,679	$1,009,000	$9,166
Kentucky	10,947	478	11,425	557,853	7,257
Louisiana[3]	100,555	3,529	104,084	13,861,836	140,386
Maryland	1,730	181	1,911	358,000	1,261
Massachusetts	215,808	334	216,142	80,844,528	285,495
Michigan	20,712	381	21,093	2,664,680	20,719
Minnesota	5,389	47	5,436	929,115	4,297
Mississippi[4]	9,518	0	9,518	592,423	7,431
Missouri	3,957	162	4,119	230,213	2,380
New Jersey	15,826	416	16,242	2,283,978	10,261
New Mexico	11,514	298	11,812	105,842	4,771
North Carolina	165,189	3,166	168,355	15,663,995	72,832
Ohio	25,648	533	26,181	6,157,943	22,391
Oregon	1,867	53	1,920	289,475	1,063
Pennsylvania	17,515	1,329	18,844	1,568,967	8,006
Rhode Island	17,497	131	17,628	4,372,091	23,006
Texas[4]	165,073	0	165,073	22,154,369	132,879
Virginia	33,325	510	33,835	4,654,544	20,947
Washington	67	21	88	20,776	133
West Virginia	476	55	531	32,519	330
Wisconsin	6,382	116	6,498	407,000	3,346
Total	**1,728,423**	**51,443**	**1,779,866**	**$373,829,442**	**$2,198,182**

[1]Excludes the FAIR Plans of Arkansas and Hawaii. [2]Exposure is the estimate of the aggregate value of all insurance in force in all FAIR Plans in all lines (except liability, where applicable, and crime) for 12 months ending September through December. [3]Citizens Property Insurance Corp., which combined the FAIR and Beach Plans. [4]The Mississippi and Texas FAIR Plans do not offer a commercial policy.

Source: Property Insurance Plans Service Office (PIPSO).

Insurance Provided By Beach And Windstorm Plans

Beach and Windstorm Plans ensure that insurance is available against damage from hurricanes and other windstorms. In Georgia, Massachusetts and New York, FAIR Plans provide wind and hail coverage for certain coastal communities. These states do not have Beach and Windstorm Plans.

Insurance Provided By Beach And Windstorm Plans, Fiscal Year 2015[1]

State	Number of policies			Exposure[2] ($000)	Direct premiums written ($000)
	Habitational	Commercial	Total		
Alabama	31,530	92	31,622	$5,502,703	$41,685
Mississippi	37,524	853	38,377	5,869,340	64,209
North Carolina	243,172	11,959	255,131	88,605,091	386,893
South Carolina	34,499	691	35,190	12,250,367	73,587
Texas	272,304	14,556	286,860	78,551,742	503,824
Total	**619,029**	**28,151**	**647,180**	**$190,779,243**	**$1,070,198**

[1]The Florida and Louisiana Beach Plans merged with their FAIR Plans, see chart on page 104. [2]Exposure is the estimate of the aggregate value of all insurance in force in each state's Beach and Windstorm Plan in all lines (except liability, where applicable, and crime) for 12 months ending September through December. Source: Property Insurance Plans Service Office (PIPSO).

HOMEOWNERS: COSTS/EXPENDITURES

The average homeowners insurance premium rose by 6.0 percent in 2013, following a 5.6 percent increase in 2012, according to a February 2016 study by the National Association of Insurance Commissioners. The average renters insurance premium rose 0.5 percent in 2013 and was unchanged in 2012. A 2016 Insurance Information Institute poll conducted by ORC International found that 93 percent of homeowners had homeowners insurance but only 41 percent of renters had renters insurance.

U.S. homeownership rate was 62.9 percent in second-quarter 2016, down from 63.4 percent a year ago to the lowest rate since the third quarter of 1965, according to the U.S. Census Bureau. The 2010 Census showed that in some of the largest cities renters outnumbered owners, including New York, where 69.0 percent of households were occupied by renters, followed by Los Angeles (61.8 percent), Chicago (55.1 percent) and Houston (54.6 percent).

Average Premiums For Homeowners And Renters Insurance, United States, 2004-2013

Year	Homeowners[1]	Percent change	Renters[2]	Percent change
2004	$729	9.1%	$195	-1.6%
2005	764	4.8	193	-1.0
2006	804	5.2	189	-2.1
2007	822	2.2	182	-3.7
2008	830	1.0	182	[3]
2009	880	6.0	184	1.1
2010	909	3.3	185	0.5
2011	979	7.7	187	1.1
2012	1,034	5.6	187	[3]
2013	1,096	6.0	188	0.5

[1]Based on the HO-3 homeowner package policy for owner-occupied dwellings, 1 to 4 family units. Provides all risks coverage (except those specifically excluded in the policy) on buildings and broad named-peril coverage on personal property, and is the most common package written. [2]Based on the HO-4 renters insurance policy for tenants. Includes broad named-peril coverage for the personal property of tenants. [3]Less than 0.1 percent. Source: © 2016 National Association of Insurance Commissioners (NAIC). Reprinted with permission. Further reprint or distribution strictly prohibited without written permission of NAIC.

Average Premiums For Homeowners And Renters Insurance By State, 2013[1]

State	Homeowners Average premium[2]	Rank[3]	Renters Average premium[4]	Rank[3]	State	Homeowners Average premium[2]	Rank[3]	Renters Average premium[4]	Rank[3]
Alabama	$1,323	8	$245	4	Montana	$938	29	$143	48
Alaska	980	25	168	28	Nebraska	1,151	16	149	41
Arizona	724	44	192	17	Nevada	687	46	191	18
Arkansas	1,183	14	212	9	New Hampshire	885	36	149	41
California[5]	966	26	203	13	New Jersey	1,058	21	163	31
Colorado	1,160	15	168	28	New Mexico	898	34	186	20
Connecticut	1,274	9	200	14	New York	1,213	13	209	10
Delaware	709	45	152	40	North Carolina	1,008	23	146	46
D.C.	1,150	17	158	33	North Dakota	1,078	20	113	51
Florida	2,115	1	208	11	Ohio	763	43	188	19
Georgia	1,044	22	226	6	Oklahoma	1,654	4	245	4
Hawaii	953	27	215	7	Oregon	568	50	163	31
Idaho	561	51	155	38	Pennsylvania	863	37	157	35
Illinois	938	29	172	26	Rhode Island	1,334	7	178	24
Indiana	887	35	183	21	South Carolina	1,214	12	195	16
Iowa	832	40	147	43	South Dakota	915	31	120	50
Kansas	1,343	6	176	25	Tennessee	1,090	19	213	8
Kentucky	981	24	170	27	Texas[6]	1,837	2	247	2
Louisiana	1,822	3	246	3	Utah	609	49	146	46
Maine	776	42	147	43	Vermont	814	41	153	39
Maryland	904	33	158	33	Virginia	911	32	156	36
Massachusetts	1,263	10	198	15	Washington	676	47	165	30
Michigan	839	39	204	12	West Virginia	844	38	179	22
Minnesota	1,222	11	147	43	Wisconsin	665	48	130	49
Mississippi	1,395	5	250	1	Wyoming	952	28	156	36
Missouri	1,143	18	179	22	**United States**	**$1,096**		**$188**	

[1]Includes state funds and residual markets. [2]Based on the HO-3 homeowner package policy for owner-occupied dwellings, 1 to 4 family units. Provides all risks coverage (except those specifically excluded in the policy) on buildings and broad named-peril coverage on personal property and is the most common package written. [3]Ranked from highest to lowest. States with the same premium receive the same rank. [4]Based on the HO-4 renters insurance policy for tenants. Includes broad named-peril coverage for the personal property of tenants. [5]Data provided by the California Department of Insurance. [6]The Texas Department of Insurance developed home insurance policy forms that are similar but not identical to the standard forms. In addition, due to the Texas Windstorm Association (which writes wind-only policies) classifying HO-1, 2 and 5 premiums as HO-3, the average premium for homeowners insurance is artificially high.
Note: Average premium=Premiums/exposure per house years. A house year is equal to 365 days of insured coverage for a single dwelling. The NAIC does not rank state average expenditures and does not endorse any conclusions drawn from this data.

Source: © 2016 National Association of Insurance Commissioners (NAIC). Reprinted with permission. Further reprint or distribution strictly prohibited without written permission of NAIC.

Homeowners Insurance Industry Underwriting Expenses, 2015[1]

Expense	Percent of premiums
Losses and related expenses[2]	
Loss and loss adjustment expense (LAE) ratio	**61.6%**
Incurred losses	52.5
Defense and cost containment expenses incurred	1.5
Adjusting and other expenses incurred	7.5
Operating expenses[3]	
Expense ratio	**29.1%**
Net commissions and brokerage expenses incurred	12.6
Taxes, licenses and fees	2.6
Other acquisition and field supervision expenses incurred	8.6
General expenses incurred	5.3
Dividends to policyholders[2]	**0.5%**
Combined ratio after dividends[4]	**91.3%**

[1]After reinsurance transactions [2]As a percent of net premiums earned ($78.6 billion in 2015). [3]As a percent of net premiums written ($79.9 billion in 2015). [4]Sum of loss and LAE, expense and dividends ratios.

Source: NAIC data, sourced from S&P Global Market Intelligence, Insurance Information Institute.

HOMEOWNERS: CLAIMS

In 2014, 5.3 percent of insured homes experienced a claim.

Homeowners insurance losses, net of reinsurance, rose to $41.2 billion in 2015 from $39.9 billion in 2014, according to S&P Global Market Intelligence.

Homeowners Insurance Losses, 2010-2014[1]

Year	Total homeowners losses Claim frequency[2]	Total homeowners losses Claim severity[3]	Year	Total homeowners losses Claim frequency[2]	Total homeowners losses Claim severity[3]
2010	6.77	$8,568	2013	5.01	$10,397
2011	9.98	8,431	2014	5.27	10,750
2012	7.70	8,797	**Average[4]**	**6.98**	**$9,155**

[1]For homeowners multiple peril policies (HO-2, HO-3, HO-5 and HE-7 for North Carolina). Excludes tenants and condominium policies. Excludes Arkansas and Texas. [2]Claims per 100 house years (policies). [3]Average amount paid per claim; based on accident year incurred losses, excluding loss adjustment expenses, i.e., indemnity costs per accident year incurred claims. [4]Weighted average, 2010-2014.

Source: ISO®, a Verisk Analytics® business.

Causes Of Homeowners Insurance Losses

Property damage, including theft, accounted for 97.3 percent of homeowners insurance claims in 2014. Changes in the type of homeowners loss from one year to another are partially influenced by fluctuations in the number and severity of weather-related events such as hurricanes and winter storms. There are two ways of looking at losses: by the average number of claims filed per 100 policies (frequency) and by the average amount paid for each claim (severity). The loss category "water damage and freezing" includes damage caused by mold, if covered.

Homeowners Insurance Losses By Cause, 2010-2014[1] (Percent of losses incurred)

Cause of loss	2010	2011	2012	2013	2014
Property damage[2]	**95.2%**	**97.0%**	**96.7%**	**95.9%**	**97.3%**
Fire and lightning	25.0	18.4	23.3	29.2	25.9
Wind and hail	36.1	46.6	49.1	30.8	27.3
Water damage and freezing	21.1	21.4	16.9	25.9	33.7
Theft	3.1	2.3	2.9	3.4	2.5
All other property damage[3]	9.9	8.3	4.5	6.6	7.9
Liability[4]	**4.8%**	**3.0%**	**3.3%**	**4.1%**	**2.7%**
Bodily injury and property damage	4.7	2.9	3.1	3.8	2.5
Medical payments and other	0.2	0.1	0.2	0.3	0.2
Credit card and other[5]	6	6	6	6	6
Total	**100.0%**	**100.0%**	**100.0%**	**100.0%**	**100.0%**

[1]For homeowners multiple peril policies (HO-2, HO-3, HO-5). Excludes tenants and condominium owners policies. Excludes Arkansas and Texas. [2]First party, i.e., covers damage to policyholder's own property. [3]Includes vandalism and malicious mischief. [4]Payments to others for which policyholder is responsible. [5]Includes coverage for unauthorized use of various cards, forgery, counterfeit money and losses not otherwise classified. [6]Less than 0.1 percent.

Source: ISO®, a Verisk Analytics® business.

Homeowners Insurance Claims Frequency*

- Homeowners claims related to wind or hail are the most frequent; the costliest are related to fire and lightning.
- About one in 15 insured homes has a claim each year.
- About one in 30 insured homes has a property damage claim related to wind or hail each year.
- About one in 55 insured homes has a property damage claim caused by water damage or freezing each year.
- About one in 215 insured homes has a property damage claim due to theft each year.
- About one in 265 insured homes has a property damage claim related to fire and lightning.
- About one in 1,000 homeowners policies has a liability claim related to the cost of lawsuits for bodily injury or property damage that the policyholder or family members cause to others.

*Insurance Information Institute calculations, based on ISO®, a Verisk Analytics® business, data for homeowners insurance claims from 2010-2014 (see table below).

Average Homeowners Losses, 2010-2014[1]
(Weighted average, 2010-2014)

In the five-year period, 2010-2014, 7.0 percent of insured homes had a claim. Wind and hail accounted for the largest share of claims, with 3.1 percent of insured homes having such a loss.

Cause of loss	Claim frequency[2]	Claim severity[3]
Property damage[4]	**6.83**	**$9,024**
Fire and lightning	0.38	39,791
Wind and hail	3.13	8,041
Water damage and freezing	1.86	7,958
Theft	0.47	3,786
All other[5]	0.99	4,800
Liability[6]	**0.15**	**$15,221**
Bodily injury and property damage	0.10	20,453
Medical payments and other	0.04	2,598
Credit card and other[7]	[8]	**$554**
Average (property damage and liability), 2010-2014	**6.98**	**$9,155**

[1]For homeowners multiple peril policies (HO-2, HO-3, HO-5 and HE-7 for North Carolina). Excludes tenants and condominium owners policies. Excludes Arkansas and Texas. [2]Claims per 100 house years (policies). [3]Accident year incurred losses, excluding loss adjustment expenses, i.e., indemnity costs per accident year incurred claims. [4]First party, i.e., covers damage to policyholder's own property. [5]Includes vandalism and malicious mischief. [6]Payments to others for which policyholder is responsible. [7]Includes coverage for unauthorized use of various cards, forgery, counterfeit money and losses not otherwise classified. [8]Less than 0.01.

Source: ISO®, a Verisk Analytics® business.

Lightning

In 2015 there were 27 direct lightning fatalities, up from 26 in 2014 and higher than the record low of 23 in 2013. From 2006 to 2015 on average about 31 people died each year from lightning strikes in the United States, according to the National Weather Service.

Homeowners Insurance Claims And Payout For Lightning Losses, 2011-2015

	2011	2012	2013	2014	2015	Percent change	
						2014-2015	2011-2015
Number of paid claims	186,307	151,000	114,740	99,871	99,423	-0.4%	-46.6%
Insured losses ($ millions)	$952.5	$969.0	$673.5	$739.0	$790.1	6.9	-17.0
Average cost per claim	$5,112	$6,400	$5,869	$7,400	$7,947	7.4	55.5

Source: Insurance Information Institute, State Farm®.

Top 10 States For Homeowners Insurance Lightning Losses By Number Of Claims, 2015

Rank	State	Number of paid claims	Insured losses ($ millions)	Average cost per claim
1	Florida	11,898	$156.2	$13,131
2	Georgia	10,442	61.0	5,844
3	Texas	8,844	84.9	9,595
4	Louisiana	5,333	24.4	4,578
5	Alabama	4,508	28.3	6,280
6	North Carolina	4,226	28.8	6,810
7	Pennsylvania	3,686	13.2	3,579
8	Tennessee	3,397	24.5	7,212
9	Virginia	3,174	21.0	6,607
10	South Carolina	3,163	13.7	4,318
	Total, top 10	58,671	$455.9	$7,771

Source: Insurance Information Institute, State Farm®.

As of July 2016, 77 insurance companies participated in the Write Your Own (WYO) program, started in 1983, in which insurers issue policies and adjust flood claims on behalf of the federal government under their own names.

In 2015, 86.5 percent of NFIP policies were held in the WYO program.

As of May 2016, 68 percent of NFIP policies covered single family homes, 21 percent covered condominiums, and 5 percent covered businesses and other non-residential properties. Two- to four-family units and other residential policies accounted for the remainder.

Superstorm Sandy which occurred in October 2012 resulted in $8.2 billion in NFIP payouts as of June 2016, second only to 2005's Hurricane Katrina with $16.3 billion in payouts.

FLOOD INSURANCE

National Flood Insurance Program

Flood damage is excluded under standard homeowners and renters insurance policies. However, flood coverage is available in the form of a separate policy both from the National Flood Insurance Program (NFIP) and from a few private insurers.

Congress created the NFIP in 1968 in response to the rising cost of taxpayer-funded disaster relief for flood victims and the increasing amount of damage caused by floods. The NFIP makes federally backed flood insurance available in communities that agree to adopt and enforce flood-plain management ordinances to reduce future flood damage. The NFIP is self-supporting for the average historical loss year. This means that unless there is a widespread disaster, operating expenses and flood insurance claims are financed through premiums collected.

The 2016 Insurance Information Institute *Annual Pulse Survey* found that 12 percent of American homeowners had a flood insurance policy, fewer than the 14 percent who had the coverage in 2015, as shown in the chart below.

Homeowners With Flood Insurance, 2012-2016

	2012	2013	2014	2015	2016
Total	**14%**	**14%**	**14%**	**14%**	**12%**
By region					
Northeast	14	10	11	11	13
Midwest	6	12	7	10	8
South	21	15	20	21	14
West	6	11	8	9	10

Source: Insurance Information Institute *Annual Pulse Survey*.

Flood Insurance Losses

National Flood Insurance Program (NFIP) payouts vary widely from year to year. Flood loss payments totaled $792 million in 2015, higher than the 2014 losses of $377 million and down significantly from $9.3 billion in 2012, the year of superstorm Sandy. In 2005 loss payments totaled $17.8 billion, the highest amount on record, including losses from Hurricanes Katrina, Rita and Wilma. (See page 145 for information on flood insurance losses.)

There were 130,214 NFIP claims from superstorm Sandy as of June 2016. The average paid loss was $63,352, compared with 167,984 claims from Katrina, with an average paid loss of $97,142.

In 2015 the average amount of flood coverage was $243,189, and the average premium was $663.

The average flood claim in 2015 was $39,184, down from $60,488 in 2012, the year of Sandy.

NFIP earned premiums fell slightly to $3.45 billion in 2015 from $3.54 billion in 2014.

As of the end of June the federal government had declared 17 major flood disasters in 2016, compared with 27 in all of 2015.

National Flood Insurance Program, 1980-2015

Year	Policies in force at year-end	Losses paid	
		Number	Amount ($000)
1980	2,103,851	41,918	$230,414
1985	2,016,785	38,676	368,239
1990	2,477,861	14,766	167,897
1995	3,476,829	62,441	1,295,578
2000	4,369,087	16,362	251,721
2005	4,962,011	213,587	17,770,118
2007	5,655,919	23,189	614,014
2008	5,684,275	74,907	3,487,967
2009	5,700,235	31,033	779,898
2010	5,645,436	29,155	773,575
2011	5,646,144	78,183	2,427,274
2012	5,620,017	150,832	9,266,395
2013	5,568,642	18,101	491,415
2014	5,406,725	12,887	376,648
2015	5,206,241	20,208	791,837

Source: U.S. Department of Homeland Security, Federal Emergency Management Agency.

Flood Insurance In The United States, 2015[1]

State	Direct NFIP business		WYO business		Total NFIP/WYO	
	Number of policies	Insurance in force[2] ($ millions)	Number of policies	Insurance in force[2] ($ millions)	Number of policies	Insurance in force[2] ($ millions)
Alabama	10,645	$2,141.1	44,619	$10,145.6	55,264	$12,286.7
Alaska	762	168.3	2,033	548.2	2,795	716.5
Arizona	6,416	1,479.3	29,286	7,070.7	35,702	8,550.0
Arkansas	3,468	525.9	15,225	2,570.9	18,693	3,096.8
California	47,099	12,730.0	238,038	66,521.0	285,137	79,251.1
Colorado	4,379	1,011.0	18,888	4,635.6	23,267	5,646.7
Connecticut	2,649	612.8	38,011	9,560.3	40,660	10,173.1
Delaware	4,674	1,231.6	22,169	5,619.8	26,843	6,851.3
D.C.	106	27.7	2,039	444.4	2,145	472.1
Florida	139,718	36,132.2	1,682,198	400,138.6	1,821,916	436,270.8
Georgia	17,484	4,278.5	71,251	18,358.9	88,735	22,637.3
Hawaii	2,546	574.8	57,416	12,742.8	59,962	13,317.6
Idaho	1,097	247.3	5,096	1,202.8	6,193	1,450.0
Illinois	12,269	2,126.3	33,302	6,454.1	45,571	8,580.4
Indiana	6,246	983.1	20,291	3,994.7	26,537	4,977.8
Iowa	2,804	436.1	11,564	2,313.2	14,368	2,749.3
Kansas	2,568	405.9	8,643	1,582.4	11,211	1,988.3
Kentucky	3,853	535.8	18,945	3,137.5	22,798	3,673.3
Louisiana	118,622	28,635.0	334,201	82,497.7	452,823	111,132.7
Maine	654	132.9	8,081	1,880.5	8,735	2,013.4
Maryland	7,006	1,674.1	62,034	14,092.7	69,040	15,766.8
Massachusetts	5,156	1,147.8	58,558	14,664.4	63,714	15,812.2
Michigan	4,745	691.9	18,717	3,542.2	23,462	4,234.2
Minnesota	1,877	400.9	8,654	1,965.7	10,531	2,366.6
Mississippi	14,844	3,460.2	51,598	12,165.7	66,442	15,625.8
Missouri	4,294	687.7	18,641	3,488.7	22,935	4,176.4
Montana	880	170.1	4,340	868.5	5,220	1,038.6
Nebraska	2,426	380.1	8,579	1,623.4	11,005	2,003.5
Nevada	2,342	533.5	10,572	2,768.8	12,914	3,302.3
New Hampshire	644	132.1	8,218	1,778.0	8,862	1,910.1

(table continues)

Flood Insurance In The United States, 2015[1] (Cont'd)

State	Direct NFIP business		WYO business		Total NFIP/WYO	
	Number of policies	Insurance in force[2] ($ millions)	Number of policies	Insurance in force[2] ($ millions)	Number of policies	Insurance in force[2] ($ millions)
New Jersey	18,246	$4,021.9	215,534	$53,049.4	233,780	$57,071.3
New Mexico	2,444	451.4	11,938	2,407.1	14,382	2,858.5
New York	20,998	5,227.3	167,204	44,945.4	188,202	50,172.7
North Carolina	15,143	3,730.9	114,864	27,914.4	130,007	31,645.3
North Dakota	2,021	528.4	10,234	2,714.5	12,255	3,242.9
Ohio	7,623	1,107.3	30,744	5,665.4	38,367	6,772.7
Oklahoma	3,669	651.2	12,124	2,448.3	15,793	3,099.6
Oregon	6,573	1,528.3	24,191	5,827.8	30,764	7,356.1
Pennsylvania	10,136	1,639.2	55,270	11,393.4	65,406	13,032.6
Rhode Island	591	144.4	14,512	3,731.4	15,103	3,875.8
South Carolina	24,133	6,548.6	175,949	44,510.7	200,082	51,059.3
South Dakota	952	201.4	3,862	886.5	4,814	1,087.9
Tennessee	5,560	1,254.5	24,782	5,732.6	30,342	6,987.1
Texas	105,268	28,419.4	482,424	127,454.0	587,692	155,873.4
Utah	669	147.6	3,317	827.7	3,986	975.3
Vermont	365	65.2	3,731	827.4	4,096	892.6
Virginia	17,375	4,300.7	87,697	22,247.2	105,072	26,547.9
Washington	6,178	1,385.1	33,694	8,298.4	39,872	9,683.5
West Virginia	4,646	549.6	13,181	1,966.6	17,827	2,516.2
Wisconsin	2,038	332.7	12,004	2,317.4	14,042	2,650.1
Wyoming	408	90.7	1,613	388.1	2,021	478.8
American Samoa	0	0.0	0	0.0	0	0.0
Guam	159	31.1	72	14.8	231	45.9
N. Mariana Islands	5	0.4	10	1.8	15	2.1
Puerto Rico	118	15.3	9,497	1,353.9	9,615	1,369.3
Virgin Islands	279	52.2	1,342	262.2	1,621	314.4
United States[3]	687,870	$166,118.7	4,421,000	$1,075,564.7	5,108,870	$1,241,683.4

[1] Direct and Write Your Own (WYO) business may not add to total due to rounding. [2] Total limits of liability for all policies in force.
[3] Includes WYO policies written in unknown areas.

Source: U.S. Department of Homeland Security, Federal Emergency Management Agency.

EARTHQUAKE INSURANCE

Standard homeowners, renters and business insurance policies do not cover damage from earthquakes. Coverage is available either in the form of an endorsement or as a separate policy. Earthquake insurance provides protection from the shaking and cracking that can destroy buildings and personal possessions. Coverage for other kinds of damage that may result from earthquakes, such as fire and water damage due to burst gas and water pipes, is provided by standard home and business insurance policies. Earthquake coverage is available mostly from private insurance companies. In California homeowners can also get coverage from the California Earthquake Authority (CEA), a privately funded, publicly managed organization. Only about 10 percent of California residents currently have earthquake coverage, down from about 30 percent in 1996, two years after the Northridge, California, earthquake.

Eight percent of homeowners nationwide responding to a May 2016 poll by the Insurance Information Institute said they have earthquake insurance. Homeowners in the West were most likely to have earthquake insurance with 14 percent saying they had the coverage followed by the Midwest at 7 percent; and the South and Northeast at 6 percent. See page 150 for information on earthquake insurance losses.

Earthquake Insurance, 2006-2015 ($000)

Year	Net premiums written[1]	Annual percent change	Combined ratio[2]	Annual point change[3]
2006	$1,315,423	18.9%	40.4	-10.5 pts.
2007	1,246,538	-5.2	30.0	-10.4
2008	1,259,872	1.1	33.5	3.5
2009	1,288,353	2.3	36.3	2.8
2010	1,443,598	12.0	41.4	5.1
2011	1,467,372	1.6	55.8	14.4
2012	1,593,451	8.6	36.3	-19.5
2013	1,586,985	-0.4	30.3	-6.0
2014	1,641,847	3.5	34.1	3.8
2015	1,650,225	0.5	28.1	-6.0

[1]After reinsurance transactions, excludes state funds. [2]After dividends to policyholders. A drop in the combined ratio represents an improvement; an increase represents a deterioration. [3]Calculated from unrounded numbers.

Source: NAIC data, sourced from S&P Global Market Intelligence, Insurance Information Institute.

Leading Writers Of Earthquake Insurance

The California Earthquake Authority (CEA), a publicly managed, largely privately funded organization that sells its policies through participating private insurance companies, was the leading writer of earthquake insurance in the United States, based on direct premiums written in 2015, according to data from S&P Global Market Intelligence. The CEA had $636 million in direct premiums written in 2015, all of which covered residential California properties. It accounted for 22 percent of the total U.S. earthquake insurance market in 2015. The nine other largest earthquake insurers in 2015 were all private insurance companies.

Top 10 Writers Of Earthquake Insurance By Direct Premiums Written, 2015 ($000)

Rank	Group/company	Direct premiums written[1]	Market share[2]
1	California Earthquake Authority	$635,955	22.0%
2	State Farm Mutual Automobile Insurance	244,245	8.4
3	Zurich Insurance Group[3]	201,147	6.9
4	American International Group (AIG)	150,119	5.2
5	Chubb Ltd.[4]	148,712	5.1
6	Travelers Companies Inc.	140,949	4.9
7	GeoVera Insurance Holdings Ltd.	114,353	4.0
8	Liberty Mutual	79,177	2.7
9	Berkshire Hathaway Inc.	78,007	2.7
10	Swiss Re Ltd.	73,634	2.5

[1]Before reinsurance transactions, includes state funds. [2]Based on U.S. total, includes territories. [3]Data for Farmers Insurance Group of Companies and Zurich Financial Group (which owns Farmers' management company) are reported separately by S&P Global Market Intelligence. [4]Chubb Ltd. data reflect the 2015 merger with Ace Ltd.

Source: NAIC data, sourced from S&P Global Market Intelligence, Insurance Information Institute.

COMMERCIAL LINES

The commercial lines sector of the property/casualty insurance industry generally provides insurance products for businesses as opposed to the personal lines sector, which offers products for individuals. However, the division between commercial and personal coverages is not precise. For example, inland marine insurance, which is included in the commercial lines sector, may cover some personal property such as expensive jewelry and fine art.

Leading Companies

Top 10 Writers Of Commercial Lines Insurance By Direct Premiums Written, 2015 ($000)

Rank	Group/company	Direct premiums written[1]	Market share[2]
1	American International Group (AIG)	$16,980,061	5.8%
2	Chubb Ltd.[3]	16,675,193	5.7
3	Travelers Companies Inc.	16,347,492	5.6
4	Liberty Mutual	13,801,267	4.7
5	Zurich Insurance Group[4]	13,403,445	4.6
6	CNA Financial Corp.	9,203,419	3.2
7	Nationwide Mutual Group	8,401,984	2.9
8	Hartford Financial Services	7,478,308	2.6
9	Berkshire Hathaway Inc.	7,056,856	2.4
10	Tokio Marine Group	5,956,554	2.0

[1]Before reinsurance transactions, includes state funds. [2]Based on U.S. total, includes territories. [3]Chubb Ltd. data reflect the 2015 merger with Ace Ltd. [4]Data for Farmers Insurance Group of Companies and Zurich Financial Group (which owns Farmers' management company) are reported separately by S&P Global Market Intelligence.

Source: NAIC data, sourced from S&P Global Market Intelligence, Insurance Information Institute.

Top 10 Commercial Insurance Brokers Of U.S. Business By Revenue, 2015[1] ($ millions)

Rank	Company	Brokerage revenues
1	Marsh & McLennan Cos. Inc.[2]	$6,327
2	Aon P.L.C.	6,052
3	Willis Towers Watson P.L.C.[2]	3,981
4	Arthur J. Gallagher & Co.	2,713
5	BB&T Insurance Holdings Inc.	1,676
6	Brown & Brown Inc.	1,657
7	Wells Fargo Insurance Services USA Inc.	1,316
8	Hub International Ltd.	1,147
9	USI Insurance Services L.L.C.	1,028
10	Lockton Cos. L.L.C.[3]	996

[1]Companies that derive less than 50 percent of revenues from commercial retail brokerage or employee benefits are not ranked. [2]Reported U.S. acquisitions in 2015. [3]Fiscal year ending April 30.

Source: Business Insurance July 18, 2016.

Workers Compensation Insurance And Excess Workers Compensation

Workers compensation insurance provides for the cost of medical care and rehabilitation for injured workers and lost wages and death benefits for the dependents of persons killed in work-related accidents. Workers compensation systems vary from state to state. Workers compensation combined ratios are expressed in two ways. Calendar year results reflect claim payments and changes in reserves for accidents that happened in that year or earlier. Accident year results only include losses from a particular year. Excess workers compensation, a coverage geared to employers that self-insure for workers compensation, comes into play when claims exceed a designated dollar amount.

Workers Compensation Insurance, 2006-2015 ($000)

| Year | Net premiums written[2] | Annual percent change | Combined ratio[1] | | | |
			Calendar year[3]	Annual point change[4]	Accident year[5]	Annual point change
2006	$41,820,419	7.3%	95.4	-6.7 pts.	85	-2 pts.
2007	40,610,991	-2.9	101.7	6.3	97	12
2008	36,939,016	-9.0	101.5	-0.2	104	7
2009	32,247,870	-12.7	107.9	6.4	108	4
2010	31,643,087	-1.9	116.1	8.2	116	8
2011	35,664,230	12.7	117.6	1.5	112	-4
2012	38,747,594	8.6	110.4	-7.3	103	-9
2013	41,147,216	6.2	103.0	-7.3	100	-3
2014	43,546,737	5.8	102.4	-0.6	97	-3
2015	45,090,509	3.5	95.4	-7.0	98[6]	1

[1]After dividends to policyholders. A drop in the combined ratio represents an improvement; an increase represents a deterioration. [2]After reinsurance transactions, excludes state funds. [3]Calendar year data are from S&P Global Market Intelligence. [4]Calculated from unrounded data. [5]Accident year data are from the National Council on Compensation Insurance (NCCI). [6]Estimated by NCCI.

Source: NAIC data, sourced from S&P Global Market Intelligence, Insurance Information Institute; © National Council on Compensation Insurance.

Excess Workers Compensation Insurance, 2008-2015 ($000)

Year	Net premiums written[1]	Annual percent change	Combined ratio[2]	Annual point change[3]
2008	$926,487	NA	148.3	NA
2009	941,117	1.6%	34.8	-113.5 pts.
2010	799,733	-15.0	50.9	16.0
2011	816,435	2.1	134.7	83.8
2012	815,770	-0.1	153.6	18.9
2013	844,098	3.5	69.3	-84.3
2014	920,223	9.0	112.3	43.0
2015	924,261	0.4	114.0	1.7

[1]After reinsurance transactions, excludes state funds. [2]After dividends to policyholders. A drop in the combined ratio represents an improvement; an increase represents a deterioration. [3]Calculated from unrounded numbers. NA=Data not available. Source: NAIC data, sourced from S&P Global Market Intelligence, Insurance Information Institute.

Workers Compensation Medical Costs, 2006-2015

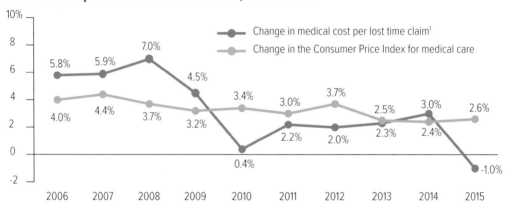

[1]Based on states where the National Council on Compensation Insurance provides ratemaking services. Represents costs for injuries that resulted in time off from work. Data for 2015 are preliminary. Source: U.S. Bureau of Labor Statistics; © National Council on Compensation Insurance.

Workers Compensation Benefits, Coverage And Costs, 2013-2014

	2013	2014	Percent change
Covered workers (000)	130,245	132,673	1.9%
Covered wages ($ billions)	$6,466	$6,820	5.5
Workers compensation benefits paid ($ billions)	62.5	62.3	-1.2
Medical benefits	31.4	31.4	[1]
Cash benefits	31.1	30.9	-0.6
Employer costs for workers compensation ($ billions)	87.6	91.8	4.9

[1]Less than 0.1 percent.

Source: Workers Compensation: Benefits, Coverage, and Costs, 2014, National Academy of Social Insurance.

Other Liability Insurance

Other liability insurance protects the policyholder from legal liability arising from negligence, carelessness or a failure to act that causes property damage or personal injury to others. It includes errors and omissions, umbrella liability and liquor liability. Product liability, a separate line of insurance, protects the manufacturer, distributor or seller of a product from legal liability resulting from a defective condition that caused personal injury or damage associated with the use of the product.

Other Liability Insurance, 2006-2015 ($000)

Year	Net premiums written[1]	Annual percent change	Combined ratio[2]	Annual point change[3]
2006	$42,229,148	7.5%	94.8	-15.8 pts.
2007	40,997,132	-2.9	99.2	4.4
2008	38,602,734	-5.8	93.8	-5.4
2009	36,184,065	-6.3	105.5	11.7
2010	35,802,772	-1.1	108.1	2.6
2011	36,511,575	2.0	96.1	-12.0
2012	38,307,679	4.9	103.2	7.0
2013	42,075,315	9.8	96.8	-6.4
2014	44,181,272	5.0	94.8	-2.0
2015	45,585,279	3.2	101.6	6.8

[1]After reinsurance transactions, excludes state funds. [2]After dividends to policyholders. A drop in the combined ratio represents an improvement; an increase represents a deterioration. [3]Calculated from unrounded data.

Source: NAIC data, sourced from S&P Global Market Intelligence, Insurance Information Institute.

Product Liability Insurance, 2006-2015 ($000)

Year	Net premiums written[1]	Annual percent change	Combined ratio[2]	Annual point change[3]
2006	$3,621,671	2.1%	77.8	-53.3 pts.
2007	3,265,035	-9.8	99.8	22.0
2008	2,777,587	-14.9	124.0	24.2
2009	2,365,681	-14.8	124.0	[4]
2010	2,050,619	-13.3	157.1	33.1
2011	2,320,540	13.2	160.0	2.9
2012	2,575,225	11.0	102.7	-57.3
2013	2,718,879	5.6	155.3	52.6
2014	2,674,183	-1.6	138.4	-16.8
2015	2,796,758	4.6	130.6	-7.8

[1]After reinsurance transactions, excludes state funds. [2]After dividends to policyholders. A drop in the combined ratio represents an improvement; an increase represents a deterioration. [3]Calculated from unrounded data. [4]Less than 0.1 point.

Source: NAIC data, sourced from S&P Global Market Intelligence, Insurance Information Institute.

Commercial And Farmowners Multiple Peril Insurance

Commercial multiple peril insurance is a package policy that includes property, boiler and machinery, crime and general liability coverages. Farmowners multiple peril insurance, similar to homeowners insurance, provides coverage to farmowners and ranchowners against a number of named perils and liabilities. It covers a dwelling and its contents, as well as barns, stables and other structures.

Commercial Multiple Peril Insurance, 2006-2015

Total ($000)					
Year	Net premiums written[1]	Annual percent change	Year	Net premiums written[1]	Annual percent change
2006	$31,856,902	7.7%	2011	$29,995,201	3.7%
2007	31,261,039	-1.9	2012	31,502,689	5.0
2008	30,306,109	-3.1	2013	33,245,146	5.5
2009	28,926,363	-4.6	2014	34,375,127	3.4
2010	28,913,516	[2]	2015	34,741,532	1.1

Nonliability Portion ($000)									
Year	Net premiums written[1]	Annual percent change	Combined ratio[3]	Annual point change[4]	Year	Net premiums written[1]	Annual percent change	Combined ratio[3]	Annual point change[4]
2006	$18,250,773	3.3%	83.9	-11.5 pts.	2011	$18,657,799	2.5%	119.1	16.2 pts.
2007	18,334,139	0.5	89.6	5.7	2012	19,513,568	4.6	113.9	-5.1
2008	18,235,095	-0.5	107.7	18.1	2013	21,058,709	7.9	93.3	-20.6
2009	17,927,074	-1.7	98.3	-9.4	2014	21,983,697	4.4	96.9	3.6
2010	18,210,612	1.6	102.9	4.5	2015	21,478,035	-2.3	91.6	-5.4

Liability Portion ($000)									
Year	Net premiums written[1]	Annual percent change	Combined ratio[3]	Annual point change[4]	Year	Net premiums written[1]	Annual percent change	Combined Rratio[3]	Annual point change[4]
2006	$13,606,129	14.3%	104.0	1.1 pts.	2011	$11,337,402	5.9%	101.8	5.8 pts.
2007	12,926,900	-5.0	95.4	-8.6	2012	11,989,121	5.7	94.1	-7.7
2008	12,071,014	-6.6	97.5	2.1	2013	12,186,437	1.6	103.8	9.7
2009	10,999,289	-8.9	94.2	-3.2	2014	12,391,430	1.7	103.6	-0.2
2010	10,702,904	-2.7	96.0	1.8	2015	13,263,497	7.0	99.2	-4.4

[1]After reinsurance transactions, excludes state funds. [2]Less than 0.1 percent. [3]After dividends to policyholders. A drop in the combined ratio represents an improvement; an increase represents a deterioration. [4]Calculated from unrounded data.

Source: NAIC data, sourced from S&P Global Market Intelligence, Insurance Information Institute.

Farmowners Multiple Peril Insurance, 2006-2015 ($000)

Year	Net premiums written[1]	Annual percent change	Combined ratio[2]	Annual point change[3]
2006	$2,300,728	1.9%	123.2	28.0 pts.
2007	2,413,562	4.9	98.1	-25.0
2008	2,586,861	7.2	119.5	21.3
2009	2,612,262	1.0	107.9	-11.6
2010	2,754,955	5.5	108.2	0.3
2011	2,932,576	6.4	117.4	9.2
2012	3,277,423	11.8	99.5	-17.9
2013	3,511,651	7.1	93.9	-5.6
2014	3,628,084	3.3	94.7	0.7
2015	3,762,555	3.7	89.9	-4.8

[1]After reinsurance transactions, excludes state funds. [2]After dividends to policyholders. A drop in the combined ratio represents an improvement; an increase represents a deterioration. [3]Calculated from unrounded data.

Source: NAIC data, sourced from S&P Global Market Intelligence, Insurance Information Institute.

Medical Malpractice Insurance

Medical malpractice insurance covers facilities, doctors and other professionals in the medical field for liability claims arising from the treatment of patients.

Medical Malpractice Insurance, 2006-2015 ($000)

Year	Net premiums written[1]	Annual percent change	Combined ratio[2]	Annual point change[3]
2006	$10,378,325	20.4%	90.6	-4.7 pts.
2007	9,958,513	-4.0	84.7	-5.9
2008	9,521,113	-4.4	79.2	-5.5
2009	9,206,794	-3.3	85.5	6.3
2010	9,096,345	-1.2	88.9	3.4
2011	8,833,365	-2.9	88.0	-1.0
2012	8,713,595	-1.4	93.1	5.2
2013	8,531,233	-2.1	89.4	-3.8
2014	8,475,474	-0.7	106.0	16.6
2015	8,201,438	-3.2	102.3	-3.7

[1]After reinsurance transactions, excludes state funds. [2]After dividends to policyholders. A drop in the combined ratio represents an improvement; an increase represents a deterioration. [3]Calculated from unrounded data.

Source: NAIC data, sourced from S&P Global Market Intelligence, Insurance Information Institute.

Fire And Allied Lines Insurance

Fire insurance provides coverage against losses caused by fire and lightning. It is usually sold as part of a package policy such as commercial multiple peril. Allied lines insurance includes property insurance that is usually bought in conjunction with a fire insurance policy. It includes coverage for wind and water damage and vandalism.

Fire Insurance, 2006-2015 ($000)

Year	Net premiums written[1]	Annual percent change	Combined ratio[2]	Annual point change[3]
2006	$9,365,050	18.0%	78.0	-5.3 pts.
2007	9,664,054	3.2	85.6	7.6
2008	9,906,059	2.5	92.3	6.7
2009	10,109,161	2.1	78.6	-13.7
2010	10,199,101	0.9	80.2	1.7
2011	10,317,968	1.2	94.1	13.9
2012	10,795,612	4.6	87.4	-6.7
2013	11,229,431	4.0	79.1	-8.3
2014	11,501,516	2.4	84.8	5.7
2015	11,414,797	-0.8	84.9	0.1

[1]After reinsurance transactions, excludes state funds. [2]After dividends to policyholders. A drop in the combined ratio represents an improvement; an increase represents a deterioration. [3]Calculated from unrounded data.

Source: NAIC data, sourced from S&P Global Market Intelligence, Insurance Information Institute.

Allied Lines Insurance, 2006-2015 ($000)

Year	Net premiums written[1]	Annual percent change	Combined ratio[2]	Annual point change[3]
2006	$6,593,122	10.9%	94.6	-58.6 pts.
2007	6,889,750	4.5	53.5	-41.1
2008	7,691,004	11.6	128.1	74.6
2009	7,744,256	0.7	93.6	-34.5
2010	7,494,281	-3.2	98.9	5.3
2011	7,800,211	4.1	132.7	33.8
2012	8,161,346	4.6	138.0	5.3
2013	9,251,852	13.4	90.2	-47.7
2014	9,209,843	-0.5	90.1	-0.2
2015	9,119,642	-1.0	88.1	-2.0

[1]After reinsurance transactions, excludes state funds. [2]After dividends to policyholders. A drop in the combined ratio represents an improvement; an increase represents a deterioration. [3]Calculated from unrounded data.

Source: NAIC data, sourced from S&P Global Market Intelligence, Insurance Information Institute.

Inland Marine And Ocean Marine Insurance

Inland marine insurance covers bridges and tunnels, goods in transit, movable equipment, unusual property and communications-related structures as well as expensive personal property. Ocean marine insurance provides coverage on all types of vessels, for property damage to the vessels and cargo, as well as associated liabilities.

Inland Marine Insurance, 2006-2015 ($000)

Year	Net premiums written[1]	Annual percent change	Combined ratio[2]	Annual point change[3]
2006	$9,217,002	11.7%	72.7	17.7 pts.
2007	9,775,987	6.1	79.2	6.5
2008	9,408,463	-3.8	92.7	13.5
2009	8,686,660	-7.7	89.2	-3.5
2010	8,527,512	-1.8	86.0	-3.2
2011	8,768,829	2.8	97.6	11.6
2012	9,603,749	9.5	95.9	-1.7
2013	10,147,908	5.7	83.6	-12.4
2014	10,990,045	8.3	83.4	-0.2
2015	11,417,338	3.9	83.8	0.4

[1]After reinsurance transactions, excludes state funds. [2]After dividends to policyholders. A drop in the combined ratio represents an improvement; an increase represents a deterioration. [3]Calculated from unrounded data.
Source: NAIC data, sourced from S&P Global Market Intelligence, Insurance Information Institute.

Ocean Marine Insurance, 2006-2015 ($000)

Year	Net premiums written[1]	Annual percent change	Combined ratio[2]	Annual point change[3]
2006	$3,133,674	6.3%	97.3	-17.2 pts.
2007	3,261,490	4.1	113.6	16.3
2008	3,098,438	-5.0	103.2	-10.5
2009	2,941,486	-5.1	91.8	-11.3
2010	2,740,956	-6.8	96.1	4.3
2011	2,760,853	0.7	100.9	4.8
2012	2,704,665	-2.0	109.1	8.2
2013	2,863,507	5.9	98.1	-11.0
2014	2,910,377	1.6	88.2	-9.9
2015	2,831,564	-2.7	94.3	6.1

[1]After reinsurance transactions, excludes state funds. [2]After dividends to policyholders. A drop in the combined ratio represents an improvement; an increase represents a deterioration. [3]Calculated from unrounded data.
Source: NAIC data, sourced from S&P Global Market Intelligence, Insurance Information Institute.

Surety And Fidelity

Surety bonds provide monetary compensation in the event that a policyholder fails to perform certain acts such as the proper fulfillment of a construction contract within a stated period. Surety bonds are usually purchased by the party that has contracted to complete a project. They are required for public projects in order to protect taxpayers. Fidelity bonds, which are usually purchased by an employer, protect against losses caused by employee fraud or dishonesty.

Surety Bonds, 2006-2015 ($000)

Year	Net premiums written[1]	Annual percent change	Combined ratio[2]	Annual point change[3]
2006	$4,434,780	16.2%	81.5	-20.6 pts.
2007	4,779,117	7.8	72.2	-9.3
2008	4,960,250	3.8	67.0	-5.2
2009	4,835,409	-2.5	79.5	12.6
2010	4,851,328	0.3	70.7	-8.8
2011	4,849,480	[4]	72.9	2.2
2012	4,695,782	-3.2	76.8	3.9
2013	4,868,847	3.7	72.7	-4.0
2014	5,000,382	2.7	70.6	-2.1
2015	5,139,866	2.8	73.8	3.2

[1]After reinsurance transactions, excludes state funds. [2]After dividends to policyholders. A drop in the combined ratio represents an improvement; an increase represents a deterioration. [3]Calculated from unrounded data. [4]Less than 0.1 percent.

Source: NAIC data, sourced from S&P Global Market Intelligence, Insurance Information Institute.

Fidelity Bonds, 2006-2015 ($000)

Year	Net premiums written[1]	Annual percent change	Combined ratio[2]	Annual point change[3]
2006	$1,240,822	2.0%	87.2	2.1 pts.
2007	1,239,760	-0.1	76.5	-10.7
2008	1,140,617	-8.0	84.2	7.7
2009	1,098,372	-3.7	105.4	21.2
2010	1,082,534	-1.4	95.8	-9.6
2011	1,098,225	1.4	102.0	6.2
2012	1,096,406	-0.2	99.4	-2.6
2013	1,124,199	2.5	92.9	-6.5
2014	1,165,280	3.7	92.9	[4]
2015	1,161,375	-0.3	77.3	-15.7

[1]After reinsurance transactions, excludes state funds. [2]After dividends to policyholders. A drop in the combined ratio represents an improvement; an increase represents a deterioration. [3]Calculated from unrounded data. [4]Less than 0.1 point.

Source: NAIC data, sourced from S&P Global Market Intelligence, Insurance Information Institute.

Mortgage Guaranty Insurance

Private mortgage insurance (PMI), also known as mortgage guaranty insurance, guarantees that in the event of a default, the insurer will pay the mortgage lender for any loss resulting from a property foreclosure, up to a specific amount. PMI, which is purchased by the borrower but protects the lender, is sometimes confused with mortgage life insurance, a life insurance product that pays off the mortgage if the borrower dies before the loan is repaid. Banks generally require PMI for all borrowers with down payments of less than 20 percent of the home price. The industry's combined ratio, a measure of profitability, deteriorated (i.e., rose) significantly in 2007 and 2008, reflecting the economic downturn and the subsequent rise in mortgage defaults, and remained at high levels through 2012. In 2015 the combined ratio fell to 58.1, the lowest level since it was 52.1 in 2001.

Mortgage Guaranty Insurance, 2006-2015 ($000)

Year	Net premiums written[1]	Annual percent change	Combined ratio[2]	Annual point change[3]
2006	$4,565,899	2.5%	71.0	-4.2 pts.
2007	5,192,104	13.7	129.0	58.1
2008	5,371,878	3.5	219.8	90.8
2009	4,564,406	-15.0	201.9	-17.9
2010	4,248,798	-6.9	198.4	-3.6
2011	4,242,340	-0.2	219.0	20.7
2012	3,965,896	-6.5	189.7	-29.4
2013	4,329,947	9.2	98.0	-91.7
2014	4,180,006	-3.5	70.2	-27.7
2015	4,681,917	12.0	58.1	-12.1

[1]After reinsurance transactions, excludes state funds. [2]After dividends to policyholders. A drop in the combined ratio represents an improvement; an increase represents a deterioration. [3]Calculated from unrounded data.

Source: NAIC data, sourced from S&P Global Market Intelligence, Insurance Information Institute.

Top 10 Writers Of Mortgage Guaranty Insurance By Direct Premiums Written, 2015 ($000)

Rank	Group/company	Direct premiums written[1]	Market share[2]
1	MGIC Investment Corp.	$1,098,133	22.5%
2	American International Group (AIG)[3]	1,018,306	20.9
3	Radian Group Inc.	1,008,565	20.7
4	Genworth Financial Inc.	698,691	14.3
5	Essent US Holdings Inc.	368,930	7.6
6	PMI Group Inc.	235,589	4.8
7	Old Republic International Corp.	193,703	4.0
8	Arch Capital Group Ltd.[3]	134,841	2.8
9	NMI Holdings Inc.	114,211	2.3
10	Chubb Ltd.[4]	96	[5]

[1]Before reinsurance transactions, includes state funds. [2]Based on U.S. total, includes territories. [3]In 2016 AIG agreed to sell its mortgage guaranty business to Arch Capital Group Ltd. [4]Chubb Ltd. data reflect the 2015 merger with Ace Ltd. [5]Less than 0.1 percent.

Source: NAIC data, sourced from S&P Global Market Intelligence, Insurance Information Institute

Financial Guaranty Insurance

Financial guaranty insurance, also known as bond insurance, helps expand the financial markets by increasing borrower and lender leverage. It guarantees the principal and interest payments on municipal obligations.

Financial guaranty insurers are specialized, highly capitalized companies that traditionally had the highest rating. The insurer's high rating attaches to the bonds thus lowering the risk of the bonds to investors. With their credit rating thus enhanced, municipalities can issue bonds that pay a lower interest rate, enabling them to borrow more for the same outlay of funds. The combined ratio climbed to 421.4 in 2008 at the height of the economic downturn. In 2013 the combined ratio fell below zero as several companies reduced loss reserves by more than $2 billion combined as a result of strains created by the financial crisis. Over the years financial guaranty insurers have expanded their reach beyond municipal bonds and now insure a wide array of products, including mortgage-backed securities, pools of credit default swaps and other structured transactions.

Financial Guaranty Insurance, 2006-2015[1] ($000)

Year	Net premiums written[2]	Annual percent change	Combined ratio[3]	Annual point change[4]
2006	$2,163,324	7.4%	47.7	17.8 pts.
2007	3,038,889	40.5	152.4	104.8
2008	3,171,560	4.4	421.4	268.9
2009	1,793,410	-43.5	100.6	-320.7
2010	1,371,908	-23.5	228.4	127.8
2011	968,898	-29.4	219.0	-9.4
2012	692,541	-28.5	181.6	-37.4
2013	710,480	2.6	-3.4	-184.9
2014	488,482	-31.2	91.3	94.7
2015	418,792	-14.3	99.0	7.8

[1]Based on Insurance Expense Exhibit (IEE) data. Ambac did not file an IEE in 2006; Financial Guaranty Insurance Co. did not file an IEE in 2012. Several companies in 2013 reduced loss reserves as a result of strains from the financial crisis, creating a negative combined ratio. [2]After reinsurance transactions, excludes state funds. [3]After dividends to policyholders. A drop in the combined ratio represents an improvement; an increase represents a deterioration. [4]Calculated from unrounded numbers.

Source: NAIC data, sourced from S&P Global Market Intelligence, Insurance Information Institute.

Top 10 Writers Of Financial Guaranty Insurance By Direct Premiums Written, 2015 ($000)

Rank	Group/company	Direct premiums written[1]	Market share[2]
1	Assured Guaranty Ltd.	$236,927	43.7%
2	MBIA Inc.	102,715	18.9
3	Syncora Holdings Ltd.	78,390	14.5
4	Ambac Financial Group Inc.	58,457	10.8
5	Build America Mutual Assurance Co.	25,306	4.7
6	Berkshire Hathaway Inc.	12,573	2.3
7	Financial Guaranty Insurance Co.	12,406	2.3
8	CIFG Assurance North America Inc.	11,789	2.2
9	Transamerica Casualty Insurance Co.	3,000	0.6
10	Radian Group Inc.	844	0.2

[1]Before reinsurance transactions, includes state funds. [2]Based on U.S. total, includes territories.

Source: NAIC data, sourced from S&P Global Market Intelligence, Insurance Information Institute.

Burglary And Theft Insurance And Boiler And Machinery Insurance

Burglary and theft insurance covers the loss of property, money and securities due to burglary, robbery or larceny. Boiler and machinery insurance is also known as mechanical breakdown, equipment breakdown or systems breakdown coverage. Among the types of equipment covered by this insurance are heating, cooling, electrical, telephone/communications and computer equipment.

Burglary And Theft Insurance, 2006-2015 ($000)

Year	Net premiums written[1]	Annual percent change	Combined ratio[2]	Annual point change[3]
2006	$143,132	19.1%	64.3	0.7 pts.
2007	160,703	12.3	56.4	-7.9
2008	160,434	-0.2	48.2	-8.3
2009	152,197	-5.1	59.6	11.5
2010	167,152	9.8	69.4	9.8
2011	194,661	16.5	61.6	-7.8
2012	220,831	13.4	58.6	-3.0
2013	207,225	-6.2	42.2	-16.4
2014	226,247	9.2	60.3	18.1
2015	230,393	1.8	61.3	1.0

[1]After reinsurance transactions, excludes state funds. [2]After dividends to policyholders. A drop in the combined ratio represents an improvement; an increase represents a deterioration. [3]Calculated from unrounded numbers.

Source: NAIC data, sourced from S&P Global Market Intelligence, Insurance Information Institute.

Boiler And Machinery Insurance, 2006-2015 ($000)

Year	Net premiums written[1]	Annual percent change	Combined ratio[2]	Annual point change[3]
2006	$1,675,347	5.8%	73.1	12.9 pts.
2007	1,741,099	3.9	73.1	[4]
2008	1,728,595	-0.7	87.7	14.6
2009	1,803,376	4.3	71.7	-16.1
2010	1,721,764	-4.5	71.5	-0.2
2011	1,810,941	5.2	75.0	3.5
2012	1,887,625	4.2	80.8	5.8
2013	1,979,514	4.9	72.2	-8.6
2014	1,998,967	1.0	76.6	4.4
2015	1,682,090	-15.9	69.3	-7.2

[1]After reinsurance transactions, excludes state funds. [2]After dividends to policyholders. A drop in the combined ratio represents an improvement; an increase represents a deterioration. [3]Calculated from unrounded numbers. [4]Less than 0.1 point.

Source: NAIC data, sourced from S&P Global Market Intelligence, Insurance Information Institute.

Crop Insurance

Crop-hail insurance is provided by the private market and covers just hail, fire and wind. Federally sponsored multiple peril crop insurance covers other causes of loss and is serviced by the private market but subsidized and reinsured by the federal government.

Crop-Hail Insurance, 2006-2015 ($000)

Year	Direct premiums written[1]	Annual percent change	Loss ratio[2]	Annual point change
2006	$405,254	-6.8%	50	6 pts.
2007	489,649	20.8	48	-2
2008	669,436	36.7	83	35
2009	621,322	-7.2	91	8
2010	682,188	9.8	67	-24
2011	843,801	23.7	116	49
2012	958,163	13.6	74	-42
2013	958,857	0.1	67	-7
2014	991,984	3.5	122	55
2015	979,703	-1.2	76	-46

[1]Before reinsurance transactions, total for all policyholders of crop-hail insurance. [2]The percentage of each premium dollar spent on claims and associated costs. A drop in the loss ratio represents an improvement; an increase represents a deterioration.

Source: National Crop Insurance Services.

Multiple Peril Crop Insurance, 2006-2015[1] ($000)

Year	Net premiums written[2]	Annual percent change	Combined ratio[3]	Annual point change[4]
2006	$2,824,769	26.4%	77.9	-13.3 pts.
2007	3,648,996	29.2	74.7	-3.2
2008	5,077,625	39.2	90.1	15.3
2009	3,964,690	-21.9	79.7	-10.4
2010	3,501,631	-11.7	73.9	-5.8
2011	5,456,991	55.8	90.6	16.8
2012	5,321,811	-2.5	104.0	13.3
2013	4,942,547	-7.1	103.3	-0.7
2014	4,189,765	-15.2	104.9	1.6
2015	3,680,768	-12.1	99.9	-5.1

[1]Includes private crop-hail insurance from 2006 to 2013. Data for 2014 and 2015 exclude private crop-hail insurance. [2]After reinsurance transactions, excludes state funds. [3]After dividends to policyholders. A drop in the combined ratio represents an improvement; an increase represents a deterioration. [4]Calculated from unrounded numbers.

Source: NAIC data, sourced from S&P Global Market Intelligence, Insurance Information Institute.

Top 10 Writers Of Multiple Peril Crop Insurance By Direct Premiums Written, 2015 ($000)

Rank	Group/company	Direct premiums written[1]	Market share[2]
1	Chubb Ltd.[3]	$1,750,152	18.3%
2	Zurich Insurance Group[4]	1,742,209	18.2
3	QBE Insurance Group Ltd.	1,264,485	13.2
4	American Financial Group Inc.	892,516	9.3
5	Endurance Specialty Holdings	768,612	8.0
6	Farmers Mutual Hail Insurance Co. of Iowa	655,868	6.9
7	CGB Insurance Co.	555,989	5.8
8	Tokio Marine Group	493,235	5.2
9	Archer-Daniels-Midland Co.	401,456	4.2
10	Everest Re Group Ltd.	209,066	2.2

[1]Before reinsurance transactions, includes state funds. [2]Based on U.S. total, includes territories. [3]Chubb Ltd. data reflect the 2015 merger with Ace Ltd. [4]Data for Farmers Insurance Group of Companies and Zurich Financial Group (which owns Farmers' management company) are reported separately by S&P Global Market Intelligence.

Source: NAIC data, sourced from S&P Global Market Intelligence, Insurance Information Institute.

Warranty Insurance

Warranty insurance coverage compensates for the cost of repairing or replacing defective products past the normal warranty period provided by manufacturers.

Warranty Insurance, 2008-2015 ($000)

Year	Net premiums written[1]	Annual percent change	Combined ratio[2]	Annual point change[3]
2008	$2,086,935	NA	94.3	NA
2009	1,757,247	-15.8%	97.9	3.6 pts.
2010	1,864,139	6.1	106.4	8.5
2011	1,695,799	-9.0	97.1	-9.3
2012	1,386,404	-18.2	99.5	2.5
2013	1,155,338	-16.7	104.2	4.7
2014	1,020,188	-11.7	93.5	-10.8
2015	1,017,790	-0.2	107.9	14.4

[1]After reinsurance transactions, excludes state funds. [2]After dividends to policyholders. A drop in the combined ratio represents an improvement; an increase represents a deterioration. [3]Calculated from unrounded numbers. NA=Data not available.

Source: NAIC data, sourced from S&P Global Market Intelligence, Insurance Information Institute.

MAJOR CATASTROPHIES: WORLD

Natural catastrophes and man-made disasters resulted in $37 billion in insured losses in 2015, compared with $36 billion in 2014 and well below the inflation-adjusted previous 10-year average of $62 billion, according to Swiss Re. Explosions at Tianjin port in China comprised the largest insured-loss event of the year and largest man-made loss event ever in Asia. There were 353 disaster events in 2015, of which 198 were natural disasters, the most ever recorded by *sigma*, a Swiss Re publication. Natural catastrophes accounted for $28 billion in insured losses. Asia suffered the most insured losses in 2015, including the explosions in Tianjin ($2.5 billion to $3.5 billion in insured losses), Typhoon Goni in Japan ($1.1 billion) and flooding in southern India ($755 million). The earthquake in Nepal was the biggest disaster of the year globally, killing close to 9,000 people, the largest loss of life in a single event, with total losses estimated at $6 billion, only $160 million of which were insured. In the U.S., the biggest loss came from a mid-February winter storm that caused damage in 17 states, with Massachusetts hit hardest. Insured losses were $2.1 billion, mainly from burst frozen water pipes and ice weight or water damage to property.

Top 10 Costliest Insurance Losses, 2015[1] (US$ millions)

Rank	Date	Country	Event	Insured loss in U.S. dollars
1	Aug. 12	China	Port of Tianjin - explosions at a warehouse storing hazardous chemicals	$2,500 to $3,500
2	Feb. 16	U.S.	Severe winter storm, strong winds, heavy snowfall and ice accumulations	2,081
3	May 23	U.S.	Thunderstorms, tornadoes, hail, severe flooding in Texas and Oklahoma	1,461
4	Apr. 7	U.S.	Thunderstorms, large hail, tornadoes, flash floods	1,204
5	Aug. 18	Japan, Philippines, North Korea	Typhoon Goni	1,150
6	Dec. 22	U.K., Ireland	Floods (Storms Eva and Frank)	1,032
7	Mar. 30	Germany, Netherlands, et al.	Winter Storm Niklas[2]	1,009
8	Apr. 18	U.S.	Thunderstorms, large hail, tornadoes, flash floods	939
9	Sep. 12	U.S.	Wildland fire "Valley Fire"	921
10	Jun. 21	U.S.	Thunderstorms, large hail, tornadoes, flash floods	914

(1) Property and business interruption losses, excludes life and liability losses. Includes flood losses in the U.S. insured via the National Flood Insurance Program. Loss data shown here may differ from figures shown elsewhere for the same event due to differences in the date of publication, the geographical area covered and other criteria used by organizations collecting the data. (2) Loss numbers for Storm Niklas are Swiss Re estimates based on data from Perils AG. NA=Data not available. Source: Swiss Re, *sigma*, No. 1/2016; Property Claim Services (PCS®), a Verisk Analytics® business, insured losses for natural catastrophes in the United States.

World Insured Catastrophe Losses, 2006-2015[1] (2015 $ millions)

Year	Weather-related natural catastrophes	Man-made	Earthquakes	Total
2006	$14,699	$5,991	$95	$20,786
2007	26,876	6,596	640	34,113
2008	48,330	9,231	464	58,025
2009	23,747	4,338	673	28,758
2010	32,309	5,186	14,671	52,167
2011	69,311	6,768	56,486	132,564
2012	72,236	6,067	1,765	80,068
2013	36,569	7,866	46	44,480
2014	28,384	7,045	313	35,741
2015	27,279	8,983	510	36,772

[1]In order to maintain comparability of the data over the course of time, the minimum threshold for losses was adjusted annually to compensate for inflation in the United Sates. Adjusted to 2015 dollars by Swiss Re.

Source: Swiss Re.

Top 10 Costliest World Insurance Losses, 1970-2015[1] (2015 $ millions)

Rank	Date	Country	Event	Insured loss
1	Aug. 25, 2005	U.S., Gulf of Mexico	Hurricane Katrina, storm surge, damage to oil rigs	$79,663
2	Mar. 11, 2011	Japan	Earthquake (Mw 9.0) triggers tsunami	36,865
3	Oct. 24, 2012	U.S., Caribbean, Canada	Hurricane Sandy, massive storm surge	36,115
4	Aug. 23, 1992	U.S., Bahamas	Hurricane Andrew, floods	27,017
5	Sep. 11, 2001	U.S.	Terror attacks on WTC, Pentagon and other buildings	25,129
6	Jan. 17, 1994	U.S.	Northridge earthquake (Mw 6.7)	24,455
7	Sep. 6, 2008	U.S., Gulf of Mexico, Caribbean	Hurricane Ike	22,343
8	Feb. 22, 2011	New Zealand	Earthquake (Mw 6.1), aftershocks	16,853
9	Sep. 2, 2004	U.S., Caribbean, Venezuela	Hurricane Ivan, damage to oil rigs	16,180
10	Jul. 27, 2011	Thailand	Heavy monsoon rains, extreme flooding	15,799

[1]Property and business interruption losses, excludes life and liability losses. Includes flood losses in the United States insured via the National Flood Insurance Program. Adjusted to 2015 dollars by Swiss Re.

Note: Loss data shown here may differ from figures shown elsewhere for the same event due to differences in the date of publication, the geographical area covered and other criteria used by organizations collecting the data.

Source: Swiss Re, sigma, 1/2016.

Top 10 Deadliest World Catastrophes, 2015

Rank	Date	Country	Event	Victims[1]
1	Apr. 25	Nepal, India, China, Bangladesh	Earthquake (Mw 7.8), avalanche on Mount Everest, aftershocks	8,960
2	May 21	India	Heatwave	2,248
3	Jun. 1	Pakistan	Heatwave	1,270
4	Jul. 29	Europe	Heatwave	1,200
5	Apr. 19	Libyan Arab Jamahiriya	Boat carrying migrants capsizes	822
6	Sep. 23	Saudi Arabia	Stampede and crush at the annual Hajj pilgrimage	769
7	Jan. 12	Malawi, Mozambique, Zimbabwe	Severe floods	451
8	Jun. 1	China	Cruise ship hit by strong winds and rains capsizes on Yangtze River	442
9	Apr. 13	Italy, Mediterranean Sea	Boat carrying migrants capsizes	400
10	Oct. 26	Afghanistan, Pakistan, India	Earthquake (Mw 7.5)	399

[1]Dead and missing.

Source: Swiss Re, *sigma*, No. 1/2016.

Top 10 Deadliest World Catastrophes, 1970-2015

Rank	Date	Country	Event	Victims[1]
1	Nov. 11, 1970	Bangladesh	Storm and flood catastrophe	300,000
2	Jul. 28, 1976	China	Earthquake (M 7.6)	255,000
3	Jan. 12, 2010	Haiti	Earthquake (Mw 7.0), aftershocks	222,570
4	Dec. 26, 2004	Indonesia, Thailand et al.	Earthquake (Mw 9), tsunami in Indian Ocean	220,000
5	May 2, 2008	Myanmar (Burma), Bay of Bengal	Tropical cyclone Nargis, Irrawaddy Delta flooded	138,300
6	Apr. 29, 1991	Bangladesh	Tropical cyclone Gorky	138,000
7	May 12, 2008	China	Earthquake (Mw 7.9) in Sichuan, aftershocks	87,449
8	Oct. 8, 2005	Pakistan, India, Afghanistan	Earthquake (Mw 7.6), aftershocks, landslides	74,310
9	May 31, 1970	Peru	Earthquake (M 7.9), massive avalanche and floods	66,000
10	Jun. 15, 2010	Russia, Czech Republic	Heat wave with temperatures up to 40° Celsius	55,630

[1]Dead and missing.

Source: Swiss Re, *sigma*, No. 1/2016.

Top 10 Costliest World Earthquakes And Tsunamis By Insured Losses, 1980-2015[1]

($ millions)

Rank	Date	Location	Losses when occurred		Fatalities
			Overall	Insured[2]	
1	Mar. 11, 2011	Japan: Aomori, Chiba, Fukushima, Ibaraki, Iwate, Miyagi, Tochigi, Tokyo, Yamagata. Includes tsunami.	$210,000	$40,000	15,880
2	Feb. 22, 2011	New Zealand: Canterbury, Christchurch, Lyttelton	24,000	16,500	185
3	Jan. 17, 1994	U.S. (CA): Northridge, Los Angeles, San Fernando Valley, Ventura, Orange	44,000	15,300	61
4	Feb. 27, 2010	Chile: Concepcion, Metropolitana, Rancagua, Talca, Temuco, Valparaiso. Includes tsunami.	30,000	8,000	520
5	Sep. 4, 2010	New Zealand: Canterbury, Christchurch, Avonside, Omihi, Timaru, Kaiapoi, Lyttelton	10,000	7,400	0
6	Jan. 17, 1995	Japan: Hyogo, Kobe, Osaka, Kyoto	100,000	3,000	6,430
7	Jun. 13, 2011	New Zealand: Canterbury, Christchurch, Lyttelton	2,700	2,100	1
8	May 20 and May 29, 2012	Italy: Emilia-Romagna, San Felice del Panaro, Cavezzo, Rovereto di Novi, Carpi, Concordia. Series of earthquakes.	16,000	1,600	18
9	Dec. 26, 2004	Sri Lanka, Indonesia, Thailand, India, Bangladesh, Myanmar, Maldives, Malaysia. Includes tsunami.	10,000	1,000	220,000
10	Oct. 17, 1989	U.S. (CA): Loma Prieta, Santa Cruz, San Francisco, Oakland, Berkeley, Silicon Valley	10,000	960	68

[1]As of March 2016. Ranked on insured losses when occurred. [2]Based on property losses including, if applicable, agricultural, offshore, marine, aviation and National Flood Insurance Program losses in the United States and may differ from data shown elsewhere.

Source: © 2016 Munich Re, Geo Risks Research, NatCatSERVICE.

MAJOR CATASTROPHES: UNITED STATES

Property Claim Services (PCS®), a Verisk Analytics® business, defines a catastrophe as an event that causes $25 million or more in insured property losses and affects a significant number of property/casualty (P/C) policyholders and insurers. PCS estimates represent anticipated insured losses from natural and man-made catastrophes on an industrywide basis, reflecting the total net insurance payment for personal and commercial property lines of insurance covering fixed property; vehicles; boats; related-property items; business interruption; and additional living expenses. They exclude loss adjustment expenses. P/C insurance industry catastrophes losses in the United States fell slightly to $15.2 billion in 2015 from $15.5 billion in 2014, according to PCS. The number of claims totaled 2.0 million compared with 2.1 million in 2014. The number of catastrophes rose to 39 from 31 in 2014, the highest number of catastrophes in the 10 years from 2006 to 2015. Munich Re estimates shown below are for natural catastrophes only.

Natural Catastrophe Losses In The United States, 2015[1] ($ millions)

Event	Number of relevant events[2]	Fatalities	Overall losses	Insured losses[3]
Severe thunderstorm	37	114	$13,400	$9,600
Winter storms and cold waves	11	98	4,700	3,500
Flood, flash flood	12	86	3,800	1,100
Earthquake and geophysical	0	0	minor	minor
Tropical cyclone	2	5	100	60
Wildfire, heat waves and drought	19	14	4,400	1,900
Other	4	7	minor	minor
Total	**85**	**324**	**$26,400**	**$16,100**

[1]As of February 2016. [2]Events that have caused at least one fatality or losses of $3 million or more. [3]Based on property losses including, if applicable, agricultural, offshore, marine, aviation and National Flood Insurance Program losses and may differ from data shown elsewhere.

Source: Munich Re NatCatSERVICE; Property Claim Services®, a unit of ISO®, a Verisk Analytics® business. © 2016 Munich Re, NatCatSERVICE.

Catastrophes By Quarter, 2015[1] ($ millions)

Quarter	Estimated insured losses	Number of catastrophes
1	$3,584	9
2	7,048	15
3	2,451	5
4	2,129	10
Full year	**$15,212**	**39**

[1]Includes catastrophes causing insured property losses of at least $25 million in 1997 dollars and affecting a significant number of policy-holders and insurers. Excludes losses covered by the federally administered National Flood Insurance Program.

Source: Property Claim Services®, a unit of ISO®, a Verisk Analytics® business.

Top Five States By Insured Catastrophe Losses, 2015[1] ($ millions)

Rank	State	Estimated insured loss
1	Texas	$3,382.9
2	California	1,229.8
3	Massachusetts	1,192.0
4	Illinois	969.2
5	Oklahoma	942.6

[1]Includes catastrophes causing insured property losses of at least $25 million in 1997 dollars and affecting a significant number of policy-holders and insurers. Excludes losses covered by the federally administered National Flood Insurance Program.

Source: Property Claim Services (PCS®), a Verisk Analytics® business.

8. LOSSES

Major Catastrophes: United States

Estimated Insured Property Losses, U.S. Catastrophes, 2006-2015[1]

Year	Number of catastrophes	Number of claims (millions)	Dollars when occurred ($ billions)	In 2015 dollars[2] ($ billions)
2006	31	2.3	$9.2	$10.7
2007	23	1.2	6.7	7.6
2008	36	4.1	27.0	29.9
2009	27	2.2	10.5	11.6
2010	33	2.4	14.3	15.5
2011	30	4.9	33.6	35.7
2012	26	4.0	35.0	36.5
2013	28	1.8	12.9	13.2
2014	31	2.1	15.5	15.6
2015	39	2.0	15.2	15.2

[1]Includes catastrophes causing insured property losses of at least $25 million in 1997 dollars and affecting a significant number of policyholders and insurers. Excludes losses covered by the federally administered National Flood Insurance Program. [2]Adjusted for inflation through 2015 by ISO using the GDP implicit price deflator.

Source: Property Claim Services (PCS®), a Verisk Analytics® business.

Top 10 Costliest Catastrophes, United States[1] ($ millions)

Rank	Date	Peril	Estimated insured property loss	
			Dollars when occurred	In 2015 dollars [2]
1	Aug. 2005	Hurricane Katrina	$41,100	$49,047
2	Sep. 2001	Fire, explosion: World Trade Center, Pentagon terrorist attacks	18,779	24,613
3	Aug. 1992	Hurricane Andrew	15,500	24,111
4	Oct. 2012	Hurricane Sandy	18,750	19,563
5	Jan. 1994	Northridge, CA earthquake	12,500	18,597
6	Sep. 2008	Hurricane Ike	12,500	13,826
7	Oct. 2005	Hurricane Wilma	10,300	12,292
8	Aug. 2004	Hurricane Charley	7,475	9,207
9	Sep. 2004	Hurricane Ivan	7,110	8,758
10	Apr. 2011	Flooding, hail and wind including the tornadoes that struck Tuscaloosa and other locations	7,300	7,757

[1]Property losses only. Excludes flood damage covered by the federally administered National Flood Insurance Program. [2]Adjusted for inflation through 2015 by ISO using the GDP implicit price deflator.

Source: Property Claim Services (PCS®), a Verisk Analytics® business.

Inflation-Adjusted U.S. Insured Catastrophe Losses By Cause Of Loss, 1996-2015[1]
(2015 $ billions)

	Events including tornadoes[2]	$162.5	40.2%
	Hurricanes and tropical storms	158.6	39.3
	Winter storms	30.4	7.5
	Terrorism	24.6	6.1
	Other wind/hail/flood	19.9	4.9
	Fires[3]	7.3	1.8
	Other[4]	0.8	0.2
	Total	**$404.1**	**100.0%**

[1]Adjusted for inflation through 2015 by ISO using the GDP implicit price deflator. Excludes catastrophes causing direct losses less than $25 million in 1997 dollars. Excludes flood damage covered by the federally administered National Flood Insurance Program. [2]Includes other wind, hail, and/or flood losses associated with catastrophes involving tornadoes. [3]Includes wildland fires. [4]Includes losses from civil disorders, water damage, utility service disruptions, and any workers compensation catastrophes generating losses in excess of PCS's threshold after adjusting for inflation.

Source: Property Claim Services (PCS®), a Verisk Analytics® business.

Top Three States By Inflation-Adjusted Insured Catastrophe Losses, 1986-2015[1]
(2015 $ billions)

	Rest of the U.S.[2]	$347.8	67.5%
	Florida	68.6	13.3
	Texas	55.0	10.7
	New York	44.0	8.5
	Total	**$515.4**	**100.0%**

[1]Adjusted for inflation through 2015 by ISO using the GDP implicit price deflator. Excludes catastrophes causing direct losses less than $25 million in 1997 dollars. Excludes flood damage covered by the federally administered National Flood Insurance Program. [2]Includes the other 47 states plus Washington, D.C., Puerto Rico and the U.S. Virgin Islands.

Source: Property Claim Services (PCS®), a Verisk Analytics® business.

HURRICANES

Hurricanes are tropical cyclones. A hurricane's winds revolve around a center of low pressure, expressed in millibars (mb) or inches of mercury. Hurricanes are categorized on the Saffir-Simpson Hurricane Wind Scale, which has a range of from 1 to 5, based on the hurricane's intensity at the time of landfall at the location experiencing the strongest winds. The scale provides examples of the type of damage and impacts in the United States associated with winds of the indicated intensity. It does not address the potential for other hurricane-related phenomena such as storm surge, rainfall-induced floods and tornadoes. The Saffir-Simpson Hurricane Wind Scale was introduced in 2009 and modified in 2010 and 2012. It replaced the Saffir-Simpson Scale, which tied specific storm surge and flooding effects to each category of hurricane. The National Oceanic and Atmospheric Administration found that storm surge values varied widely, depending on the size of the storm, among several other factors, and thus often fell significantly outside the ranges suggested in the original scale.

Insured losses from hurricanes rose in the past decade as hurricane activity intensified. When adjusted for inflation, eight of the 10 costliest hurricanes in U.S. history have struck since 2004. In addition to the increase in storm activity, construction along the Gulf and East Coasts has continued to develop and property values have increased, resulting in higher loss exposure.

The Saffir-Simpson Hurricane Wind Scale

Category [1]	Sustained wind speed (mph)	Wind damage	Historical example
1	74-95	Very dangerous winds will produce some damage	Hurricane Dolly, 2008, South Padre Island, Texas
2	96-110	Extremely dangerous winds will cause extensive damage	Hurricane Frances, 2004, Port St. Lucie, Florida
3	111-129	Devastating damage will occur	Hurricane Ivan, 2004, Gulf Shores, Alabama
4	130-156	Catastrophic damage will occur	Hurricane Charley, 2004, Punta Gorda, Florida
5	157 or higher	Catastrophic damage will occur	Hurricane Andrew, 1992, Cutler Ridge, Florida

[1]Category 3 or higher storms are classified as "major".

Source: U.S. Department of Commerce, National Oceanic and Atmospheric Administration, National Hurricane Center.

Catastrophic Hurricane Losses In The United States, 2006-2015 ($ billions)

Year	Number of catastrophic hurricanes[1]	Estimated insured loss		Year	Number of catastrophic hurricanes[1]	Estimated insured loss	
		Dollars when occurred	In 2015 dollars[2]			Dollars when occurred	In 2015 dollars[2]
2006	0[3]	NA	NA	2011	1	$4.3	$4.6
2007	0[3]	NA	NA	2012	2	19.7	20.5
2008	3	$15.2	$16.8	2013	0[3]	NA	NA
2009	0[3]	NA	NA	2014	0[3]	NA	NA
2010	0[3]	NA	NA	2015	0[3]	NA	NA

[1]Hurricanes causing insured property losses of at least $25 million in 1997 dollars and affecting a significant number of policyholders and insurers. Excludes losses covered by the federally administered National Flood Insurance Program. [2]Adjusted for inflation through 2015 by ISO using the GDP implicit price deflator. [3]No hurricane met the PCS definition of a catastrophe. NA=Not applicable.

Source: Property Claim Services (PCS®), a Verisk Analytics® business.

The following chart from PCS ranks historic hurricanes based on their insured losses, adjusted for inflation. The chart beneath it, from AIR Worldwide, estimates insured property losses from notable hurricanes from past years, if they were to hit the nation again today with the same meteorological parameters.

Top 10 Costliest Hurricanes In The United States[1] ($ millions)

Rank	Date	Location	Hurricane	Estimated insured loss[2]	
				Dollars when occurred	In 2015 dollars[3]
1	Aug. 25-30, 2005	AL, FL, GA, LA, MS, TN	Hurricane Katrina	$41,100	$49,047
2	Aug. 24-26, 1992	FL, LA	Hurricane Andrew	15,500	24,111
3	Oct. 28-31, 2012	CT, DC, DE, MA, MD, ME, NC, NH, NJ, NY, OH, PA, RI, VA, VT, WV	Hurricane Sandy	18,750	19,563
4	Sep. 12-14, 2008	AR, IL, IN, KY, LA, MO, OH, PA, TX	Hurricane Ike	12,500	13,826
5	Oct. 24, 2005	FL	Hurricane Wilma	10,300	12,292
6	Aug. 13-14, 2004	FL, NC, SC	Hurricane Charley	7,475	9,207
7	Sep. 15-21, 2004	AL, DE, FL, GA, LA, MD, MS, NC, NJ, NY, OH, PA, TN, VA, WV	Hurricane Ivan	7,110	8,758
8	Sep. 17-22, 1989	GA, NC, PR, SC, UV, VA	Hurricane Hugo	4,195	7,152
9	Sep. 20-26, 2005	AL, AR, FL, LA, MS, TN, TX	Hurricane Rita	5,627	6,715
10	Sep. 3-9, 2004	FL, GA, NC, NY, SC	Hurricane Frances	4,595	5,660

[1]Includes hurricanes occurring through 2015. [2]Property coverage only. Excludes flood damage covered by the federally administered National Flood Insurance Program. [3]Adjusted for inflation through 2015 by ISO using the GDP implicit price deflator.

Source: Property Claim Services (PCS®), a Verisk Analytics® business.

Estimated Insured Losses For The Top 10 Historical Hurricanes Based On Current Exposures[1] ($ billions)

Rank	Date	Event	Category	Insured loss (current exposures)
1	Sep. 18, 1926	Miami Hurricane	4	$125
2	Aug. 24, 1992	Hurricane Andrew	5	57
3	Sep. 17, 1947	1947 Fort Lauderdale Hurricane	4	53
4	Sep. 17, 1928	Great Okeechobee Hurricane	5	51
5	Aug. 29, 2005	Hurricane Katrina	3[2]	45
6	Sep. 9, 1965	Hurricane Betsy	3	45
7	Sep. 9, 1900	Galveston Hurricane of 1900	4	41
8	Sep. 10, 1960	Hurricane Donna	4	35
9	Sep. 21, 1938	The Great New England Hurricane	3	33
10	Sep. 15, 1950	Hurricane Easy	3	23

[1]Modeled loss to property, contents and business interruption and additional living expenses for residential, mobile home, commercial and auto exposures as of December 31, 2011. Losses include demand surge. [2]Refers to Katrina's second landfall in Louisiana.

Source: AIR Worldwide Corporation.

Hurricanes And Related Deaths In The United States, 1996-2015

Year	Total hurricanes[1]	Made landfall as hurricane in the U.S.	Deaths[2]	Year	Total hurricanes[1]	Made landfall as hurricane in the U.S.	Deaths[2]
1996	3	2	59	2006	5	0	0
1997	1	1	6	2007	6	1	1
1998	10	3	23	2008	8	4[4]	41
1999	8	2	60	2009	3	1[5]	6
2000	8	0	4	2010	12	0	11
2001	9	0	42	2011	7	1	44
2002	4	1	5	2012	10	1[6]	83
2003	7	2	24	2013	2	0	1
2004	9	6[3]	59	2014	6	1	2
2005	15	7	1,518	2015	4	0	3

[1]Atlantic Basin. [2]Includes fatalities from high winds of less than hurricane force from tropical storms. [3]One hurricane (Alex) is considered a strike but not technically a landfall. [4]Includes one hurricane (Hanna) which made landfall as a tropical storm. [5]Hurricane Ida, which made landfall as a tropical storm. [6]Excludes Hurricane Sandy which made landfall as a post-tropical storm.

Source: Insurance Information Institute from data supplied by the U.S. Department of Commerce, National Oceanic and Atmospheric Administration, National Hurricane Center.

Top 10 Deadliest Mainland U.S. Hurricanes[1]

Rank	Year	Hurricane/location	Category	Deaths
1	1900	Texas (Galveston)	4	8,000[2]
2	1928	Florida (Southeast; Lake Okeechobee)	4	2,500[3]
3	2005	Hurricane Katrina (Southeast Louisiana; Mississippi)	3	1,200
4	1893	Louisiana (Cheniere Caminanda)	4	1,100-1,400[4]
5	1893	South Carolina; Georgia (Sea Islands)	3	1,000-2,000
6	1881	Georgia; South Carolina	2	700
7	1957	Hurricane Audrey (Southwest Louisiana; North Texas)	4	416
8	1935	Florida (Keys)	5	408
9	1856	Louisiana (Last Island)	4	400
10	1926	Florida (Miami, Pensacola); Mississippi; Alabama	4	372

[1]Based on a National Hurricane Center analysis of mainland tropical cyclones from 1851-2010. [2]Could be as high as 12,000. [3]Could be as high as 3,000. [4]Total including offshore deaths is near 2,000.

Source: U.S. Department of Commerce, National Oceanic and Atmospheric Administration, National Hurricane Center.

WINTER STORMS

Top 15 Costliest U.S. Winter Events By Insured Losses, 1980-2015[1] ($ millions)

Rank	Date	Event	Location	Losses when occurred		Deaths
				Overall	Insured[2]	
1	Feb. 16-25, 2015	Winter storm, winter damage	CT, DC, DE, IL, KY, MA, MD, ME, MI, NC, NH, NJ, NY, OH, PA, RI, SC, TN, VA, VT	$2,800	$2,100	39
2	Mar. 11-14, 1993	Blizzard	AL, CT, DE, FL, GA, KY, LA, MA, MD, ME, MS, NC, NH, NJ, NY, OH, PA, RI, SC, TN, TX, VA, VT, WV	5,000	2,000	270
3	Jan. 5-8, 2014	Winter damage, cold wave	AL, CT, GA, IL, IN, KY, MA, MD, ME, MI, MN, MO, MS, NC, NE, NJ, NY, OH, PA, SC, TN, VA, WI	2,500	1,700	NA
4	Apr. 13-17, 2007	Winter storm, tornadoes, floods	CT, DE, DC, GA, LA, MA, MD, ME, MS, NC, NH, NJ, NY, PA, RI, SC, TX, VA, VT, WV	2,000	1,600	19
5	Mar. 13-15, 2010	Winter storm, floods	CT, MA, NH, NJ, NY, PA, RI	1,700	1,200	11
6	Apr. 7-11, 2013	Winter storm	CA, IN, KS, MO, NE, SD, WI	1,500	1,200	NA
7	Dec. 10-13, 1992	Winter storm	CT, DE, NJ, NY, MA, MD, NE, PA, RI, VA	3,000	1,000	19
8	Jan. 31-Feb. 3, 2011	Winter storm, snowstorms, winter damage	CT, IA, IL, IN, KS, MA, ME, MO, NY, OH, PA, RI, TX, WI	1,300	980	36
9	Dec. 17-30, 1983	Winter damage, cold wave	FL, GA, ID, IL, IN, IA, KS, KY, LA, MD, MA, MI, MN, MS, MO, MT, NE, NJ, NY, NC, ND, OH, OK, OR, PA, RI, SC, SD, TN, TX, UT, VA, WA, WV, WI, WY	1,000	880	500
10	Jan. 17-20, 1994	Winter damage, cold wave	CT, DE, IN, IL, KY, MA, ME, MD, NC, NH, NJ, NY, OH, PA, RI, SC, TN, VA, VT, WV	1,000	800	70
11	Feb. 10-12, 1994	Winter damage	AL, AR, GA, LA, MS, NC, OK, SC, TN, TX, VA	3,000	800	9
12	Jan. 1-4, 1999	Winter storm	AL, AR, CT, DE, FL, GA, IL, IN, LA, MO, MA, MD, ME, MS, NC, NJ, NY,OH, OK, PA, RI, SC, TN, TX, VA, WV	1,000	780	25
13	Jan. 4-9, 2008	Winter storm	AR, CA, CO, IL, IN, KS, MI, MO, NV, NY, OH, OK, OR, WA, WI	1,000	750	12
14	Jan. 31-Feb. 6, 1996	Winter damage	AL, AR, CT, DE, FL, GA, IA, IL, IN, KS, KY, LA, MA, MD, MI, MO, MS, NC, NE, NJ, NY, OH, OK, PA, SC, TN, TX, VA, WV, WI	1,500	740	16
15	Feb. 24-25, 2013	Blizzard, winter damage	LA, OK, TX	1,000	690	1

[1]Costliest U.S. blizzards and winter storms/damages based on insured losses when occurred. [2]Based on property losses including, if applicable, agricultural, offshore, marine, aviation and National Flood Insurance Program losses in the United States and may differ from data shown elsewhere. NA=Data not available.

Source: © 2016 Munich Re, NatCatSERVICE, as of September 2016.

FLOODS

Superstorm Sandy was the second costliest U.S. flood, based on National Flood Insurance Program payouts as of June 2016. The figures below are preliminary, as claims are still being processed.

Top 10 Most Significant Flood Events By National Flood Insurance Program Payouts[1]

Rank	Date	Event	Location	Number of paid losses	Amount paid ($ millions)	Average paid loss
1	Aug. 2005	Hurricane Katrina	AL, FL, GA, LA, MS, TN	167,985	$16,318	$97,140
2	Oct. 2012	Superstorm Sandy	CT, DC, DE, MA, MD, ME, NC, NH, NJ, NY, OH, PA, RI, VA, VT, WV	130,352	8,309	63,745
3	Sep. 2008	Hurricane Ike	AR, IL, IN, KY, LA, MO, OH, PA, TX	46,658	2,697	57,796
4	Sep. 2004	Hurricane Ivan	AL, DE, FL, GA, LA, MD, MS, NJ, NY, NC, OH, PA, TN, VA, WV	28,297	1,612	56,974
5	Aug. 2011	Hurricane Irene	CT, DC, DE, MA, MD, ME, NC, NH, NJ, NY, PA, RI, VA, VT	44,271	1,340	30,278
6	Jun. 2001	Tropical Storm Allison	FL, LA, MS, NJ, PA, TX	30,671	1,105	36,028
7	May 1995	Louisiana Flood	LA	31,343	585	18,667
8	Aug. 2012	Tropical Storm Isaac	AL, FL, LA, MS	12,041	555	46,073
9	Sep. 2003	Hurricane Isabel	DE, MD, NJ, NY, NC, PA, VA, WV	19,938	500	25,091
10	Sep. 2005	Hurricane Rita	AL, AR, FL, LA, MS, TN, TX	9,529	475	49,821

[1]Includes events from 1978 to June 30, 2016, as of September 9, 2016. Defined by the National Flood Insurance Program as an event that produces at least 1,500 paid losses. Stated in dollars when occurred.

Source: U.S. Department of Homeland Security, Federal Emergency Management Agency; U.S. Department of Commerce, National Oceanic and Atmospheric Administration, National Hurricane Center.

TORNADOES

A tornado is a violently rotating column of air that extends from a thunderstorm and comes into contact with the ground, according to the National Oceanic and Atmospheric Administration (NOAA). In an average year about 1,000 tornadoes are reported nationwide, according to NOAA. Tornado intensity is measured by the enhanced Fujita (EF) scale. The scale rates tornadoes on a scale of 0 through 5, based on the amount and type of wind damage. It incorporates 28 different damage indicators, based on damage to a wide variety of structures ranging from trees to shopping malls.

The Fujita Scale For Tornadoes

Category	Damage	Original F scale[1] Wind speed (mph)	Enhanced F scale[2] 3-second gust (mph)
F-0	Light	40-72	65-85
F-1	Moderate	73-112	86-110
F-2	Considerable	113-157	111-135
F-3	Severe	158-207	136-165
F-4	Devastating	208-260	166-200
F-5	Incredible	261-318	Over 200

[1]Original scale: wind speeds represent fastest estimated speeds over one quarter of a mile. [2]Enhanced scale: wind speeds represent maximum 3-second gusts.

Source: U.S. Department of Commerce, National Oceanic and Atmospheric Administration.

Tornado Losses

Tornadoes accounted for 40.2 percent of inflation-adjusted insured catastrophe losses from 1996 to 2015, according to Property Claim Services (PCS®), a Verisk Analytics® business. In 2015 insured losses from U.S. tornadoes/thunderstorms totaled $9.6 billion, down from $12.3 billion in 2014. The number of tornadoes rose to 1,177 in 2015 from 886 in 2014, according to the National Oceanic and Atmospheric Administration (NOAA). There were 36 direct fatalities from tornadoes in 2015, down from 47 in 2014, according to NOAA. May was the top month for tornadoes in 2015, with 381 tornadoes. The United States experiences more tornadoes than any other country, according to a 2013 report by Lloyd's of London.

Preliminary NOAA data show that there were almost 900 tornadoes in 2016 through early October, compared with 955 during the same period in 2015. On January 17 tornadoes developed in Florida with two fatalities. On February 23 and 24 tornadoes formed in Louisiana, Mississippi and Virginia resulting in two fatalities in Louisiana, one in Mississippi and four in Virginia. On April 27 one fatality resulted from a tornado in Texas and on May 9 tornadoes in Oklahoma killed two people. As of early October, 2016 fatalities reached 12.

Top 10 Costliest U.S. Catastrophes Involving Tornadoes[1]
($ millions)

Rank	Date	Location	Estimated insured loss[2]	
			Dollars when occurred	In 2015 dollars[3]
1	Apr. 22-28, 2011	AL, AR, GA, IL, KY, LA, MO, MS, OH, OK, TN, TX, VA	$7,300	$7,757
2	May 20-27, 2011	AR, GA, IA, IL, IN, KS, KY, MI, MN, MO, NC, NE, NY, OH, OK, PA, TN, TX, VA, WI	6,900	7,332
3	May 2-11, 2003	AL, AR, CO, GA, IA, IL, IN, KS, KY, MO, MS, NC, NE, OH, OK, SC, SD, TN	3,205	4,056
4	Oct. 4-6, 2010	AZ	2,700	2,928
5	Apr. 6-12, 2001	AR, CO, IA, IL, IN, KS, KY, MI, MN, MO, NE, OH, OK, PA, TX, WI	2,200	2,884
6	Mar. 2-3, 2012	AL, GA, IN, KY, OH, TN	2,500	2,608
7	Apr. 28-29, 2012	IL, IN, KY, MO, TX	2,500	2,608
8	May 12-16, 2010	IL, MD, OK, PA, TX	2,000	2,169
9	Apr. 27-May 3, 2002	AR, GA, IL, IN, KS, KY, MD, MO, MS, NC, NY, OH, PA, TN, TX, VA, WV	1,675	2,162
10	Apr. 13-15, 2006	IA, IL, IN, WI	1,850	2,142

[1]Based on data through May 31, 2016. [2]Property coverage only. In addition to losses due to tornadoes themselves, amounts may include losses due to hail, wind and flooding during the same event. [3]Adjusted for inflation through 2015 by ISO using the GDP implicit price deflator.

Source: Property Claim Services (PCS®), a Verisk Analytics® business.

The costliest U.S. catastrophe involving tornadoes occurred in April 2011, when a spate of twisters hit Tuscaloosa, Alabama, and other areas, causing $7.8 billion in insured losses in 2015 dollars.

The second costliest were the tornadoes that struck Joplin, Missouri, and other locations in May 2011, resulting in $7.3 billion in insured losses in 2015 dollars.

Number Of Tornadoes And Related Deaths Per Month, 2015[1]

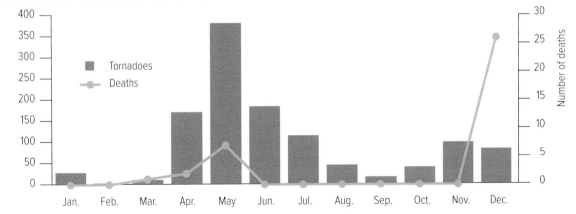

[1]Excludes Puerto Rico. A tornado that crosses state lines is counted as a single event in this chart.

Source: U.S. Department of Commerce, Storm Prediction Center, National Weather Service.

Tornadoes And Related Deaths In The United States, 1996-2015[1]

Year	Tornadoes	Deaths	Year	Tornadoes	Deaths
1996	1,173	25	2006	1,103	67
1997	1,148	67	2007	1,098	81
1998	1,424	130	2008	1,692	126
1999	1,345	94	2009	1,156	21
2000	1,071	40	2010	1,282	45
2001	1,216	40	2011	1,691	553
2002	941	55	2012	938	70
2003	1,376	54	2013	906	55
2004	1,819	36	2014	886	47
2005	1,264	38	2015	1,177	36

[1]Excludes Puerto Rico. A tornado that crosses state lines counts as one event.

Source: U.S. Department of Commerce, Storm Prediction Center, National Weather Service.

Top 10 States By Number Of Tornadoes, 2015[1]

Rank	State	Number of tornadoes
1	Texas	228
2	Kansas	178
3	Oklahoma	111
4	Illinois	82
5	Mississippi	63
6	Colorado	52
7	Missouri	48
8	Iowa	46
9	Nebraska	38
10	North Dakota	35

[1]Tornadoes that cross state lines are counted in every state in which they touch down.

Source: U.S. Department of Commerce, Storm Prediction Center, National Weather Service.

Tornadoes And Related Deaths By State, 2015[1]

State	Tornadoes	Fatalities	Rank[2]	State	Tornadoes	Fatalities	Rank[2]
Alabama	32	0	12	Montana	1	0	39
Alaska	0	0	[3]	Nebraska	38	0	9
Arizona	3	0	32	Nevada	2	0	37
Arkansas	25	2	14	New Hampshire	1	0	39
California	13	0	23	New Jersey	0	0	[3]
Colorado	52	0	6	New Mexico	4	0	30
Connecticut	0	0	[3]	New York	3	0	32
Delaware	1	0	39	North Carolina	10	0	26
D.C.	0	0	[3]	North Dakota	35	0	10
Florida	24	0	15	Ohio	6	0	29
Georgia	24	0	15	Oklahoma	111	2	3
Hawaii	0	0	[3]	Oregon	1	0	39
Idaho	1	0	39	Pennsylvania	12	0	25
Illinois	82	2	4	Rhode Island	0	0	[3]
Indiana	17	0	20	South Carolina	13	0	23
Iowa	46	0	8	South Dakota	26	0	13
Kansas	178	0	2	Tennessee	18	2	19
Kentucky	17	0	20	Texas	228	17	1
Louisiana	34	0	11	Utah	3	0	32
Maine	0	0	[3]	Vermont	0	0	[3]
Maryland	3	0	32	Virginia	7	0	28
Massachusetts	2	0	37	Washington	4	0	30
Michigan	9	0	27	West Virginia	3	0	32
Minnesota	24	0	15	Wisconsin	20	0	18
Mississippi	63	11	5	Wyoming	15	0	22
Missouri	48	0	7	**United States**	**1,259[4]**	**36**	

[1]Ranked by total number of tornadoes. [2]States with the same number receive the same ranking. [3]State had no tornadoes in 2015. [4]The U.S. total will not match data used in other charts because it counts tornadoes that cross state lines.

Source: U.S. Department of Commerce, Storm Prediction Center, National Weather Service.

EARTHQUAKES

The costliest U.S. earthquake, the 1994 Northridge quake, caused $15.3 billion in insured damages when it occurred (about $25 billion in 2015 dollars). It ranks as the fifth costliest U.S. disaster, based on insured property losses (in 2015 dollars), topped only by Hurricane Katrina, the attacks on the World Trade Center, Hurricane Andrew and superstorm Sandy. Eight of the costliest U.S. quakes, based on inflation-adjusted insured losses, were in California, according to Munich Re. In 2015 the biggest earthquake to strike the United States was a magnitude 6.9 quake that occurred on July 27 southwest of Umnak Island, Alaska. There was no damage due to the remote location. Seismicity continued to rise in 2015 in the central United States, with 32 earthquakes of magnitude 4.0 and greater in Kansas, Oklahoma and Texas compared with 17 in 2014. A magnitude 5.0 quake east of Challis, Idaho, hit on January 3, 2015.

Top 10 Costliest U.S. Earthquakes By Inflation-Adjusted Insured Losses[1]

| Rank | Date | Location | Overall losses when occurred | Insured losses[2] | | Fatalities |
				Dollars when occurred	In 2015 dollars[3]	
1	Jan. 17, 1994	California: Northridge, Los Angeles, San Fernando Valley, Ventura, Orange	$44,000	$15,300	$24,470	61
2	Apr. 18, 1906	California: San Francisco, Santa Rosa, San Jose	525	180	4,310[4]	3,000
3	Oct. 17, 1989	California: Loma Prieta, Santa Cruz, Oakland, San Francisco, Berkeley, Silicon Valley	10,000	960	1,830	68
4	Feb. 28, 2001	Washington: Olympia, Seattle, Tacoma; Oregon	2,000	300	400	1
5	Mar. 27-28, 1964	Alaska: Anchorage, Kodiak Island, Seward, Valdez, Portage, Whittier, Cordova, Homer, Seldovia	540	45	340	131
6	Feb. 9, 1971	California: San Fernando Valley, Los Angeles	550	35	200	65
7	Oct. 1, 1987	California: Los Angeles, Whittier	360	75	160	8
8	Aug. 24, 2014	California: Napa, Vallejo, Solano, Sonoma, American Canyon	700	150	150	1
9	Apr. 4, 2010	California: San Diego, Calexico, El Centro, Los Angeles, Imperial; Arizona: Phoenix, Yuma	150	100	110	0
10	Sep. 3, 2000	California: Napa	80	50	70	0

[1]Costliest U.S. earthquakes occurring from 1950 to 2015, based on insured losses when occurred. Includes the 1906 San Francisco, California, earthquake, for which reliable insured losses are available. [2]Based on property losses including, if applicable, agricultural, offshore, marine, aviation and National Flood Insurance Program losses in the United States and may differ from data shown elsewhere. [3]Inflation-adjusted to 2015 dollars by Munich Re. [4]Inflation-adjusted to 2015 dollars based on 1913 Bureau of Labor Statistics data (earliest year available).

Source: © 2016 Munich Re, NatCatSERVICE.

The previous chart ranks historic earthquakes based on their total insured property losses, adjusted for inflation. The chart below uses a computer model to measure the estimated impact of historical quakes according to current exposures. The 2012 analysis is based on AIR Worldwide's U.S. earthquake model. It makes use of the firm's property exposure database and takes into account the current number and value of exposed properties.

Estimated Insured Losses For The Top 10 Historical Earthquakes Based On Current Exposures[1] ($ billions)

Rank	Date	Location	Magnitude	Insured loss (current exposures)
1	Feb. 7, 1812	New Madrid, MO	7.7	$112
2	Apr. 18, 1906	San Francisco, CA	7.8	93
3	Aug. 31, 1886	Charleston, SC	7.3	44
4	Jun. 1, 1838	San Francisco, CA	7.4	30
5	Jan. 17, 1994	Northridge, CA	6.7	23
6	Oct. 21, 1868	Hayward, CA	7.0	23
7	Jan. 9, 1857	Fort Tejon, CA	7.9	8
8	Oct. 17, 1989	Loma Prieta, CA	6.3	7
9	Mar. 10, 1933	Long Beach, CA	6.4	5
10	Jul. 1, 1911	Calaveras, CA	6.4	4

[1]Modeled loss to property, contents, business interruption and additional living expenses for residential, mobile home, commercial and auto exposures as of December 31, 2011. Losses include demand surge and fire following earthquake. Policy conditions and earthquake insurance take-up rates are based on estimates by state insurance departments and client claims data.

Source: AIR Worldwide Corporation.

TERRORISM

Nearly 3,000 people perished in the September 11, 2001, terrorist attacks in New York, Washington and Pennsylvania, excluding the 19 hijackers. Total insured losses from the terrorist attacks on the World Trade Center in New York City and the Pentagon were about $43.6 billion in 2015 dollars, including property, life and liability insurance claim costs. Loss estimates may differ from estimates calculated by other organizations. It is the worst terrorist attack on record in terms of fatalities and insured property losses, which totaled about $25.2 billion (in 2015 dollars).

Top 20 Costliest Terrorist Acts By Insured Property Losses (2015 $ millions)

Rank	Date	Country	Location	Event	Insured property loss[1]	Fatalities
1	Sep. 11, 2001	U.S.	New York, Washington, DC, Pennsylvania	Hijacked airliners crash into World Trade Center and Pentagon	$25,152[2]	2,982
2	Apr. 24, 1993	U.K.	London	Bomb explodes near NatWest tower in the financial district	1,215	1
3	Jun. 15, 1996	U.K.	Manchester	Irish Republican Army (IRA) car bomb explodes near shopping mall	996	0
4	Apr. 10, 1992	U.K.	London	Bomb explodes in financial district	899	3
5	Feb. 26, 1993	U.S.	New York	Bomb explodes in garage of World Trade Center	837	6
6	Jul. 24, 2001	Sri Lanka	Colombo	Rebels destroy 3 airliners, 8 military aircraft and heavily damage 3 civilian aircraft	533	20
7	Feb. 9, 1996	U.K.	London	IRA bomb explodes in South Key Docklands	347	2
8	Jun. 23, 1985	North Atlantic	Irish Sea	Bomb explodes on board of an Air India Boeing 747	217	329
9	Apr. 19, 1995	U.S.	Oklahoma City, OK	Truck bomb crashes into government building	195	168
10	Sep. 12, 1970	Jordan	Zerqa, Dawson's Field (disused RAF airstrip in desert)	Hijacked Swissair DC-8, TWA Boeing 707, BOAC VC-10 dynamited on ground	170	0
11	Sep. 6, 1970	Egypt	Cairo	Hijacked PanAm B-747 dynamited on ground	148	0
12	Apr. 11, 1992	U.K.	London	Bomb explodes in financial district	128	0
13	Nov. 26, 2008	India	Mumbai	Attack on two hotels; Jewish center	113	172
14	Mar. 27, 1993	Germany	Weiterstadt	Bomb attack on a newly built, still unoccupied prison	95	0
15	Dec. 30, 2006	Spain	Madrid	Bomb explodes in car garage at Barajas Airport	78	2
16	Dec. 21, 1988	U.K.	Lockerbie	Bomb explodes on board of a PanAm Boeing 747	76	270
17	Jul. 25, 1983	Sri Lanka		Riot	63	0
18	Jul. 7, 2005	U.K.	London	Four bombs explode during rush hour in a tube and bus	63	52
19	Nov. 23, 1996	Comoros	Indian Ocean	Hijacked Ethiopian Airlines Boeing 767-260 ditched at sea	60	127
20	Mar. 17, 1992	Argentina	Buenos Aires	Bomb attack on Israel's embassy in Buenos Aires	51	24

[1]Includes bodily injury and aviation hull losses. Updated to 2015 dollars by the Insurance Information Institute using the U.S. Bureau of Labor Statistics CPI Inflation Calculator. [2]Differs from inflation-adjusted estimates made by other organizations due to the use of different deflators.
Source: Swiss Re.

NUCLEAR INCIDENTS

The International Atomic Energy Agency (IAEA) rates the severity of nuclear incidents on the International Nuclear and Radiological Event Scale (INES) from one (indicating an anomaly) to seven (indicating a major event). The scale considers an event's impact based on three criteria: its effect on people and the environment; whether it caused unsafe levels of radiation in a facility; and if preventive measures did not function as intended. Scales six and seven designate full meltdowns, where the nuclear fuel reactor core overheats and melts. Partial meltdowns, in which the fuel is damaged, are rated four or five.

Japan's Nuclear and Industrial Safety Agency assigned a provisional rating of seven to the March 2011 accident at Japan's Fukushima Daiichi nuclear power plant. The 1986 Chernobyl accident in the former Soviet Union is the only other incident to rate a seven. The Chernobyl incident killed 56 people directly and thousands of others indirectly through cancer and other diseases. The 2011 incident in Japan released high amounts of radiation and caused widespread evacuations in affected areas but no deaths to date.

The 1979 Three Mile Island accident in Harrisburg, Pennsylvania, the worst nuclear accident in the United States, was designated a five. Insurers paid about $71 million in liability claims and litigation costs associated with the accident. In addition to the liability payments to the public under the Price-Anderson Act, $300 million was paid by a pool of insurers to the operator of the damaged nuclear power plant under its property insurance policy.

Selected Examples Of Historic Nuclear Events, Classified By The INES[1]

Level	INES description	Example
1	Anomaly	Breach of operating limits at nuclear facilities
2	Incident	Atucha, Argentina, 2005 - Overexposure of a worker at a power reactor exceeding the annual limit
3	Serious incident	Sellafield, U.K., 2005 - Release of large quantity of radioactive material, contained within the installation
4	Accident with local consequences	Tokaimura, Japan, 1999 - Fatal exposure of workers following an event at a nuclear facility
5	Accident with wider consequences	3 Mile Island, U.S., 1979 - Severe damage to reactor core. Minimal breach of outside environment
6	Serious accident	Kyshtym, Russia, 1957 - Significant release of radioactive material from the explosion of high activity waste tank
7	Major accident	Chernobyl, Ukraine, 1986 - Widespread health and environmental effects from explosion in power plant

[1]International Nuclear and Radiological Event Scale.
Source: International Atomic Energy Agency. INES Flyer.

HAIL

Hail causes about $1 billion in damage to crops and property each year, according to the National Oceanic Atmospheric Administration (NOAA). Events involving wind, hail or flood accounted for $19.9 billion in insured catastrophe losses in 2015 dollars from 1996 to 2015 (not including payouts from the National Flood Insurance Program), according to Property Claim Services (PCS®), a Verisk Analytics® business. There were 5,412 major hail storms in 2015, according to the NOAA's Severe Storms database.

A report issued by Verisk Insurance Solutions® in August 2014 showed that over the 14 years from 2000 to 2013 U.S. insurers paid almost 9 million claims for hail losses, totaling more than $54 billion. Most of those losses—70 percent—occurred during the past six years. In addition to the higher number of claims, the average claim severity during the past six years was 65 percent higher than the period 2000 through 2007.

Hail Fatalities, Injuries And Damage, 2011-2015[1]

Year	Fatalities	Injuries	Property damage ($ millions)	Crop damage ($ millions)	Total damage ($ millions)
2011	0	31	$450.5	$81.9	$532.4
2012	0	54	2,414.4	93.9	2,508.3
2013	0	4	1,245.5	75.0	1,320.5
2014	0	23	1,416.9	293.2	1,710.1
2015	0	0	586.0	133.0	719.0

[1]Includes the 50 states, Puerto Rico, Guam and the Virgin Islands.
Source: U.S. Department of Commerce, National Oceanic and Atmospheric Administration, National Weather Service.

Top Five States By Number of Major Hail Events, 2015[1]

Rank	State	Number of hail events
1	Texas	783
2	Kansas	519
3	Nebraska	458
4	Oklahoma	349
5	South Dakota	283
	United States	**5,411**

[1]One inch in diameter or larger.
Source: U.S. Department of Commerce, National Oceanic and Atmospheric Administration, National Weather Service.

WILDFIRES

Fire plays an important role in the life of a forest, clearing away dead wood and undergrowth to make way for younger trees. But for much of the last century, fire-suppression policies have sought to extinguish wildfires as quickly as possible to preserve timber and real estate. This approach has led to the accumulation of brush and other vegetation that is easily ignited and serves as fuel for wildfires. Most of the large fires with significant property damage have occurred in California, where some of the fastest developing counties are in forest areas.

Wildfire Losses In The United States, 2006-2015[1] (2015 $ millions)

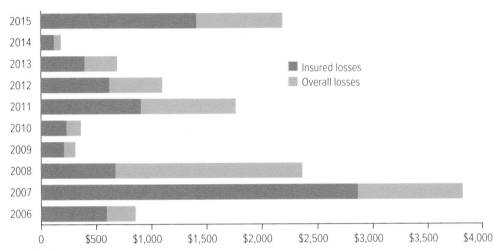

[1]Adjusted for inflation.

Source: © 2016 Munich Re, Geo Risks Research, NatCatSERVICE.

2015 And 2016 Wildfires

The 2015 fire season set a new record for the number of acres burned in the United States. Between January 1 and December 30, 2015, there were 68,151 wildfires, which burned 10,125,149 acres, according to the National Interagency Fire Center. During the same period in 2014, 63,417 fires burned 3,577,620 acres. The previous record was set in 2006 at 9,873,745 acres.

From January 1 to October 7, 2016, there were 46,618 wildfires, compared to 51,023 wildfires in the same period in 2015. About 4.8 million acres were burned in the 2016 period, compared with 9.1 million in 2015.

In May 2016 a wildfire broke out in Fort McMurray, Alberta, Canada. According to the Insurance Bureau of Canada damage caused by the wildfires totaled $3.58 billion, making it the most expensive disaster for insurers in the country's history.

Two fatalities were attributed to the fire and the entire population of about 90,000 were evacuated. About 2,400 homes and buildings were destroyed. More than 27,000 personal property claims were filed, averaging $81,000 each. The smoke from the fire could be seen as far south as Iowa.

Top 10 States For Wildfires Ranked By Number Of Fires And By Number Of Acres Burned, 2015

Rank	State	Number of fires		Rank	State	Number of acres burned
1	Texas	9,272		1	Alaska	5,111,404
2	California	8,745		2	Washington	1,137,664
3	North Carolina	3,828		3	California	893,362
4	Alabama	3,198		4	Idaho	804,094
5	Missouri	3,161		5	Oregon	685,809
6	Oregon	2,588		6	Montana	351,264
7	Montana	2,432		7	Texas	184,418
8	Florida	2,422		8	Arizona	160,152
9	Georgia	2,331		9	Oklahoma	100,382
10	Mississippi	2,294		10	Florida	73,432

Source: National Interagency Fire Center.

Top 10 Costliest Wildland Fires In The United States[1] ($ millions)

Rank	Date	Name, Location	Estimated insured loss	
			Dollars when occurred	In 2015 dollars[2]
1	Oct. 20-21, 1991	Oakland Hills Fire, CA	$1,700	$2,705
2	Oct. 21-24, 2007	Witch Fire, CA	1,300	1,466
3	Oct. 25-Nov. 4, 2003	Cedar Fire, CA	1,060	1,342
4	Oct. 25-Nov. 3, 2003	Old Fire, CA	975	1,234
5	Sep. 12-14, 2015	Valley Fire, CA	921	921
6	Nov. 2-3, 1993	Topanga Fire, CA	375	570
7	Sep. 4-9, 2011	Bastrop County Complex Fire, TX	530	563
8	Oct. 27-28, 1993	Laguna Canyon Fire, CA	350	532
9	Jun. 24-28, 2012	Waldo Canyon Fire, CO	450	470
10	Jun. 27-Jul. 2, 1990	Painted Cave Fire, CA	265	436

[1]Property coverage only for catastrophic fires. Effective January 1, 1997, ISO's Property Claim Services (PCS) unit defines catastrophes as events that cause more than $25 million in insured property damage and that affect a significant number of insureds and insurers. From 1982 to 1996, PCS used a $5 million threshold in defining catastrophes. Before 1982, PCS used a $1 million threshold. [2]Adjusted for inflation through 2015 by ISO using the GDP implicit price deflator.

Source: Property Claim Services (PCS®), a Verisk Analytics® business.

Wildfire Exposure

A 2015 study by CoreLogic identifies almost 900,000 residential properties across 13 states in the western U.S. currently at high or very high risk of wildfire damage. They represent a combined total property value estimated at more than $237 billion. Of the total properties identified, 192,000 homes fall into the very high risk category, with total residential exposure valued at more than $49 billion. Another analysis, conducted by Verisk Analytics®, identified the 10 states most prone to wildfire, based on the number and percentage of homes at high or extreme wildfire risk. California had the most households at risk (about 2 million), while Idaho had the highest percentage of households at risk (24 percent).

Total Potential Exposure To Wildfire Damage By Risk Category, 2014[1] ($ billions)

State	Low	Moderate	High	Very high
Arizona	$9.64	$0.98	$1.76	$1.57
California	75.84	61.92	89.35	16.10
Colorado	18.63	11.53	14.58	13.91
Idaho	9.20	5.56	3.71	2.62
Montana	14.63	4.43	2.29	2.40
Nevada	4.24	5.19	4.57	0.16
New Mexico	11.65	4.62	7.07	2.46
Oklahoma	31.92	16.77	0.03	0.00
Oregon	8.24	9.49	11.91	3.20
Texas	59.53	147.68	48.26	6.33
Utah	2.85	3.93	0.77	0.01
Washington	84.07	18.08	2.88	0.51
Wyoming	3.68	2.62	0.49	0.33
Total, states shown	$331.27	$292.81	$187.66	$49.61

[1]Reconstruction value of single-family residences at risk.

Source: CoreLogic, Inc., a data and analytics company.

Top 10 Most Wildfire-Prone States, 2013

By households			By percent		
Rank	State	Households at high or extreme risk from wildfires[1]	Rank	State	Percent of households at high or extreme risk from wildfires
1	California	1,989,100	1	Idaho	24.1%
2	Texas	1,299,800	2	Colorado	16.9
3	Colorado	373,600	3	California	14.5
4	Washington	163,400	4	New Mexico	13.6
5	Idaho	160,800	5	Texas	13.0
6	Oregon	159,800	6	Utah	12.8
7	Arizona	159,100	7	Oregon	9.5
8	Utah	125,500	8	Washington	5.7
9	New Mexico	122,600	9	Arizona	5.6
10	Nevada	59,100	10	Nevada	5.1

By insured wildfire loss		
Rank	State	Largest insured wildfire loss (year)
1	California	$1.7 billion (1991)
2	Texas	530 million (2011)
3	Colorado	450 million (2012)
4	New Mexico	140 million (2000)
5	Arizona	120 million (2002)
6	Idaho	NA
7	Nevada	NA
8	Oregon	NA
9	Utah	NA
10	Washington	NA

[1]Number of households is based on data from the 2010 U.S. Census.

NA=Data not available.

Source: Verisk Insurance Solutions – Underwriting and Verisk Climate units of Verisk Analytics®.

FIRE

Great strides have been made in constructing fire-resistant buildings and improving fire-suppression techniques, both of which have reduced the incidence of fire. However, in terms of property losses, these advances have been somewhat offset by increases in the number of and value of buildings. In 2015, on average, a fire department responded to a fire every 23 seconds in the United States, according to the National Fire Protection Association. A structure fire occurred every 63 seconds, a residential structure fire occurred every 86 seconds and an outside property fire occurred every 52 seconds.

Fire Losses In The United States, 2006-2015[1]

Year	Property loss ($ millions)	Loss per capita[2]
2006	$20,340	$68.17
2007	24,399	81.00
2008	24,734	81.34
2009	22,911	74.68
2010	20,486	66.22
2011	19,511	62.59
2012	23,977	76.33
2013	19,054	60.22
2014	21,801	68.36
2015	21,020	65.40

[1]Including allowances for FAIR Plan and uninsured losses. [2]Calculated by the Insurance Information Institute using ISO property loss and population estimates from the U.S. Census Bureau, Population Division.
Source: ISO®, a Verisk Analytics® business; U.S. Census Bureau, Population Division.

Fire Losses In The United States, By Line Of Insurance, 2015[1]

Homeowners	52.1%
Fire	32.3
Commercial multiple peril	15.6

[1]Estimated. Includes FAIR plan and uninsured losses.
Source: ISO®, a Verisk Analytics® business.

Structure fires caused $10.3 billion in damage in 2015. The majority of the damage ($7.2 billion) was to residential properties, according to the National Fire Protection Association.

Structure Fires, 2006-2015[1]

Year	Number of fires	Year	Number of fires
2006	524,000	2011	484,500
2007	530,500	2012	480,500
2008	515,000	2013	487,500
2009	480,500	2014	494,000
2010	482,000	2015	501,500

Source: Reproduced with permission from *Fire Loss in the United States During 2015* by Hylton J.G. Haynes, ©National Fire Protection Association.

Civilian (Nonfirefighter) Fire Deaths And Injuries By Property Use, 2015

Property use	Civilian fire deaths	Percent change from 2014	Percent of all civilian fire deaths	Civilian fire injuries
Residential	2,605	6.8%	79.4%	11,575
1 and 2 family homes[1]	2,155	-8.1	65.7	8,050
Apartments	405	1.3	12.3	3,025
Other residential[2]	45	-10.0	1.4	500
Nonresidential structures[3]	80	23.1	2.4	1,425
Highway vehicles	445	43.5	13.6	1,550
Other vehicles[4]	55	57.1	1.7	325
All other fires[5]	95	35.7	2.9	825
Total	**3,280**	**1.1%**	**100.0%**	**15,700**

[1]Includes manufactured homes. [2]Includes hotels and motels, college dormitories, boarding houses, etc. [3]Includes public assembly, educational, institutional, store and office, industry, utility, storage and special structure properties. [4]Includes trains, boats, ships, farm vehicles and construction vehicles. [5]Includes outside properties with value, as well as brush, rubbish and other outside locations.

Source: Reproduced with permission from *Fire Loss in the United States During 2015* by Hylton J.G. Haynes, ©National Fire Protection Association.

Structure Fires By Type Of Use, 2015[1]

Property use	Estimated number of fires	Percent change from 2014	Property loss[2] ($ millions)	Percent change from 2014
Public assembly	17,000	21.4%	$323	-24.7%
Educational	5,000	0.0	40	-32.2
Institutional	6,500	0.0	51	27.5
Residential	388,000	0.4	7,210	3.1
1 and 2 family homes[3]	270,500	-1.1	5,799	-0.8
Apartments	95,000	1.1	1,161	18.3
Other[4]	22,500	18.4	250	50.6
Stores and offices	16,500	-5.7	635	-10.3
Industry, utility, defense[5]	9,000	-10.0	924	47.6
Storage in structures	30,500	10.9	1,032	32.1
Special structures	29,000	7.4	65	-69.2
Total	**501,500**	**1.5%**	**$10,280**	**4.4%**

[1]Estimates based on data reported by fire departments responding to the 2015 National Fire Experience Survey. May exclude reports from all fire departments. [2]Includes overall direct property loss to contents, structures, vehicles, machinery, vegetation or any other property involved in a fire. Excludes indirect losses, such as business interruption or temporary shelter costs. [3]Includes manufactured homes. [4]Includes hotels and motels, college dormitories, boarding houses, etc. [5]Excludes incidents handled only by private brigades or fixed suppression systems.

Source: Reproduced with permission from *Fire Loss in the United States During 2015* by Hylton J.G. Haynes, ©National Fire Protection Association.

Top 10 Costliest Large-Loss Fires, 2015 ($ millions)

Rank	Month	State	Type of facility	Estimated loss
1	September	California	Wildland urban interface fire	$1,500.0
2	September	California	Wildland urban interface fire	450.0
3	April	Kentucky	Appliance parts warehouse	110.0
4	April	Nebraska	Military fighter jet	62.0
5	March	Pennsylvania	Glass manufacturing plant	55.0
6	June	Pennsylvania	Fertilizer manufacturing plant	40.0
7	July	California	Church	31.0
8	September	California	Silk screening product plant	31.0
9	March	Idaho	Grain processing plant	24.0
10	August	Washington	Wildland urban interface fire	22.0

Source: Reproduced with permission from *Large-Loss Fires in the United States, 2015* by Stephen G. Badger, ©National Fire Protection Association.

Top 10 Costliest Large-Loss Fires In U.S. History ($ millions)

Rank	Date	Location/event	Estimated loss[1]	
			Dollars when occurred	In 2015 dollars[2]
1	Sep. 11, 2001	World Trade Center (terrorist attacks)	$33,400[3]	$44,770[3]
2	Apr. 18, 1906	San Francisco Earthquake and Fire	350	9,160
3	Oct. 8-9, 1871	Great Chicago Fire	168	3,360
4	Oct. 20, 1991	Oakland, CA, firestorm	1,500	2,650
5	Oct. 20, 2007	San Diego County, CA, The Southern California Firestorm	1,800	2,030
6	Nov. 9, 1872	Great Boston Fire	75	1,530
7	Sep. 12, 2015	Valley Fire, CA, wildland urban interface fire	1,500	1,500
8	Oct. 23, 1989	Pasadena, Texas, polyolefin plant	750	1,420
9	May 4, 2000	Los Alamos, NM, Cerro Grande wildland fire	1,000	1,420
10	Oct. 25, 2003	Julian, CA, Cedar wildland fire	1,100	1,320

[1]Loss estimates are from National Fire Protection Association (NFPA) records. The list is limited to fires for which some reliable dollar loss estimates exists. [2]Adjustment to 2013 dollars made by the NFPA using the Consumer Price Index, including the U.S. Census Bureau's estimates of the index for historical times; adjusted to 2015 dollars by the Insurance Information Institute using the Bureau of Labor Statistics Inflation Calculator. [3]Differs from inflation-adjusted estimates made by other organizations due to the use of different deflators.

Source: Reproduced with permission from Large-Loss Fires in the United States, 2015 by Stephen G. Badger, ©National Fire Protection Association.

Top Nine Most Catastrophic Multiple-Death Fires, 2015[1]

Rank	Month	State	Type of facility	Deaths
1	March	New York	Three-story single-family home	7
2	January	Maryland	Three-story single-family home	6
3	January	Ohio	One-story single-family home	5
4	October	Kentucky	Three-story single-family home and a two-unit home	5
5	December	California	One-story single-family dwelling	5
6	September	California	Wildland/urban interface	4
7	November	Ohio	Small business jet aircraft and four-unit apartment building	4
8	April	California	One-story tire shop	3
9	August	Washington	Wildland/urban interface	3

[1]Fires that kill five or more people in residential property, or three or more people in nonhome or nonstructural property. There were only nine castastrophic fires in 2015 that met this criteria.

Source: Based on data from Catastrophic Multiple-Death Fires in 2015 by Stephen G. Badger, ©National Fire Protection Association. Used with permission.

Top 10 Most Catastrophic Multiple-Death Fires In U.S. History[1]

Rank	Date	Location/event	Deaths
1	Sep. 11, 2001	New York, NY, World Trade Center terrorist attack	2,666[2]
2	Apr. 27, 1865	Mississippi River, SS Sultana steamship	1,547
3	Oct. 8, 1871	Peshtigo, WI, forest fire	1,152
4	Jun. 15, 1904	New York, NY, General Slocum steamship	1,030
5	Dec. 30, 1903	Chicago, IL, Iroquois Theater	602
6	Oct. 12, 1918	Cloquet, MN, forest fire	559
7	Nov. 28, 1942	Boston, MA, Cocoanut Grove night club	492
8	Apr. 16, 1947	Texas City, TX, SS Grandcamp and Monsanto Chemical Co. plant	468
9	Sep. 1, 1894	Hinckley, MN, forest fire	418
10	Dec. 6, 1907	Monongha, WV, coal mine explosion	361

[1]Fires that kill five or more people in home property, or three or more people in nonhome or nonstructural property. [2]Revised to 2,976 by government officials.

Source: ©National Fire Protection Association.

CRIME: ARSON

Arson is the act of deliberately setting fire to a building, car or other property for fraudulent or malicious purposes. It is a crime in all states. According to the National Fire Protection Association (NFPA), there were about 23,000 fires intentionally set in 2015, an increase of 21.1 percent over the year before. Intentionally set fires in structures resulted in 205 civilian deaths in 2015, an increase of 30.6 percent from 2014. A 1982 study by the Insurance Research Council found that about 14 percent of arson cases are insurance-motivated. Once a major problem in the 1990s, church arsons have dropped significantly. Intentional fires in religious and funeral properties fell 82 percent from 1,320 in 1980 to 240 in 2002, the last year such figures were tracked. There were 1,600 structural fires in houses of worship which caused $105 million in property damage on average from 2007 to 2011, according to the NFPA. Fires in a larger category, religious and funeral properties, averaged 1,780 during the same five years. Among those fires, 16 percent, or about 285 each year, were intentional. The U.S. Fire Administration determined arson to also be a leading cause of wildfires.

In 2015 property loss from intentionally set structure fires decreased 25 percent from 2014, according to the National Fire Protection Association, although the number of fires rose 21 percent.

Intentionally set fires in vehicles rose 25.0 percent in 2015 while the property loss from those fires fell 36.2 percent.

The property loss from all intentionally set fires (structures and vehicles) was $534 million in 2015, down 26.7 percent from $729 million in 2014.

Intentionally Set Fires, 2006-2015

Year	Structures		Vehicles[2]	
	Number of fires	Property loss ($ millions)[1]	Number of fires	Property loss ($ millions)[1]
2006	31,100	$755	20,500	$134
2007	32,500	733	20,500	145
2008	30,500	866	17,500	139
2009	26,500	684	15,000	108
2010	27,500	585	14,000	89
2011	26,500	601	14,000	88
2012	26,000	581	12,500	480[3]
2013	22,500	577	10,500	86
2014	19,000	613	8,000	116
2015	23,000	460	10,000	74

[1]Includes overall direct property loss to contents, structures, vehicles, machinery, vegetation or any other property involved in a fire. Excludes indirect losses, such as business interruption or temporary shelter costs. [2]Includes highway vehicles, trains, boats, ships, aircraft and farm and construction vehicles. [3]Includes $400 million in property loss from an intentionally set fire aboard the submarine USS Miami.

Source: Reproduced with permission from *Fire Loss in the United States During 2015* by Hylton J.G. Haynes, ©National Fire Protection Association; earlier data from prior reports.

CRIME: PROPERTY

The Federal Bureau of Investigation's (FBI) *Uniform Crime Reports* defines property crime as larceny-theft, motor vehicle theft and burglary. These crimes involve the unlawful taking of money or property without the use of force or threat of force against the victims. Larceny theft involves the successful or attempted taking of property from another; it includes shoplifting, pick-pocketing, purse-snatching and bicycle theft. While the theft of motor vehicles is a separate offense category, the thefts of motor vehicle parts and accessories are considered larceny. Burglary involves the unlawful entry into a structure such as a home or business. The burglary rate for renters was about 80 percent higher than for owners in 2011, according to a 2013 Bureau of Justice Statistics report. Home burglaries accounted for 73.2 percent of burglary offenses in 2014, according to the FBI.

Number And Rate Of Property Crime Offenses In The United States, 2006-2015[1]

| Year | Burglary | | Larceny-theft | |
	Number	Rate	Number	Rate
2006	2,194,993	733.1	6,626,363	2,213.2
2007	2,190,198	726.1	6,591,542	2,185.4
2008	2,228,887	733.0	6,586,206	2,166.1
2009	2,203,313	717.7	6,338,095	2,064.5
2010	2,168,459	701.0	6,204,601	2,005.8
2011	2,185,140	701.3	6,151,095	1,974.1
2012	2,109,932	672.2	6,168,874	1,965.4
2013	1,932,139	610.5	6,019,465	1,901.9
2014	1,713,153	537.2	5,809,054	1,821.5
2015	1,579,527	491.4	5,706,346	1,775.4

| Year | Motor vehicle theft | | Total property crime[2] | |
	Number	Rate	Number	Rate
2006	1,198,245	400.2	10,019,601	3,346.6
2007	1,100,472	364.9	9,882,212	3,276.4
2008	959,059	315.4	9,774,152	3,214.6
2009	795,652	259.2	9,337,060	3,041.3
2010	739,565	239.1	9,112,625	2,945.9
2011	716,508	230.0	9,052,743	2,905.4
2012	723,186	230.4	9,001,992	2,868.0
2013	700,288	221.3	8,651,892	2,733.6
2014	686,803	215.4	8,209,010	2,574.1
2015	707,758	220.2	7,993,631	2,487.0

[1]Rate is per 100,000 inhabitants. [2]Property crimes are the offenses of burglary, larceny-theft and motor vehicle theft.
Source: U.S. Department of Justice, Federal Bureau of Investigation, *Uniform Crime Reports*.

CRIME: CYBER AND IDENTITY THEFT

As businesses increasingly depend on electronic data and computer networks to conduct their daily operations, growing pools of personal and financial information are being transferred and stored online. This can leave individuals exposed to privacy violations, and financial institutions and other businesses exposed to potentially enormous liability if and when a breach in data security occurs.

Interest in cyber insurance and risk continues to grow as a result of high-profile data breaches and awareness of the almost endless range of exposure businesses face. A 2016 data leak, called the Panama Papers in the media, exposed millions of documents from the electronic files of Panamanian law firm Mossack Fonseka. In 2015, two health insurers, Anthem and Premera Blue Cross, were breached, exposing the data of 79 million and 11 million customers, respectively. The U.S. government has also been the target of hackers. Recent breaches at the Federal Deposit Insurance Corp. and the Internal Revenue Service follow multiple breaches in May 2015 of the Office of Personnel Management and the Department of the Interior where the records of 22 million current and former U.S. government employees were compromised.

Cyberattacks and breaches have grown in frequency, and losses are on the rise. In 2014 the number of U.S. data breaches hit a record 783, with 85.6 million records exposed, not counting Yahoo's 2014 breach, announced in September 2016, which affected over 500 million users and was suspected of being a state-sponsored attack. The number of breaches in 2015 was about the same at 781, but the number of records exposed doubled to about 169 million. The majority of the data breaches in 2015 affected medical/healthcare organizations (66.7 percent of total breaches) and government/military (20.2 percent), according to the Identity Theft Resource Center. These figures do not include the many attacks that go unreported. In addition, many attacks go undetected. Despite conflicting analyses, the costs associated with these losses are increasing. McAfee and the Center for Strategic and International Studies (CSIS) estimated the likely annual cost to the global economy from cybercrime is $445 billion a year, with a range of between $375 billion and $575 billion.

The costs of cybercrime are growing. An annual study of U.S. companies by the Ponemon Institute cites estimated average costs at $15 million in 2015, up 21 percent from $12.7 million in 2014. These costs ranged among the 58 organizations surveyed from a low of $1.9 million to a high of $65 million each year per company. Cyber insurance evolved as a product in the United States in the mid- to late-1990s as insurers have had to expand coverage for a risk that is rapidly shifting in scope and nature. More than 60 carriers offer stand-alone policies in a market encompassing $2.75 billion in gross written premiums in 2015. By mid-2016 gross premiums written was estimated at $3.25 billion.

Number Of Data Breaches And Records Exposed, 2006-2016

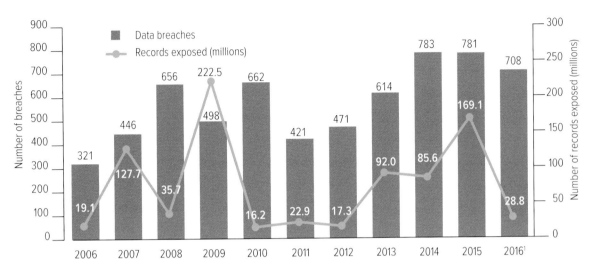

¹As of September 27, 2016.

Source: Identity Theft Resource Center.

The Internet Crime Complaint Center (IC3), a joint project of the Federal Bureau of Investigation, the National White Collar Crime Center and the Bureau of Justice Assistance monitors internet-related criminal complaints. In 2015 the IC3 received and processed 288,012 complaints. The IC3 reports that 127,145 of these complaints involved a dollar loss and puts total dollar losses at $1.1 billion. The most common complaints received in 2015 involved nonpayment or nondelivery of goods or services, accounting for about 67,000 complaints. About 31,000 complaints involved other payment scams—where a person is asked to facilitate the transfer of a large sum of money by sending a portion of it to the scammers in return for a commission or share in the profits, and scenarios where a person is sent a payment, is instructed to keep a portion and send the rest to another party. Identity theft—where a person's name or Social Security number is used without permission, was cited about 22,000 times in complaints.

Special Report

Interest in cyber insurance and risk continues to grow beyond expectations in 2016. As a bonus to readers of this year's Fact Book, we have excerpted our white paper, *Cyberrisk: Threat and Opportunity* (p. 211). The full report and more I.I.I. white papers and slides are available online for download at http://bit.ly/2gcHp0f.

Cybercrime Complaints, 2011-2015[1]

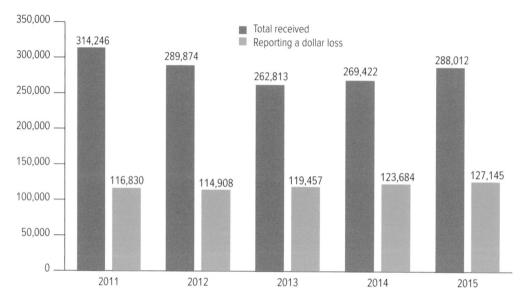

Legend:
■ Total received
■ Reporting a dollar loss

Year	Total received	Reporting a dollar loss
2011	314,246	116,830
2012	289,874	114,908
2013	262,813	119,457
2014	269,422	123,684
2015	288,012	127,145

[1]Based on complaints submitted to the Internet Crime Complaint Center.
Source: Internet Crime Complaint Center.

Top 10 States By Percent of Total U.S. Cybercrime Victims, 2015

Rank	State	Percent
1	California	14.53%
2	Florida	8.47
3	Texas	7.67
4	New York	6.30
5	Illinois	3.51
6	Pennsylvania	3.31
7	Virginia	3.14
8	New Jersey	3.01
9	Washington	2.72
10	Ohio	2.69

[1]Based on the total number of complaints submitted to the Internet Crime Complaint Center via its website from each state and the District of Columbia where the complainant provided state information.
Source: Internet Crime Complaint Center.

Consumer Fraud and Identity Theft

The Consumer Sentinel Network, maintained by the Federal Trade Commission (FTC), tracks consumer fraud and identity theft complaints that have been filed with federal, state and local law enforcement agencies and private organizations. Of the 3.1 million complaints received in 2015, 16 percent were related to identity theft. Identity theft complaints increased by more than 47 percent from 2014, and they were the second most reported after illegal debt collection. The FTC identifies 30 types of complaints. In 2015 debt collection complaints displaced identity theft in the top spot among complaint categories for the first time in 16 years, due in large part to a surge in complaints related to unwanted debt collection mobile phone calls.

Identity Theft And Fraud Complaints, 2012-2015[1]

[1]Percentages are based on the total number of Consumer Sentinel Network complaints by calendar year. These figures exclude "Do Not Call" registry complaints.

Source: Federal Trade Commission, Consumer Sentinel Network.

How Victims' Information Is Misused, 2015[1]

Type of identity theft fraud	Percent
Government documents or benefits fraud	49.2%
Other identity theft	19.2
Credit card fraud	15.8
Phone or utilities fraud	9.9
Bank fraud[2]	5.9
Attempted identity theft	3.7
Loan fraud	3.5
Employment-related fraud	3.3

[1]Percentages are based on the total number of complaints in the Federal Trade Commission's Consumer Sentinel Network (490,220 in 2015). Percentages total to more than 100 because some victims reported experiencing more than one type of identity theft. [2]Includes fraud involving checking, savings, and other deposit accounts and electronic fund transfers.

Source: Federal Trade Commission, Consumer Sentinel Network.

Identity Theft By State, 2015

State	Complaints per 100,000 population[1]	Number of complaints	Rank[2]	State	Complaints per 100,000 population[1]	Number of complaints	Rank[2]
Alabama	102.3	4,973	30	Montana	87.2	901	43
Alaska	94.3	696	40	Nebraska	100.5	1,905	34
Arizona	133.8	9,136	14	Nevada	125.0	3,613	19
Arkansas	97.7	2,911	37	New Hampshire	142.0	1,890	9
California	141.3	55,305	10	New Jersey	125.8	11,266	17
Colorado	123.2	6,724	21	New Mexico	101.1	2,109	33
Connecticut	225	8,078	2	New York	122.0	24,157	23
Delaware	124.9	1,181	20	North Carolina	106.0	10,646	29
Florida	217.4	44,063	3	North Dakota	76.0	575	48
Georgia	149.1	15,230	7	Ohio	134.4	15,611	12
Hawaii	62.6	896	50	Oklahoma	120.0	4,695	24
Idaho	101.3	1,676	32	Oregon	126.1	5,081	15
Illinois	158.7	20,414	5	Pennsylvania	116.2	14,877	25
Indiana	93.9	6,217	41	Rhode Island	141.2	1,491	11
Iowa	89.7	2,803	42	South Carolina	102.3	5,010	30
Kansas	112.7	3,282	27	South Dakota	63.1	542	49
Kentucky	80.9	3,581	46	Tennessee	107.9	7,121	28
Louisiana	94.4	4,410	39	Texas	144.3	39,630	8
Maine	113.9	1,514	26	Utah	85.7	2,567	44
Maryland	183.2	11,006	4	Vermont	83.9	525	45
Massachusetts	125.5	8,530	18	Virginia	123.2	10,329	21
Michigan	158.1	15,684	6	Washington	126.1	9,043	15
Minnesota	97.8	5,368	36	West Virginia	79.9	1,474	47
Mississippi	98.8	2,955	35	Wisconsin	134.4	7,756	12
Missouri	364.3	22,164	1	Wyoming	96.6	566	38

[1]Population figures are based on the 2015 U.S. Census population estimates. [2]Ranked by complaints per 100,000 population. The District of Columbia had 228.0 complaints per 100,000 population and 1,533 victims. States with the same ratio of complaints per 100,000 population receive the same rank.

Source: Federal Trade Commission, Consumer Sentinel Network.

MOTOR VEHICLES: CRASHES

The National Highway Traffic Safety Administration (NHTSA) reports that 35,092 people died in motor vehicle crashes in 2015, up 7.2 percent from 32,744 in 2014. The 2015 increase was the largest since 1966, almost fifty years ago. The fatality rate, measured as deaths per 100 million vehicle miles traveled, rose to 1.12 in 2015, from 1.08 in 2014. The 2014 fatality rate was the lowest fatality rate on record. NHTSA property damage figures shown below are based on accidents reported to the police and exclude fender-benders.

Traffic Deaths, 2006-2015

Year	Fatalities	Annual percent change	Fatality rate per 100 million vehicle miles traveled	Fatality rate per 100,000 registered vehicles
2006	42,708	-1.8%	1.42	16.99
2007	41,259	-3.4	1.36	16.02
2008	37,423	-9.3	1.26	14.43
2009	33,883	-9.5	1.15	13.08
2010	32,999	-2.6	1.11	12.82
2011	32,479	-1.6	1.10	12.25
2012	33,782	4.0	1.14	12.72
2013	32,894	-2.6	1.10	12.21
2014	32,744	-0.5	1.08	11.89
2015	35,092	7.2	1.12	NA

NA=Data not available.
Source: U.S. Department of Transportation, National Highway Traffic Safety Administration.

In 2015 about 2.4 million people were injured in motor vehicle crashes, an increase from 2.3 million in 2014.

The injury rate per 100 million vehicle miles traveled was 78 in 2015, up from 77 in 2014.

Motor Vehicle Crashes, 2006-2015

Year	Fatal	Injury	Property damage only	Total crashes
2006	38,648	1,746,000	4,189,000	5,973,000
2007	37,435	1,711,000	4,275,000	6,024,000
2008	34,172	1,630,000	4,146,000	5,811,000
2009	30,862	1,517,000	3,957,000	5,505,000
2010	30,296	1,542,000	3,847,000	5,419,000
2011	29,757	1,530,000	3,778,000	5,338,000
2012	31,006	1,634,000	3,950,000	5,615,000
2013	30,057	1,591,000	4,066,000	5,687,000
2014	30,056	1,648,000	4,387,000	6,064,000
2015	32,166	1,715,000	4,548,000	6,296,000

Source: U.S. Department of Transportation, National Highway Traffic Safety Administration.

According to the National Highway Traffic Safety Administration, vehicle occupants accounted for 66 percent of traffic deaths in 2015. Motorcycle riders accounted for 14 percent. Pedestrians accounted for another 15 percent; pedalcyclists, bus and other nonoccupants accounted for the remainder.

Motor Vehicle Traffic Deaths By State, 2014-2015

State	Number of Deaths 2014	2015	Percent change	State	Number of Deaths 2014	2015	Percent change
Alabama	820	849	3.5%	Montana	192	224	16.7%
Alaska	73	65	-11.0	Nebraska	225	246	9.3
Arizona	773	893	15.5	Nevada	291	325	11.7
Arkansas	470	531	13.0	New Hampshire	95	114	20.0
California	3,102	3,176	2.4	New Jersey	556	562	1.1
Colorado	488	546	11.9	New Mexico	386	298	-22.8
Connecticut	248	266	7.3	New York	1,041	1,121	7.7
Delaware	124	126	1.6	North Carolina	1,284	1,379	7.4
D.C.	23	23	0.0	North Dakota	135	131	-3.0
Florida	2,494	2,939	17.8	Ohio	1,006	1,110	10.3
Georgia	1,164	1,430	22.9	Oklahoma	669	643	-3.9
Hawaii	95	94	-1.1	Oregon	357	447	25.2
Idaho	186	216	16.1	Pennsylvania	1,195	1,200	0.4
Illinois	924	998	8.0	Rhode Island	51	45	-11.8
Indiana	745	821	10.2	South Carolina	823	977	18.7
Iowa	322	320	-0.6	South Dakota	136	133	-2.2
Kansas	385	355	-7.8	Tennessee	963	958	-0.5
Kentucky	672	761	13.2	Texas	3,536	3,516	-0.6
Louisiana	740	726	-1.9	Utah	256	276	7.8
Maine	131	156	19.1	Vermont	44	57	29.5
Maryland	442	513	16.1	Virginia	703	753	7.1
Massachusetts	354	306	-13.6	Washington	462	568	22.9
Michigan	901	963	6.9	West Virginia	272	268	-1.5
Minnesota	361	411	13.9	Wisconsin	506	566	11.9
Mississippi	607	677	11.5	Wyoming	150	145	-3.3
Missouri	766	869	13.4	**United States**	**32,744**	**35,092**	**7.2%**

Source: U.S. Department of Transportation, National Highway Traffic Safety Administration.

Vehicles Involved In Crashes By Vehicle Type And Crash Severity, 2005 And 2014

	Fatal crashes		Injury crashes		Property damage-only crashes	
	2005	2014	2005	2014	2005	2014
Passenger cars						
Involved in crashes	25,169	17,848	1,893,000	1,685,000	4,169,000	4,279,000
Rate per 100 million vehicle miles traveled	1.56	1.28	117	121	258	306
Rate per 100,000 registered vehicles	18.60	13.61	1,399	1,285	3,081	3,263
Light trucks[1]						
Involved in crashes	22,964	17,136	1,209,000	1,138,000	2,919,000	3,028,000
Rate per 100 million vehicle miles traveled	2.03	1.30	107	87	258	230
Rate per 100,000 registered vehicles	24.23	13.88	1,275	922	3,080	2,452
Motorcycles						
Involved in crashes	4,682	4,694	80,000	87,000	18,000	19,000
Rate per 100 million vehicle miles traveled	44.79	23.51	769	435	174	94
Rate per 100,000 registered vehicles	75.19	55.76	1,291	1,033	291	224

[1]Trucks with 10,000 pounds or less gross vehicle weight. Includes pickups, vans, truck-based station wagons and utility vehicles.

Source: U.S. Department of Transportation (USDOT), National Highway Traffic Safety Administration (NHTSA). Vehicle miles traveled - USDOT, Federal Highway Administration, revised by NHTSA; Registered passenger cars and light trucks - R.L. Polk & Co; Registered motorcycles - USDOT, Federal Highway Administration.

Motor Vehicle Deaths By Activity Of Person Killed, 2014

■ Drivers	50.4%
■ Passengers	17.6
■ Pedestrians	14.9
■ Motorcycle riders	14.0
■ Pedalcyclists	2.2
■ Other[1]	0.6
■ Unknown occupants	0.2

[1]Includes other non-occupants.

Source: U.S. Department of Transportation, National Highway Traffic Safety Administration

Sex Of Drivers Involved In Crashes, 2005-2014[1]

	Fatal crashes				Injury crashes			
	Male		Female		Male		Female	
Year	Number	Rate[2]	Number	Rate[2]	Number	Rate[2]	Number	Rate[2]
2005	42,947	42.84	14,967	14.92	1,836,711	1,832	1,425,161	1,421
2006	41,912	41.49	14,661	14.43	1,762,552	1,745	1,387,324	1,366
2007	40,804	39.82	14,099	13.65	1,719,000	1,677	1,339,000	1,296
2008	36,881	35.59	12,568	12.00	1,609,000	1,553	1,280,000	1,223
2009	32,807	31.47	11,825	11.22	1,499,561	1,438	1,224,613	1,162
2010	31,965	30.63	11,811	11.17	1,516,000	1,453	1,265,000	1,196
2011	31,809	30.32	11,209	10.48	1,507,000	1,436	1,244,000	1,163
2012	33,124	31.55	11,509	10.77	1,634,884	1,557	1,314,534	1,230
2013	32,442	30.89	11,364	10.61	1,584,000	1,509	1,331,000	1,242
2014	32,572	30.76	11,258	10.41	1,659,000	1,567	1,351,000	1,249

	Property damage-only crashes				Total crashes			
	Male		Female		Male		Female	
Year	Number	Rate[2]	Number	Rate[2]	Number	Rate[2]	Number	Rate[2]
2005	4,357,188	4,347	3,007,038	2,998	6,236,846	6,222	4,447,166	4,435
2006	4,232,184	4,190	2,967,964	2,922	6,036,648	5,976	4,369,949	4,302
2007	4,345,000	4,241	3,066,000	2,968	6,105,000	5,968	4,418,000	4,278
2008	4,174,000	4,028	2,967,000	2,834	5,820,000	5,617	4,260,000	4,069
2009	3,913,473	3,753	2,931,260	2,782	5,445,840	5,223	4,167,698	3,956
2010	3,854,000	3,693	2,862,000	2,707	5,402,000	5,176	4,139,000	3,915
2011	3,675,000	3,503	2,921,000	2,730	5,213,000	4,970	4,176,000	3,904
2012	3,880,163	3,696	3,006,762	3,251	5,548,171	5,285	4,332,806	4,056
2013	3,990,000	3,800	3,092,000	2,886	5,607,000	5,340	4,434,000	4,138
2014	4,383,000	4,139	3,335,000	3,082	6,075,000	5,736	4,697,000	4,342

[1]Includes motorcycle riders and restricted and graduated drivers license holders in some states. [2]Rate per 100,000 licensed drivers.

Source: U.S. Department of Transportation, National Highway Traffic Safety Administration.

Teenage Drivers

Motor vehicle crashes are a leading cause of death among teenagers. According to the U.S. Department of Transportation (DOT), 1,678 drivers between the ages of 16 to 20 died in motor vehicle crashes in 2014, compared with 1,651 drivers in this age group in 2013.

Drivers In Motor Vehicle Crashes By Age, 2014

Age group	Number of licensed drivers	Percent of total	Drivers in fatal crashes	Involvement rate[1]	Drivers in all crashes	Involvement rate[1]
16 to 20	11,649,902	5.5%	3,803	32.64	1,298,000	11,138
21 to 24	14,358,484	6.8	4,654	32.41	1,202,000	8,373
25 to 34	37,360,848	17.6	8,972	24.01	2,331,000	6,238
35 to 44	35,863,375	16.9	6,894	19.22	1,804,000	5,029
45 to 54	39,497,005	18.6	7,350	18.61	1,705,000	4,318
55 to 64	36,852,500	17.4	5,997	16.27	1,318,000	3,576
65 to 74	23,832,010	11.2	3,314	13.91	640,000	2,686
Over 74	14,616,177	6.9	2,641	18.07	363,000	2,486
Total	**214,092,472**	**100.0%**	**44,583[2]**	**20.82**	**10,773,000[2]**	**5,032**

[1] Per 100,000 licensed drivers. [2] Includes drivers under the age of 16 and of unknown age.

Source: U.S. Department of Transportation, National Highway Traffic Safety Administration; Federal Highway Administration.

Motor Vehicle Deaths Per 100,000 Persons By Age, 2014

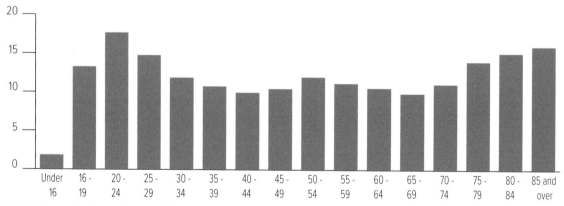

Source: Insurance Institute for Highway Safety.

Driving Behaviors Reported For Drivers And Motorcycle Operators Involved In Fatal Crashes, 2014

Behavior	Number of drivers	Percent
Driving too fast for conditions or in excess of posted speed limit	8,360	18.8%
Under the influence of alcohol, drugs or medication	5,492	12.3
Failure to keep in proper lane or running off road	3,770	8.5
Failure to yield right of way	3,094	6.9
Distracted (phone, talking, eating, object, etc.)	3,000	6.7
Operating vehicle in a careless manner	2,122	4.8
Overcorrecting/oversteering	1,814	4.1
Failure to obey traffic signs, signals or officer	1,796	4.0
Operating vehicle in erratic, reckless or negligent manner	1,548	3.5
Swerving or avoiding due to wind, slippery surface, other vehicle, object, nonmotorist in roadway, etc.	1,510	3.4
Drowsy, asleep, fatigued, ill or blacked out	1,309	2.9
Vision obscured (rain, snow, glare, lights, buildings, trees, etc.)	1,241	2.8
Driving wrong way on one-way trafficway or on wrong side of road	879	2.0
Making improper turn	765	1.7
Other factors	5,212	11.7
None reported	13,885	31.1
Unknown	5,740	12.9
Total drivers[1]	**44,583**	**100.0%**

[1] The sum of percentages is greater than total drivers as more than one factor may be present for the same driver.

Source: U.S. Department of Transportation, National Highway Traffic Safety Administration.

In 2015, 10,265 people were killed in crashes where a driver had a blood alcohol concentration (BAC) of 0.08 percent or higher, up 3.2 percent from 9,943 in 2014, according to the National Highway Traffic Safety Administration.

In 2014, the majority of alcohol-impaired crash fatalities involved drivers with a BAC of 0.15 or higher—nearly double the legal limit.

Alcohol-Impaired Crash Fatalities, 2006-2015[1]

Year	Number	As a percent of all crash deaths
2006	13,491	32%
2007	13,041	32
2008	11,711	31
2009	10,759	32
2010	10,136	31
2011	9,865	30
2012	10,336	31
2013	10,110	31
2014	9,943	30
2015	10,265	29

[1]Alcohol-impaired driving crashes are crashes that involve at least one driver or a motorcycle operator with a blood alcohol concentration (BAC) of 0.08 percent or above, the legal definition of drunk driving.
Source: U.S. Department of Transportation, National Highway Traffic Safety Administration.

Percent Of Alcohol-Impaired Drivers Involved In Fatal Crashes By Age, 2005 And 2014[1]

Age	2005	2014	Point change
16 to 20	17%	17%	0 pt.
21 to 24	33	30	-3
25 to 34	29	29	0
35 to 44	24	24	0
45 to 54	19	20	1
55 to 64	13	16	3
65 to 74	7	10	3
Over 74	4	6	2

[1]Alcohol-impaired driving crashes are crashes that involve at least one driver or a motorcycle operator with a blood alcohol concentration of 0.08 percent or above, the legal definition of drunk driving.
Source: U.S. Department of Transportation, National Highway Traffic Safety Administration.

Persons Killed In Total And Alcohol-Impaired Crashes By Person Type, 2014

Person type	Total killed	Alcohol-impaired driving fatalities[1]	
		Number	Percent of total killed
Vehicle occupants			
Driver	16,454	5,792	35%
Passenger	5,751	1,769	31
Unknown occupant	71	5	6
Total	**22,276**	**7,565**	**34%**
Motorcyclists	**4,586**	**1,577**	**34%**
Nonoccupants			
Pedestrian	4,884	696	14
Pedalcyclist	726	98	13
Other/unknown	203	30	15
Total	**5,813**	**824**	**14%**
Total	**32,675**	**9,967**	**31%**

[1]Alcohol-impaired driving crashes are crashes that involve at least one driver or a motorcycle operator with a blood alcohol concentration of 0.08 percent or above, the legal definition of drunk driving.

Source: U.S. Department of Transportation, National Highway Traffic Safety Administration.

Motorcycle Helmet Use, 1996-2015[1]

Year	Percent	Year	Percent
1996	64%	2009	67%
1998	67	2010	54
2000	71	2011	66
2005	48	2012	60
2006	51	2013	60
2007	58	2014	64
2008	63	2015	61

[1]Based on surveys of motorcyclists using helmets meeting Department of Transportation standards. Surveys conducted in October for 1996-2000 and in June thereafter.

Source: U.S. Department of Transportation, National Occupant Protection Use Survey, National Highway Traffic Safety Administration's National Center for Statistics and Analysis.

Motorcycle helmet usage fell to 61 percent in June 2015 compared with 64 percent 2014, a change that NHTSA indicates is not statistically significant.

Helmet use was highest in the Northeast, at 77 percent, up from 56 percent in 2014. In the West, helmet use fell to 75 percent from 85 percent in 2014.

Helmet use was 60 percent in the South, down from 78 percent in 2014 and 44 percent in the Midwest, the lowest of all the regions, down from 47 percent.

Collision Losses

The chart below shows the claim frequency and average loss payment per claim and average loss payment per insured vehicle year under collision coverage for recent model vehicles. The claim frequency is expressed as a rate per 100 insured vehicle years. A vehicle year is equal to 365 days of insurance coverage for a single vehicle.

Passenger Vehicle Collision Coverage Insurance Losses, 2013-2015 Model Years

	Claim frequency[1]	Claim severity
Passenger cars and minivans	8.2	$4,929
Pickups	6.3	4,868
SUVs	6.4	4,902
All passenger vehicles[2]	**7.4**	**$4,916**

[1]Per 100 insured vehicle years. [2]Includes claims from cargo/passenger vans.
Source: Highway Loss Data Institute.

Aggressive Driving

Aggressive driving is a major factor in U.S. traffic accidents, playing a role not just in well-publicized incidents of road rage, but in a large number of fatal highway collisions each year. The National Highway Traffic Safety Administration (NHTSA) defines aggressive driving as occurring when "an individual commits a combination of moving traffic offenses so as to endanger other persons or property." While aggressive driving is difficult to quantify, a 2009 study by the American Automobile Association reported that, based on data tracked by NHTSA's Fatal Accident Reporting System, aggressive driving played a role in 56 percent of fatal crashes from 2003 through 2007, with excessive speed being the No. 1 factor. Speeding was also the leading driving behavior associated with fatal crashes in 2014 (18.8 percent), followed by driving under the influence (12.3 percent), according to NHTSA. (See chart, page 177.)

Distracted Driving

Activities that take drivers' attention off the road, including talking or texting on cellphones, eating, conversing with passengers and other distractions, are a major safety threat. The National Highway Traffic Safety Administration (NHTSA) gauges distracted driving by collecting data on distraction-affected crashes, which focus on distractions that are most likely to affect crash involvement such as dialing a cellphone or texting and being distracted by another person or an outside event. In 2014, 3,179 people were killed in distraction-affected crashes, and 431,000 people were injured. There were 2,955 distraction-affected fatal crashes, accounting for 10 percent of all fatal crashes in the nation, 18 percent of injury crashes and 16 percent of all motor vehicle crashes in 2014.

Driver Hand-Held Cellphone Use By Age, 2006-2015[1]

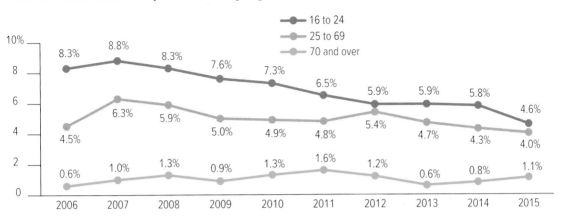

Legend:
- 16 to 24
- 25 to 69
- 70 and over

16 to 24: 8.3% (2006), 8.8% (2007), 8.3% (2008), 7.6% (2009), 7.3% (2010), 6.5% (2011), 5.9% (2012), 5.9% (2013), 5.8% (2014), 4.6% (2015)

25 to 69: 4.5% (2006), 6.3% (2007), 5.9% (2008), 5.0% (2009), 4.9% (2010), 4.8% (2011), 5.4% (2012), 4.7% (2013), 4.3% (2014), 4.0% (2015)

70 and over: 0.6% (2006), 1.0% (2007), 1.3% (2008), 0.9% (2009), 1.3% (2010), 1.6% (2011), 1.2% (2012), 0.6% (2013), 0.8% (2014), 1.1% (2015)

[1]Percent of drivers using hand-held cellphones.

Source: U.S. Department of Transportation, National Highway Traffic Safety Administration.

Fatal Crashes Affected By Distracted Drivers, 2014

	Crashes	Drivers	Fatalities
Total fatal crashes	**29,989**	**44,583**	**32,675**
Distracted-affected fatal crashes			
Number of distracted-affected fatal crashes	2,955	3,000	3,179
Percent of total fatal crashes	10%	7%	10%
Cellphone in use in distracted-affected fatal crashes			
Number of cellphone distracted-affected fatal crashes	385	398	404
Percent of fatal distracted-affected crashes	13%	13%	13%

Source: U.S. Department of Transportation, National Highway Traffic Safety Administration.

Distraction was a factor in 10 percent of fatal crashes reported in 2014.

Cellphone use was a factor in 13 percent of all fatal distracted-affected crashes, but in only 1 percent of the 29,989 fatal crashes reported in 2014.

MOTOR VEHICLES: THEFT

The FBI includes the theft or attempted theft of automobiles, trucks, buses, motorcycles, scooters, snowmobiles and other vehicles in its definition of motor vehicle theft. A motor vehicle was stolen on average every 45 seconds in the United States in 2015.

Motor vehicles were stolen at a rate of 220.2 per 100,000 people in 2015, up 2.2 percent from 2014 but down 45.0 percent from 2006.

More than $4.9 billion was lost to motor vehicle theft in 2015. The average dollar loss per theft was $7,001.

Motor Vehicle Theft In The United States, 2006-2015

Year	Vehicles stolen	Percent change	Year	Vehicles stolen	Percent change
2006	1,198,245	-3.0%	2011	716,508	-3.1%
2007	1,100,472	-8.2	2012	723,186	0.9
2008	959,059	-12.9	2013	700,288	-3.2
2009	795,652	-17.0	2014	686,803	-1.9
2010	739,565	-7.0	2015	707,758	3.1

Source: U.S. Department of Justice, Federal Bureau of Investigation, *Uniform Crime Reports.*

Eight of the top 10 U.S. Metropolitan Statistical Areas for motor vehicle theft were in California in 2015. The other two were in New Mexico and Colorado.

Top 10 U.S. Metropolitan Statistical Areas By Motor Vehicle Theft Rate, 2015

Rank	Metropolitan Statistical Area[1]	Vehicles stolen	Rate[2]
1	Modesto, CA	4,072	756.33
2	Albuquerque, NM	6,657	733.71
3	Bakersfield, CA	6,000	680.14
4	Salinas, CA	2,934	676.20
5	San Francisco-Oakland-Hayward, CA	30,554	656.21
6	Stockton-Lodi, CA	4,656	641.23
7	Pueblo, CO	983	600.89
8	Merced, CA	1,605	597.87
9	Riverside-San Bernardino-Ontario, CA	25,001	556.92
10	Vallejo-Fairfield, CA	2,352	539.34

[1]Metropolitan Statistical Areas are designated by the federal Office of Management and Budget and usually include areas much larger than the cities for which they are named.
[2]Rate of vehicle thefts reported per 100,000 people based on the 2015 U.S. Census Population Estimates.
Source: National Insurance Crime Bureau.

Top 10 States With The Most And The Fewest Number Of Motor Vehicle Thefts, 2015

Most motor vehicle thefts			Fewest motor vehicle thefts		
Rank	State	Vehicles stolen	Rank	State	Vehicles stolen
1	California	170,993	1	Vermont	178
2	Texas	67,485	2	Wyoming	592
3	Florida	40,661	3	Maine	814
4	Washington	26,867	4	New Hampshire	891
5	Georgia	26,482	5	Delaware	1,181
6	Illinois	17,652	6	South Dakota	1,188
7	Ohio	17,229	7	Rhode Island	1,389
8	Missouri	16,999	8	North Dakota	1,583
9	Arizona	16,785	9	Idaho	1,871
10	Colorado	16,000	10	Alaska	2,046

Source: U.S. Department of Justice, Federal Bureau of Investigation, *Uniform Crime Reports*.

Top 10 Most Frequently Stolen Vehicles, 2015

All model years[1]			2015 model year vehicles only		
Rank	Model	Thefts	Rank	Model	Thefts
1	Honda Accord	52,244	1	Nissan Altima	1,104
2	Honda Civic	49,430	2	Chrysler 200	1,069
3	Ford Pickup (Full size)	29,396	3	Toyota Camry	923
4	Chevrolet Pickup (Full size)	27,771	4	Toyota Corolla	776
5	Toyota Camry	15,446	5	GMC Sierra	670
6	Dodge Pickup (Full size)	11,212	6	Dodge Charger	666
7	Toyota Corolla	10,547	7	Hyundai Sonata	632
8	Nissan Altima	10,374	8	Chevrolet Malibu	629
9	Dodge Caravan	9,798	9	Chevrolet Impala	594
10	Chevrolet Impala	9,225	10	Chevrolet Cruze	586

[1]Includes all model years for each vehicle.
Source: National Insurance Crime Bureau.

RECREATION

Watercraft Accidents

Federal law requires owners of recreational boats and watercraft (non-commercial) to register them. In 2015 there were 11.9 million registered recreational watercraft, up from 11.8 million in 2014. A recreational boating accident must be reported to the U.S. Coast Guard if a person dies or is injured and requires medical treatment beyond first aid; if damage to the boat or other property exceeds $2,000; if the boat is lost; or if a person disappears from the boat.

The U.S. Coast Guard says that alcohol, combined with typical conditions such as motion, vibration, engine noise, sun, wind and spray can impair a person's abilities much faster than alcohol consumption on land. Operators with a blood alcohol concentration (BAC) above 0.10 percent are estimated to be more than 10 times more likely to be killed in an accident than watercraft operators with zero BAC. Alcohol was a contributing factor in 306 recreational watercraft accidents in 2015 (7.4 percent of all accidents), accounting for 122 deaths (19.5 percent of all deaths) and 258 injuries (9.9 percent of all injuries). Other primary contributing factors were operator inattention, resulting in 58 deaths; and operator inexperience, accounting for 37 deaths.

76 percent of fatal boating accident victims died by drowning in 2015, and of those, 85 percent were not wearing life jackets.

The most common types of watercraft involved in reported accidents in 2015 were open motorboats (45 percent), personal watercraft (Jet Skis) (19 percent) and cabin motorboats (17 percent).

Recreational Watercraft Accidents, 2011-2015[1]

Year	Accidents		Fatalities		Injuries	Property damage ($ millions)
	Total	Involving alcohol use[2]	Total	Involving alcohol use[2]		
2011	4,588	361	758	149	3,081	$52
2012	4,515	368	651	139	3,000	38
2013	4,062	305	560	94	2,620	39
2014	4,064	345	610	137	2,678	39
2015	4,158	306	626	122	2,613	42

[1]Includes accidents involving $2,000 or more in property damage. [2]The use of alcohol by a boat's occupants was a direct or indirect cause of the accident.

Source: U.S. Department of Transportation, U.S. Coast Guard.

Top 10 States By Recreational Watercraft Accidents, 2015[1]

Rank	State	Accidents	Deaths	People injured	Property damage ($000)
1	Florida	671	52	390	$9,770
2	California	369	48	227	3,101
3	New York	174	16	96	1,120
4	North Carolina	162	20	90	1,492
5	Texas	154	44	105	792
6	Maryland	146	21	125	1,074
7	South Carolina	123	17	80	958
7	New Jersey	122	8	64	134
9	Missouri	109	17	70	817
10	Tennessee	107	13	65	493

[1]Includes accidents involving $2,000 or more in property damage. Includes watercraft such as motorboats and sailboats and other vessels such as Jet Skis.

Source: U.S. Department of Transportation, U.S. Coast Guard.

Watercraft Thefts

There were 5,031 watercraft thefts in the United States in 2015, down 3 percent from 2014, according to an analysis of federal government data by the National Insurance Crime Bureau. Watercraft include motor boats, sailboats and other vessels such as Jet Skis. Of these thefts, 2,114, or 42 percent, were recovered by May 15, 2016. Personal watercraft such as Jet Skis were the most frequently stolen watercraft, with 1,108 thefts, followed by runabouts (678), utility boats (278), cruisers (181) and sailboats (52). July saw the highest number of reported thefts (612), and February had the fewest (251).

Top 10 States By Watercraft Theft, 2015

Rank	State	Thefts[1]	Rank	State	Thefts[1]
1	Florida	1,205	6	Alabama	171
2	California	528	7	Georgia	170
3	Texas	399	8	South Carolina	154
4	North Carolina	192	9	Louisiana	137
5	Washington	173	10	Tennessee	119

[1]Watercraft include motorboats and sailboats and other vessels such as Jet Skis.

Source: National Insurance Crime Bureau.

Sports Injuries

Basketball was the most dangerous sport in 2014, with 522,817 injuries reported followed by biking, with 502,104 injuries and football, with 396,457 injuries.

   The National Safety Council says that there were 179,188 swimming injuries treated in emergency rooms in 2014. About 42 percent of the injuries involved children between the ages of five and 14. A report by the Consumer Product Safety Commission found that 174 children between the ages of one and 14 drowned from Memorial Day to Labor Day in 2014. Concern is growing about the risks of sports-related concussions as lawsuits filed by injured professional football players have generated national headlines. The problem also affects thousands of young people who engage in a variety of sports. The Centers for Disease Control and Prevention reports that in 2009, an estimated 248,418 children (age 19 or younger) were treated in U.S. emergency departments for sports and recreation-related injuries that included a diagnosis of concussion or traumatic brain injury.

Sports Injuries By Number of Injuries, 2014

Sport or activity	Injuries[1]	Percent of injuries by age				
		0 to 4	5 to 14	15 to 24	25 to 64	65 and over
Basketball	522,817	0.4%	34.3%	47.0%	18.1%	0.2%
Bicycle riding[2]	502,104	4.5	33.8	17.2	38.3	6.2
Football	396,457	0.4	50.6	40.0	8.9	0.1
Exercise[3]	368,904	1.6	12.0	19.3	54.9	12.2
Soccer	239,943	1.1	43.7	38.8	16.4	[4]
Swimming[5]	179,188	9.6	42.4	16.1	26.5	5.4
Baseball	130,376	2.9	49.4	29.4	17.5	0.8
Skateboarding	119,760	0.8	34.0	49.7	15.4	0.1
Weight lifting	100,904	2.5	7.7	32.8	53.6	3.5
Softball	95,465	0.1	31.4	33.1	33.8	1.6
Roller skating[6]	66,601	1.1	56.4	11.3	30.0	1.1
Fishing	66,290	3.7	17.8	16.2	51.6	10.7
Volleyball	52,548	0.1	36.0	41.9	21.4	0.6
Horseback riding	50,688	1.0	20.4	23.0	47.7	7.9
Wrestling	39,700	[4]	41.8	53.3	5.0	[4]
Cheerleading	35,894	0.2	49.7	48.5	1.5	[4]
Gymnastics[7]	34,550	1.8	75.9	19.8	2.4	0.1
Snowboarding	31,847	0.4	23.2	51.3	25.1	[4]
Golf[8]	30,047	3.5	13.2	6.6	40.0	36.6
Martial arts	30,043	0.4	31.7	28.7	38.6	0.6

(table continues)

Sports Injuries By Number of Injuries, 2014 (Cont'd)

Sport or activity	Injuries[1]	Percent of injuries by age				
		0 to 4	5 to 14	15 to 24	25 to 64	65 and over
Track and field	29,484	[4]	39.5%	43.5%	16.3%	0.7%
Ice skating[9]	20,127	1.5%	45.7	19.5	30.0	3.3
Tennis	19,800	0.3	14.3	19.2	36.3	30.0
Ice hockey	17,627	0.1	36.9	42.0	20.6	0.4
Boxing	16,673	0.1	8.8	43.7	46.8	0.6
Bowling	16,613	9.1	13.8	15.5	45.0	16.6
Rugby	11,925	[4]	6.8	74.7	18.5	[4]
Mountain biking	8,822	[4]	5.5	18.7	74.1	1.8
Snowmobiling	6,641	1.2	2.5	24.5	70.1	1.6
Hockey, field	5,782	1.7	35.8	49.2	13.3	[4]
Mountain climbing	5,395	0.3	8.2	40.0	49.9	1.6
Water skiing	4,807	[4]	9.8	40.1	50.1	[4]
Archery	3,948	2.0	16.9	19.1	50.2	11.9
Billiards, pool	3,500	15.7	14.1	9.1	57.9	3.2
Racquetball, squash and paddleball	3,375	2.2	6.4	21.7	61.0	8.7
Horseshoe pitching[10]	1,449	5.4	6.9	12.4	64.7	10.6
Scuba diving	1,220	1.3	10.8	21.2	65.4	1.3

[1]Treated in hospital emergency departments. Excludes skiing. [2]Excludes mountain biking. [3]Includes exercise equipment (62,665 injuries) and exercise activity (306,239 injuries). [4]Less than 0.1 percent. [5]Includes injuries associated with swimming, swimming pools, pool slides, diving or diving boards and swimming pool equipment. [6]Includes roller skating (54,796 injuries) and in-line skating (11,805 injuries). [7]Excludes trampolines (104,691 injuries). [8]Excludes golf carts (15,225 injuries). [9]Excludes 5,247 injuries in skating, unspecified. [10]Data for 2013.

Source: National Safety Council. *Injury Facts®*, 2016 Edition. Itasca, IL.

ATV-Related Deaths And Injuries, 2010-2014[1]

Year	Estimated number of deaths			Estimated number of injuries[2]		
	Total	Younger than 16		Total	Younger than 16	
		Number	Percent of total		Number	Percent of total
2010	654	90	14%	115,000	28,300	25%
2011	626	81	13	107,500	29,000	27
2012	574	67	12	107,900	26,500	25
2013	547	69	13	99,600	25,000	25
2014	385	61	16	93,700	24,800	26

[1]ATVs are open-air vehicles with 3, 4 or unknown number of wheels designed for off-road use. [2]Emergency room-treated.

Source: U.S. Consumer Product Safety Commission.

AVIATION

There were 1,280 civil aviation accidents in 2015, down from 1,291 in 2014. Total fatalities fell to 404 in 2015 from 444 in 2014.

There were no fatalities on large scheduled commercial airlines in 2015 for the sixth consecutive year. There were no fatalities on large nonscheduled airlines (charter airlines) in 2015 and 2014. There were nine fatalities in 2013.

Small commuter airlines had five accidents in 2015 compared with four accidents in 2014. There was one fatality in 2015 following none in 2014.

The number of small on-demand airline (air taxi) accidents rose to 38 in 2015 compared with 35 in 2014 and 44 in 2013.

There were 1,209 general aviation (noncommercial) accidents in 2015, down from 1,223 in 2014. 2015 accidents resulted in 376 deaths, down from 424 in 2014.

United States

In the United States, the National Transportation Safety Board compiles data on aviation flight hours, accidents and fatalities for commercial and general aviation.

Commercial airlines are divided into two categories according to the type of aircraft used: aircraft with 10 or more seats and aircraft with fewer than 10 seats. The nonscheduled commercial aircraft with more than 10 seats are also called charter airlines. Commercial airlines flying aircraft with fewer than 10 seats include commuter (scheduled) airlines and on-demand air taxis. General aviation includes all U.S. noncommercial or privately owned aircraft.

In fiscal year 2015 about 786 million people flew on commercial airlines in the United States, up 4.0 percent from 2014. The Federal Aviation Administration projects that more than 1 billion people will fly on scheduled commercial airlines in the United States annually by 2031.

Aircraft Accidents In The United States, 2015[1]

	Flight hours (000)	Number of accidents		Number of fatalities[2]	Accidents per 100,000 flight hours
		Total	Fatal		
Commercial airlines					
10 or more seats					
Scheduled	17,435	27	0	0	0.155
Nonscheduled	385	1	0	0	0.260
Less than 10 seats					
Commuter	343	5	1	1	1.458
On-demand	3,566	38	7	27	1.066
General aviation	20,576	1,209	229	376	5.851
Total civil aviation	**NA**	**1,280**	**237**	**404**	**NA**

[1]Preliminary data. Totals do not add because of collisions involving aircraft in different categories. [2]Includes nonpassenger deaths.
NA=Data not available.
Source: National Transportation Safety Board.

Large Airline Accidents In The United States, 2006-2015[1]

Year	Flight hours	Total accidents	Fatal accidents	Total fatalities[2]	Total accidents per 100,000 flight hours
2006	19,263,209	33	2	50	0.171
2007	19,637,322	28	1	1	0.143
2008	19,126,766	28	2	3	0.146
2009	17,626,832	30	2	52	0.170
2010	17,750,986	30	1	2	0.169
2011	17,962,965	32	0	0	0.178
2012	17,722,236	26	0	0	0.147
2013	17,717,957	23	2	9	0.130
2014	17,646,147	29	0	0	0.164
2015[3]	17,820,000	28	0	0	0.157

[1]Scheduled and unscheduled planes with more than 10 seats. [2]Includes nonpassenger deaths. [3]Preliminary.
Source: National Transportation Safety Board.

World Aviation Losses

In 2015 more than 3.5 billion people flew safely on 37.6 million flights, according to the International Air Transport Association. The global accident rate (as measured by the rate of hull losses on Western-built jets) was 0.32 in 2015, or about one major accident for every 3.1 million flights. This compares with an accident rate of 0.27 in 2014. A hull loss is an accident in which the aircraft is destroyed or substantially damaged and is not subsequently repaired. There were 68 accidents in 2015 (on Eastern- and Western-built aircraft), down from 77 in 2014. The Germanwings 9525 and Metrojet 9268 losses that resulted in the deaths of 374 passengers and crew are not included in the statistics because they were caused by deliberate acts of unlawful interference, namely pilot suicide and suspected terrorism.

World Aviation Accidents, 2011-2015[1]

Year	Accidents[2]		Fatalities[2]	Total accident rate[3]
	Total	Fatal		
2011	96	22	490	0.58
2012	78	15	414	0.28
2013	88	15	177	0.38
2014	77	12	641	0.27
2015	68	4	136	0.32

[1]Accident information is current at the time of publication, but is subject to future revision. [2]On Eastern and Western built jet aircraft. [3]Measured in hull losses per million flights of Western built jet aircraft. A hull loss is an accident in which the aircraft is destroyed or substantially damaged and is not subsequently repaired.
Source: International Air Transport Association.

Top 10 Deadliest World Aviation Crashes

Rank	Date	Location	Country	Operator	Fatalities
1	Mar. 27, 1977	Tenerife	Spain	Pan Am, KLM	583
2	Aug. 12, 1985	Yokota AFB	Japan	JAL	520
3	Nov. 12, 1996	New Delhi	India	Saudi Arabian Airlines, Kazakhstan Airlines	349
4	Mar. 3, 1974	Ermenonville	France	Turkish Airlines	346
5	Jun. 23, 1985	Atlantic Ocean		Air India	329
6	Aug. 19, 1980	Jedda	Saudi Arabia	Saudi Arabian Airlines	301
7	Jul. 17, 2014	Grabovo	Ukraine	Malaysia Airlines	298
8	Jul. 3, 1988	Persian Gulf		Iran Air	290
9	Feb. 19, 2003	Kerman	Iran	Islamic Republic of Iran Air Force	275
10	May 25, 1979	Chicago	U.S.	American Airlines	273

Source: Aircraft Crashes Record Office, Geneva.

WORKPLACE

According to the National Safety Council (NSC), the total cost of unintentional workplace deaths and injuries in 2014 was an estimated $140 billion. This figure includes wage and productivity losses of injured workers of $45.7 billion, medical costs of $31.7 billion and administrative expenses of $44.7 billion. Other employers' costs include their uninsured costs that add another $11.5 billion and included are $3.5 billion in motor vehicle damage and fire losses of $2.9 billion. Economic losses from work injuries are not comparable from year to year; as additional or more precise data become available to the NSC, they are used from that year forward. Previously estimated figures are not revised.

Workplace Losses And Deaths, 2005-2014

Year	Workers[3] (000)	Economic loss[1] ($ millions)		Loss per worker (In 2014 dollars)[4]	Fatalities[2]	
		Dollars when occurred	In 2014 dollars[4]		Number	Per 100,000 workers
2005	142,946	$160,400	$194,431	$1,360	4,984	3.5
2006	145,607	164,700	193,405	1,328	5,088	3.5
2007	147,203	175,300	200,152	1,360	4,829	3.3
2008	146,535	183,000	201,217	1,373	4,423	3.3
2009	141,102	168,900	186,377	1,321	3,744	2.9
2010	140,298	176,900	192,054	1,369	3,896	3.0
2011	140,298	188,900	198,807	1,417	3,901	3.0
2012	143,709	198,200	204,365	1,422	3,903	3.0
2013	145,171	206,100	209,443	1,443	3,899	2.9
2014	146,307	140,000	140,000[5]	957	4,005	2.9

[1]Economic loss from unintentional injuries. These estimates are not comparable from year to year. [2]From unintentional injuries. [3]Age 16 and over, gainfully employed, including owners, managers and other paid employees, the self-employed, unpaid family workers and active duty resident military personnel. [4]Adjusted to 2014 dollars by the Insurance Information Institute using the Bureau of Labor Statistics' Inflation Calculator. [5]The 2015 National Safety Council cost estimate model represents a complete redesign and is not comparable to previous cost estimates. The 2014 estimate should be considered a data break from previous years.

Source: National Safety Council. *Injury Facts®*, 2016 Edition. Itasca, IL; U.S. Department of Labor, Bureau of Labor Statistics.

Private Industries With The Largest Number Of Nonfatal Occupational Injuries And Illnesses, 2015[1]

Rank	Industry	Number (000)	Incidence rate[2]
1	General medical and surgical hospitals	214.1	6.0
2	Restaurants and other eating places	185.2	3.0
3	Nursing and residential care facilities	171.9	6.8
4	Specialty trade contractors	138.0	3.7
5	Ambulatory health care services	130.0	2.4
6	General merchandise stores	103.3	4.5
	Total, private industry	**2,905.9**	**3.0**

Combined the six industries accounted for almost one-third (32.4 percent) of all cases reported among private industry workplaces in 2015.

[1]Based on industries with 100,000 or more cases in 2015. Excludes farms with fewer than 11 employees. [2]The incidence rates represent the number of injuries and illnesses per 100 full-time workers.

Source: U.S. Department of Labor, Bureau of Labor Statistics.

Top 10 Occupations With The Largest Number Of Injuries And Illnesses, 2014[1]

Rank	Occupation	Number	Percent of total
1	Truck drivers, heavy and tractor-trailer	55,710	6.1%
2	Laborers (nonconstruction)	55,370	6.0
3	Janitors and cleaners	39,290	4.3
4	Nursing assistants	39,020	4.3
5	Police and sheriff's patrol officers	27,660	3.0
6	General maintenance and repair workers	27,460	3.0
7	Registered nurses	26,830	2.9
8	Stock clerks and order fillers	25,250	2.8
9	Retail salespersons	23,500	2.6
10	Light truck and delivery service drivers	22,420	2.4
	Total, top 10	**342,510**	**37.4%**
	Total, all occupations	**916,440**	**100.0%**

[1]Nonfatal injuries and illnesses involving days off from work for private industries; excludes farms with fewer than 11 employees.

Source: U.S. Department of Labor, Bureau of Labor Statistics

Causes Of Workplace Deaths

According to the U.S. Department of Labor, the highest rate of workplace fatalities in 2014 was among logging workers, with 109.5 deaths per 100,000 full-time employees, followed by fishing workers, aircraft pilots and flight engineers, and roofers. The all-industry average was 3.3 deaths per 100,000 workers.

Workplace Deaths By Cause, 2013-2014[1]

Cause	2013	2014	
	Number	Number	Percent of total
All transportation (includes vehicle crashes)	1,865	1,891	40%
Vehicle crashes[2]	1,099	1,075	23
Falls	724	793	17
Assaults and violence (includes homicides)	773	749	16
Homicides	404	403	9
Contact with objects and equipment	721	708	15
Exposure to harmful substances or environments	335	390	8
Fires and explosions	149	137	3
Total workplace fatalities	**4,585**	**4,679**	**100%**

[1]From intentional and unintentional sources. [2]Roadway incidents involving motorized land vehicles.

Source: U.S. Department of Labor, Bureau of Labor Statistics, Census of Fatal Occupational Injuries.

Asbestos-Related Illness

Exposure to asbestos can cause lung cancer and other respiratory diseases. The first asbestos-related lawsuit was filed in 1966. A large number of workers who may have physical signs of exposure but not a debilitating disease are filing claims now out of concern that if they later develop an illness, the company responsible may be bankrupt, due to other asbestos claims. It can take as long as 40 years after exposure for someone to be diagnosed with an asbestos-related illness.

Estimated Asbestos Losses, 2006-2015[1] ($ billions)

Year	Beginning reserve	Losses Incurred[2]	Paid	Ending reserve[3]
2006	$25.2	$1.7	$2.6	$24.1
2007	23.2	2.5	2.5	23.5
2008	23.5	1.1	3.7	20.5
2009	20.6	1.9	2.0	20.4
2010	20.5	2.4	2.3	20.6
2011	20.6	1.8	1.8	20.6
2012	20.4	1.9	2.0	20.3
2013	20.4	2.0	2.1	20.3
2014	20.3	1.5	2.4	19.4
2015	19.4	1.7	2.8	18.3

Over the 10 years 2006 to 2015, incurred losses for asbestos claims have averaged $1.8 billion. Losses in 2007 at $2.5 billion and 2010 at $2.4 billion were significantly above average.

[1]All amounts are net of reinsurance recoveries. [2]Incurred losses are losses related to events that have occurred, regardless of whether or not the claims have been paid, net of reinsurance. Includes loss adjustment expenses. [3]Because of changes in the population of insurers reporting data each year, the beginning reserve may not equal the ending reserve of the prior year.

Source: NAIC data, sourced from S&P Global Market Intelligence, Insurance Information Institute.

HOME

In 2014, 20.2 million Americans, or one in 16 people, experienced an unintentional injury in the home that required aid from a medical professional, according to an analysis by the National Safety Council (NSC). Injuries requiring medical attention occur more often at home than in public places, the workplace and motor vehicle crashes combined, according to the NSC. There were 69,500 deaths from unintentional home injuries in 2014. Despite population growth and a corresponding rise in the number of fatal injuries, the rate of fatal home injuries has declined dramatically over the past 100 years, falling by 22 percent to 21.8 deaths per 100,000 people in 2014 from 28 deaths per 100,000 people in 1912. However, the number and rate of unintentional home injury deaths has been steadily rising since 2000, largely due to increases in unintentional poisonings and falls.

Unintentional Home Deaths And Injuries, 2014

Deaths	69,500
Medically consulted injuries	20,200,000
Death rate per 100,000 population	21.8
Costs	$241.9 billion

Source: National Safety Council. *Injury Facts®*, 2016 Edition. Itasca, IL.

Principal Types Of Home Unintentional Injury Deaths, 2014

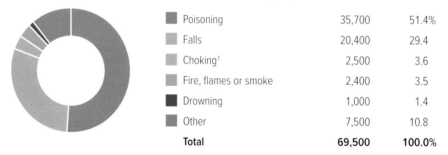

◼	Poisoning	35,700	51.4%
◼	Falls	20,400	29.4
◼	Choking[1]	2,500	3.6
◼	Fire, flames or smoke	2,400	3.5
◼	Drowning	1,000	1.4
◼	Other	7,500	10.8
	Total	**69,500**	**100.0%**

[1]Inhalation and ingestion of food or other object that obstructs breathing.
Source: National Safety Council. *Injury Facts®*, 2016 Edition. Itasca, IL.

CAUSES OF DEATH

Mortality risks

Heart disease is the leading cause of death in the United States, accounting for 614,000 fatalities in 2014, according to the Centers for Disease Control and Prevention. Influenza and pneumonia ranked eighth in 2014, with some 55,000 fatalities. However, pandemic influenza viruses have the potential to be far more deadly. An estimated 675,000 Americans died during the 1918 Spanish influenza pandemic, the deadliest and most infectious known influenza strain to date.

Top 15 Major Causes of Death, 2014

Rank	Cause of death	Number of deaths	Age-adjusted death rate[1]	
			Rate	Percent change from 2013
1	Heart disease	614,348	167.0	-1.6%
2	Malignant neoplasms (tumors)	591,699	161.2	-1.2
3	Chronic lower respiratory diseases	147,101	40.5	-3.8
4	Accidents (unintentional injuries)	136,053	40.5	2.8
5	Cerebrovascular diseases (stroke)	133,103	36.5	0.8
6	Alzheimer's disease	93,541	25.4	8.1
7	Diabetes	76,488	20.9	-1.4
8	Influenza and pneumonia	55,227	15.1	-5.0
9	Kidney disease	48,146	13.2	[2]
10	Intentional self-harm (suicide)	42,773	13.0	3.2
11	Septicemia	38,940	10.7	[2]
12	Chronic liver disease and cirrhosis	38,170	10.4	2.0
13	Hypertension[3]	30,221	8.2	-3.5
14	Parkinson's disease	26,150	7.4	1.4
15	Pneumonitis due to solids and liquids	18,792	5.1	1.9
	All deaths	**2,626,418**	**724.6**	**-1.0%**

[1]Per 100,000 population; factors out differences based on age. [2]Less than 0.1 percent. [3]Essential (primary) hypertension and hypertensive renal disease.

Source: National Center for Health Statistics.

Gun Deaths And Injuries

The societal cost of U.S. injuries from firearms, including lost work time, medical care, insurance, criminal-justice expenses, pain, suffering and lost quality of life, amounted to about $174 billion in 2010, according to an analysis of Centers for Disease Control and Prevention data by the Pacific Institute for Research and Evaluation. Fatal injuries accounted for $153.3 billion, or nearly 90 percent of the costs. Suicides accounted for 53 percent of the societal cost of firearm injuries, followed by homicides and assaults, accounting for 41 percent. Unintentional acts, legal intervention and acts of undetermined intent make up the remainder.

Deaths By Firearms, 2013 And 2014

Deaths caused by firearms	Number		Percent of total	
	2013	2014[1]	2013	2014[1]
Accidental discharge of firearms	505	586	1.5%	1.7%
Suicide by firearms	21,175	21,334	63.8	63.5
Assault (homicide) by firearms	11,208	10,945	33.8	32.6
Undetermined intent	281	270	0.8	0.8
Total[2]	33,169	33,599	100.0%	100.0%

[1]Preliminary. [2]Excludes deaths resulting from legal intervention.

Source: Centers for Disease Control and Prevention, National Vital Statistics Report.

Chapter 9
Factors Affecting Costs

COST OF GOODS AND SERVICES

The Bureau of Labor Statistics *Consumer Expenditures Survey* describes the buying habits of American consumers, using household expenditure records and surveys. Expenditures include goods and services purchased, whether or not payment was made at the time of purchase and all sales and excise taxes.

Income, age of family members, geographic location, taste and personal preference influence expenditures. Location often affects the cost of auto and homeowners insurance. Rural households spend less than urban households on auto insurance; regional variations in residential building costs affect spending on homeowners insurance. In addition to the number and types of cars, where they are driven and by whom, auto insurance prices are influenced by such factors as the degree of competition in the marketplace and how claimants are compensated, through the no-fault or traditional tort systems.

Insurance And Other Consumer Expenditures As A Percent Of Total Household Spending, 1990-2015[1]

	1990	1995	2000	2005	2010	2013	2014	2015
Housing	30.0%	31.7%	31.7%	31.9%	33.7%	32.8%	32.6%	32.1%
Transportation	15.9	16.4	17.5	16.0	13.9	15.6	14.9	15.0
Food	15.0	14.0	13.6	12.8	12.7	12.9	12.6	12.5
Retirement[2]	8.8	8.0	7.8	10.4	10.5	10.2	10.1	10.7
Other	10.6	10.2	10.5	10.4	10.4	10.0	10.0	10.1
Total insurance	5.8	6.8	6.3	6.5	7.3	7.7	8.8	8.7
Health	2.0	2.7	2.6	2.9	3.8	4.4	5.4	5.3
Vehicle	2.0	2.2	2.0	2.0	2.1	2.0	2.1	1.9
Homeowners	0.5	0.7	0.7	0.7	0.8	0.7	0.7	0.8
Life	1.2	1.1	1.0	0.8	0.6	0.6	0.6	0.6
Other	0.1	0.1	0.1	0.1	[3]	[3]	0.1	[3]
Entertainment	5.0	5.0	4.9	5.1	5.2	4.9	5.1	5.1
Clothing	5.7	5.3	4.9	4.1	3.5	3.1	3.3	3.3
Healthcare	3.1	2.7	2.8	2.8	2.8	2.7	2.7	2.4

[1]Ranked by 2015 expenditures. [2]Mostly payroll deductions for retirement purposes such as Social Security (74 percent of retirement expenditures), government and private pension plans (13 percent) and nonpayroll deposits such as IRAs (13 percent) in 2015. [3]Less than 0.1 percent.
Note: Percentages do not add to 100 percent due to rounding.

Source: U.S. Department of Labor, Bureau of Labor Statistics.

Insurance Expenditures As A Percentage Of Total Household Spending, 2015

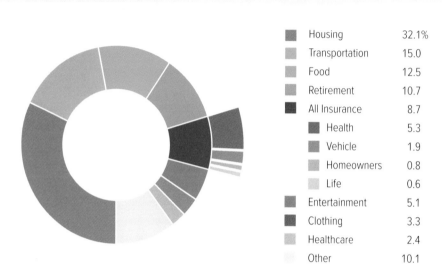

Housing	32.1%
Transportation	15.0
Food	12.5
Retirement	10.7
All Insurance	8.7
Health	5.3
Vehicle	1.9
Homeowners	0.8
Life	0.6
Entertainment	5.1
Clothing	3.3
Healthcare	2.4
Other	10.1

Note: Percentages do not add up to 100 percent due to rounding.

Source: U.S. Department of Labor, Bureau of Labor Statistics.

Insurance accounted for 8.7 percent of household spending in 2015, down 0.1 percentage points from 2014. Of this, the share spent on health insurance fell 0.1 percentage points and the vehicle insurance share fell 0.2 percentage points. The share spent on homeowners insurance rose 0.1 percentage point and the life insurance share remained the same.

Consumer Prices

The Bureau of Labor Statistics consumer price index (CPI) tracks changes in the prices paid by consumers for a representative basket of goods and services. The cost of living (all items) rose 0.1 percent in 2015. The cost of motor vehicle insurance and hospital services rose more (5.4 percent and 4.1 percent, respectively). The cost of tenants and household insurance rose 3.2 percent and medical care rose 2.6 percent.

Consumer Price Indices For Insurance And Related Items And Annual Rates Of Change, 2006-2015 (Base: 1982-84=100)

Year	Cost of living (all items)		Motor vehicle insurance		Medical care items		Physicians' services		Hospital services[1]	
	Index	Percent change	Index	Percent change	Index	Percent change	Index	Percent change	Index	Percent change
2006	201.6	3.2%	331.8	0.6%	336.2	4.0%	291.9	1.5%	172.1	6.5%
2007	207.3	2.8	333.1	0.4	351.1	4.4	303.2	3.9	183.6	6.7
2008	215.3	3.8	341.5	2.5	364.1	3.7	311.3	2.7	197.2	7.4
2009	214.5	-0.4	357.0	4.5	375.6	3.2	320.8	3.0	210.7	6.9
2010	218.1	1.6	375.2	5.1	388.4	3.4	331.3	3.3	227.2	7.8
2011	224.9	3.2	388.7	3.6	400.3	3.0	340.3	2.7	241.2	6.2
2012	229.6	2.1	402.5	3.6	414.9	3.7	347.3	2.1	253.6	5.1
2013	233.0	1.5	419.4	4.2	425.1	2.5	354.2	2.0	265.4	4.7
2014	236.7	1.6	437.2	4.2	435.3	2.4	359.1	1.4	278.8	5.0
2015	237.0	0.1	460.6	5.4	446.8	2.6	366.1	1.9	290.1	4.1
Percent change, 2006-2015		17.6%		38.8%		32.9%		25.4%		68.6%

Year	Motor vehicle body work		New vehicles		New cars		New trucks[2]		Used cars and trucks	
	Index	Percent change	Index	Percent change	Index	Percent change	Index	Percent change	Index	Percent change
2006	224.8	4.6%	137.6	-0.2%	136.4	0.9%	142.9	-1.7%	140.0	0.4%
2007	232.2	3.3	136.3	-1.0	135.9	-0.4	140.7	-1.5	135.7	-3.0
2008	239.7	3.2	134.2	-1.5	135.4	-0.3	137.1	-2.6	134.0	-1.3
2009	248.5	3.7	135.6	1.1	136.7	0.9	138.8	1.3	127.0	-5.2
2010	254.4	2.4	138.0	1.8	138.1	1.0	142.7	2.8	143.1	12.7
2011	259.9	2.2	141.9	2.8	142.2	3.0	146.5	2.7	149.0	4.1
2012	264.9	1.9	144.2	1.7	144.2	1.4	149.4	1.9	150.3	0.9
2013	271.0	2.3	145.8	1.1	144.9	0.5	151.8	1.6	149.9	-0.3
2014	278.0	2.6	146.3	0.3	144.5	-0.3	153.6	1.1	149.1	-0.5
2015	280.8	1.0	147.1	0.6	144.4	-0.1	155.4	1.2	147.1	-1.3
Percent change, 2006-2015		24.9%		6.9%		5.9%		8.8%		5.1%

(table continues)

Consumer Price Indices For Insurance And Related Items And Annual Rates Of Change, 2006-2015 (Base: 1982-84=100) (Cont'd)

Year	Tenants and household insurance[3,4]		Repair of household items[3,5]		Legal services		Existing single- family homes	
	Index	Percent change	Index	Percent change	Index	Percent change	Median price ($000)	Percent change
2006	116.5	-0.9%	154.7	5.0%	250.0	3.4%	$222	1.0%
2007	117.0	0.4	161.2	4.2	260.3	4.1	219	-1.3
2008	118.8	1.6	170.0	5.5	270.7	4.0	198	-9.5
2009	121.5	2.2	176.0	3.5	278.1	2.7	173	-12.9
2010	125.7	3.5	181.7	3.2	288.1	3.6	173	0.3
2011	127.4	1.4	NA	NA	297.4	3.2	166	-4.0
2012	131.3	3.1	198.7	NA	303.5	2.0	177	6.6
2013	135.4	3.1	206.7	4.0	311.8	2.8	197	11.4
2014	141.9	4.8	212.4	2.8	318.5	2.1	208	5.7
2015	146.4	3.2	220.1	3.6	323.6	1.6	222	6.8
Percent change, 2006-2015		25.7%		42.3%		29.4%		0.2%

[1]December 1996=100. [2]December 1983=100. [3]December 1997=100. [4]Only includes insurance covering rental properties. [5]Includes appliances, reupholstery and inside home maintenance. NA=Data not available. Note: Percent changes after 2007 for consumer price indices and all years for the median price of existing single-family homes calculated from unrounded data.

Source: U.S. Department of Labor, Bureau of Labor Statistics; National Association of Realtors.

FRAUD

Insurance fraud is a deliberate deception perpetrated against or by an insurance company or agent for the purpose of financial gain. Fraud may be committed at different points in the insurance transaction by applicants for insurance, policyholders, third-party claimants or professionals who provide services to claimants. Insurance agents and company employees may also commit insurance fraud. Common fraud include padding, or inflating actual claims, misrepresenting facts on an insurance application, submitting claims for injuries or damage that never occurred and staging accidents.

Size Of The Problem

The exact amount of fraud committed is difficult to determine. In the late 1980s, the Insurance Informatic Institute interviewed claims adjusters and concluded that fraud accounted for about 10 percent of the property/casualty insurance industry's incurred losses and loss adjustment expenses each year. Using this measure, over the five-year period from 2011 to 2015, property/casualty fraud amounted to about $34 billion each year. The figure can fluctuate based on line of business, economic conditions and othe factors. The nature of fraud is constantly evolving.

Insurance fraud is the second costliest white collar crime, according to the National Insurance Crime Bureau (NICB), trailing only tax evasion. The NICB is a not-for-profit organization that works with insurers and law enforcement to identify, detect and prosecute insurance crime, including insurance fraud. The bureau fosters fraud awareness, see nicb.org.

The Insurance Research Council estimated that between $5.6 billion and $7.7 billion was fraudulently added to paid claims for auto insurance bodily injury payments in 2012. The IRC studied more than 35,000 auto injury claims closed with payment and reported the results in its 2016 report, *Fraud and Buildup in Auto Injury Claims*. Fraud accounted for between 15 percent and 17 percent of total claims payments for auto insurance bodily injury.

Fighting Insurance Fraud

Insurers are at the front line in combatting insurance fraud despite the increase in the number of states that have passed laws to criminalize the practice. By 2016 every state and the District of Columbia had enacted laws that classify fraud as a crime at least for some lines of insurance and have instituted immunity for reporting insurance fraud. Forty-three states and the District of Columbia had fraud bureaus or divisions where fraud can be reported, investigated and prosecuted. Twenty-two states and the District of Columbia required insurers to create and implement programs to reduce insurance fraud. Many property/casualty insurers have created Special Investigative Units within their companies. These use specially trained professionals to look into suspicious claims, then work with law enforcement officials and organizations like the NICB to catch perpetrators.

One of the most effective means of combatting fraud is the adoption of data technologies that cut the time needed to recognize fraud. Advances in analytical technology are crucial in the fight against fraud to keep pace with sophisticated rings that constantly develop new scams. According to a company that develops insurance fraud analytics, insurers typically see evidence of organized staged accidents shortly after they start a direct internet channel for their customers. These websites allow criminals to exploit loopholes in consumer applications and underwriting and they test the systems by filing many applications and observing which ones are flagged for additional information.

Traditional approaches that concentrate on detection after payments are made (pay and chase programs) have been improved by predictive modeling, claims scoring and other tools that attempt to uncover fraud before a payment is made. Newer strategies are employed when claims are first filed. Suspicious claims are flagged for further review while those with no suspicious elements are processed normally. Data-mining programs that scan many insurance claims have been improved by the consolidation of insurance industry claims databases, such as ISO's ClaimSearch, the world's largest comprehensive database of claims information. Systems that identify anomalies in a database can be used to develop algorithms that enable an insurer to automatically stop claim payments. An insurance technology expert said that this approach has produced 20 to 50 percent reductions in fraud loss for some insurers. Newer programs that analyze patterns and text, such as adjuster notes, can search various kinds of data formats for key terms and word patterns. Investigators scan social media sites such as Facebook, Twitter and YouTube when they examine workers compensation claims. Software developers offer systems that scan publicly accessible sites for claimants who post activities from which they would be physically restricted due to claims, according to an A.M. Best article.

In 2014 the Coalition Against Insurance Fraud and the SAS Institute published a report entitled, *State of Insurance Fraud Technology*, to track how insurers deploy technology to combat insurance fraud. An online survey of 42 insurers reported that 95 percent use anti-fraud technology, up from 88 percent in 2012. Fifty-one percent of the survey participants said suspected fraud has increased to some degree. Seven percent said it has increased significantly.

Payment Attributable To Fraud In Auto Insurance Bodily Injury Claims, 2002-2012[1]
($ billions)

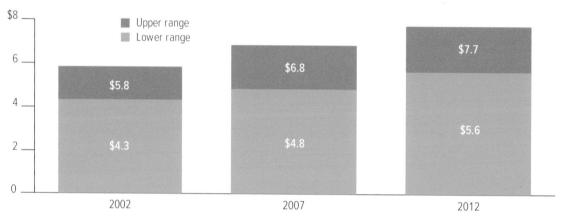

[1]Portion of paid claim dollars attributable to fraud or buildup among auto insurance bodily injury coverages: bodily injury, personal injury protection, medical payments, uninsured motorists and underinsured motorists.

Source: Insurance Research Council.

LITIGIOUSNESS

Insurers' Legal Defense Costs

Lawsuits against businesses affect the cost of insurance and the products and services of the industries sued. Travelers Insurance 2016 *Business Risk Index* showed that legal liability was the fourth-highest rated worry for business leaders in the United States for the second year in a row. Of 1,202 business leaders surveyed, 51 percent indicated they worry about it somewhat or a great deal.

Businesses address their liability concerns through many types of risk management, of which insurance is an important component. Swiss Re data show that in 2014 the United States had the largest commercial liability insurance market in the world both in premium volume ($87 billion) and as a percentage of gross domestic product (0.52 percent). More than half of all global liability premiums were written in the United States.

Top 10 Largest World Commercial Liability Markets, 2014 (US$ billions)

Rank	Country	Direct premiums written		GDP[1]	Liability as a percentage of	
		Liability	Total nonlife		Total nonlife	GDP[1]
1	United States	$86.6	$539.3	$16,805.4	16.1%	0.52%
2	United Kingdom	10.6	101.0	2,713.9	10.5	0.39
3	Germany	8.6	92.9	3,751.9	9.2	0.23
4	France	6.7	83.3	2,812.5	8.1	0.24
5	Japan	6.3	85.5	4,913.0	7.3	0.13
6	Canada	5.0	50.6	1,831.0	9.9	0.27
7	Italy	5.0	46.3	2,133.5	10.8	0.23
8	Australia	4.9	32.7	1,501.0	14.9	0.33
9	China	4.2	105.5	9,603.2	3.9	0.04
10	Spain	2.1	31.2	1,369.5	6.9	0.16
	Total, countries shown	$140.0	$1,170.0	$47,400.0	12.0%	0.30%
	Total, all countries	$165.0	$1,600.0	$77,400.0	10.3%	0.21%

[1]Gross domestic product.
Source: Swiss Re.

9. FACTORS AFFECTING COSTS
Litigiousness

Insurers are required to defend their policyholders against lawsuits. The costs of settling a claim are reported on insurers' financial statements as defense and cost containment expenses incurred. These expenses include defense, litigation and medical cost containment. Expenditures for surveillance, litigation management and fees for appraisers, private investigators, hearing representatives and fraud investigators are included. In addition, attorney legal fees may be incurred owing to a duty to defend, even when coverage does not exist, because attorneys must be hired to issue opinions about coverage. Insurers' defense costs as a percentage of incurred losses are relatively high in some lines such as product liability and medical malpractice, reflecting the high cost of defending certain types of lawsuits, such as medical injury cases and class actions against pharmaceutical companies. For example, in 2015, in addition to $1.5 billion in product liability incurred losses, insurers spent $1.04 billion on settlement expenses, equivalent to 70.5 percent of the losses.

Defense Costs And Cost Containment Expenses As A Percent Of Incurred Losses, 2013-2015[1] ($000)

	2013		2014		2015	
	Amount	As a percent of incurred losses	Amount	As a percent of incurred losses	Amount	As a percent of incurred losses
Product liability	$1,166,236	75.1%	$952,997	77.4%	$1,037,576	70.5%
Medical malpractice	1,656,257	53.3	1,873,835	43.2	1,871,109	53.8
Commercial multiple peril[2]	2,096,543	37.7	2,083,103	39.1	1,977,804	34.7
Other liability	4,914,500	25.4	4,366,030	21.1	4,786,370	19.9
Workers compensation	3,035,186	12.3	3,357,813	12.9	3,305,927	13.7
Commercial auto liability	1,207,682	10.7	1,266,051	10.6	1,541,787	11.4
Private passenger auto liability	4,600,395	6.8	4,714,942	6.5	4,923,908	6.2
All liability lines	**$18,676,799**	**14.0%**	**$18,614,771**	**13.1%**	**$19,444,481**	**12.8%**

[1]Net of reinsurance, excluding state funds. [2]Liability portion only.

Source: NAIC data, sourced from S&P Global Market Intelligence, Insurance Information Institute.

9. FACTORS AFFECTING COSTS
Litigiousness

Personal Injury Awards

Most lawsuits are settled out of court. Of those that are tried and proceed to verdict, Jury Verdict Research data from Thomson Reuters show that in 2014 (latest data available) the median (or midpoint) award in personal injury cases was $75,000, up from $70,000 in 2013. The average award also rose in 2014 and was $1,055,480 compared with $1,010,069 in 2013. Thomson Reuters notes that average awards can be skewed by a few very high awards and that medians are more representative. In cases of product liability the highest median award in 2014 was in industrial/construction products cases ($2,541,000). In disputes concerning medical malpractice the highest median award was in childbirth cases ($2,160,420). In cases involving business negligence the highest median award was against manufacturing industries ($743,000).

Awards of $1 million or more accounted for 18 percent of all personal injury awards in 2013 and 2014, up from 17 percent in the prior two-year period. In 2013 and 2014, 76 percent of product liability awards and 51 percent of medical malpractice awards amounted to $1 million or more, the highest proportion of awards. Vehicular liability, and premises and personal negligence liability cases had the lowest proportion of awards of $1 million or more, at 8 percent and 11 percent, respectively.

Trends In Personal Injury Lawsuits, 2008-2014[1]

Year	Award median	Probability range[2]	Award range	Award mean
2008	$40,000	$10,000 - $225,780	$1 - $188,000,000	$836,978
2009	40,000	9,887 - 207,828	1 - 77,418,670	750,392
2010	39,216	10,000 - 200,000	1 - 71,000,000	653,898
2011	60,924	12,249 - 343,958	1 - 58,619,989	782,912
2012	75,000	19,100 - 356,481	1 - 155,237,000	1,097,759
2013	70,000	16,000 - 300,000	1 - 165,972,503	1,010,069
2014	75,000	16,412 - 400,000	1 - 172,061,728	1,055,480
Overall, 2008-2014	$50,000	$11,303 - $268,402	$1 - $188,000,000	$857,730

[1]Excludes punitive damages. [2]Twenty-five percent above and below the median award. The median represents the midpoint jury award. Half of the awards are above the median and half are below. This helps establish where awards tend to cluster.

Source: Reprinted with permission of Thomson Reuters, *Current Award Trends in Personal Injury*, 55th edition.

Median And Average Personal Injury Jury Awards By Type Of Liability, 2014

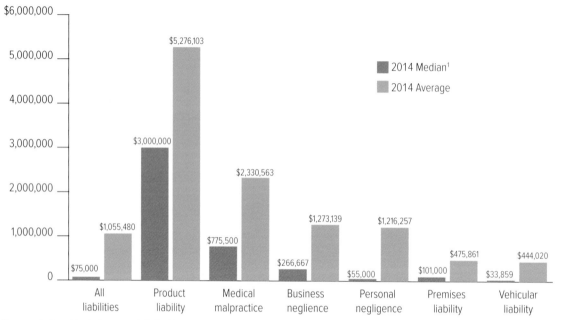

[1]Represents the midpoint jury award. Half of the awards are above the median and half are below.

Source: Reprinted with permission of Thomson Reuters, *Current Award Trends in Personal Injury*, 55th edition.

Directors And Liability Insurance

Directors and officers liability insurance (D&O) covers directors and officers of a company for negligent acts or omissions and for misleading statements that result in suits against the company. There are various forms of D&O coverage. Corporate reimbursement coverage indemnifies directors and officers of the organization. Side-A coverage provides D&O coverage for personal liability when directors and officers are not indemnified by the firm. Entity coverage for claims made specifically against the company is also available. D&O policies may be broadened to include coverage for employment practices liability (EPL). EPL coverage may also be purchased as a stand-alone policy.

Sixty-three percent of corporations purchased D&O coverage in 2015, according to the 2016 *RIMS Benchmark Survey* from the Risk and Insurance Management Society, based on a survey of 1,248 organizations. Banks were the most likely to purchase D&O coverage, with 88 percent of industry respondents purchasing the coverage, followed by 86 percent of respondents in telecommunication services. JLT Specialty's *2015 U.S. Directors and Officers Liability Survey* of 157 U.S. organizations that purchase D&O liability insurance found that the group's average D&O limits that were purchased was $131 million and the median limit purchased was $105 million. For public companies the average limit was $170 million. For private companies the average was $98 million. Twenty-four percent of public companies and 17 percent of private companies increased their D&O limits from their previous purchase. According to the 2014 survey 31 percent of respondents reported having had a claim in the past five years, with nonprofits reporting the highest proportion of claims (58 percent).

Types Of Directors And Officers Liability Claims By Ownership, 2011-2014[1]

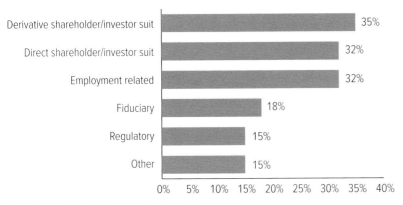

- Derivative shareholder/investor suit — 35%
- Direct shareholder/investor suit — 32%
- Employment related — 32%
- Fiduciary — 18%
- Regulatory — 15%
- Other — 15%

The percentage of respondents reporting derivative shareholder/investor lawsuits, the most widespread claim, dropped to 35 percent in 2014 from 38 percent in 2013.

[1]Based on participants in the survey that reported one or more claims over the five-year period.
Source: JLT Specialty *2015 U.S. Directors and Officers Liability Survey,*

Top 10 Writers Of Directors And Officers Liability Insurance By Direct Premiums Written, 2015[1] ($000)

Rank	Group/company	Direct premiums written	Market share
1	American International Group (AIG)	$1,071,634	16.7%
2	Chubb Ltd.[2]	923,802	14.4
3	XL Group plc	657,581	10.2
4	Tokio Marine Group	563,507	8.8
5	CNA Financial Corp.	415,477	6.5
6	Travelers Companies Inc.	312,749	4.9
7	American Financial Group Inc.	232,852	3.6
8	Zurich Insurance Group[3]	205,291	3.2
9	Alleghany Corp.	167,857	2.6
10	W. R. Berkley Corp.	159,354	2.5

Directors and officers liability insurance direct premiums written totaled $6.4 billion in 2015, according to S&P Global Market Intelligence.

[1]Includes property/casualty insurers that provided monoline directors and officers policies. The coverage may also be purchased as part of a package commercial multiperil policy. Includes some state funds.
[2]Chubb Ltd. data reflect the 2015 merger with Ace Ltd. [3]Data for Farmers Insurance Group of Companies and Zurich Financial Group (which owns Farmers' management company) are reported separately by S&P Global Market Intelligence.
Source: NAIC data, sourced from S&P Global Market Intelligence, Insurance Information Institute.

Directors And Officers Liability Claims By Type Of Claimant In The United States, 2011-2014[1]

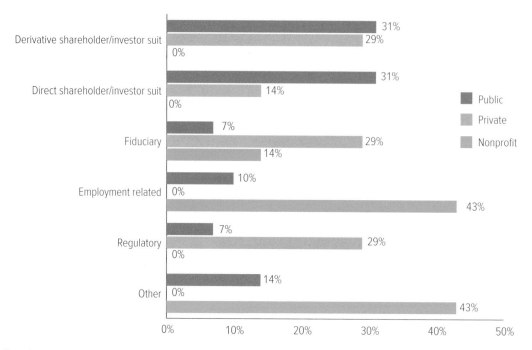

Derivative shareholder/investor suit — Public 31%, Private 29%, Nonprofit 0%

Direct shareholder/investor suit — Public 31%, Private 14%, Nonprofit 0%

Fiduciary — Public 7%, Private 29%, Nonprofit 14%

Employment related — Public 10%, Private 0%, Nonprofit 43%

Regulatory — Public 7%, Private 29%, Nonprofit 0%

Other — Public 14%, Private 0%, Nonprofit 43%

Legend: Public, Private, Nonprofit

[1]Based on participants in the survey that reported one or more claims over the four-year period.
Source: JLT Specialty *2015 U.S. Directors and Officers Liability Survey*.

Employment Practices Liability

Employment practices are a frequent source of claims against directors, officers and their organizations. Organizations that purchase insurance for employment practices liability (EPL) claims typically either buy a stand-alone EPL insurance policy or endorse their directors and officers liability (D&O) policy to cover employment practices liability. In 2014, 9 percent of public companies responding to a JLT Specialty survey shared or blended their D&O limits with another coverage such as EPL or fiduciary liability, compared with 44 percent of private companies and 67 percent of nonprofits.

In 2015, 33 percent of the 1,248 respondents to the *2016 RIMS Benchmark Survey* from the Risk and Insurance Management Society said they bought EPL policies. Banks were the most likely to purchase EPL coverage, with 68 percent of industry respondents purchasing the coverage, followed by information technology companies (46 percent), nonbank financials (44 percent), consumer discretionary firms (42 percent), and professional services (41 percent). American International Group Inc. was the leading writer, based on EPL premiums written, with a 23.7 percent market share in 2015, followed by Zurich Insurance Group Ltd. (11.3 percent), Markel (10.4 percent), XL Catlin (10.4 percent) and AXIS Capital Holdings Ltd. (8.1 percent).

Trends In Employment Practices Liability, 2010-2014

Year	Median (midpoint) award	Probability range[1]
2010	$172,000	$50,000 - $385,000
2011	271,000	83,811 - 552,500
2012	68,195	11,598 - 256,254
2013	100,000	15,772 - 250,497
2014	87,975	20,000 - 306,108

[1]The middle 50 percent of all awards arranged in ascending order in a sampling, 25 percent above and below the median award.

Source: Reprinted with permission of Thomson Reuters, *Employment Practice Liability: Jury Award Trends and Statistics*, 2015 edition.

Employment Practices Liability, By Defendant Type, 2008-2014[1]

Service/retail companies	47%
Government entities	38
Manufacturing/industrial companies	9
Transportation companies	4
Other	2

[1]Based on plaintiff and defendant verdicts rendered.

Source: Reprinted with permission of Thomson Reuters, Employment Practice Liability: Jury Award Trends And Statistics, 2015 edition.

Shareholder Lawsuits

Cornerstone Research has conducted annual studies of securities class-action settlements and filings each year since the passage of the 1995 Private Securities Litigation Reform Act, enacted to curb frivolous shareholder lawsuits.

At 189, new filings in 2015 were the highest since 2008.

2015 filings were dominated by consumer noncyclical companies such as biotechology, pharmaceutical and healthcare companies.

Post-Reform Act Class-Action Filings Of Securities Lawsuits By Industry, 1997-2015[1]

Industry	Average 1997-2014	2014	2015
Consumer	67	81	77
Communications	29	17	26
Technology	24	14	24
Industrial	17	10	19
Financial	35	26	17
Energy	8	15	11
Basic materials	4	4	9
Utilities	3	1	4
Other	1	2	2
Total	**188**	**170**	**189**

[1]Private Securities Litigation Reform Act of 1995.
Source: Cornerstone Research.

The number of settlements grew to 80 in 2015 from 63 in 2014 due in part to three years of increases in case filings.

There were eight mega-settlements in 2015 ($100 million or more) compared with one in 2014, contributing to the increase in total settlement dollars.

Post-Reform Act Class-Action Filings Of Securities Lawsuits, 1996-2015[1] (2015 dollars)

Settlements	1996-2013	2014	2015
Minimum	$0.1 million	$0.3 million	$0.4 million
Median	8.2 million	6.0 million	6.1 million
Average	55.6 million	17.0 million	37.9 million
Maximum	8.5 billion	265.3 million	970.5 million
Total settlements	**$80.9 billion**	**$1.1 billion**	**$3.0 billion**
Number of settlements	**1,457**	**63**	**80**

[1]Private Securities Litigation Reform Act of 1995; adjusted for inflation by Cornerstone Research.
Source: Cornerstone Research.

SPECIAL REPORT

Cyberrisk: Threat And Opportunity

Robert P. Hartwig, Ph.D., CPCU, and Claire Wilkinson
October 2016

I. Growth In Interest In Cyber Liability

An explosion of data and digital technologies, combined with the increasing complexity of threats and changing regulatory expectations, is propelling the cyberrisk landscape into uncharted territory.

Economic thought leaders have warned that failing to understand and address risks related to technology, primarily the systemic cascading effects of cyberrisks or the breakdown of critical information infrastructure, could have far-reaching consequences for national economics, economic sectors and global enterprises. As the Internet of Things (IoT) leads to more connections between people and machines, cyber dependency will increase, raising the odds of an attack with potential cascading effects across the cyber ecosystem.[1]

Emerging technologies such as drones, additive manufacturing (3-D printing, for example), smart city projects, internet-connected home appliances and autonomous vehicles could also disrupt established business practices and create new security threats, fundamentally changing the nature of risks.[2] Effective global governance will be critical to manage evolving security and privacy risks going forward.

Number And Impact Of Data Breaches Continues To Rise

In 2015 a total of 781 U.S. data breaches were tracked, with 169 million records exposed, according

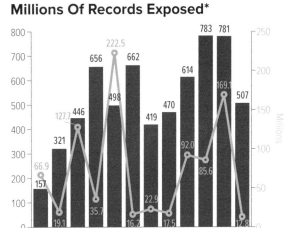

Fig. 1

Number Of Data Breaches/ Millions Of Records Exposed*

*Figures as of July 7, 2016.
Source: Identity Theft Resource Center.

to the Identity Theft Resource Center (Fig. 1).[3] This represents the second highest year since the center began tracking breaches in 2005.

The ongoing trend of record high numbers of breaches continues—in the first half of 2016, some 507 data breach events had been publicly disclosed as of July 7, 2016, with 12.8 million records exposed.

A high profile global breach with massive fallout is the Panama Papers online leak targeting Pana-manian law firm Mossack Fonseca. This email hack included 2.6 terabytes of data, including 4.8 million email messages and 2.2 million PDFs. The leaked information allegedly details the ways dozens of high-ranking politicians, their relatives or close associ-ates in more than 40 countries used offshore companies to hide income and avoid paying taxes. More than 100 news organizations published reports based on the leaked information starting in early April 2016. Mean-while, the just-disclosed 2014 Yahoo breach believed to have been the work of a state-sponsored group, compromised a record 500 million accounts. It high-lights the scope of the threat and widespread impact as users scramble to reset passwords. Disclosure of the breach comes as Yahoo tries to complete its pending deal with Verizon. Both events serve as a reminder of the importance of having a robust insurance program and cybersecurity strategy.

Breaches targeting medical/healthcare providers continue apace in 2016. A ransomware attack in February against a Hollywood hospital forced its computer systems offline for more than one week. While patient records were not compromised in this attack, Hollywood Presby-terian Medical Center paid a $17,000 ransom in bitcoin to the hacker to regain control of its systems. In July 2015, hackers accessed as many as 4.5 million patient records in UCLA Health System's computer network.

Insurers are also coming under attack. Two high profile breaches in 2015 occurred at health insurers Anthem and Premera Blue Cross. At Anthem, hackers gained access to a corporate database containing the personally identifiable information on 78.8 million current and former U.S. customers and employees. Anthem also stated that anywhere from 8.8 million to 18.8 million non-customers could have been impacted. Meanwhile, Premera Blue Cross suffered a network intrusion in March 2015 that compromised the financial and medical records of 11 million customers.

The U.S. government continues to be a target of hackers. Recent breaches at the Federal Deposit Insurance Corp. (FDIC) and the IRS follow multiple breaches in May 2015 of the Office of Personnel Management and Interior Department systems, when

hackers stole records on as many as 22 million current and former civilian U.S. government employees. The U.S. Federal Reserve is also reported to have been the target of multiple attacks.

Other recent victims include well-known brands such as Wendy's, Verizon Enterprise Solutions, Ashley Madison, Sony Pictures, Staples, Home Depot, JP Morgan Chase, PF Chang's, eBay, Snapchat and Target.

Yet despite the large number reported, the actual number of breaches and exposed records is without a doubt much higher as many, if not most, attacks go unreported and undetected.

The majority of the 781 data breaches in 2015 hit business and medical/healthcare organizations, according to the Identity Theft Resource Center (Fig. 2).

Fig. 2

2015 Data Breaches By Business Category, By Number Of Breaches

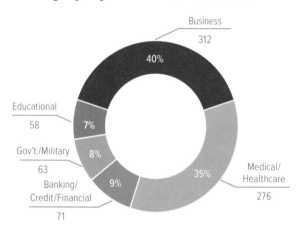

Total may not equal 100% due to rounding.
Source: Identity Theft Resource Center.

Medical and healthcare organizations accounted for the majority of records exposed by data breaches in 2015 (Fig. 3).

High profile breaches have triggered greater awareness of the risk and need for insurance. One legal

Fig. 3

Medical And Healthcare Records Were More Than Half Of All Records Stolen

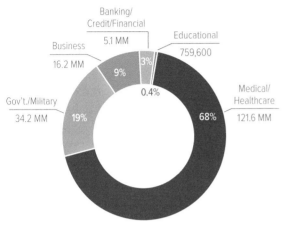

Banking/ Credit/Financial
5.1 MM

Business
16.2 MM
9%

Educational
759,600
3%

0.4%

Gov't./Military
34.2 MM
19%

Medical/ Healthcare
121.6 MM
68%

Source: Identity Theft Resource Center.
Total may not equal 100% due to rounding.

expert described the 2013 Target data breach as "the equivalent of 10 free Super Bowl ads for insurers selling cyber policies."[4]

The fact that Target had $100 million in network security insurance was widely reported.[5] As of January 2016, Target estimated it had already accrued $291 million in expenses related to the data breach, with some $90 million expected to be offset by insurance.

Health insurer Anthem is understood to have some $150 million to $200 million in cyber insurance, including excess layers of coverage. It is also reported that Home Depot had $105 million in coverage and that insurance would cover some $27 million in recovery costs from the retailer's 2014 breach.

The Threat To Businesses

No industry sector appears to be safe. For any business or government entity that stores confidential customer and client information online, a massive data breach can leave it fighting to maintain reputation and brand value.

Cyber incidents (crime, data breaches, IT failures) moved into the top 3 global business risks in 2016, according to the fifth annual Allianz Risk Barometer Survey, climbing up to rank 3 from No. 5 (Fig. 4).[6]

Cyber incidents also ranked as the top long-term risk, according to the Allianz survey, while impact of digitalization and new technology also feature among the top 10 risks identified by companies.

Other survey highlights:

- Loss of reputation (69 percent) is the main cause of economic loss after an attack, followed by business

Fig. 4

In 2016 Cyber Incidents Were Ranked The No. 3 Global Business Risk

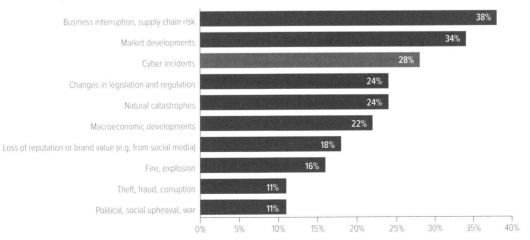

Business interruption, supply chain risk	38%
Market developments	34%
Cyber incidents	28%
Changes in legislation and regulation	24%
Natural catastrophes	24%
Macroeconomic developments	22%
Loss of reputation or brand value (e.g. from social media)	18%
Fire, explosion	16%
Theft, fraud, corruption	11%
Political, social upheaval, war	11%

Source: Allianz Risk Barometer on Business Risks 2016.

interruption (BI) (60 percent) and liability claims after a data breach (52 percent).

- The increasing sophistication of attacks is the impact of digitalization that companies fear most (52 percent), according to Allianz. Respondents also fear data fraud or theft (50 percent) and breakdown of critical infrastructure (38 percent).

- A lack of understanding (48 percent) of the complexity of the risks involved is cited as the main factor preventing companies from being better prepared to combat threats. Not having a concrete assessment of the cost of the risks involved (46 percent) ranks second, while budgetary constraints (39 percent) rank third.

Emerging Technology Risks

As technologies evolve, companies of all sizes are potentially exposed to even greater risks from data breaches.

The Internet of Things (IoT) means that billions of connected things, from autonomous vehicles, to smart home devices, to medical devices, to wearable devices could be vulnerable to attack and the onus is on manufacturers to prioritize security and reduce the risks.[7] Gartner forecasts that 6.4 billion connected things will be in use worldwide in 2016, up 30 percent from 2015, and will reach 20.8 billion by 2020.[8]

Even automobiles are now vulnerable to hacking. Laptop computers are now being used to bypass key fobs and hijack electronic ignition systems to steal cars. In August 2016 two men were accused of using a laptop to steal more than 100 vehicles in the Houston area.[9] And in July 2015, Chrysler announced the recall of 1.4 million Jeep vehicles after it was demonstrated that dashboard functions, steering, transmission and braking systems could be hacked and manipulated wirelessly.[10]

Smart home devices, including smart door locks and alarms, in millions of homes are a potential target of attacks. Symantec research found multiple vulnerabilities in 50 commercially available devices.

Researchers have also discovered potentially life-threatening vulnerabilities in medical devices, such as insulin pumps, smart pacemakers and X-ray machines.[11] In January, the U.S. Food and Drug Administration issued draft guidance outlining steps medical device manufacturers should continuously take to address cyberrisks.

Security concerns surround the adoption of cloud computing—the use of a network of remote servers over the internet to store, manage and process data, rather than a local server—by both companies and government agencies.

Mobile security and privacy is another concern. Growing numbers of mobile devices are being used to access confidential and critical information, leaving corporate networks even more vulnerable to attack.

Ransomware And Social Engineering Risks

Ransomware and social engineering attacks are on the rise. A $16,000 ransom paid by the University of Calgary to restore data following a ransomware attack, a $500 bitcoin payment made by a NASCAR racing team after critical team data was held hostage, and a $17,000 bitcoin payment made by Hollywood Presbyterian Medical Center after a hacker gained control of its systems are just some recent attacks that have raised concerns among businesses and insurers.

Nearly 40 percent of businesses have experienced a ransomware attack in the last year, and of these, more than one-third lost revenue while one in five had to stop business completely, according to recent research.[12] More than 20 percent of attacks demanded more than $10,000 in ransom. In April, the Federal Bureau of Investigation (FBI) reported that law enforcement had seen an increase in ransomware attacks in 2015, particularly targeting organizations because the payoffs are higher. Ransomware attacks are not only proliferating, but becoming more sophisticated, the FBI warned.[13] Symantec reports that crypto-style ransomware (encrypting files) grew by 35 percent in 2015 and predicted that this extremely profitable type of attack will continue to ensnare PC users and expand to any network-connected device that can be held hostage for a profit.[14] McAfee Labs predicted that ransomware will remain a major and rapidly growing threat in 2016.[15]

A growing financial fraud—and form of social engineering—is business email compromise (BEC) fraud, also known as CEO fraud, which last year was described by the FBI as an emerging global threat.[16] These sophisticated phishing attacks occur when cyber criminals send fake email messages from company CEOs, often when a CEO is known to be out of the office, asking company accountants to transfer funds to a supplier. Instead, the funds go to a criminal account.

Since the FBI's Internet Crime Complaint Center (IC3) began tracking BEC scams in late 2013, more than 7,000 U.S. companies have been targeted by such attacks with total dollar losses exceeding $740 million. That figure is likely much higher when non-U.S. victims and unreported losses are included.

Impact On Small, Midsize Businesses

While data breaches on larger companies tend to dominate the headlines, small and medium-sized businesses are increasingly vulnerable.

Their exposure is much the same as that of larger companies, according to experts, but many do not realize they are the "soft underbelly" of cybersecurity, mistakenly believing they are too small to be attacked.[17]

Attacks are growing more common, with Travelers estimating that 62 percent of all breach victims are small to medium-sized businesses.[18]

A recent U.K. government report also suggested that one-third (33 percent) of small businesses have had a breach in the past 12 months, while for medium businesses that number is at just over one-half (51 percent).[19]

While concerns have grown amid increasing frequency and costs of attacks, security spending is on the rise, a recent Gartner report found. The worldwide cybersecurity market will increase to $170 billion by 2020, up from $75.4 billion in 2015.[20]

In 2015, 38 percent more security incidents were detected than in 2014, and companies of all sizes boosted their information security budgets by 24 percent in 2015, PwC found.[21] Interestingly, 46 percent of survey respondents said their board participates in information security budgets.

The Threat To Government

Governments are facing an unprecedented level of attacks and threats with the potential to undermine national security and critical infrastructure.

U.S. President Obama has stated that cyber terrorism is one of the biggest threats facing the United States today, noting in his 2015 State of the Union speech:

"No foreign nation, no hacker, should be able to shut down our networks, steal our trade secrets, or invade the privacy of American families, especially our kids.

"We are making sure our government integrates intelligence to combat cyber threats, just as we have done to combat terrorism."[22]

After the 2014 Sony Pictures breach, President Obama declared malicious cyberattacks a national emergency and signed an executive order April 1, 2015, establishing new sanctions to curb this "unusual and extraordinary threat to the national security, foreign policy and economy of the United States."[23]

For government the threat extends beyond dollars and cents. The International Institute for Counter Terrorism (ICT) reports that global jihad groups and other terrorist organizations are increasingly venturing into cyberspace, engaging in what they call "electronic jihad," attacking the enemy by sabotaging its online infrastructure, using the information available to them from the virtual world to cause mayhem in the real world, and developing their own defensive capabilities.[24]

Such attacks are the work of an evolving list of perpetrators, including state-sponsored groups, criminal organizations, hacktivists, insiders, and terrorists.

The rising popularity of digital currencies, such as bitcoin, has also resulted in their acceptance as payment by a growing number of establishments, despite potential risks and illegal uses. The ICT noted the technological aspects of bitcoin that make it an ideal means of fundraising for illegal activities, such as terrorism. Separately, there have also been several well-publicized hacker attacks on bitcoin exchanges, which is a growing risk for companies.

There were two noteworthy critical infrastructure attacks in 2014. A Russian hacker group called "Energetic Bear" launched a malware attack that caused significant disruption for U.S. energy sector companies, and an attack against a steel plant in Germany disrupted control systems, leaving operators unable to shut down a blast furnace, resulting in massive physical damage.

The Department of Homeland Security's Industrial Control Systems Cyber Emergency Response Team (ICS-CERT) received reports of approximately 295 attacks on critical infrastructure control systems in the United States in fiscal year 2015 (October 2014 through September 2015), a 20 percent increase over the prior year.[25] The critical manufacturing sector saw the most reported incidents, accounting for one-third (33 percent), followed by the energy sector with 46 incidents (16 percent).

Government Fights Back

In July, the White House announced a new policy directive spelling out how the government will coordinate its response to large-scale cyber incidents. As part of this initiative a new metric designed to gauge the severity of attacks and how the government responds to them will assign a rating of 0 through 5 (with 5 being the most severe) to significant incidents.

In February 2014, the National Institute of Standards and Technology (NIST) released a new framework for improving critical infrastructure cybersecurity. The framework gathers existing global standards

and practices to help organizations understand, communicate and manage their risks. A year earlier President Obama issued an executive order that promoted increased information sharing about threats between government and private companies that oversee critical infrastructure such as electrical grids.

In 2011, a report from the Pentagon concluded that computer sabotage coming from another country can constitute an act of war.[26] It noted that the Laws of Armed Conflict—which guide traditional wars and are derived from various international treaties such as the Geneva Convention—apply in cyberspace as in traditional warfare.

A number of federal legislative/regulatory proposals on cybersecurity have been passed or are under consideration by Congress. At the state level, some 47 states have breach notification laws in effect.

Since October 2011 the Securities and Exchange Commission (SEC) has provided guidance for publicly traded companies to disclose significant instances of cyberrisks and events.[27] Descriptions of relevant insurance coverage were included in the SEC's list of appropriate disclosures.

This raises the important question of whether and how adequately businesses are protected by insurance coverage in the event of an attack. For insurers, the increasingly complex and ever evolving nature of threats and attacks presents both a challenging risk and an opportunity.

Two key security bills passed by the House in late April 2015 would shield from liability companies that share cyber threat information with the government.

Cyber Terrorism Coverage

Language regarding acts of war or terrorism in cyber insurance policies is typically vague. For example, a cyberattack or data breach caused by a state-sponsored group classified by the U.S. government as a terrorist organization falls into a gray area, bringing up questions over insurance coverage.

The most recent extension of the terrorism risk insurance program [the Terrorism Risk Insurance Program Reauthorization Act of 2015 (TRIPRA)] does not explicitly or directly address cyberattacks.

The general view is that if a cyber terrorism attack resulted in damage ordinarily covered by a terrorism insurance policy such as fire or explosion, there would be coverage under the terrorism risk insurance law, so long as the event meets all the criteria set forth in the act leading to a certification of the event as an act of terrorism.[28]

For example, if a cyber terrorism attack led to a major explosion at a power plant, that damage would likely be covered by terrorism insurance. However, costs resulting from an attack such as notification to customers after a data breach, the cost of fines and penalties, the theft of confidential information and lawsuits would be far beyond the scope of the program.[29]

In response to a growing number of incidents and cyber threats targeting commercial industries that can lead to equipment failure, physical damage to property and/or injury to people, several insurers now offer expanded coverage. These products include coverage for property damage and bodily injury, specifically for companies in critical infrastructure industries, such as oil and gas, chemicals, power and utilities.

II. Cyberattacks: Rising Frequency And Severity

Latest industry research points to the rising frequency and severity of cybercrimes and attacks.

A joint report by McAfee and the Center for Strategic and International Studies (CSIS) found that governments and companies underestimate how much risk they face from cybercrime and how quickly this risk can grow.[30]

McAfee and CSIS estimated the likely annual cost to the global economy from cybercrime is $445 billion a year, with a range of between $375 billion and $575 billion. This figure is more than the national income of most countries, the report noted.

The most important cost comes from its damage to company performance and to national economies. Cybercrime damages trade, competitiveness, innovation and global economic growth, according to the report.

Cybercrime remains a growth industry. CSIS research predicts that opportunities will grow as more business activities move online and more consumers around the world connect to the Internet, and as autonomous devices are connected.

Losses from the theft of intellectual property will also increase as acquiring countries improve their ability to make use of it to manufacture competing goods.

Fig. 5

Malicious Code, Denial Of Service And Phishing Were The Most Costly Cyber Crimes In 2015

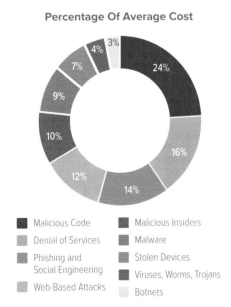

Percentage Of Average Cost

- Malicious Code — 24%
- 16%
- 14%
- 12%
- 10%
- 9%
- 7%
- 4%
- 3%

Legend:
- Malicious Code
- Denial of Services
- Phishing and Social Engineering
- Web-Based Attacks
- Malicious Insiders
- Malware
- Stolen Devices
- Viruses, Worms, Trojans
- Botnets

Total may not equal 100% due to rounding.
Source: 2015 Cost of Cyber Crime: United States, Ponemon Institute.

Fig. 6

Information Theft And Business Disruption Account For The Bulk Of External Costs

Percentage Of Total External Cost

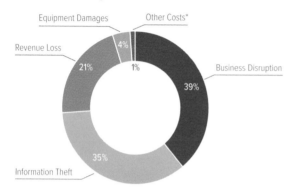

*Other costs include direct and indirect costs that could not be allocated to a main external cost category. Total may not equal 100% due to rounding.
Source: Ponemon Institute.

The Cost of Cybercrime

The cost of the typical incident continues to grow, often into millions of dollars.

An annual study of U.S. companies by the Ponemon Institute estimates the average annualized cost of cybercrime at $15.4 million, up 21 percent from $12.7 million per year the previous year, and an increase of 33 percent from $11.6 million two years ago.[31]

The total annualized cost for the 2015 benchmark sample of 58 organizations ranged from a low of $1.9 million to a high of $65 million each year per company.

The most costly crimes as a percentage of the average cost of cybercrime are those caused by malicious code and denial of service attacks, Ponemon said (Fig. 5).

Information theft continues to represent the highest external cost, followed by costs associated with business disruption, the study revealed (Fig. 6).

On an annualized basis, information theft accounted for 35 percent of total external costs (consistent with the six-year average). Costs associated with disruption to

business or lost productivity accounted for 39 percent of external costs (up 4 percent from the six-year average).[32]

The cost grows if the attack is not resolved quickly. According to the study, the average time to resolve an attack was 46 days, with an average cost to participating companies of $2 million during this 46-day period. This represents a 22 percent increase from last year's estimated average cost of $1.6 million based on a 45-day resolution period. Results show that malicious insider attacks can take more than 60 days on average to contain.

International studies also show the breadth and depth of the risk, in the United States and elsewhere.

A global benchmark study by the Ponemon Institute of 383 companies representing 12 countries, including

Fig. 7

The Average Cost Of A Breach In The U.S. Reached $7 Million in 2016*

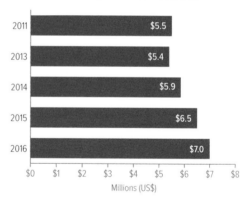

Millions (US$)

*The 2016 study examines the costs incurred by 383 companies across 16 industries representing 12 countries, including 64 U.S. case studies. Total breach costs include: lost business resulting from diminished trust or confidence of customers; costs related to detection, escalation, and notification of the breach; and ex-post response activities, such as credit report monitoring. Source: Ponemon Institute.

the United States, found that data breaches are becoming far more costly to manage and that U.S. companies suffered, on average, the most costly breaches.

This study did not include catastrophic or mega data breaches of more than approximately 100,000 compromised records because these are not typical of

Fig. 8

Malicious Or Criminal Attacks Cause Almost Half Of All Breaches

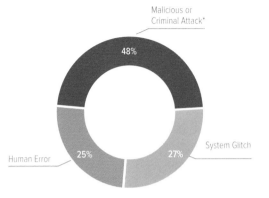

Malicious or Criminal Attack*

48%

25%

27%

Human Error

System Glitch

*The most common types of malicious or criminal attacks include malware infections, criminal insiders, phishing/social engineering and SQL injection. Total may not equal 100% due to rounding.
Source: Ponemon Institute.

the breaches most organizations experience.

For the U.S. companies participating in this research the average total cost of a breach was more than $7.0 million in 2016—the highest total average cost of the 12 countries—up 7 percent from $6.5 million in 2015 (Fig. 7).[33] Germany had the next highest total average cost at $5.0 million. In contrast, samples of Indian and South African companies experienced the lowest total average cost at $1.6 million and $1.9 million, respectively.

The average per capita cost of a data breach for U.S. companies was $221, compared to a $217 average cost calculated in 2015. Ponemon defines per capita cost as the total cost of data breach divided by the size of a data breach (i.e. the number of lost or stolen records). Also, on average U.S. companies had data breaches that resulted in among the greatest number of exposed or compromised records, at 29,611.

Malicious or criminal attacks are most often the cause of a data breach globally and also the most costly data breach incidents in all 12 countries, the Ponemon study found (Fig. 8). U.S. companies that had a data breach due to malicious or criminal attacks experienced a cost of $236 per compromised record, significantly

above the mean of $221.

The Ponemon study also found that U.S. organizations have the highest lost business costs at an average of $4.0 million. These costs include abnormal turnover of customers (a higher than average loss of customers for the industry or organization), increased customer acquisition activities, reputation losses and diminished goodwill.

Conflicting Information On Data Breach Costs

An earlier study by Verizon suggests that these data breach cost estimates may be overstated.[34] Compared to the 2014 Ponemon estimates that breaches cost companies $201 per lost record that year, Verizon's cost-per-record estimate was just 58 cents.[35]

The wildly different cost estimates arise because Verizon's 2015 Data Breach Investigations Report uses only cyber liability insurance claims data from insurers to look at the data breach cost impact, rather than a broader formula that includes both direct and indirect costs.

In its analysis Verizon did acknowledge that the 58 cent cost-per-record is a very poor estimate of loss. It goes on to set out a new breach-cost model that accounts for uncertainty as the volume of records lost increases. As a result it found that a small data breach where only 100 records are lost would most likely cost an organization between $18,120 and $35,730. At the other end of the scale, a massive data breach of 100 million records would have an average cost of between $5 million and $15.6 million, Verizon said.

The 2014 Ponemon study did find that certain organizational factors can reduce the overall cost of a data breach. Companies that had a strong security posture at the time of the data breach could reduce the average cost per record by $14.14 to $131.86—the greatest decrease in cost. Companies that had an incident response plan in place also reduced the average cost per record by $12.77.

However, the specific attributes or factors of a data breach can also increase the overall cost. For example, the study found that if the data breach involved lost or stolen devices the cost per record could increase by $16.10 to $161.10. Third party involvement in the breach incident also increases the per capita cost of a data breach by $14.80.

III. The Insurance Industry And Cyberrisk

Historical Development Of Cyber Insurance

Cyber insurance in the United States evolved as a product in the mid- to late-1990s, and the market is still seen as being in its infancy. Insurers have had to expand coverage for a risk that is rapidly shifting in scope and nature.

More than 60 carriers offer stand-alone policies, and Marsh, a major insurance broker, estimates the U.S. market was worth $2.75 billion in gross written premiums in 2015, up from $2 billion in 2014. Today, market experts suggest gross written premiums have increased to $3.25 billion.[36]

Estimates also project the European market at between €700 million and €900 million by 2018 (US$765 million to US$983 million).[37] Industry experts say the European market is likely to get a boost from expected reform of European Union (EU) data protection rules that would force companies to disclose breaches of customer data.

PwC estimates the global market could grow to at least $7.5 billion in annual premiums by the end of the decade. Insurers need to move quickly to innovate before a disruptor such as Google enters the market.

The Lloyd's insurance market estimates that the growing global market will be worth $85 billion and is positioning itself to be a global hub for coverage.[38]

Why Reliance On Traditional Policies Is Not Enough

While traditional insurance policies typically have not handled the emerging risk, limited coverage under traditional policies may be available.

For example, there may be coverage under a traditional property insurance policy if an incident resulted in a covered cause of loss, such as a fire or explosion, which caused property damage.

Traditional property insurance policies often contain express provisions covering damage or disruption to electronic data. The package policy known as the Business Owners Policy (BOP) that is often purchased by medium- and smaller-sized businesses includes coverage for electronic data loss (up to a specified limit).

If electronic data is destroyed or damaged as the result of a covered cause of loss, the insurer will pay the cost to replace or restore it. Causes of loss that apply to this coverage include a computer virus, harmful code or other harmful instructions entered into a computer system or network to which it is connected. There is no coverage, however, for loss or damage caused by the actions of any employee.

Forms now allow insurers to tailor coverage for small and midsize businesses. Optional endorsements to the standard BOP cover data breaches, data replacement and restoration, cyber extortion and business interruption.[39]

Most traditional commercial general liability policies do not cover cyberrisks, however.[40] In the United States, Insurance Services Office (ISO), a subsidiary of Verisk Analytics, is a key supplier of statistical, actuarial and underwriting claims information for property/casualty insurers. ISO also develops standard insurance policy forms. ISO's revisions to its general liability policy form in 2014 and 2013 consist primarily of a mandatory exclusion of coverage for personal and advertising injury claims arising from access or disclosure of confidential information.

Reliance on traditional insurance policies is therefore not enough, so specialized policies have been developed by insurers.

Stand-Alone Cyber Coverage

Specialized cyberrisk coverage is available primarily as a stand-alone policy. Each policy is tailored to the specific needs of a company, depending on the technology being used and the level of risk involved. Both first- and third-party coverages are available.

Coverages include:

Loss/Corruption Of Data: Covers damage to, or destruction of, valuable information assets as a result of viruses, malicious code and Trojan horses.

Business Interruption: Covers loss of business income as a result of an attack on a company's network that limits its ability to conduct business, such as a denial-of-service computer attack. Coverage also includes extra expenses, forensic expenses and dependent business interruption.

Liability: Covers defense costs, settlements, judgments and, sometimes, punitive damages incurred by a company as a result of:

- Breach of privacy due to theft of data
- Transmission of a computer virus or other liabilities resulting from a computer attack, which causes financial loss to third parties
- Failure of security which causes network systems to be unavailable to third parties
- Allegations of copyright or trademark infringement, libel, slander, defamation or other "media" activities on the company's website, such as postings by visitors on bulletin boards and in chat rooms.

D&O/Management Liability: Newly developed and tailored D&O products provide broad all risks coverage, meaning that the risk is covered unless specifically excluded.

Cyber Extortion: Covers the "settlement" of an extortion threat against a company's network, as well as the cost of hiring a security firm to track down and negotiate with blackmailers.

Crisis Management: Covers the costs to retain public relations assistance or advertising to rebuild a company's reputation after an incident.

Criminal Rewards: Covers the cost of posting a criminal reward fund for information leading to the arrest and conviction of a criminal who has attacked a company's computer systems.

Data Breach: Covers the expenses and legal liability resulting from a data breach. Policies may also provide access to services helping business owners to comply with regulatory requirements and to address customer concerns.

Identity Theft: Provides access to an identity theft call center in the event of stolen customer or employee personal information.

Depending on the individual policy, specialized coverage can apply to both internally and externally launched attacks, as well as to viruses that are specifically targeted against the insured or widely distributed across the internet. Premiums can range from a few thousand dollars for base coverage for small businesses (less than $10 million in revenue) to several hundred thousand dollars for major corporations desiring comprehensive coverage.

New Areas Of Development

As quickly as insurers develop cyber policies, new exposures are emerging.

Individual Risks: Insurers are starting to offer cyber insurance programs for individuals. Such programs typically bundle coverages previously available only to businesses, but increasingly important to individuals as they access and store data online. Coverage can be added to homeowners or renters policies and may include coverage and services for computer attacks, cyber extortion, online fraud and the breach of personal information involving smart phones, computers and connected home devices.

Individuals seek to better protect themselves from the risks created by their participation in social media. While traditional homeowners insurance policies include liability protection that covers the insured against lawsuits for bodily injury or property damage, coverage may be limited and individual policies may differ by company and by state. Case law is also evolving. However, umbrella or excess liability policies provide broader protection, including claims against the insured for libel and slander, as well as higher liability limits. Specialized insurance products that protect an individual from social media related risks are under development.

Cloud Computing: Insurers are developing products to provide coverage for cloud providers and the businesses that utilize them. Recruiting new business can be challenging for cloud providers as businesses have concerns over data security. Traditional cyber liability policies typically exclude losses incurred by a third party such as a cloud provider. The cloud coverage being developed by insurers would apply to loss, theft and liability of the data stored within the cloud, whether the loss occurs from hacking, a virus or a subsequent liability event.

Deceptive Funds Transfer (Social Engineering Coverage): Coverage for theft losses resulting from deceptive funds transfer (sometimes known as social engineering coverage) is in demand in response to the rise in losses from business email compromise (BEC) scams. A number of cyber insurers have started offering cyber crime policies that provide coverage for losses due to funds transfer fraud and cyber deception.

Property Damage And Bodily Injury: Several insurers have started offering limited coverage that addresses property damage and bodily injury from a cyberattack. These products have been developed in response to the increasing incidence and threats of attacks targeting commercial industries that can lead to equipment failure, physical damage to property and physical harm to people. Companies in critical infrastructure industries, such as oil and gas, chemicals, power and utility, and transportation have a growing need for this type of cover. Products

typically address coverage gaps in a customer's existing commercial lines program.

Social Media/Networking: Insurers have developed products that can be added to cyber policies to cover a company's media and/or social networking activities. Some policies now provide coverage for certain social media liability exposures such as online defamation, advertising, libel and slander. Intellectual property rights may also be covered.

Cyber Insurance: Legal Environment

In its *sigma* publication Swiss Re noted that the recent rise in cyber-related litigation is only expected to increase.[41] There have been several recent legal developments in the cyber arena.

Data Breach Liability

An organization may be found liable if a breach resulting from a systems failure or lax security compromises the security of customer personal information or data. A variety of legal actions may be pursued, including allegations of negligence, breach of fiduciary duty and breach of contract.

Increased regulation at both the federal and state level related to information security and breach notification is expanding the legal avenues that may be pursued. Many states have enacted laws requiring companies to notify consumers of breaches of personal data. Federal laws, such as the HIPAA, the Gramm Leach Bliley Act and the Fair Credit Reporting Act have requirements to safeguard the privacy of personal information.

A federal court in New Jersey in 2014 upheld the power of the Federal Trade Commission (FTC) to sue companies that fail to protect their customers' data.[42] The ruling rebuffed a challenge from Wyndham hotels, which argued that the FTC overstepped its authority with a 2012 lawsuit against the global hotel chain.

Class Action Lawsuits

Mega data breaches have prompted class action lawsuits against companies seeking damages collectively on behalf of individuals whose personal information was lost or stolen. Legal experts note that the scope and number of data breach class actions is unprecedented, with more cases being filed in the aftermath of recent massive data breaches.[43]

For example, more than 70 class actions lawsuits alone were filed against Target following its 2013 breach. According to one legal expert, for some plaintiffs' lawyers this was "the Black Friday door buster to end all others."[44] And an April 2011 hacking of Sony's PlayStation online services led to the filing of more than 50 class action complaints in the United States.

Plaintiffs typically allege that businesses failed to adequately safeguard consumer information and gave insufficient and untimely notice of the breach. In the Target class actions some of the plaintiffs are even seeking damages for emotional distress as well as punitive damages. Target and other companies may also face class actions from banks and credit unions seeking damages for administrative expenses, lost interest, transaction fees and lost customers.

Settlements can be huge. In March 2015, a federal judge gave preliminary approval to a $10 million settlement in just one Target class action.[45] In August 2015, Target agreed to pay up to $67 million to settle with Visa Inc. on behalf of banks and other firms that issue credit and debit cards. The amount would compensate card issuers for the costs of issuing new cards, adding more call center staff to handle customer queries and the costs of the actual fraud. In December 2015, Target also agreed to a $39 million settlement with several U.S. banks that service MasterCard.

As of January 2016, Target estimated it had already accrued $291 million in expenses related to the data

breach, with some $90 million expected to be offset by insurance. That estimate was based on the prospect of settling many lawsuits.

Data Breach Insurance Coverage

Companies that have suffered a data breach look to their insurance policies for coverage to help mitigate some of the enormous costs. The increasing uptake of cyber liability policies and rising claims makes it inevitable that coverage disputes will arise. The fact that there is no standard cyber insurance form means that individual policy terms and conditions may vary greatly.

In one of the first decisions interpreting a cyber insurance policy, the U.S. District Court in Arizona on May 31, 2016, held that a cyber insurance policy issued by Federal Insurance Co. (Chubb) does not cover liabilities to credit card issuers arising from a 2014 data breach at P.F. Chang's China Bistro.

When a stolen credit card number is fraudulently used, the bank that issued the credit card is financially responsible for paying the fraudulent charge. It also incurs the cost of delivering a new credit card to the consumer. If a retailer's data breach was behind the fraud, the bank has legal agreements that let it indirectly recover its costs from the retailer responsible for the breach. One such agreement left P.F. Chang with an assessment of just under $2 million. The restaurant chain filed a claim against its cyber insurance policy.

P.F. Chang lost. The court found that losses arising from these assessments are not covered losses, at least not under this specific insurance policy. It's important to note that in reaching its decision, the court turned to cases analyzing commercial general liability (CGL) policies for guidance because cyber policies are relatively new to the market, but the fundamental principles are the same. Also of note is the fact that Federal Insurance did pay approximately $1.7 million for P.F. Chang's damages related to forensic and defense costs. These damages were not at issue under the policy.[46]

Changes In Cyber Insurance Pricing And Capacity

While the market is growing rapidly, the exact number of companies in the United States and elsewhere that have a policy has been difficult to determine. But new reporting requirements developed by the National Association of Insurance Commissioners (NAIC) give us a first glimpse of the cyber insurance policies issued in the U.S. marketplace.

Based on the NAIC Cybersecurity and Identity Theft Coverage Supplement for insurer financial statements, a total of 117 U.S. insurers reported writing some cyber insurance premiums in 2015. Direct premiums written were $993 million in 2015, while the number of in-force policies totaled 1.5 million.

Aon Benfield reports that 48 insurers wrote more than $1 million in cyber premiums in 2015. Only seven insurers reported written premiums over $50 million. The top five accounted for 61 percent of premiums, and the top 10 accounted for 80 percent. As the market expands, premiums for the smaller insurers are expected to expand as well, broadening the distribution of premium in the market.[47]

Cyber insurance was profitable in 2015, with a 49.0 percent average loss ratio across all insurers, though individual insurer results deviated greatly. Loss ratios among the top 20 underwriters varied between zero percent at the low end to 161 percent at the high end, according to Aon's analysis.

Of the $993 million in total premium reported in 2015, package cybersecurity policies accounted for $515.1 million, or 52 percent, while stand-alone cybersecurity policies accounted for $480.7 million, or 48 percent (Fig. 9).

Since a significant amount of the coverage is written via Lloyd's and other international insurance markets that do not report to the NAIC, actual U.S. premiums are likely considerably higher.

Fig. 9

Package Policies Make Up Just More Than Half Of All Cyber Insurance Premium

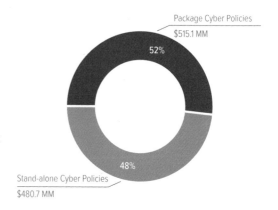

Package Cyber Policies
$515.1 MM
52%

48%
Stand-alone Cyber Policies
$480.7 MM

Source: NAIC Cybersecurity and Identity Theft Coverage Supplement, 2015.

Whatever the precise number of U.S. companies buying cyber insurance may be, Swiss Re estimates that by 2025 cyber coverage will be included in every retail, commercial and industrial insurance policy.[48]

Latest market analysis indicates a continued pattern of strong growth in cyber insurance purchasing.[49] A March 2016 market briefing from broker Marsh notes an increasing awareness and appreciation of the risk, from the boardroom to the data center. In the face of an evolving risk landscape and an aggressive regulatory environment, organizations no longer treat cyber as a problem to be fixed, but rather as a risk to be managed, Marsh said.

In 2015, the number of Marsh clients purchasing stand-alone cyber insurance increased by 27 percent over 2014 (Fig. 10). Critical infrastructure industries—including chemical, communications, energy, health care, and transportation—show more interest in the coverage, particularly related to business interruption losses. After the 2015 blackout caused by a cyberattack on an electricity provider in Ukraine, the power and utilities sector showed notable growth in the purchase of cyber insurance, with a 28 percent increase in the number of

Fig. 10

Stand-Alone Policies Grew By More Than 25 Percent Among Marsh Clients

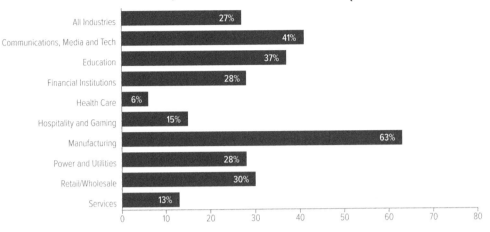

Marsh clients purchasing coverage in 2015 over 2014.

Companies are also buying higher limits. Cyber insurance limits purchased in 2015 averaged $16.9 million across all industries and all company sizes, a 15 percent increase over the average of $14.7 million in 2014, Marsh says.

Among larger companies, which tend to have greater exposure to cyberrisk, average limits purchased were $39.2 million, up 15 percent from an average of $34.2 million in 2014.

Large communications, media and technology organizations purchased the highest average limits—$86.7 million—of any industry. Large financial institutions witnessed an 18 percent increase in average limits purchased in 2015 over 2014.

Companies may not be buying enough cover, however. An earlier study by Marsh based on the data output of its proprietary statistical model—the Cyber IDEAL—found that the exposure facing many organizations eclipses the risk transfer programs they have implemented.[50] For example, retailers with revenues between $5 billion and $20 billion on average will buy an aggregate limit of $23 million. However, a hypothetical retailer in that bracket may have a much higher exposure than that average limit (Fig. 11).

For a retailer with $12 billion in annual revenues that holds a maximum 75 million records, Cyber IDEAL indicates that a one-in-100 data breach event could result in the exposure of more than 21 million records with costs exceeding $340 million, or nearly 12 times the average limits purchased. Such an event could

Fig. 11

A One-In-100 Data Breach Could Cost $340 Million

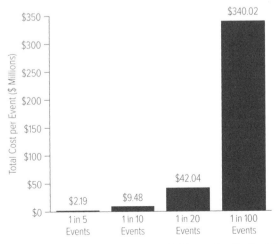

Source: A Cybersecurity Call to Action, Marsh & McLennan Cos, The Chertoff Group, November 2014

potentially create an enterprise-threatening risk, before even accounting for the risk to reputation, Marsh said.

As for rates, during 2015 markets remained challenging for certain industries—notably retail and health care—and for insureds with significant losses. Insurer competition remains strong for business outside of high-exposure classes, however. Average rate increases at renewal for both primary layers and total programs—as measured by average annual changes in the year-over-year price per million of limits—were lower in the latter half of the year than in the first half of 2015. The average primary rate per million rose at 18.5 percent in the first quarter of 2015, dropping to 12.1 percent in the fourth quarter (Fig. 12).

Marsh reports that the market was challenged by a growing recognition that organizations increasingly rely upon technology for essential operations, and are thus looking for coverage beyond indemnification for privacy breach costs.

Market capacity remained abundant at more than $500 million, but total program size varied by industry as well as the types of coverage options elected. Most large towers comprise between $200 million and $400 million in limits, Marsh noted. No insurers of significant size entered the market in the last quarter of 2015, but individual insurer appetites continued to develop, with carriers differentiating around such areas as attachment points, deployed limits and followed coverages.

Obstacles To Writing Cyber Coverage

Cyberrisk remains difficult for insurance underwriters to quantify for a number of reasons, including:

- **Complexity Of Risk:** The definition of cyber risk is rapidly evolving and expanding. Attacks are increasing sophisticated. The range of perpetrators, targets and exposures at stake ever broadens. It is a constant challenge for C-suite executives, boards of directors, cybersecurity experts, IT professionals,

Fig. 12

Rates For Cyber Cover Rose In 2015 For Both Primary And Excess Layers, But At A Declining Rate

Source: *Benchmarking Trends: Operational Risks Drive Cyber Insurance Purchases,* Marsh Global Analytics, March 2016.

law enforcement, governments and insurers to keep pace. In addition to damaged or lost assets and business interruption, attacks can result in costly investigations, litigation and settlements as well as reputation damage, with the potential knock-on effect on a company's customer base, stock price and earnings. Insurance industry leaders have acknowledged that there could be inescapable limitations on the capacity of the market to handle the demand for cyber insurance for both public and private sectors.[51]

- **Lack Of Historical Data:** Although many costly events have occurred, there is a lack of historical data for cyberrisk, making it difficult for insurers to write and price policies appropriately. While there is no standard form for the coverage, catastrophe modelers and insurers are working together to develop common data standards for use in risk models. Earlier this year Lloyd's and the Lloyd's Market Association teamed up with catastrophe modelers AIR Worldwide and RMS along with the Cambridge Center for Risk Studies, to develop a set of common core data

requirements.[52] The goal is to develop a standardized approach to identify, quantify and report
cyber exposure data across the insurance industry.
Several catastrophe modelers and brokers have
launched tools and models to manage cyberrisks.[53]
Aggregation and accumulation risk is a particular
focus of modelers. Guy Carpenter recently formed
a strategic alliance with cybersecurity specialist
Symantec to create a cyber aggregation model.[54]
Surveys can help identify and track trends, but
they do not provide an adequate basis for actuarial
analysis. Last year ratings agency A.M. Best[55]
noted: "The quantifying of risks and rewards to insureds has not reached a reliable level of actuarial
data and consequence-oriented analytics, which is
needed for accurate pricing of the premiums and
establishing appropriate reserves." This lack of
actuarial data is holding back the growth in market
capacity, industry players say.[56]

- **Risk Accumulation and Aggregation
  Uncertainty:** Cyberattacks have the potential

to be massive and wide-ranging. Risk accumulation—in which a single event spans multiple risks
affecting companies, countries, industries and lines
of business—is a growing concern and creates the
potential for catastrophic risk.[57] A "cyber hurricane"
event, in which tens or hundreds of thousands of
systems are compromised by a common event
could result in potentially catastrophic numbers of
insurance claims.[58] The Heartbleed security flaw,
disclosed in April 2014, is just one example of this
type of vulnerability. Another source of concern is
cloud computing. The breach of a cloud service
provider could affect many customers around the
world, many of whom might share the same insurer.
Several insurers have warned that the scope of
the exposures is too broad to be covered by the
private sector alone.[59] At least one has described
cyber as a "systemic risk" and proposed government cover akin to the terrorism risk insurance
programs in place in several countries.[60]

For full text and more I.I.I. white papers, visit http://bit.ly/2gcHp0f.

Sources And Endnotes

1. World Economic Forum, *Global Risks 2016, 11th Edition*.

2. ESADEgeo (Center for Global Economy and Geopolitics) and Zurich, *Global cyber governance: preparing for new business risks*, Risk Nexus, April 2015.

3. Current statistics found at Identity Theft Resource Center.

4. Randy Maniloff, White and Williams LLP, "There Aren't As Many Cos. With Cyberinsurance As You Think," *Law360.com*, February 24, 2014.

5. Craig A. Newman, "Target's Cyber Insurance: A $100 Million Policy vs. $300 Million (So Far) In Costs,"*The Data Security Law Blog of Patterson Belknap Webb & Tyler LLP*, April 7, 2016.

6. Allianz Risk Barometer 2016, January 2016.

7. Symantec, 2016 Internet Security Threat Report, Volume 21, April 2016.

8. Gartner, press release, November 10, 2015.

9. "Two arrested for stealing Jeeps—using laptops", *USA Today* and *KHOU-TV*, August 4, 2016.

10. Andy Greenberg, "After Jeep Hack, Chrysler Recalls 1.4M Vehicles for Bug Fix," *Wired*, July 24, 2015.

11. Kim Zetter, "Medical Devices That Are Vulnerable To Life-Threatening Hacks," *Wired*, November 24, 2015.

12. Malwarebytes™, "Major International Study Finds Nearly 40 Percent of Enterprises Hit By Ransomware in the Last Year," press release, August 3, 2016.

13. Federal Bureau of Investigation, *Incidents of Ransomware on the Rise*, April 29, 2016.

14. Symantec, 2016 Internet Security Threat Report, Volume 21, April 2016.

15. McAfee Labs, *2016 Threats Predictions*, November 2015.

16. Federal Bureau of Investigation, *Business Email Compromise: An Emerging Global Threat*, August, 28, 2015.

17. Rick Betterley, editor of the *Betterley Report*, interviewed on WRIN.tv, February 20, 2015.

18. Rosalie Donlon, "Small, mid-sized businesses hit by 62% of all cyber attacks," *Propertycasualty360.com*, May 27, 2015.

19. Oliver Ralph, "Cyber Villains Pose Greater Threats to Smaller Companies," *The Financial Times*, June 1, 2016.

20. Steve Morgan, "CyberSecurity Market Reaches $75 billion in 2015; Expected to Reach $170 Billion By 2020," *Forbes*, December 20, 2015.

21. PwC, *The Global State of Information Security Survey 2016*.

22. Damian Paletta, "Obama Calls For Tough Legislation to Combat Cyber-Attacks," *The Wall Street Journal*, January 20, 2015.

23. Statement by the President on Executive Order *Blocking the Property of Certain Persons Engaging in Significant Malicious Cyber-Enabled Activities*.

24. International Institute for Counter-Terrorism (ICT), Cyber-Terrorism Activities, Report No. 14, July–September 2015, and Report No. 10, July-September 2014.

25. ICS-CERT Monitor, November/December 2015.

26. Siobhan Gorman and Julian E. Barnes, "Cyber Combat: Act of War," *The Wall Street Journal*, May 30, 2011.

27. Division of Corporation Finance, Securities and Exchange Commission, CF Disclosure Guidance: Topic No. 2 – Cybersecurity, October 13, 2011.

28. Robert Hartwig, interview by Kenneth Simon, WRIN.tv, April 13, 2015. At the time, Dr. Hartwig was president of the Insurance Information Institute.

29. Matthew Sturdevant, "When Terrorists Attack Online, Is Cyber-Insurance Enough?," *Hartford Courant*, January 26, 2015.

30. McAfee and the Center for Strategic and International Studies, *Net Losses: Estimating the Global Cost of Cybercrime, Economic Impact of Cybercrime II*, June 2014.

31. Ponemon Institute, *2015 Cost of Cyber Crime Study: United States*, October 2015.

32. In the context of the Ponemon study, an external cost is one that is created by external factors such as fines and litigation of marketability of stolen intellectual properties.

33. Ponemon Institute (research sponsored by IBM), *2016 Cost of a Data Breach Study: Global Analysis*, June 2016.

34. Verizon, *2015 Data Breach Investigations Report*, April 2015.

35. Ponemon Institute (research sponsored by IBM), *2014 Cost of a Data Breach Study: Global Analysis*, May 2014.

36. Richard Betterley, "Cyber/Privacy Insurance Market Survey—2016," *The Betterley Report*, June 2016.

37. Allianz Global Corporate & Specialty, press release, July 10, 2013.

38. Stuart Poole-Robb, "Here's why the cyber insurance industry is worth £55.6 billion," *ITProPortal.com*, February 7, 2015.

39. "New ISO Cyber Endorsements for Small, Medium Businesses Now Available," *Insurance Journal*, March 4, 2015.

40. *Cybersecurity Brief*, National Association of Insurance Commissioners, updated February 13, 2015.

41. "Liability Claims Trends: Emerging Risks And Rebounding Economic Drivers," Swiss Re *sigma* No. 4/2014.

42. "Court Upholds FTC's Power to Sue Hacked Companies," *National Journal Online*, April 7, 2014.

43. *Trends in Data Breach Cybersecurity Regulation, Legislation and Litigation*, Mayer Brown, April 17, 2014.

44. Randy J. Maniloff, "Measuring the Bull's-Eye on Target's Back: Lessons From the T.J. Maxx Data Breach Class Actions," *Coverage Opinions*, January 15, 2014.

45. Hiroko Tabuchi, "$10 Million Settlement in Target Data Breach Gets Preliminary Approval," *The New York Times*, March 19, 2015.

46. Tressler LLP, "The Future is Now: Court Finds No Coverage Under Cyber Policy For P.F. Chang's Data Breach," *Privacy Risk Report*, June 9, 2016.

47. *Cyber Update: 2015 Cyber Insurance Profits and Performance*, May 2016, Aon Benfield Analytics.

48. Michel M. Lies, "How Do You Insure Against Cybercrime?," *The Experts* (blog), *The Wall Street Journal*, April 21, 2015. Lies is group chief executive of Swiss Re.

49. "Benchmarking Trends: Operational Risks Drive Cyber Insurance Purchases," *Marsh Risk Management Research Briefing*, March 2016.

50. *A Cybersecurity Call to Action*, Marsh & McLennan Cos., The Chertoff Group, November 2014.

51. Mark Hollmer, "Cyber Attacks Increasing on Public-Sector and Non-Profit Targets," *Carrier Management*, March 12, 2015.

52. "Lloyd's Develops Standardized Data Requirements for Cyber Risks," *Insurance Journal*, January 19, 2016.

53. Robert Lenihan, "Modeling Firms Take First Look at Cyber Risks," *Business Insurance,* May 29, 2016.

54. Guy Carpenter, "Guy Carpenter Forms Strategic Alliance to Develop Cyber Aggregation Model," press release, May 17, 2016.

55. A.M. Best, "Cyber Security Presents Challenging Landscape for Insurers and Insureds," *Best's Special Report*, Issue Review, December 5, 2014.

56. Ben Beeson, vice president, Cyber Security and Privacy, Lockton Cos, testimony before the U.S. Senate Commerce Committee Subcommittee on Consumer Protection, Product Safety, Insurance, and Data Security Hearing: *Examining the Evolving Cyber Insurance Marketplace*, March 19, 2015.

57. "Liability Claims Trends: Emerging Risks And Rebounding Economic Drivers," Swiss Re *sigma* No. 4/2014.

58. *The Betterley Report*, " 'Maybe Next Year' Turns Into 'I Need It Now,'" Cyber Privacy/Insurance Market Survey – 2014, June 2014.

59. Catherine Mulligan, senior vice president, Management Solutions Group, Zurich, testimony before the U.S. Senate Commerce Committee Subcommittee on Consumer Protection, Product Safety, Insurance, and Data Security Hearing: *Examining the Evolving Cyber Insurance Marketplace*, March 19, 2015.

60. Alistair Gray, "Cyber risks too big to cover, says Lloyd's insurer," *The Financial Times*, February 5, 2015.

I.I.I. Store

The I.I.I. Store is your gateway to a wide array of books and brochures from the Insurance Information Institute.

Publications are available in print and PDF formats, and some may be ordered from Amazon.com as ebooks. Quantity discounts are available for many products. Order online at www.iii.org/store, call 212-346-5500 or email publications@iii.org.

Insurance Fact Book

Thousands of insurance facts, figures, tables and graphs designed for quick and easy reference.

Insurance Handbook

A guide to the insurance industry for reporters, public policymakers, students, insurance company employees, regulators and others. Online version available at www.iii.org/insurancehandbook

Insuring Your Business: A Small Business Owners' Guide To Insurance

A comprehensive insurance guide for small business owners. Online version available at www.iii.org/smallbusiness

A Firm Foundation Online: How Insurance Supports The Economy

Shows the myriad ways in which insurance provides economic support—from offering employment and fueling the capital markets, to providing financial security and income to individuals and businesses. Provides national and state data. Selected state versions are also available.

Available at www.iii.org/economics

International Insurance Fact Book Online

Facts and statistics on the property/casualty and life insurance industries of dozens of countries.

Available at www.iii.org/international

Commercial Insurance Online

A guide to the commercial insurance market—what it does, how it functions and its key players.

Available at www.iii.org/commerciallines

I.I.I. Insurance Daily

Keeps thousands of readers up-to-date on important events, issues and trends in the insurance industry, available by subscription. Transmitted early each business day via email.

Contact: daily@iii.org

Consumer Brochures

Renters Insurance
Your Home Inventory
Nine Ways To Lower Your Auto Insurance Costs
Settling Insurance Claims After A Disaster
Twelve Ways To Lower Your Homeowners Insurance Costs ...and many others

Apps

 Know Your Plan™ is the award-winning disaster preparedness app that helps you, your family and even your pets be ready to safely get out of harm's way before trouble starts.

 Know Your Stuff® – **Home Inventory** ensures you'll always have an up-to-date record of your belongings. An upgraded and redesigned version is available in the Apple App Store and Google Play for free, and on the Web at www.KnowYourStuff.org.

Social

Find us on:

 facebook.com/InsuranceInformationInstitute

 @iiiorg   @IIIindustryblog
@III_Research   @InsuringFLA
@InsuringCAL

 youtube.com/user/iiivideo

 linkedin.com/company/insurance-information-institute

 pinterest.com/iiiorg

 plus.google.com/iii.org

 Snapchat: iiiorg

Blogs

Terms + Conditions: An inside look at the insurance industry and current issues.

Insuring Florida: Helping Florida residents understand insurance coverage and related issues in the Sunshine State.

Insuring California: Helping Californians understand state-specific insurance coverage and related issues.

2016: A LOOK BACK

Autonomous Vehicles

- On May 7, 2016, the driver of a Tesla car operating in Autopilot mode was killed near Williston, Florida. His car struck the side of a turning tractor-trailer. Early reports indicated the auto's self-driving feature did not distinguish the white side of a turning tractor-trailer from a brightly lit sky. The car did not automatically activate its brakes and the driver did not take control and use the brakes. It is believed to be the first instance of a traffic fatality involving a car that was operating with advanced driver assistance features active.
- On September 14, 2016, the ride-sharing service Uber began operating self-driving automobiles in Pittsburgh. In the pilot service the vehicles have a safety driver in the front seat in case human intervention is needed.

Cybersecurity

- In September 2016, Yahoo confirmed that at least 500 million user accounts were stolen in a data breach in late 2014 that may have included names, email addresses, telephone numbers, dates of birth, and some passwords and security questions and answers.
- In October 2016, hackers using a botnet of internet-enabled devices, possibly with publicly available source code, launched a series major distributed denial of service (DDoS) attacks on DNS servers in the U.S., resulting in a major internet outage. The attacks exploited everyday Internet of Things devices, such as DVRs, baby monitors and other ordinary household appliances and devices that are networked to the internet, that lack the security that computers and phones might have.

Earthquakes

- On February 6, 2016, a strong magnitude 6.4 earthquake struck southern Taiwan killing at least 117 people and injuring 550 others. Damage was most significant in the city of Tainan, where several multi-story buildings collapsed. According to Aon Benfield, the Taiwan government allocated $750 million for recovery and rebuilding. The Financial Supervisory Commission cited preliminary insured losses at only $8.0 million.
- On April 14, 2016, a magnitude 6.5 earthquake struck the Kumamoto prefecture of Japan. Twenty-eight hours later a magnitude 7.3 quake struck the region. Japanese officials have confirmed 41 deaths.
- On April 16, 2016, a magnitude 7.8 earthquake struck Ecuador. At least 272 people died, and more than 2,500 others were injured.

Hurricanes/Inland Flooding

- In 2015 and 2016 Texas, Louisiana, Mississippi, South Carolina and West Virginia have experienced devastating rainfall-induced flooding which resulted in billions of dollars in economic losses. In 2015, flash and river floods claimed 176 lives, up dramatically from 38 in 2014.
- In late September into October 2016, Hurricane Matthew made its way across the Caribbean,

causing extensive damage to Haiti and the Bahamas, and then moved up the coast of the Southeastern U.S. Parts of northern Florida and the Carolinas were particularly hard hit, with North Carolina experiencing historic flooding. Estimates of insured losses for Hurricane Matthew range from $1.5 billion to $7 billion in the U.S. The death toll from the storm is at 46 in the United States.

Mergers & Acquisitions

- In the first 10 months of 2016, there were 55 insurance deals affecting whole insurance companies in the United States, compared with 78 in all of 2015. There were 31 property/casualty company deals so far in 2016, only five deals fewer than in all of 2015.

Regulation

- In March 2016 a U.S. District Court removed MetLife Inc.'s designation as a systemically important financial institution, which was imposed by the Financial Stability Oversight Council (FSOC) within the U.S Treasury Department. The ruling freed the company from adhering to the FSOC's capital standards. The Treasury Department is appealing the decision.

Terrorism

- On June 12, 2016, a gunman killed 49 people and wounded 53 others in an Orlando, Florida nightclub.
- On September 17, 2016, a pipe bomb exploded in a garbage can near a Marine Corps charity run in Seaside Heights, New Jersey.
- Also on September 17, 2016, a bomb exploded in the Chelsea neighborhood of New York City. Thirty-one civilians were injured. A second bomb was discovered by authorities four blocks away.
- On September 18, 2016, multiple bombs were discovered inside a suspicious package at a New Jersey train station.

Wildfires

- From January 1 to October 7, 2016, there were 46,618 wildfires, compared to 51,023 wildfires in the same period in 2015. About 4.8 million acres were burned in the 2016 period, compared with 9.1 million in 2015.
- In May 2016 a wildfire broke out in the Alberta, Canada, city of Fort McMurray. The fire is set to become the costliest ever Canadian natural disaster for insurers, with 1,600 buildings destroyed and more under threat. Two fatalities are attributed to the fire and the entire population of about 90,000 were evacuated. The smoke from the fire could be seen as far south as Iowa.

Workers Compensation Opt-Out

- In September 2016 the Oklahoma Supreme Court ruled that the state's Opt Out Act is unconstitutional in Vasquez v. Dillards. The Opt Out Act allowed qualified employers to opt out of the Oklahoma workers' compensation system by establishing an Employee Benefit Plan (Plan) under the provisions of federal law, the Employee Retirement Income Security Act (ERISA).

STATE INSURANCE DEPARTMENTS

The majority of state commissioners are appointed by state governors and serve at their pleasure. The states designated with an asterisk (*) presently elect insurance commissioners to four-year terms.

Alabama • Tel. 334-269-3550. Fax 334-241-4192. www.aldoi.gov

Alaska • Tel. 907-269-7900. Fax 907-269-7910. www.insurance.alaska.gov

American Samoa • Tel. 684-633-4116. www.americansamoa.gov

Arizona • Tel. 602-364-2499. Fax 602-364-2505. www.id.state.az.us

Arkansas • Tel. 501-371-2600. Fax 501-371-2618. www.insurance.arkansas.gov

*California • Tel. 213-897-8921. Fax 213-897-9051. www.insurance.ca.gov

Colorado • Tel. 303-894-7499. Fax 303-894-7455. www.dora.state.co.us/insurance

Connecticut • Tel. 860-297-3800. Fax 860-566-7410. www.ct.gov/cid

*Delaware • Tel. 302-674-7300. Fax 302-739-5280. www.delawareinsurance.gov

District of Columbia • Tel. 202-727-8000. Fax 202-535-1196. www.disb.dc.gov

Florida • Tel. 850-413-3140. Fax 850-488-3334. www.floir.com

*Georgia • Tel. 404-656-2070. Fax 404-657-8542. www.oci.ga.gov

Guam • Tel. 671-635-1817. Fax 671-633-2643. www.guamtax.com

Hawaii • Tel. 808-586-2790. Fax 808-586-2806. www.cca.hawaii.gov/ins

Idaho • Tel. 208-334-4250. Fax 208-334-4398. www.doi.idaho.gov

Illinois • Tel. 217-782-4515. Fax 217-782-5020. www.insurance.illinois.gov

Indiana • Tel. 317-232-2385. Fax 317-232-5251. www.in.gov/idoi

Iowa • Tel. 515-281-5705. Fax 515-281-3059. www.iid.state.ia.us

*Kansas • Tel. 785-296-3071. Fax 785-296-7805. www.ksinsurance.org

Kentucky • Tel. 502-564-3630. Fax 502-564-1453. insurance.ky.gov

*Louisiana • Tel. 225-342-1258. Fax 225-342-8622. www.ldi.la.gov

Maine • Tel. 207-624-8475. Fax 207-624-8599. www.maine.gov/pfr/insurance

Maryland • Tel. 410-468-2090. Fax 410-468-2020. www.insurance.maryland.gov

Massachusetts • Tel. 617-521-7794. Fax 617-753-6830. www.mass.gov/ocabr/government/oca-agencies/doi-lp

Michigan • Tel. 517-284-8800. Fax 517-284-8837 www.michigan.gov/difs

Minnesota • Tel. 651-539-1600. Fax 651-539-1547. www.mn.gov/commerce/industries/insurance

*Mississippi • Tel. 601-359-3569. Fax Admin 601-359-2543. www.mid.state.ms.us

Missouri • Tel. 573-751-4126. Fax 573-751-5888. www.insurance.mo.gov

*Montana • Tel. 406-444-2040. Fax 406-444-3497. www.csi.mt.gov

Nebraska • Tel. 402-471-2201. Fax 402-471-4610. www.doi.ne.gov

Nevada • Tel. 775-687-0700. Fax 775-687-0787. www.doi.state.nv.us

New Hampshire • Tel. 603-271-2261. Fax 603-271-1406. www.nh.gov/insurance

New Jersey • Tel. 609-292-7272. Fax 609-454-8468. www.dobi.nj.gov

New Mexico • Tel. 505-827-4601. Fax 505-476-0326. www.nmprc.state.nm.us/id.htm

New York • Tel. 212-480-6400. Fax 212-480-2310. www.dfs.ny.gov

*North Carolina • Tel. 919-807-6750. Fax 919-733-4264. www.ncdoi.com

*North Dakota • Tel. 701-328-2440. Fax 701-328-4880. www.nd.gov/ndins

Ohio • Tel. 614-644-2658. Fax 614-644-3743. www.insurance.ohio.gov

*Oklahoma • Tel. 405-521-2828. Fax 405-521-6635. www.oid.state.ok.us

Oregon • Tel. 503-947-7980. Fax 503-378-4351. www.cbs.state.or.us/external/ins

Pennsylvania • Tel. 717-787-2317. Fax 717-787-8585. www.insurance.pa.gov

Puerto Rico • Tel. 787-304-8686. Fax 787-273-6365. www.ocs.gobierno.pr

Rhode Island • Tel. 401-462-9500. Fax 401-462-9532. www.dbr.state.ri.us

South Carolina • Tel. 803-737-6160. Fax 803-737-6231. www.doi.sc.gov

South Dakota • Tel. 605.773.3563. Fax 605-773-5369. www.dlr.sd.gov/insurance

Tennessee • Tel. 615-741-2241. Fax 615-532-6934. www.tn.gov/commerce

Texas • Tel. 512-463-6464. Fax 512-475-2005. www.tdi.state.tx.us

Utah • Tel. 801-538-3800. Fax 801-538-3829. www.insurance.utah.gov

Vermont • Tel. 802-828-3301. Fax 802-828-3306. www.bishca.state.vt.us

Virgin Islands • Tel. 340-774-7166. Fax 340-774-9458. www.ltg.gov.vi/division-of-banking-and-insurance.html

Virginia • Tel. 804-371-9694. Fax 804-371-9349. www.scc.virginia.gov/boi

*Washington • Tel. 360-725-7100. Fax 360-586-2018. www.insurance.wa.gov

West Virginia • Tel. 304-558-3386. Fax 304-558-4965. www.wvinsurance.gov

Wisconsin • Tel. 608-266-3585. Fax 608-266-9935. www.oci.wi.gov

Wyoming • Tel. 307-777-7401. Fax 307-777-2446. insurance.state.wy.us

INSURANCE AND RELATED SERVICE ORGANIZATIONS

The following organizations are supported by insurance companies or have activities closely related to insurance. National and state organizations which subscribe to the services of the Insurance Information Institute are identified by an asterisk (*).

A.M. BEST COMPANY INC. • Ambest Road, Oldwick, NJ 08858. Tel. 908-439-2200. www.ambest.com — Rating organization and publisher of reference books and periodicals relating to the insurance industry.

ACORD • One Blue Hill Plaza, 15th Floor, P.O. Box 1529, Pearl River, NY 10965-8529. Tel. 845-620-1700. www.acord.com — An industry-sponsored institute serving as the focal point for improving the computer processing of insurance transactions through the insurance agency system.

THE ACTUARIAL FOUNDATION • 475 North Martingale Road, Suite 600, Schaumburg, IL 60173-2226. Tel. 847-706-3535. www.actuarialfoundation.org — Develops, funds and executes education and research programs that serve the public by harnessing the talents of actuaries.

ADVOCATES FOR HIGHWAY AND AUTO SAFETY • 750 First Street NE, Suite 1130, Washington, DC 20002. Tel. 202-408-1711. www.saferoads.org — An alliance of consumer, safety and insurance organizations dedicated to highway and auto safety.

AIR WORLDWIDE CORPORATION • 131 Dartmouth Street, Boston, MA 02116. Tel. 617-267-6645. www.air-worldwide.com — Risk modeling and technology firm that develops models of global natural hazards, enabling companies to identify, quantify and plan for the financial consequences of catastrophic events.

ALTERNATIVE DISPUTE RESOLUTION (ADR) FORUM • P.O. Box 50191, Minneapolis, MN 55405-0191. Tel. 800-474-2371. www.adrforum.com — A leading neutral administrator of arbitration, mediation and other forms of alternative dispute resolution worldwide.

AMERICA'S HEALTH INSURANCE PLANS (AHIP) • 601 Pennsylvania Avenue, NW, South Building, Suite 500, Washington, DC 20004. Tel. 202-778-3200. www.ahip.org — National trade association representing the health insurance industry.

AMERICAN ACADEMY OF ACTUARIES • 1850 M Street NW, Suite 300, Washington, DC 20036. Tel. 202-223-8196. www.actuary.org — Professional association for actuaries. Issues standards of conduct and provides government liaison and advisory opinions.

AMERICAN ASSOCIATION FOR LONG-TERM CARE INSURANCE • 3835 E. Thousand Oaks Blvd., Suite 336, Westlake Village, CA 91362. Tel. 818-597-3227. www.aaltci.org — A national professional organization exclusively dedicated to promoting the importance of planning for long-term care needs.

AMERICAN ASSOCIATION OF CROP INSURERS • 1 Massachusetts Avenue NW, Suite 800, Washington, DC 20001-1401. Tel. 202-789-4100. www.cropinsurers.com — Trade association of insurance companies to promote crop insurance.

AMERICAN ASSOCIATION OF INSURANCE SERVICES • 701 Warrenville Road, Lisle, IL 60532. Tel. 800-564-AAIS. www.aaisonline.com — Rating, statistical and advisory organization, made up principally of small and medium-sized property/casualty companies.

AMERICAN ASSOCIATION OF MANAGING GENERAL AGENTS • 610 Freedom Business Center, Suite 110, King of Prussia, PA 19406. Tel. 610-992-0022. www.aamga.org — Membership association of managing general agents of insurers.

AMERICAN BANKERS INSURANCE ASSOCIATION • 1120 Connecticut Avenue, NW, Washington, DC 20036. Tel. 202-663-5172. www.aba.com — A separately chartered affiliate of the American Bankers Association. A full service association for bank insurance interests dedicated to furthering the policy and business objectives of banks in insurance.

THE AMERICAN COLLEGE OF FINANCIAL SERVICES • 270 South Bryn Mawr Avenue, Bryn Mawr, PA 19010. Tel. 610-526-1000. www.theamericancollege.edu — An independent, accredited nonprofit institution, originally The American College of Life Underwriters. Provides graduate and professional education in insurance and other financial services.

AMERICAN COUNCIL OF LIFE INSURERS (ACLI) • 101 Constitution Avenue NW, Suite 700, Washington, DC 20001-2133. Tel. 202-624-2000. www.acli.com — Trade association responsible for the public affairs, government, legislative and research aspects of the life insurance business.

*AMERICAN INSTITUTE OF MARINE UNDERWRITERS • 14 Wall Street, New York, NY 10005. Tel. 212-233-0550. www.aimu.org — Provides information of concern to marine underwriters and promotes their interests.

AMERICAN INSURANCE ASSOCIATION (AIA) - NATIONAL OFFICE • 555 12th St, NW, Suite 550, Washington, DC 20004. Tel. 202-828-7100. www.aiadc.org — Trade and service organization for property/casualty insurance companies. Provides a forum for the discussion of problems as well as safety, promotional and legislative services.

AMERICAN LAND TITLE ASSOCIATION • 1800 M Street, NW, Suite 300S, Washington, DC 20036-5828. Tel. 202-296-3671. www.alta.org — Trade organization for title insurers, abstractors and agents. Performs statistical research and lobbying services.

AMERICAN NUCLEAR INSURERS • 95 Glastonbury Boulevard, Suite 300, Glastonbury, CT 06033. Tel. 860-682-1301. www.amnucins.com — A nonprofit unincorporated association through which liability insurance protection is provided against hazards arising out of nuclear reactor installations and their operations.

AMERICAN RISK AND INSURANCE ASSOCIATION • 716 Providence Road, Malvern, PA 19355-3402. Tel. 610-640-1997. www.aria.org — Association of scholars in the field of risk management and insurance, dedicated to advancing knowledge in the field and enhancing the career development of its members.

AMERICAN TORT REFORM ASSOCIATION • 1101 Connecticut Avenue NW, Suite 400, Washington, DC 20036. Tel. 202-682-1163. www.atra.org — A broad based, bipartisan coalition of more than 300 businesses, corporations, municipalities, associations and professional firms that support civil justice reform.

APIW: A PROFESSIONAL ASSOCIATION OF WOMEN IN INSURANCE • 990 Cedar Bridge Ave, Brick, NJ 08723-4157. Tel. 973-941-6024. www.apiw.org — A professional association of women in the insurance and reinsurance industry and related fields. Provides professional education, networking and support services to encourage the development of professional leadership among its members.

ARBITRATION FORUMS, INC. • 3820 Northdale Boulevard, Suite 200A, Tampa, FL 33624. Tel. 866-977-3434. www.arbfile.org — Nonprofit provider of interinsurance dispute resolution services for self-insureds, insurers and claim service organizations.

ASSOCIATION OF FINANCIAL GUARANTY INSURERS • Mackin & Casey LLC, 139 Lancaster Street, Albany, NY 12210. Tel. 518-449-4698. www.afgi.org — Trade association of the insurers and reinsurers of municipal bonds and asset-backed securities.

ASSOCIATION OF GOVERNMENTAL RISK POOLS • 9 Cornell Rd., Latham, NY 12110. Tel. 518-389-2782. www.agrip.org — Organization for public entity risk and benefits pools in North America.

AUTOMOBILE INSURANCE PLANS SERVICE OFFICE • 302 Central Avenue, Johnston, RI 02919. Tel. 401-946-2310. www.aipso.com — Develops and files rates and provides other services for state-mandated automobile insurance plans.

BANK INSURANCE & SECURITIES ASSOCIATION • 2025 M Street, NW, Suite 800, Washington, DC 20036. Tel. 202-367-1111. www.bisanet.org — Fosters the full integration of securities and insurance businesses with depository institutions' traditional banking businesses. Participants include executives from the securities, insurance, investment advisory, trust, private banking, retail, capital markets and commercial divisions of depository institutions.

BISRA - BANK INSURANCE & SECURITIES RESEARCH ASSOCIATES • 300 Day Hill Road, Windsor, CT 06095-4761. Tel. 860-298-3935. www.bisra.com — Consultant focusing on the financial services marketplace. Conducts studies of sales penetration, profitability, compensation and compliance. (formerly Kehrer-LIMRA).

CAPTIVE INSURANCE COMPANIES ASSOCIATION • 4248 Park Glen Rd., Minneapolis, MN 55416. Tel. 952-928-4655. www.cicaworld.com — Organization that disseminates information useful to firms that utilize the captive insurance company concept to solve corporate insurance problems.

*CASUALTY ACTUARIAL SOCIETY • 4350 North Fairfax Drive, Suite 250, Arlington, VA 22203. Tel. 703-276-3100. www.casact.org — Promotes actuarial and statistical science in property/casualty insurance fields.

CERTIFIED AUTOMOTIVE PARTS ASSOCIATION • 1000 Vermont Ave., NW Suite 1010, Washington, DC 20005. Tel. 202-737-2212. www.capacertified.org — Nonprofit organization formed to develop and oversee a test program guaranteeing the suitability and quality of automotive parts.

COALITION AGAINST INSURANCE FRAUD • 1012 14th Street NW, Suite 200, Washington, DC 20005. Tel. 202-393-7330. www.insurancefraud.org — An alliance of consumer, law enforcement, and insurance industry groups dedicated to reducing all forms of insurance fraud through public advocacy and education.

THE COMMITTEE OF ANNUITY INSURERS • c/o Davis & Harman LLP, 1455 Pennsylvania Avenue, NW, Suite 1200, Washington, DC 20004. Tel. 202-347-2230. www.annuity-insurers.org — Group whose goal is to address federal legislative and regulatory issues relevant to the annuity industry and to participate in the development of federal tax and securities policies regarding annuities.

CONNING RESEARCH AND CONSULTING, INC. • One Financial Plaza, Hartford, CT 06103-2627. Tel. 860-299-2000. www.conningresearch.com — Research and consulting firm that offers an array of specialty information products, insights and analyses of key issues confronting the insurance industry.

CORELOGIC • 40 Pacifica, Suite 900, Irvine, CA 92618. Tel. 800-426-1466. www.corelogic.com — Provides comprehensive data, analytics and services to financial services and real estate professionals.

COUNCIL OF INSURANCE AGENTS AND BROKERS • 701 Pennsylvania Avenue NW, Suite 750, Washington, DC 20004-2608. Tel. 202-783-4400. www.ciab.com — A trade organization representing leading commercial insurance agencies and brokerage firms.

CROP INSURANCE AND REINSURANCE BUREAU • 440 First St NW, Suite 500, Washington, DC 20001. Tel. 202-544-0067. www.cropinsurance.org — Crop insurance trade organization.

DEFENSE RESEARCH INSTITUTE • 55 W. Monroe St., Suite 2000, Chicago, IL 60603. Tel. 312-795-1101. www.dri.org — A national and international membership association of lawyers and others concerned with the defense of civil actions.

EASTBRIDGE CONSULTING GROUP, INC. • 50 Avon Meadow Lane, #101, Avon, CT 06001. Tel. 860-676-9633. www.eastbridge.com — Provides consulting, marketing, training and research services to financial services firms, including those involved in worksite marketing and the distribution of individual and employee benefits products.

EMPLOYEE BENEFIT RESEARCH INSTITUTE • 1100 13th Street NW, Suite 878, Washington, DC 20005-4051. Tel. 202-659-0670. www.ebri.org — The institute's mission is to advance the public's, the media's and policymakers' knowledge and understanding of employee benefits and their importance to the U.S. economy.

EQECAT • 475 14th Street, Suite 550, Oakland, CA 94612-1938. Tel. 510-817-3100. www.eqecat.com — Provider of products and services for managing natural and man-made risks. Provides innovative catastrophe management solutions for property and casualty insurance underwriting, accumulation management and transfer of natural hazard and terrorism risk.

THE FINANCIAL SERVICES ROUNDTABLE • 600 13th Street NW, Suite 400, Washington, DC 20005. Tel. 202-289-4322. www.fsroundtable.org — A forum for U.S. financial industry leaders working together to determine and influence the most critical public policy concerns related to the integration of the financial services.

FITCH CREDIT RATING COMPANY • 33 Whitehall Street, New York, NY 10004. Tel. 212-908-0500. www.fitchratings.com — Assigns claims-paying ability ratings to insurance companies.

GLOBAL AEROSPACE, INC. • One Sylvan Way, Parsippany, NJ 07054. Tel. 973-490-8500. www.global-aero.com — A pool of property/casualty companies engaged in writing all classes of aviation insurance.

GLOBAL ASSOCIATION OF RISK PROFESSIONALS • 111 Town Square Place, 14th Floor, Jersey City, NJ 07310. Tel. 201-719-7210. www.garp.com — International group whose aim is to encourage and enhance communications between risk professionals, practitioners and regulators worldwide.

GRIFFITH INSURANCE EDUCATION FOUNDATION • 720 Providence Rd, Suite 100, Malvern, PA 19355. Tel. 855-288-7743. www.griffithfoundation.org — The foundation promotes the teaching and study of risk management and insurance at colleges and universities nationwide and provides education programs for public policymakers on the basic principles of risk management and insurance.

GROUP LEGAL SERVICES ASSOCIATION • 321 North Clark Street, Chicago, IL 60654. Tel. 312-988-5751. www.glsaonline.org — National membership organization providing information and technical assistance to lawyers, insurance companies, administrators, marketers and consumers regarding group and prepaid legal service plans.

HIGHWAY LOSS DATA INSTITUTE • 1005 North Glebe Road, Suite 700, Arlington, VA 22201. Tel. 703-247-1600. www.hldi.org — Nonprofit organization to gather, process and provide the public with insurance data concerned with human and economic losses resulting from highway accidents.

INDEPENDENT INSURANCE AGENTS & BROKERS OF AMERICA, INC. • 127 South Peyton Street, Alexandria, VA 22314. Tel. 800-221-7917. www.independentagent.com — Trade association of independent insurance agents.

INLAND MARINE UNDERWRITERS ASSOCIATION • 14 Wall Street, 8th Floor, New York, NY 10005. Tel. 212-233-0550. www.imua.org — Forum for discussion of problems of common concern to inland marine insurers.

INSURANCE ACCOUNTING AND SYSTEMS ASSOCIATION, INC. • P.O. Box 51340, Durham, NC 27717. Tel. 919-489-0991. www.iasa.org — Promotes the study, research and development of modern techniques in insurance accounting and systems.

INSURANCE COMMITTEE FOR ARSON CONTROL • 3601 Vincennes Road, Indianapolis, IN 46268. Tel. 317-876-6226. www.arsoncontrol.org — All-industry coalition that serves as a catalyst for insurers' anti-arson efforts and a liaison with government agencies and other groups devoted to arson control.

INSURANCE DATA MANAGEMENT ASSOCIATION, INC. • 545 Washington Boulevard, Jersey City, NJ 07310-1686. Tel. 201-469-3069. www.idma.org — An independent, nonprofit, professional, learned association dedicated to increasing the level of professionalism, knowledge and visibility of insurance data management.

INSURANCE INDUSTRY CHARITABLE FOUNDATION • 1999 Avenue of the Stars, Suite 1100, Los Angeles, CA 90067. Tel. 424-253-1107. www.iicf.org — Seeks to help communities and enrich lives by combining the collective strengths of the industry to provide grants, volunteer service and leadership.

INSURANCE INFORMATION INSTITUTE (I.I.I.) • 110 William Street, 18th Floor, New York, NY 10038. Tel. 212-346-5500. www.iii.org — A primary source for information, analysis and reference on insurance subjects.

INSURANCE INSTITUTE FOR BUSINESS & HOME SAFETY • 4775 East Fowler Avenue, Tampa, FL 33617. Tel. 813-286-3400. www.DisasterSafety.org — An insurance industry-sponsored nonprofit organization dedicated to reducing losses, deaths, injuries and property damage resulting from natural hazards.

INSURANCE INSTITUTE FOR HIGHWAY SAFETY • 1005 North Glebe Road, Suite 800, Arlington, VA 22201. Tel. 703-247-1500. www.iihs.org — Research and education organization dedicated to reducing loss, death, injury and property damage on the highways. Fully funded by property/casualty insurers.

INSURANCE LIBRARY ASSOCIATION OF BOSTON • 156 State Street, Second Floor, Boston, MA 02109. Tel. 617-227-2087. www.insurancelibrary.org — The Insurance Library Association of Boston founded in 1887, is a nonprofit insurance association that has an extensive insurance library on all lines of insurance.

INSURANCE REGULATORY EXAMINERS SOCIETY • 1611 County Rd B West, Suite 320 St. Paul, MN 55113. Tel. 651-917-6250. www.go-ires.org — Nonprofit professional and educational association for examiners and other professionals working in insurance industry.

INSURANCE RESEARCH COUNCIL (A DIVISION OF THE INSTITUTES) • 718 Providence Road, Malvern, PA 19355-0725. Tel. 610-644-2212. www.insurance-research.org — Provides research relevant to public policy issues affecting risk and insurance.

INSURED RETIREMENT INSTITUTE • 1100 Vermont Avenue, NW, 10th Floor, Washington, DC 20005. Tel. 202-469-3000. www.irionline.org — Source of knowledge pertaining to annuities, insured retirement products and retirement planning; provides educational and informational resources. Formerly the National Association for Variable Annuities (NAVA).

INTEGRATED BENEFITS INSTITUTE • 595 Market Street, Suite 810, San Francisco, CA 94105. Tel. 415-222-7280. www.ibiweb.org — A private, nonprofit organization that provides research, discussion and analysis, data services and legislative review to measure and improve integrated benefits programs, enhance efficiency in delivery of all employee-based benefits and promote effective return-to-work.

INTERMEDIARIES AND REINSURANCE UNDERWRITERS ASSOCIATION, INC. • c/o The Beaumont Group, Inc., 3626 East Tremont Avenue, Suite 203, Throggs Neck, NY 10465. Tel. 718-892 0228. www.irua.com — Educational association to encourage the exchange of ideas among reinsurers worldwide writing principally treaty reinsurance.

INTERNATIONAL ASSOCIATION OF INSURANCE PROFESSIONALS • 3525 Piedmont Road, Building 5, Suite 300, Atlanta, GA 30305. Tel. 800-766-6249. www.internationalinsuranceprofessionals.org — Provides insurance education, skills enhancement and leadership development to its members.

INTERNATIONAL ASSOCIATION OF SPECIAL INVESTIGATION UNITS • N83 W13410 Leon Road, Menomonee Falls, WI 53051. Tel. 414-375-2992. www.iasiu.org — Group whose goals are to promote a coordinated effort within the industry to combat insurance fraud and to provide education and training for insurance investigators.

INTERNATIONAL INSURANCE SOCIETY, INC. • 101 Astor Place, Suite 202, New York, NY 10003. Tel. 212-277-5171. www.internationalinsurance.org — A nonprofit membership organization whose mission is to facilitate international understandings, the transfer of ideas and innovations, and the development of personal networks across insurance markets through a joint effort of leading executives and academics throughout the world.

IVANS (INSURANCE VALUE ADDED NETWORK SERVICES) • 5405 Cypress Center Drive, Suite 150, Tampa, FL 33609. Tel. 855-233-9128. www.ivans.com — An industry-sponsored organization offering a data communications network linking agencies, companies and providers of data to the insurance industry.

KAREN CLARK & COMPANY • 2 Copley Place, Tower 2, 1st Floor, Boston, MA 02116. Tel. 617-423-2800. www.karenclarkandco.com — Catastrophe risk assessment and modeling firm.

KINETIC ANALYSIS CORPORATION • 8070 Georgia Avenue, Suite 413, Silver Spring, MD 20910. Tel. 240-821-1202. www.kinanco.com — Specializes in estimating the impact of natural and man-made hazards on the structures and the economy for clients in engineering, land development, and risk management.

LATIN AMERICAN AGENTS ASSOCIATION • 520 S. Curson Ave., Los Angeles, CA 90036. Tel. 213-290-8930. Facebook.com/LAAAFanPage. — An independent group of Hispanic agents and brokers, whose goal is to educate, influence and inform the insurance community about the specific needs of the Latino community in the United States.

LATIN AMERICAN ASSOCIATION OF INSURANCE AGENCIES • P.O. Box 520844, Miami, FL 33152-2844. Tel. 305-477-1442. facebook/LAAA fan Page — An association of insurance professionals whose purpose is to protect the rights of its members, benefit the consumer through education, provide information and networking services, and promote active participation in the political environment and community service.

LIFE HAPPENS • 1655 North Fort Myer Drive, Suite 610, Arlington, VA 22209. Tel. 888-LIFE-777. www.lifehappens.org — Nonprofit organization dedicated to addressing the public's growing need for information and education about life, health, disability and long-term care insurance.

LIFE INSURANCE SETTLEMENT ASSOCIATION • 280 W. Canton Ave, Suite 430, Winter Park, FL 32789. Tel. 407-894-3797. www.lisa.org — Promotes the development, integrity and reputation of the life settlement industry.

*LIGHTNING PROTECTION INSTITUTE • P.O. Box 99, Maryville, MO 64468. Tel. 800-488-6864. www.lightning.org — Nonprofit organization dedicated to ensuring that its members' lightning protection systems are the best possible quality in design, materials and installation.

LIMRA INTERNATIONAL • 300 Day Hill Road, Windsor, CT 06095. Tel. 800-235-4672. www.limra.com — Worldwide association providing research, consulting and other services to insurance and financial services companies in more than 60 countries. LIMRA helps its member companies maximize their marketing effectiveness.

LOMA (LIFE OFFICE MANAGEMENT ASSOCIATION) • 6190 Powers Ferry Road, Suite 600, Atlanta, GA 30339. Tel. 770-951-1770. www.loma.org — Worldwide association of insurance companies specializing in research and education, with a primary focus on home office management.

LOSS EXECUTIVES ASSOCIATION • P.O. Box 37, Tenafly, NJ 07670. Tel. 201-569-3346. www.lossexecutives.com — A professional association of property loss executives providing education to the industry.

MARSHALL & SWIFT • 777 South Figueroa St., 12th Floor, Los Angeles, CA 90017. Tel. 800-421-8042. www.msbinfo.com — Building cost research company providing data and estimating technologies to the property insurance industry.

MIB, INC. • 50 Braintree Hill Park, Suite 400, Braintree, MA 02184-8734. Tel. 781-751-6000. www.mib.com/lost_life_insurance.html — Database of individual life insurance applications processed since 1995.

MICHAEL WHITE ASSOCIATES • 823 King of Prussia Road, Radnor, PA 19087. Tel. 610-254-0440. www.bankinsurance.com — Consulting firm that helps clients plan, develop and implement bank insurance sales programs. Conducts research on and benchmarks performance of bank insurance and

MOODY'S INVESTORS SERVICE • 7 World Trade Center, at 250 Greenwich Street, New York, NY 10007. Tel. 212-553-1653. www.moodys.com — Global credit analysis and financial information firm.

NATIONAL AFRICAN-AMERICAN INSURANCE ASSOCIATION • 1718 M Street NW, P.O. Box 1110, Washington, DC 20036. Tel. 866-56-NAAIA. www.naaia.org — NAAIA fosters the nationwide presence, participation and long-term financial success of African-American insurance professionals within the greater insurance community and provides its members and the insurance industry a forum for sharing information and ideas that enhance business and professional development.

THE NATIONAL ALLIANCE FOR INSURANCE EDUCATION & RESEARCH • P.O. Box 27027, Austin, TX 78755-2027. Tel. 800-633-2165. www.scic.com — National education program in property, liability and life insurance, with a continuing education requirement upon designation.

NATIONAL ASSOCIATION OF HEALTH UNDERWRITERS • 1212 New York Avenue NW, Suite 1100, Washington, DC 20005. Tel. 202-552-5060. www.nahu.org — Professional association of people who sell and service disability income, and hospitalization and major medical health insurance companies.

NATIONAL ASSOCIATION OF INDEPENDENT INSURANCE ADJUSTERS • 1880 Radcliff Ct., Tracy, CA 95376. Tel. 209-832-6962. www.naiia.com — Association of claims adjusters and firms operating independently on a fee basis for all insurance companies.

NATIONAL ASSOCIATION OF INSURANCE AND FINANCIAL ADVISORS • 2901 Telestar Court, Falls Church, VA 22042-1205. Tel. 877-866-2432. www.naifa.org — Professional association representing health and life insurance agents.

NATIONAL ASSOCIATION OF INSURANCE COMMISSIONERS • 1100 Walnut Street, Suite 1500, Kansas City, MO 64106-2197. Tel. 816-842-3600. www.naic.org — Organization of state insurance commissioners to promote uniformity in state supervision of insurance matters and to recommend legislation in state legislatures.

NATIONAL ASSOCIATION OF MUTUAL INSURANCE COMPANIES (NAMIC) • 3601 Vincennes Road, Indianapolis, IN 46268. Tel. 317-875-5250. www.namic.org — National property/casualty insurance trade and political advocacy association.

NATIONAL ASSOCIATION OF PROFESSIONAL INSURANCE AGENTS • 400 North Washington Street, Alexandria, VA 22314-2353. Tel. 703-836-1279. www.pianet.org — Trade association of independent insurance agents. Operations: Lobbying, Education, Communications, Business Building Tools and Insurance Products

NATIONAL ASSOCIATION OF PROFESSIONAL SURPLUS LINES OFFICES, LTD. • 4131 North Mulberry Drive, Ste. 200, Kansas City, MO 64116. Tel. 816-741-3910. www.napslo.org — Professional association of wholesale brokers, excess and surplus lines companies, affiliates and supporting members.

NATIONAL ASSOCIATION OF SURETY BOND PRODUCERS (NASBP) • 1140 19th Street, Suite 800, Washington, DC 20036-5104. Tel. 202-686-3700. www.nasbp.org — NASBP members are professionals who specialize in providing surety bonds for construction and other commercial purposes to companies and individuals needing the assurance offered by surety bonds. Its members have broad knowledge of the surety marketplace and the business strategies and underwriting differences among surety companies.

***NATIONAL CONFERENCE OF INSURANCE GUARANTY FUNDS** • 300 North Meridian Street, Suite 1020, Indianapolis, IN 46204. Tel. 317-464-8199. www.ncigf.org — Advisory organization to the state guaranty fund boards; gathers and disseminates information regarding insurer insolvencies.

NATIONAL CONFERENCE OF INSURANCE LEGISLATORS • 2317 Route 34, Suite 2B, Manasquan, NJ, 08736. Tel. 732-201-4133. www.ncoil.org — Organization of state legislators whose main area of public policy concern is insurance and insurance regulation.

NATIONAL CROP INSURANCE SERVICES, INC. • 8900 Indian Creek Parkway, Suite 600, Overland Park, KS 66210-1567. Tel. 913-685-2767. www.ag-risk.org — National trade association of insurance companies writing hail insurance, fire insurance and insurance against other weather perils to growing crops, with rating and research services for crop-hail and rain insurers.

NATIONAL FIRE PROTECTION ASSOCIATION • One Batterymarch Park, Quincy, MA 02169-7471. Tel. 617-770-3000. www.nfpa.org — Independent, nonprofit source of information on fire protection, prevention and suppression. Develops and publishes consensus fire safety standards; sponsors national Learn Not to Burn campaign.

NATIONAL FLOOD INSURANCE PROGRAM (NFIP) • 500 C Street SW, Washington, DC 20472. Tel. 800-621-FEMA. www.floodsmart.gov — The NFIP offers flood insurance to homeowners, renters and business owners if their community participates in the program. Participating communities agree to adopt and enforce ordinances that meet or exceed FEMA requirements to reduce the risk of flooding.

NATIONAL HIGHWAY TRAFFIC SAFETY ADMINISTRATION (NHTSA) • 1200 New Jersey Avenue SE, West Building, Washington, DC 20590. Tel. 888-327-4236. www.nhtsa.gov — Carries out programs and studies aimed at reducing economic losses in motor vehicle crashes and repairs.

NATIONAL INDEPENDENT STATISTICAL SERVICE • 3601 Vincennes Road, P.O. Box 68950, Indianapolis, IN 46268. Tel. 317-876-6200. www.niss-stat.org — National statistical agent and advisory organization for all lines of insurance, except workers compensation.

*NATIONAL INSURANCE CRIME BUREAU • 1111 East Touhy Avenue, Suite 400, Des Plaines, IL 60018. Tel. 800-447-6282. www.nicb.org — A nonprofit organization dedicated to preventing, detecting and defeating insurance fraud.

NATIONAL OCEANIC AND ATMOSPHERIC ADMINISTRATION (NOAA) • 1401 Constitution Avenue NW, Room 5128, Washington, DC 20230. Tel. 828-271-4800. www.noaa.gov — Government agency focused on keeping citizens informed of the changing environment through monitoring climate change, issuing storm warnings and coastal restoration.

NATIONAL ORGANIZATION OF LIFE AND HEALTH INSURANCE GUARANTY ASSOCIATIONS (NOLHGA) • 13873 Park Center Road, Suite 505, Herndon, VA 20171. Tel. 703-481-5206. www.nolhga.com — A voluntary association composed of the life and health insurance guaranty associations of all 50 states, the District of Columbia and Puerto Rico.

NATIONAL RISK RETENTION ASSOCIATION • 16133 Ventura Blvd., Suite 1055, Encino, CA 91436. Tel. 800-421-5981. www.riskretention.org — The voice of risk retention group and purchasing group liability insurance programs, organized pursuant to the Federal Liability Risk Retention Act.

NATIONAL SAFETY COUNCIL • 1121 Spring Lake Drive, Itasca, IL 60143-3201. Tel. 630-285-1121. www.nsc.org — Provides national support and leadership in the field of safety, publishes safety material and conducts public information and publicity programs.

NATIONAL STRUCTURED SETTLEMENTS TRADE ASSOCIATION • 1100 New York Avenue, NW, Suite 750W, Washington, DC 20005. Tel. 202 289 4004. www.nssta.com — Trade association representing consultants, insurers and others who are interested in the resolution and financing of tort claims through periodic payments.

*NCCI HOLDINGS, INC. • 901 Peninsula Corporate Circle, Boca Raton, FL 33487. Tel. 561-893-1000. www.ncci.com — Develops and administers rating plans and systems for workers compensation insurance.

NEIGHBORWORKS AMERICA • 999 North Capitol Street NE, Suite 900, Washington, DC 20002. Tel. 202-760-4000. www.nw.org — The goal of this group is to develop partnerships between the insurance industry and NeighborWorks organizations to better market the products and services of both, for the benefit of the customers and communities they serve.

NEW YORK ALLIANCE AGAINST INSURANCE FRAUD • 1450 Western Ave., Suite 101, Albany, NY 12203. Tel. 518-432-3576. www.fraudny.com — A cooperative effort of insurance companies in New York State to educate the industry about the costs of insurance fraud, the many forms is can take and what can be done to fight it.

NEW YORK INSURANCE ASSOCIATION, INC. • 130 Washington Ave., Albany, NY 12210. Tel. 518-432-4227. www.nyia.org — Domestic and non-domestic property/casualty companies operations: lobbying.

NEW YORK PROPERTY INSURANCE UNDERWRITING ASSOCIATION • 100 William St., 4th Fl., New York, NY 10038. Tel. 212-208-9700. www.nypiua.com — Provides basic property insurance for New York State residents not able to obtain the coverage through the voluntary market. Administers the C-MAP and FAIR Plan.

NONPROFIT RISK MANAGEMENT CENTER • 204 South King Street, Leesburg, VA 20175. Tel. 703-777-3504. www.nonprofitrisk.org — Conducts research and education on risk management and insurance issues of special concern to nonprofit organizations.

NORTH AMERICAN PET HEALTH INSURANCE ASSOCIATION • P.O. Box 37940, Raleigh, NC 27627. Tel. 877-962-7442. www.naphia.org — Group whose members work collaboratively towards establishing and maintaining universal and professional standards for terminology, best practices, quality and ethics in the pet health industry.

OPIC • 1100 New York Avenue, NW, Washington, DC 20527. Tel. 202-336-8400. www.opic.gov — Self-sustaining U.S. government agency providing political risk insurance and finance services for U.S. investment in developing countries.

PHYSICIAN INSURERS ASSOCIATION OF AMERICA • 2275 Research Boulevard, Suite 250, Rockville, MD 20850. Tel. 301-947-9000. www.thepiaa.org — Trade association representing physician-owned mutual insurance companies that provide medical malpractice insurance.

PROFESSIONAL LIABILITY UNDERWRITING SOCIETY (PLUS) • 5353 Wayzata Boulevard, Suite 600, Minneapolis, MN 55416. Tel. 800-845-0778. www.plusweb.org — An international, nonprofit association that provides educational opportunities and programs about the professional liability industry.

PROPERTY CASUALTY INSURERS ASSOCIATION OF AMERICA (PCI) • 8700 West Bryn Mawr, Suite 1200S, Chicago, IL 60031-3512. Tel. 847-297-7800. www.pciaa.net — Serves as a voice on public policy issues and advocates positions that foster a competitive market place for property/casualty insurers and insurance consumers.

PROPERTY INSURANCE PLANS SERVICE OFFICE • 27 School Street, Suite 302, Boston, MA 02108. Tel. 617-371-4175. www.pipso.com — Provides technical and administrative services to state property insurance plans.

PROPERTY LOSS RESEARCH BUREAU • 3025 Highland Parkway, Suite 800, Downers Grove, IL 60515. Tel. 630-724-2200. www.plrb.org — This property/casualty trade organization promotes productivity and efficiency in the property and liability loss and claim adjustment processes, disseminates information on property and liability issues and fosters education and new and beneficial developments within the industry.

PUBLIC RISK MANAGEMENT ASSOCIATION • 700 S. Washington St., Suite 218, Alexandria, VA 22314. Tel. 703-528-7701. www.primacentral.org — Membership organization representing risk managers in state and local public entities.

RAND INSTITUTE FOR CIVIL JUSTICE • 1776 Main Street, Santa Monica, CA 90407-2138. Tel. 310-393-0411. www.rand.org — Organization formed within The Rand Corporation to perform independent, objective research and analysis concerning the civil justice system.

REINSURANCE ASSOCIATION OF AMERICA • 1445 New York Ave, NW, 7th Fl., Washington, DC 20005. Tel. 202-638-3690. www.reinsurance.org — Trade association of property/casualty reinsurers; provides legislative services for members.

RISK AND INSURANCE MANAGEMENT SOCIETY, INC. • 5 Bryant Park, 13th Floor, New York, NY 10018. Tel. 212-286-9292. www.rims.org — Organization of corporate buyers of insurance, which makes known to insurers the insurance needs of business and industry, supports loss prevention and provides a forum for the discussion of common objectives and problems.

RISK MANAGEMENT SOLUTIONS, INC. • 7575 Gateway Boulevard, Newark, CA 94560. Tel. 510-505-2500. www.rms.com — Provides products and services for the quantification and management of catastrophe risk associated with natural perils as well as products for weather derivatives and enterprise risk management for the property/casualty insurance industry.

RUNZHEIMER INTERNATIONAL • 1 Runzheimer Parkway, Waterford, WI 53185. Tel. 800-558-1702. www.runzheimer.com — Management consulting firm that provides workforce mobility solutions relating to business vehicles, relocation, travel management, corporate aircraft and mobile device management programs.

SCHOOL OF RISK MANAGEMENT, INSURANCE AND ACTUARIAL SCIENCE OF THE TOBIN COLLEGE OF BUSINESS AT ST. JOHN'S UNIVERSITY (FORMERLY THE COLLEGE OF INSURANCE) • 101 Astor Place, New York, NY 10003. Tel. 212-277-5198. www.stjohns.edu/academics/graduate/tobin/srm — Insurance industry-supported college providing a curriculum leading to bachelor's and master's degrees in business administration, financial management of risk, insurance finance and actuarial science. The Kathryn and Shelby Cullom Davis Library (212-277-5135) provides services, products and resources to its members.

SELF-INSURANCE INSTITUTE OF AMERICA • P.O. Box 1237, Simpsonville, SC 29681. Tel. 800-851-7789. www.siia.org — Organization that fosters and promotes alternative methods of risk protection.

S&P GLOBAL MARKET INTELLIGENCE • One SNL Plaza, 212 7th St. NE, Charlottesville, VA 22902. Tel. 877-863-1306. www.marketintelligence.spglobal.com/ — Research firm that collects, standardizes and disseminates all relevant corporate, financial, market and M&A data as well as news and analytics for the industries it covers: banking, specialized financial services, insurance, real estate and energy.

SOCIETY OF ACTUARIES • 475 North Martingale Road, Suite 600, Schaumburg, IL 60173. Tel. 847-706-3500. www.soa.org — An educational, research and professional organization dedicated to serving the public and its members. The Society's vision is for actuaries to be recognized as the leading professionals in the modeling and management of financial risk and contingent events.

SOCIETY OF FINANCIAL EXAMINERS • 12100 Sunset Hills Rd., Suite 130, Reston, VA 20190-3221. Tel. 703-234-4140. www.sofe.org — Professional society for examiners of insurance companies, banks, savings and loans, and credit unions.

SOCIETY OF INSURANCE RESEARCH • 4248 Park Glen Road, Minneapolis, MN 55416 . Tel. 952-928-4641. www.sirnet.org — Stimulates insurance research and fosters exchanges among society members on research methodology.

SOCIETY OF INSURANCE TRAINERS AND EDUCATORS • 2800 West Higgins Road, Suite 440, Hoffman Estates, IL 60169 . Tel. 847-852-5204 . www.insurancetrainers.org — Professional organization of trainers and educators in insurance.

STANDARD & POOR'S RATING GROUP • 55 Water Street, New York, NY 10041. Tel. 212-438-2000. www.standardandpoors.com — Monitors the credit quality of bonds and other financial instruments of corporations, governments and supranational entities.

SURETY & FIDELITY ASSOCIATION OF AMERICA (SFAA) • 1140 19th Street, NW, Suite 500, Washington, DC 20036. Tel. 202-463-0600. www.surety.org — Statistical, rating, development and advisory organization for surety and fidelity bonds in the U.S.

UNDERWRITERS' LABORATORIES, INC. • 2600 N.W. Lake Rd., Camas, WA 98607-8542. Tel. 360-817-5500. www.ul.com — Investigates and tests electrical materials and other products to determine that fire prevention and protection standards are being met.

U.S. MORTGAGE INSURERS • 1101 17th Street NW, Suite 700, Washington, DC 20036. Tel. 202-280-1820. www.usmi.org — Represents the private mortgage insurance industry. MICA provides information on related legislative and regulatory issues, and strives to enhance understanding of the role private mortgage insurance plays in housing Americans.

*VERISK/ISO • 545 Washington Boulevard, Jersey City, NJ 07310-1686. Tel. 201-469-3000. www.verisk.com — A leading source of information about property/casualty insurance risk. Provides statistical, actuarial, underwriting and claims information; policy language; information about specific locations; fraud identification tools; and technical services. Products help customers protect people, property and financial assets.

WEATHER RISK MANAGEMENT ASSOCIATION (WRMA) • 529 14th Street, NW, Suite 750, Washington, DC 20045. Tel. 202-289-3800. www.wrma.org — Serves the weather risk management industry by providing forums for discussion and interaction with others associated with financial weather products.

*WISCONSIN INSURANCE ALLIANCE • 44 E. Mifflin St., Suite 901, Madison, WI 53703-2888. Tel. 608-255-1749. www.wial.com — A state trade association of property/casualty insurance companies conducting legislative affairs and public relations on behalf of the industry.

*WORKERS COMPENSATION RESEARCH INSTITUTE • 955 Massachusetts Avenue, Cambridge, MA 02139. Tel. 617-661-9274. www.wcrinet.org — A nonpartisan, nonprofit membership organization conducting public policy research on workers' compensation, healthcare and disability issues. Members include employers, insurers, insurance regulators and state regulatory agencies, as well as several state labor organizations.

MEMBERS

I.I.I. Member Companies

ACUITY

AEGIS Insurance Services Inc.

AIG

Allianz of America, Inc.

Allied World Assurance Company

Allstate Insurance Group

American Agricultural Insurance
Company

American Family Insurance

American Integrity Insurance Company

American Reliable Insurance

Amerisafe

Amerisure Insurance Companies

Arch Insurance Group

Argo Group US

Arthur J. Gallagher

Beacon Mutual Insurance Company

BITCO Insurance Companies

Canal Insurance

Catholic Mutual Insurance

Chesapeake Employers' Insurance
Company

Chubb Limited

Church Mutual Insurance Company

The Concord Group

COUNTRY Financial

Country-Wide Insurance Company

CNA

CSAA Insurance Group

CUMIS Insurance Society, Inc.

Dryden Mutual Insurance Company

EMC Insurance Companies

Enumclaw Insurance Group

Erie & Niagara Insurance Association

Erie Insurance Group

Farm Bureau Town and Country
Insurance Company of Missouri

Farmers Group, Inc.

GEICO

Gen Re

Germania Insurance

Grange Insurance Association

Grange Insurance Companies

GuideOne Insurance

The Hanover Insurance Group Inc.

The Harford Mutual Insurance Companies

The Hartford Financial Services Group

The Horace Mann Companies

Island Insurance Companies

Kemper Corporation

Liberty Mutual Group

Lloyd's

Lockton Companies

Magna Carta Companies

MAPFRE USA

Marsh Inc.

MetLife Auto & Home

Michigan Millers Mutual Insurance
Company

Millville Mutual Insurance Company

Missouri Employers Mutual Insurance

MMG Insurance Company

Motorists Insurance Group

Munich Re

Nationwide

New York Central Mutual Fire Insurance
Company

The Norfolk & Dedham Group

Northern Neck Insurance Company

Ohio Mutual Insurance Group

OneBeacon Insurance Group

PartnerRe

Pennsylvania Lumbermens Mutual
Insurance Company

Providence Mutual Fire Insurance
Company

Scor U.S. Corporation

SECURA Insurance Companies

Selective Insurance Group

State Auto Insurance Companies

State Farm Mutual Automobile Insurance
Company

The Sullivan Group

Swiss Reinsurance America Corporation

Travelers

USAA

Utica National Insurance Group

Westfield Group

W. R. Berkley Corporation

XL Catlin

The Zenith

Zurich North America

Associate Members

ANE, Agency Network Exchange, LLC

California Earthquake Authority

Deloitte

Farmers Mutual Fire Insurance of
Tennessee

Imperial PFS

Mutual Assurance Society of Virginia

Sompo Japan Research Institute, Inc.

Transunion Insurance Solutions

Academic And Governmental Members

Babson College

Beihang University (Beijing)

Connecticut General Assembly – Office of Legislative Research

Cornell University

Drake University

East Carolina University

Eastern Connecticut State University

Florida State University

Fudan University (Shanghai, China)

Georgetown University Law Center

The Glasgow Caledonian University (London)

Illinois State University

LaSalle University

New Mexico University

Old Dominion University

Olivet College

Pennsylvania State University

Purdue University

St. John's University

St. Joseph's University

Stanford University

Temple University

TesTeachers

U.S. Department of Commerce – Bureau of Economic Analysis

U.S. Department of Commerce - Office of Finance & Insurance Industries

University of Alabama

University of Central Arkansas

University of Cyprus

University of Dammam, Saudi Arabia

University of Georgia

University of Guelph (Ontario, Canada)

University of Hawaii – West Oahu

University of Illinois at Urbana-Champaign

University of Iowa

University of Minnesota

University of Mississippi

University of Missouri Law School

University of North Texas

University of Pennsylvania

University of South Carolina

University of Southern Maine

University of Tennessee-Knoxville

University of Texas at Dallas

University of Westminster (London)

The Wharton School at the University of Pennsylvania

University of Wisconsin-Madison

Insurance Information Institute
110 William Street
New York, NY 10038
Tel. 212-346-5500. www.iii.org

STAFF

James P. Ballot, Senior Director – Marketing and Content Strategy – jamesb@iii.org
Michael Barry, Vice President – Media Relations – michaelb@iii.org
Andréa C. Basora, Executive Vice President – andreab@iii.org
Kenthaya Cadet, Executive Assistant – kenthayac@iii.org
Erica Edwards, Editorial Assistant – Publications – ericae@iii.org
Rita El-Hakim, Manager – Operations and Office Services – ritae@iii.org
Mary-Anne Firneno, Research Manager – mary-annef@iii.org
Lilia Giordano, Administrative Assistant – liliag@iii.org
Jennifer Ha, Managing Editor – jenniferh@iii.org
Sean Kevelighan, Chief Executive Officer – seank@iii.org
Katja Charlene Lewis, Manager – Publications and Web Production – charlenel@iii.org
Shorna Lewis, Director – Technology and Web Production – shornal@iii.org
Carol Liesch, Director – Payroll and Benefits Administration – caroll@iii.org
Chi Wai Lima, Creative Director – chiwail@iii.org
James Lynch, FCAS, MAAA, Chief Actuary and Vice President – Data and Information Services – jamesl@iii.org
Parmila Phillips, Senior Director – Finance – parmilap@iii.org
Diane Portantiere, Senior Director – Member Services – dianep@iii.org
Marielle Rodriguez, Digital & Social Media Coordinator – marieller@iii.org
Jeanne Salvatore, Senior Vice President and Chief Communications Officer – jeannes@iii.org
Maria Sassian, Information Specialist – marias@iii.org
Steven Weisbart, Ph.D., CLU, Senior Vice President and Chief Economist – stevenw@iii.org
Loretta Worters, Vice President – Communications – lorettaw@iii.org

REPRESENTATIVES

William J. Davis, Atlanta, Davis Communications – billjoe@bellsouth.net
Elianne González, Miami, Hispanic Press Officer – elianneg@iii.org
Robert P. Hartwig, Ph.D, CPCU, Special Consultant – bobh@iii.org
Lynne McChristian, Tampa, Florida Representative – lynnem@iii.org
Janet Ruiz, California Representative – San Francisco – janetr@iii.org
Claire Wilkinson, Consultant – clairew@iii.org

A

accident and health insurance, 67, 72
accidents. *See also* automobile/motor vehicle
  crashes
    aviation, 188–190
    recreational, 184–187
    top 10 states by recreational watercraft
      accidents, 185
    watercraft, 184–185
agency companies, 26–27
aggressive driving, 180
airline accidents. *See* aviation losses
alcohol server liability laws, 95
alcohol-impaired driving, 178–179
allied lines insurance, 124
all-terrain vehicle (ATV) accidents, 187
alternative risk transfer (ART), 7
annuities, 34–36, 40
    defined, 37
    distribution channels, 28
    fixed, 34
    retirement, 29
    sales, 34–35
    top 10 writers, 15, 35–36
    types and uses for, 34
    variable, 28, 34–35
anomaly detection, 201
arson, 163–164
asbestos-related illness, 193
ATV accidents, 187
automobile accidents. *See* automobile/motor
  vehicle crashes
automobile insurance
    add-on automobile insurance, 89
    assigned risk plans, 82
    claims, 81–82
    combined ratio, by year, 73, 75
    commercial, 66, 68, 73, 75
    compulsory, 86–88
    cost factors, 197, 199
    costs/expenditures, 76–79
        average expenditures by state, 78–79
        claims and expenses, 80
        top 10 most and least expensive cities
          for, 77
        top 10 most and least expensive states
          for, 77
        underwriting expenses, 80
    high-risk markets
        insured vehicles, 82
        private passenger cars, 83–84
        shared/residual market, 82
        uninsured motorists, 84–86
    incurred losses, 82
    laws, 86–99
        add-on, 89
        alcohol server liability, 95
        choice no-fault, 89
        definition of terms, 89

drunk driving, 93–95
financial responsibility/compulsory,
  86–88
liability coverage, 89–90
no-fault, 89
older drivers, 96–97
seatbelt, 91–92
tort liability, 89
young drivers, 92, 98–99
online distribution channels, 25
premiums, 65–66, 68, 73–75
    commercial vs. personal, 73
    liability and collision/comprehensive,
      73–74
    net written, 65–66
    top most/least expensive, by state, 77
    top 10 writers, commercial, 75
    top 10 writers, private, 74
private passenger cars, 66, 68, 73–74,
  82–84
shared/residual market, 82–83
top 10 highest/lowest states for uninsured
  motorists, 85
voluntary market, 82, 83–84
automobile/motor vehicle crashes, 171–181
    aggressive driving, 180
    alcohol-impaired driving, 178–179
    alcohol-impaired driving by age of driver,
      178
    by age of driver, 176
    by severity and vehicle type, 174
    by sex of driver, 175
    by state, 173
    by year, 171–172
    collision losses, 180
    distracted driving, 180–181
    driver behavior, 177
    motorcycle helmet use, 179
    traffic deaths
        alcohol-impaired driving, 178–179
        by activity of person killed, 174
        by age of driver, 176
        by state, 173
        by year, 172
        distracted driving, 181
automobile/motor vehicle theft, 182–183
    top 10 metropolitan statistical areas for, 182
    top 10 states with most/fewest, 183
    top 10 stolen vehicles, 183
aviation losses, 188–190
    top 10 deadliest aviation crashes, 190
    United States, 188–189
    worldwide, 189–190

B

beach and windstorm plans, 103–104, 105–106
blood alcohol concentration (BAC), 93–94,
  178–179, 184
boats. *See* watercraft accidents
boiler and machinery insurance, 130
bond insurance, 128–129
bonds, 39, 56, 57

brokers
    top 10 global, 5
    top 10 U.S., 118
burglary, 164–165
burglary and theft insurance, 67, 71, 130
business insurance. *See* commercial property/
  casualty insurance

C

California Earthquake Authority (CEA), 116
capacity, 54
captives, 7
catastrophe (cat) bonds, 8–9
    risk capital, 9
    top ten, 8
catastrophes, 133–158
    defined, 136
    earthquakes, 150–151
    floods, 145
    hail, 154
    hurricanes, 140–143
    nuclear incidents, 153
    terrorism, 151–152
    tornadoes, 146–149
    United States, 136–151
        top three states by inflation-adjusted
          insured losses, 139
        top five states by insured catastrophe
          loss, 137
        top 10 costliest earthquakes and
          tsunamis, 136
        top 10 costliest U.S. catastrophes, 138
        top 15 costliest U.S. winter events, 144
    wildfires, 155–158
    winter storms, 144
    world, 133–136, 152
        top 10 costliest world insurance
          losses, 134
        top 10 costliest earthquakes and
          tsunamis, 136
        top 10 costliest world catastrophes, 134
        top 10 deadliest world catastrophes, 135
cellphone use/driver distraction laws, 180–181
charitable contributions by insurance industry,
  17
choice no-fault automobile insurance, 89
claims
    automobile insurance, 81–82
    collision losses, 180
    fraudulent, 200–202
    homeowners insurance, 108–110
    property/casualty insurance, 62
class-action lawsuits, shareholder, 210
coastal areas
    insured properties, 103
combined ratio, 50, 55. *See also* specific lines
commercial property/casualty insurance,
  118–132
    allied lines insurance, 124
    boiler and machinery insurance, 130
    burglary and theft insurance, 130

crop insurance, 131–132
financial guaranty insurance, 65, 67, 71,
    128–129
fire insurance, 124
leading companies, 118
liability coverage (other liability), 121
marine insurance (inland and ocean), 125
medical malpractice insurance, 123
mortgage guaranty insurance, 127–128
multiple peril insurance, 122–123
surety and fidelity bonds, 126
warranty insurance, 132
workers compensation, 119–120
compulsory automobile insurance, 86–88
consumer fraud, 169–170
consumer price indices, 197–200
cost factors, 197–200
consumer prices, 198–200
fraud, 200–202
goods and services, 197–200
household spending and insurance costs,
    197–198
litigiousness, 203–210 (*see also* lawsuits
    and legal costs)
crime, 163–170
arson, 163
cyberattacks and identity theft, 166–170,
property crimes, 164
crop insurance, 66, 72, 131–132
crop-hail insurance, 131
multiple peril crop insurance, 131–132
top 10 writers of multiple peril crop
    insurance, 132
cross-border sales, 6
cybercrime
cyberattacks, frequency and severity, 217–220
cyberliability market, growth of, 211–217
cyberrisk and the insurance industry,
    220–227
Cyberrisk: Threat and Opportunity, excerpt,
    211–228
cybersecurity, 166–168, 211–228
top 10 states for, 168

D

D&O (directors and officers liability insurance),
    206–208
data breaches. *See* cybersecurity
death rates, by cause, 195–196
declinations, 58
defense and cost containment expenses, 204
defined benefit and defined contribution
    pension plans, 31
direct premiums written, 14–15, 59,65
by state, 61
life/health, by line, 35
top writers, 15, 41, 43, 74–75, 101, 117–118,
    128–129, 132
directors and officers liability insurance (D&O),
    206–208
top 10 writers of, 207
disability insurance, 43, 44

disasters. *See* catastrophes
distracted driving, 180–181
distribution channels, 25–28
agency writers vs. direct writers, 26
annuities, 28
automobile insurance, 25
life insurance, 27
online, 25
property/casualty insurance, 25, 26
dividends, policyholder, 50, 53, 55
Dodd-Frank Wall Street and Consumer
    Protection Act, 34
drunk driving, 93–95, 178–179

E

earthquake insurance, 67, 71, 100, 116–117
top 10 writers, 117
earthquakes, 150–151
top 10 costliest earthquakes and tsunamis,
    136
top 10 costliest in U.S., 150
top ten, insured losses for, 151
economic contributions of insurance industry,
    17–19
emerging markets, 9–12
Employee Retirement Income Security Act of
    1974, 32
employment in insurance, 17–18
employment practices liability (EPL) coverage,
    206, 208–209
equipment breakdown insurance, 130
errors and omissions, 121
excess workers compensation, 119
expense ratio, 55

F

Fair Access to Insurance Requirements (FAIR)
    Plans, 103–105
farmowners multiple peril insurance, 122–123.
    See also crop insurance
fatalities
automobiles/motor vehicles, 171–174,
    176–177
aviation, 188–190
distracted driving/cellphone use, 180–181
drunk driving, 178–179
fire, 159–163
hurricanes, 142–143
tornadoes, 148–149
workplace, 191
fidelity bonds, 71, 126
financial data
life/health insurance, 37–46
property/casualty insurance, 49–64
financial guaranty insurance, 128–129
top 10 writers, 129
financial responsibility laws, automobile
    insurance, 86–88
fire
by property use, 161
deaths and injuries from, 162–163

losses from, 108–109, 159–162
arson, 163–164
structure fires, 160–161
top 10 most catastrophic multiple-death
    fires, 163
top 10 most costly large-loss fires, 161
wildfires, 155–158
fire insurance, commercial, 124
firearms. *See* gun deaths and injuries
flood insurance, 100, 112–115
flood losses, 113–115
floods, 145
top 10 most significant flood events, 145
foreign reinsurers, 3
foreign sales of insurance, 6
forest fires. *See* wildfires
401(k) plans, 33
fraud. *See* insurance fraud
fraud bureaus, 201
Fujita scale for tornado classification, 146

G

generally accepted accounting principles
    (GAAP), 51
global insurers. *See* world insurance markets
gross domestic product (GDP) from insurance
    industry, 19
guaranty funds, 63–64
gun deaths and injuries, 196

H

hail, 154
top five states affected by, 154
healthcare insurance, 16. *See also* life/health
    insurance
home injuries/deaths, unintentional, 194–195
homeowners insurance, 100–111
claims, 108–111
causes of loss, 109–110
frequency of, 108–110
lightning losses, 109–110
combined ratio, 100
cost factors, 197, 198
costs/expenditures, 106–108
premiums, average, 106–107
underwriting expenses, 108
high-risk markets, 101–106
beach and windstorm plans, 105–106
coastal area properties, 102–103
Fair Access to Insurance Requirements
    (FAIR) Plans, 104–105
residual market property plans, 103–104
top 10 states, by population change, 102
mold, 109
premiums, 66, 68, 95–96, 100–101
top 10 writers by direct premiums written,
    101

hurricanes, 140–143
    coastal exposure, 103
    costliest, 141
    deadliest, 143
    losses, 141
    Saffir-Simpson Hurricane Wind Scale, 140

I

identity theft, 169–170
Individual Retirement Accounts (IRAs), 32
injuries. *See* accidents
inland marine insurance, 67, 70, 125
insolvency funds. *See* guaranty funds
insurance companies
    domestic, by state, 23
    global top 10, 4–5
    top companies, 15, 43, 47, 48, 59, 74–75,
        117–118, 128–129, 132
insurance cost factors. *See* cost factors
insurance fraud, 200–202
    payment attributable to, 202
international sales, 6
Internet crime. *See* cybercrime
Internet Crime Complaint Center (IC3), 167
investments, property/casualty insurance,
    56–57

K

Keogh plans, 32

L

larceny-theft, 164–165, 182–183
laws
    affecting drivers, 86–99 (*see also*
        automobile insurance)
    insurance fraud, 201–202
lawsuits and legal costs, 203–210
    commercial liability markets, top 10 largest,
        203
    directors and officers liability insurance
        (D&O), 206–208
    employment practices liability (EPL)
        coverage, 208–209
    insurers' legal defense costs, 203–204
    personal injury awards, 205–206
    shareholder lawsuits, 210
liability coverage
    automobile insurance, 89–90
    employment practices liability (EPL)
        coverage, 206–209
    general, 121
license renewal laws, 96–97
life insurance. *See also* life/health insurance
    annuities, 15, 29, 34–36, 41, 45–46
    distribution channels, 27
    top 10 writers, 15
life/health insurance, 27, 37–48
    benefits and claims, 40
    companies, number of, 23
    employment, 17
    income analysis, 38

investments, 39
payout data, 40
premiums by line, 41–46
    by state, 45–46
    disability insurance, 43–44
    long-term care insurance, 44
    private health insurance, 42–43
top 10 writers, group/individual, 43
top 20 writers, 47
lightning, 109–111
liquor liability, 95, 121
litigation costs, 203–204
long-term care (LTC) insurance, 44
loss ratio, 55
losses, 133–196
    asbestos-related illness, 193
    automobile/motor vehicle crashes, 171–181
    aviation, 188–190
    catastrophes (*see also* catastrophes)
        United States, 136–151
        world, 133–136, 152
    causes of death, 195–196
    crime
        arson, 163–164
        cyberattacks and identity theft, 166–
          170, 211–228
        property crimes, 164–165
    fire, 159–163
    home injuries/deaths, 194
    property/casualty insurance, 49, 62
    recreation, 184–187
    underwriting, 49, 53
    workplace, 190–193

M

malpractice insurance, 123
mandatory insurance. *See* compulsory
    automobile insurance
marine insurance (inland and ocean),
    commercial, 125
mechanical breakdown insurance, 130
medical insurance. *See* healthcare insurance
medical malpractice insurance, 123
mergers and acquisitions, insurance-related,
    20–22
    top 10, 21
microinsurance, 9
mold, 109
monetary thresholds, 89–90
mortality risks, 195
mortgage guaranty insurance, 67, 72, 127–128
    top 10 writers by direct premium written,
        128
motorcycles
    compulsory insurance, 86
    crashes/deaths, 174
    helmet use, 179
multiple peril insurance, 122–123, 131–132
    commercial, 67, 69, 122
    crops, 131–132
    farmowners, 65, 122–123
    homeowners insurance, 66, 68, 100

municipal bond holdings by insurance industry,
    19
mutual funds, 33

N

National Flood Insurance Program (NFIP),
    112–115
net premiums written, 65
no-fault automobile insurance, 89
nonlife insurance premiums, 1–2
nuclear incidents, 153

O

ocean marine insurance (commercial), 125
older drivers
    automobile/motor vehicle crashes, 176
    license renewal laws, 96–97
online distribution channels, 25
    automobile insurance, 25
    life insurance, 27
    property/casualty insurance, 25
other liability insurance, 65, 67, 70, 121

P

pension plans,29. *See also* retirement assets
personal injury awards, 205–206
personal injury protection (PIP), 89, 90
personal vs. commercial insurance, 66
premium taxes, 24
premiums. *See also* specific lines of insurance
    direct written, 1, 14–15, 61, 74, 75
    life/health insurance, 41–46
    net premiums written vs. direct premiums
        written, 65
    property/casualty insurance, 65–72
private mortgage insurance (PMI), 127
    top 10 writers by direct premium written,
        128
Private Securities Litigation Reform Act, 210
product liability insurance, 67, 69, 121
profitability, property/casualty insurance, 51
property/casualty insurance
    agency writers vs. direct writers, 26
    automobiles/motor vehicles (see
        automobile insurance)
    combined ratio, 50, 55
    commercial lines sector, 117–132
    earthquakes, 116–117
    employment, 17
    financial data, 49–64
    financial results, 49–55
        annual rate of return, 51
        income analysis, 49
        net premiums written and combined
          ratio, 50
        profitability, 51
    floods, 112–115
    guaranty funds, 63–64
    homeowners (see homeowners insurance)
    incurred losses, by state, 62
    insurance cycle, 52

invested assets, 56–57
online distribution channels, 25
operating results, 53
policyholders' surplus, 54
premiums, 65–72
    automobile, 73–75
    direct written, by state, 61, 68–72
    direct written vs. net written, 65
    net written, by line, 66–67
    personal vs. commercial, 66
reinsurance, 60
sector concentration, 59
surplus lines market, 58–59
top 10 writers, 15

R

recreation, 184–187
    ATV accidents, 187
    sports injuries, 186–187
    watercraft accidents, 184–185
    watercraft thefts, 186
reinsurance, 3–5, 67
    property/casualty market, 60
    top 10 brokers/companies, 4, 5, 60
    top 10 U.S. reinsurers, 60
renters insurance, 106–107
residual/shared market, 82, 103–104
retirement assets, 29–36
    401(k) plans, 33
    annuities, 34–36
    defined benefit and defined contribution
        plans, 31
    Individual Retirement Accounts (IRAs), 32
    mutual funds in, 33
    Roth IRAs, 32
risk export lists, 58
risk-financing options, 7–9
Roth IRAs, 32

S

Saffir-Simpson Hurricane Wind Scale, 140
SAS Institute, 202
Savings Incentive Match Plans for Employees
    (SIMPLE) plans, 32
seatbelt laws, 91–92
shared/residual market, 82–84, 103–104
shareholder lawsuits, 210
Simplified Employee Pensions (SEP), 32
special purpose vehicles, 8

state-by-state tables
    automobile insurance
        alcohol server liability laws, 95
        drunk driving laws, 93–94
        expenditures, 78–79
        financial responsibility limits, 87–88
        liability coverage laws, 90
        older drivers, 96–97
        private passenger cars insured, 83–84
        seatbelt laws, 91–92
        uninsured motorists, 85–86
        young drivers, 98–99
    automobile/motor vehicle deaths, 173
    employment in insurance, 17–18
    flood insurance, 114–115
    homeowners insurance
        beach and windstorm plans, 106
        coastal property data, 102–103
        FAIR plans data, 104–105
    identity theft, 170
    insurance companies domiciled per state,
        23
    premiums, life/health insurance, 45–46
    property/casualty insurance
        direct premiums written, 61, 68–72
        guaranty funds, 64
        incurred losses, 62
    taxes, premium, 24
    tornadoes, 149
statutory accounting principles (SAP), 51
surety bonds, 126
surplus lines market, 58–59
    top 10 companies, 59
systems breakdown insurance, 130

T

taxes, 24, 49–50, 108
teenage drivers. See young drivers
terrorist attacks, 151–152
    top 20 costliest, 152
theft
    automobiles/motor vehicles, 165, 182–183
    burglary, 165
    homeowners, 108–109
    watercraft, 185
tornadoes, 146–149
    deaths related to, 147–149
    defined, 146
    Fujita scale for classification, 146
    top 10 costliest U.S. catastrophes involving,
        147
    top 10 states, by number of tornadoes, 148
tort liability, auto insurance, 89
tsunamis, 136

U

umbrella liability, 121
underwriting expenses, 49, 80, 108
uninsured motorists, 84–86

V

verbal thresholds, automobile insurance, 89

W

warranty insurance, 132
water damage and freezing claims, 109
watercraft accidents, 184–185
    top 10 states for, 185
watercraft thefts, 185
wildfires, 155–156
    top 10 most costly, in U.S., 156
    top 10 states for, 156
windstorm plans, 105–106
winter storms, 144
workers compensation insurance, 67, 69,
    119–120
workplace losses, 190–193
    asbestos-related illness, 193
    deaths, causes of, 192
    illness and injuries, 192
    occupational disease, 192
    top 10 occupations with largest numbers of
        injuries/losses, 192
work-related illnesses, 192
world insurance markets, 1–12
    alternative risk transfer (ART) arrangements,
        7
    captives, 7
    catastrophe (cat) bonds, 8–9
    emerging markets, 10–12
    international sales, 6
    leading companies, 4–5
    microinsurance, 9
    premiums, 1–2
    reinsurance, 3–5
    risk-financing options, 7–9

Y

young drivers, 98–99